Mastering
Accounting skills

Palgrave Master Series

Accounting
Accounting Skills
Advanced English Language
Advanced Poetry
Advanced Pure Mathematics
Arabic
Basic Management
Biology
British Politics
Business Communication
Business Environment
C Programming
C++ Programming
Chemistry
COBOL Programming
Communication
Computing
Counselling Skills
Counselling Theory
Customer Relations
Database Design
Delphi Programming
Desktop Publishing
e-Business
Economic and Social History
Economics
Electrical Engineering
Electronics
Employee Development
English Grammar
English Language
English Literature
Fashion Buying and Merchandising
  Management
Fashion Styling
Financial Management
French
Geography
German

Global Information Systems
Globalization of Business
Human Resource Management
Information Technology
International Trade
Internet
Italian
Java
Language of Literature
Management Skills
Marketing Management
Mathematics
Microsoft Office
Microsoft Windows, Novell
  NetWare and UNIX
Modern British History
Modern European History
Modern United States History
Modern World History
Networks
Novels of Jane Austen
Organisational Behaviour
Pascal and Delphi Programming
Philosophy
Physics
Practical Criticism
Psychology
Public Relations
Shakespeare
Social Welfare
Sociology
Spanish
Statistics
Strategic Management
Systems Analysis and Design
Team Leadership
Theology
Twentieth-Century Russian History
Visual Basic
World Religions

www.palgravemasterseries.com

Palgrave Master Series
Series Standing Order ISBN 0–333–69343–4
(outside North America only)

You can receive future titles in this series as they are published by placing a standing order. Please contact your bookseller or, in case of difficulty, write to us at the address below with your name and address, the title of the series and the ISBN quoted above.

Customer Services Department, Macmillan Distribution Ltd
Houndmills, Basingstoke, Hampshire RG21 6XS, England

Mastering
Accounting skills

Second Edition

Margaret Nicholson

palgrave

First edition (published as *Accounting Skills*) 1989
Second edition 2000

Published by
PALGRAVE
Houndmills, Basingstoke, Hampshire RG21 6XS and
175 Fifth Avenue, New York, N. Y. 10010
Companies and representatives throughout the world

PALGRAVE is the new global academic imprint of
St. Martin's Press LLC Scholarly and Reference Division and
Palgrave Publishers Ltd (formerly Macmillan Press Ltd).

ISBN 0–333–91991–2

This book is printed on paper suitable for recycling and
made from fully managed and sustained forest sources.

A catalogue record for this book is available
from the British Library.

10   9   8   7   6
09 08 07 06 05 04

Printed and bound in Great Britain by
Creative Print and Design (Wales), Ebbw Vale

Contents

Acknowledgements

Sincere thanks to my friend Elaine Rowe who provided constant encouragement, read every word and worked through all the assignments. Thanks are also due to my husband David for his help and support.

Introduction

People often imagine that accounting involves many complex mathematical calculations; nothing could be further from the truth.

Accountancy has a language of its own and, like any other language, it sounds complicated to anyone who cannot understand it. As you begin to learn the meaning of the words, you will find that it is easier than many people would have you believe.

Mastering Accounting Skills is designed for complete beginners with no prior knowledge or experience. It is not just a textbook containing facts and information, it is also a workbook with the emphasis throughout on *learning by doing*. There are many practical assignments for you to complete, together with help on how to approach them. You cannot learn simply by reading, you need to practice accounting methods and procedures to gain the necessary skills.

You will find that the book contains many illustrations to help you gain a real understanding of the subject. At the end of each chapter there is a section headed '*Points to remember*'. These will enable you to focus on the main topics. An answer section is provided at the back of the book, giving solutions to all the assignments. Answers are fully displayed for the first two assignments in each chapter.

This book provides the underpinning knowledge for most accounting foundation courses and aims to cover the requirements of OCR (Oxford, Cambridge and RSA), Pitman and LCCI examination boards.

MARGARET NICHOLSON

▌ ▼ ▌ 1 Getting started: assets, liabilities and capital

Starting a business

There are many different types of businesses. A good way of classifying them is according to how they are owned. Among the most numerous are *sole traders*, where one person owns the business. Sole traders are the easiest form of business to set up and the owner is known as the *proprietor*. The owner has personal control over the decisions, provides all of the money and resources to run the business and receives all of the profits. Other types of businesses include partnerships, limited companies, cooperatives and public corporations.

Those people who decide to start a business feel that they have some useful product or service to offer and believe they can make money from their business dealings. We will be concerned only with the accounts of businesses owned by one person – that is, a man or woman buying and selling goods with the intention of making a profit. Typical examples of sole traders are: small retail shops, farms, cafes, hairdressers, plumbers, electricians and small building firms.

Keeping records

We all need to have some idea of our own financial position to ensure that our bills are paid on time. Keeping orderly records is of vital importance to the smooth running of any business, otherwise it would be impossible to know if the business was successful. If records are properly kept, it should be possible to quickly find out the firm's financial position at any time.

Book-keeping or *accounting* is the name given to the work of keeping the financial records of a business and special accounting terms are used to describe things.

Assets, liabilities and capital

What are assets?

Assets are the possessions of a business and include such items as: land, property and buildings, plant and machinery, motor vehicles, office furniture, office equipment, stocks of goods, money in cash, money in the bank account and money owing by *debtors*. People who owe a firm money are called debtors. (Customers who have bought goods on credit are called *debtors* until they have paid their accounts.) Anything which the business owns or is owed is called an *asset*.

What are liabilities?

Liabilities is the name given to everything the firm *owes*. They consist of money owing for goods bought on credit, loans made to the firm and for expenses such as gas, electricity, rates, rent and telephone. People who are owed money by a firm are called *creditors*. (People who have supplied goods or services on credit become *creditors* until their accounts have been paid.) Anything which the business owes is called a *liability*.

What is capital?

It is important to understand correctly the meaning of *capital* in relation to accounting. The total resources supplied by the owner of the business is known as *capital. Capital is a liability*. This may seem strange at first, but you must remember that you are keeping the books of the business and *not* the owner's personal books.

For legal reasons, business dealings must be kept entirely separate from the financial activities of the owner. Starting a new business is rather like creating a new person who has a completely different identity, so it is considered to be lending money to another person. Capital is probably best described as a *'loan'* to the new person. When the owner puts his money or some other asset into the firm he becomes a creditor of the business. Capital represents the amount *'loaned'* to the business by the owner.

Assignment tasks

1.1 In your notebook make two headings like this:
    Assets   *Liabilities*
    now place each of the following items under the correct heading:
    - Motor van
    - Creditors
    - Cash at bank
    - Office equipment
    - Stock of goods

1.2 Now place each of the following items under the correct heading:
    Assets   *Liabilities*
    - Premises
    - Debtors
    - Creditors
    - Motor vehicle

- Office furniture
- Capital
- Cash in hand

1.3 A firm has the following assets and liabilities:

	£
Capital	22,250
Debtors	5,825
Cash at bank	1,500
Creditors	2,450
Office equipment	8,425
Stock of goods	9,250

What is the total of the assets?

1.4 A firm has the following assets and liabilities:

	£
Capital	17,500
Office furniture	1,750
Motor van	6,450
Creditors	3,000
Stock of goods	3,230
Machinery	4,900
Cash at bank	420
Debtors	3,750

What is the total of the liabilities?

1.5 A firm has the following assets and liabilities:

	£
Fixtures and fittings	10,200
Office equipment	2,275
Capital	15,000
Stock of goods	1,750
Creditors	1,800
Debtors	2,825
Cash at bank	3,950

What is the total of the assets?

The accounting equation

Accounting is based upon a very simple idea. It is called the *accounting equation*, which sounds difficult, but in fact it is easy to understand. In any business the value of assets always equals the value of capital and liabilities. The formula is:

Assets = Capital + Liabilities

If we know the value of two items in this equation it is always possible to calculate the third item, for example:

- *assets less liabilities = capital* or
- *assets less capital = liabilities* or
- *capital plus liabilities = assets*

Practise the equation by completing the following Assignment tasks.

Assignment tasks

1.6 Complete the table by calculating and filling in the missing figure:

	Assets	Liabilities	Capital
(a)	42,000	17,300	?
(b)	87,500	?	61,000
(c)	?	19,950	39,800
(d)	71,450	22,750	?
(e)	64,500	?	39,500

1.7 Complete the table by calculating and filling in the missing figure:

	Assets	Liabilities	Capital
(a)	51,500	19,700	?
(b)	?	27,500	64,700
(c)	57,750	?	38,800
(d)	63,330	14,500	?
(e)	?	17,850	63,150

1.8 Complete the table by calculating and filling in the missing figure:

	Assets	Liabilities	Capital
(a)	65,000	?	32,250
(b)	?	16,750	27,900
(c)	78,350	18,900	?
(d)	?	12,750	18,350
(e)	45,000	?	20,200

1.9 Complete the table by calculating and filling in the missing figure:

	Assets	Liabilities	Capital
(a)	47,200	18,250	?
(b)	51,500	?	16,450
(c)	?	27,800	28,900
(d)	31,150	17,250	?
(e)	48,750	?	26,650

The balance sheet in action

The accounting equation is shown on a *balance sheet,* and we are now going to look at how it changes once a business starts operating. The actual assets and liabilities will alter, as illustrated in the following examples, but the formula will always hold true no matter how many transactions are entered into.

A balance sheet is always drawn up at a *specific date*. For this example, David Nicholson commenced business on 1 January 20-6 with £25,000 which he placed in a bank account for the business. His balance sheet would look like this:

Balance Sheet as at 1 January 20-6

Assets	£	Liabilities	£
Cash at bank	25,000	Capital	25,000
	25,000		25,000

Each time a transaction is made, it will affect the balance sheet. On 7 January, David Nicholson completes his first transaction – he decides to buy a motor vehicle costing £5,000 and pays for it out of his business bank account. After this transaction, his capital remains at £25,000 but the assets will change. The money in the bank will be reduced to £20,000 and there will be another asset, a motor vehicle. His balance sheet still balances, but would now look like this:

Balance Sheet as at 7 January 20-6

Assets	£	Liabilities	£
Cash at bank	20,000	Capital	25,000
Motor vehicle	5,000		
	25,000		25,000

At this point David Nicholson, decides to buy a stock of goods which he eventually hopes to re-sell. On 12 January 20-6 he buys some goods costing £600 and agrees to pay for them in one month's time. This transaction will create the liability of a creditor (a person to whom money is owed for goods or services is known as a *creditor*), and there will be another asset, a stock of goods. His balance sheet still balances, but would now look like this:

Balance Sheet as at 12 January 20-6

Assets	£	Liabilities	£
Cash at bank	20,000	Capital	25,000
Motor vehicle	5,000	Creditor	600
Stock of goods	600		
	25,600		25,600

On 16 January 20-6 goods which had cost £100 were sold to D. Davey, who agreed to pay for the goods in one month's time. This transaction will create

a new asset of a *debtor* (a person who owes the firm money is known as a *debtor*) and the stock of goods will be reduced.

Balance Sheet as at 16 January 20-6

Assets	£	Liabilities	£
Cash at bank	20,000	Capital	25,000
Motor vehicle	5,000	Creditor	600
Stock of goods	500		
Debtor	100		
	25,600		25,600

Now see if you can keep track of the changes resulting from a series of transactions by completing the following Assignment tasks.

Assignment tasks

1.10
On 21 January, David Nicholson decides to buy some office equipment costing £1,500, paying by cheque. Draw up his balance sheet to show the effect of this transaction.

1.11
On 31 January, David Nicholson bought further goods on credit, costing £1,800 and managed to persuade a business associate, A Goodson, to lend him £5,000; this was placed in the business bank account. Draw up his balance sheet as at 31 January 20-6 to show the effect of these transactions.

Points to remember

- For legal reasons the financial dealings of a business must be kept *completely separate* from those of the owner of the business.
- The total amount of resources supplied by the owner of the business is known as *capital*. It represents the amount *loaned* to the business by the owner, and is a *liability* of the business.
- Anything which the business owns or is owed is an *asset*.
- Anything which the business owes is a *liability*.
- In accounting language, the name *debtor* is given to a person who owes the firm money.
- In accounting language, people who are owed money by a firm are called *creditors*.
- A balance sheet shows the *financial position of a business at a particular point in time*.

Assignments

1.12 William Dyson sets up a new business – he has the following assets and liabilities: premises £7,000, stock of goods £3,250, motor vehicle £5,750, creditors £2,200, debtors £3,950, loan from D James £5,000, office equipment £1,750, machinery £2,700, cash at bank £5,850. You are required to calculate the amount of his capital and draw up his balance sheet as at 31 December 20-8.

1.13 From the following information calculate the amount of Andrew Foster's capital and draw up his balance sheet as at 31 March 20-8: debtors £4,950, motor vehicles £5,700, creditors £3,490, fixtures £5,500, stock of goods £2,100, cash at bank £3,250.

1.14 Peter Smart has the following balance sheet as at 31 May 20-8:

Balance Sheet as at 31 May 20-8

Assets	£	Liabilities	£
Motor vehicle	2,000	Capital	6,600
Premises	5,000	Creditors	400
Stock of goods	1,400	D Bevan (Loan)	3,000
Debtors	600		
Cash in hand	200		
Cash at bank	800		
	10,000		10,000

During the first week of June 20-8 the following transactions took place:

Jun 2 One of the debtors paid him £250 in cash
Jun 4 He bought further goods on credit costing £800
Jun 5 He bought office equipment costing £450, paying by cheque

You are required to draw up Peter Smart's balance sheet as at 6 June 20-8 after the above transactions have been completed.

1.15
Julie Chang has the following balance sheet as at 30 September 20-8:

Balance Sheet as at 30 September 20-8

Assets	£	Liabilities	£
Fixtures and fittings	2,000	Capital	10,600
Stock of goods	1,500	Creditors	1,400
Debtors	1,800		
Cash in hand	150		
Cash at bank	6,550		
	12,000		12,000

During the first week of October 20-8 the following transactions took place:

1 October   She paid a cheque of £500 to a creditor
3 October   She bought a motor vehicle costing £4,500, paying by cheque
7 October   She received a loan of £3,000 by cheque from S Wong

You are required to draw up Julie Chang's balance sheet as at 7 October 20-8 after the above transactions have been completed.

1.16
Tim Sanderson has the following balance sheet as at 30 November 20-8:

Balance Sheet as at 30 November 20-8

Assets	£	Liabilities	£
Motor vehicle	8,000	Capital	13,750
Stock of goods	700	Creditors	1,250
Debtors	1,550		
Cash in hand	450		
Cash at bank	4,300		
	15,000		15,000

During the month of December 20-8 the following transactions took place:

December 2   He bought some machinery costing £1,850, paying by cheque
December 6   He bought further goods on credit costing £960
December 12 A debtor paid him £280 by cheque
December 18 He paid a creditor £360 in cash
December 30 He bought some office furniture costing £450, paying by cheque

You are required to draw up Tim Sanderson's balance sheet as at 31 December 20-8 after the above transactions have been completed.

☑ 2 Opening the double entry accounts in the ledger

We have already seen that every transaction affects *two* items on a balance sheet. If there were only a few transactions each day we could draw up a balance sheet after each transaction, but if there were numerous transactions each day it would become impossible to draw up a balance sheet after each one.

In business, *accounts* tell the story of what is happening. Recording this information in the various accounts is called *book-keeping*. The main book used to record these transactions is known as the *ledger*. At one time all ledgers were heavy bound volumes, but today loose-leaf paper, ledger cards and computer based systems are also used. Whatever system is used to record transactions, the principles and methods are basically the same.

The *double entry* system of book-keeping is the basis of all financial accounting. To gain a clear understanding of how the system works we must put what we learn into practice. Learning how to operate the double entry system is not nearly as difficult as many people would have you believe, but you will need to practice by *'doing'* it.

Record keeping

All businesses, however small, need some form of accounting because they must keep records of all their financial dealings. They need to know how much money they *spend* and how much money they *receive*.

There are some rules which you will need to learn to ensure that your records are kept accurately and that the information can be found quickly when it is needed.

Business transactions

Any type of business deal is a *transaction*. If you go into a shop to buy a packet of mints, this is a business transaction. *Two* things happen: the shopkeeper will *receive* the money and *give* the mints.

In every business transaction there are always *two* parties involved: one is the *receiver* the other is the *giver*. It is the two aspects of every transaction which is the basis of the *double entry* system of book-keeping.

Double entry system

The most important rule to remember is that in every transaction *two* things happen, and this will affect *two* accounts:

> *Every transaction involves a debit entry in one account and a credit entry in another account.*

This means that every transaction must be recorded in *two* accounts: one account will be *debited* because it *receives value*; the other account will be *credited* because it has *given value*.

The words *debit* and *credit* can be a little confusing to begin with. Debit originates from the Latin and means *value received*. Credit also originates from the Latin and means *value given*. If you always think: '*what value is received?*' and then '*what value is given?*', you will find it quite straightforward.

The double entry system of accounting records every transaction *twice*. Two separate accounts are involved in every transaction: one account recording the *receiving* aspect (*debit* entry) and the other account recording the *giving* or *paying* aspect (*credit* entry):

> *Debit the account which receives goods, services or money*
> *Credit the account which gives goods, services or money.*

Shortened, the rule to remember is:

> *Debit the receiver*
> *Credit the giver.*

Whether they are hand written or computerised, the ledger contains accounts of each asset and liability of the business and for the capital of the owner. A separate account is kept for every item in which a business deals.

You need to appreciate that *cash* and *cheques* are different, and are kept in separate accounts. Cash consists of notes and coins, but cheques cannot be spent like money, they must be paid into a bank. The *Cash Account* is used to record cash received and paid out by the firm (notes and coins). The *Bank Account* is used to record cheques received and paid out by the firm.

Look at the illustration of some typical business transactions in figure 2.1; it shows which accounts are involved in each transaction to help you grasp the basic idea.

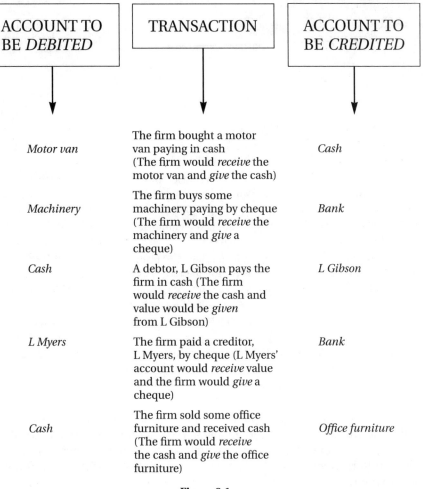

ACCOUNT TO BE *DEBITED*	TRANSACTION	ACCOUNT TO BE *CREDITED*
Motor van	The firm bought a motor van paying in cash (The firm would *receive* the motor van and *give* the cash)	Cash
Machinery	The firm buys some machinery paying by cheque (The firm would *receive* the machinery and *give* a cheque)	Bank
Cash	A debtor, L Gibson pays the firm in cash (The firm would *receive* the cash and value would be *given* from L Gibson)	L Gibson
L Myers	The firm paid a creditor, L Myers, by cheque (L Myers' account would *receive* value and the firm would *give* a cheque)	Bank
Cash	The firm sold some office furniture and received cash (The firm would *receive* the cash and *give* the office furniture)	Office furniture

Figure 2.1

Assignment tasks

2.1

Look at the following typical business transactions and work out which accounts are involved in each transaction. In every case, think what has happened and decide which account has *received value* (the account to be *debited*) and which account has *given value* (the account to be *credited*).

Complete the blank spaces by inserting the name of the account to be debited and the name of the account to be credited:

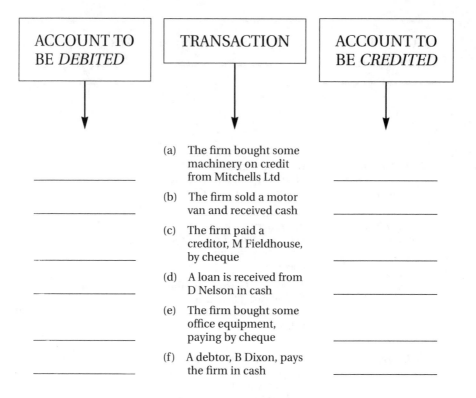

ACCOUNT TO BE *DEBITED*	TRANSACTION	ACCOUNT TO BE *CREDITED*
	(a) The firm bought some machinery on credit from Mitchells Ltd	
	(b) The firm sold a motor van and received cash	
	(c) The firm paid a creditor, M Fieldhouse, by cheque	
	(d) A loan is received from D Nelson in cash	
	(e) The firm bought some office equipment, paying by cheque	
	(f) A debtor, B Dixon, pays the firm in cash	

2.2

Look at the following typical business transactions and work out which accounts are involved in each transaction. In every case, think what has happened and decide which account has *received value* (the account to be *debited*) and which account has *given value* (the account to be *credited*).

Complete the blank spaces by inserting the name of the account to be debited and the name of the account to be credited:

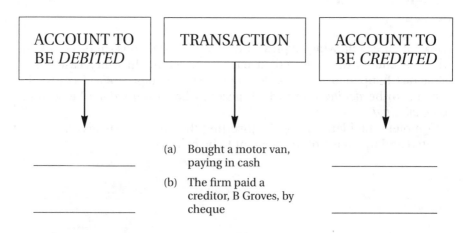

ACCOUNT TO BE *DEBITED*	TRANSACTION	ACCOUNT TO BE *CREDITED*
	(a) Bought a motor van, paying in cash	
	(b) The firm paid a creditor, B Groves, by cheque	

(c) The firm bought some office furniture on credit from Modern Offices Ltd

_____   _____

(d) A loan is received from K Williams by cheque

_____   _____

(e) The firm bought some machinery, paying in cash

_____   _____

(f) A debtor, W Preston, pays the firm in cash

_____   _____

The ledger

All the accounts of a business are kept in a book called the *ledger*. Years ago, when the book-keeper kept the books of account on a ledge, similar to a shelf fixed to a wall, the ledger was *'the book lying on the ledge'*. There was another book called the journal, or day book, but the ledger was, and still is, the main book of account.

The ledger is a book full of ruled pages, all ruled exactly the same. An account is a page in a ledger.

The ledger page is divided into two halves; think of it as a 'wall' down the centre of the page. The left-hand side of the page is called the *debit side*. The right-hand side of the page is called the *credit side*. The name of the account is written across the top of the page, in the centre.

Each account is kept on a separate page in the ledger and two accounts would *never* appear on the same page. However, when you are doing your assignments it would be a great waste of paper to show every account on a separate page, so it is usual for students to put several accounts on each page, leaving a few lines of space between each account. Ledger paper and books can be purchased from most good stationers and you will need to get a supply. This is how ledger paper is ruled:

Debit side   **Credit side**

		NAME OF ACCOUNT							
Date	Particulars	Folio	£	p	Date	Particulars	Folio	£	p

The double entry system of book-keeping is based upon the fact that every transaction has *two parts*: this is why two entries are made in the ledger for each transaction.

Entries are made in the ledger by setting up various accounts and making a *debit* entry in the account *receiving value* and a *credit* entry in the account *giving value.*

Elaine Mellor has decided to start her own business. On 1 March she started business with £5,000 in cash. This is the first transaction of the new business.

The business *receives* £5,000 in cash, so the debit entry is made in the cash account, like this:

Cash Account

	£		
Mar 1	5,000		

The credit entry will be in the capital account because the owner has *given* £5,000 to the new business. Think of the capital account as the owner's *personal account* in the new business. It shows how much the owner has *given to the business:*

Capital Account

			£
		Mar 1	5,000

The date and the amount of money will be the same in both accounts, but the particulars column is completed by *cross-reference*: it shows the name of the other account involved in the transaction. It may sound a little confusing at first but, as you will see, it is very helpful.

In real life each account is on a separate page, so when the particulars column is completed by cross-reference it always shows where the other entry has been made.

The word *capital* appears in the cash account like this:

Cash Account

		£		
Mar 1	Capital	5,000		

The word *cash* appears in the capital account, like this:

Capital Account

			£
	Mar 1	Cash	5,000

On 5 March the firm buys a motor van costing £4,500 on credit from Crossways Garage. The firm *receives* the motor van, so the debit entry is made in the motor van account, like this:

Motor Van Account

		£	
Mar 5	Crossways Garage	4,500	

The credit entry will be in Crossways Garage account because they have *given value*; the account would look like this:

Crossways Garage Account

			£
	Mar 5	Motor van	4,500

On 18 March Elaine Mellor goes to an auction and buys some machinery for the business costing £350, paying in cash. The firm *receives* the machinery, so the debit entry is made in the machinery account, like this:

Machinery Account

		£	
Mar 18	Cash	350	

The credit entry would be in the cash account because the firm has *paid out* cash; the cash account would now look like this:

Cash Account

		£			£
Mar 1	Capital	5,000	Mar 18	Machinery	350

On 24 March Elaine Mellor buys some office furniture costing £200, paying in cash. The firm *receives* the office furniture, so the debit entry is made in the office furniture account, like this:

Office Furniture Account

	£		
Mar 24 Cash	200		

The credit entry would be in the cash account because the firm has *paid out* cash. The cash account would now look like this:

Cash Account

	£			£
Mar 1 Capital	5,000	Mar 18 Machinery		350
		Mar 24 Office furniture		200

On 30 March the firm receives a loan of £2,000 in cash from John King. The firm *receives* the money in cash, so the debit entry is made in the cash account; the cash account would now look like this:

Cash Account

	£		£
Mar 1 Capital	5,000	Mar 18 Machinery	350
Mar 30 John King (Loan)	2,000	Mar 24 Office furniture	200

The credit entry would be in John King's loan account because he has *given value* to the firm:

John King (Loan) Account

		£
	Mar 30 Cash	2,000

Points to remember

- In every business transaction, *two* things happen: some form of value is *received* and some form of value is *given*.
- The double entry system of accounting means that every transaction *must* be entered *twice* in the ledger: a debit entry in one account and a credit entry in another account.
- The date of the transaction and the amount of money will be the same in both accounts; the particulars column is completed by cross-reference; it always names the account where the *corresponding entry is made*.
- A Cash Account is used to keep a record of *cash* – that is, notes and coins received and paid out by the firm.
- A Bank Account is used to keep a record of *cheques* received and paid out by the firm.

Now use your ledger to work through the following Assignments.

Assignments

2.3

K Chippendale started a new business on 1 May. In your ledger write up the double entry accounts needed to record the following transactions:

May 1 Started a new business with £2,000 in cash
    3 Bought a motor van costing £950 on credit from Crossways Garage
  12 Bought office furniture costing £500 paying in cash
  24 Received a loan of £500 in cash from L Gibson
  30 Paid Crossways Garage £950 in cash

2.4

S Curtis started a new business on 1 April. In your ledger write up the double entry accounts needed to record the following transactions:

Apr 1 Started business with £5,000 in a business bank account
    4 Bought office furniture costing £450 on credit from Design Centre
  10 Bought motor van costing £1,500 paying by cheque
  20 Received a loan of £2,000 by cheque from D Lester
  23 Bought machinery costing £500 paying by cheque
  29 Paid Design Centre £450 by cheque

2.5

J Patel started a new business on 1 June. In your ledger write up the double entry accounts needed to record the following transactions:

Jun 1 Started a new business with £7,000 in cash
  3 Opened a bank account for the business and paid £6,500 of the cash into the bank account
  6 Bought a motor van costing £1,950 paying by cheque
  9 Bought office furniture costing £500 on credit from Elite Supplies
 14 Received a loan of £1,000 in cash from P Wilson
 20 Returned some of the office furniture costing £150 to Elite Supplies because it was faulty
 23 Bought machinery costing £750 paying by cheque
 30 Paid Elite Supplies the amount owing to them £350 by cheque

2.6

M Sanchez started a new business on 1 October. In your ledger write up the double entry accounts needed to record the following transactions:

Oct 1 Started business by placing £5,000 in a business bank account
  3 Bought office equipment costing £750 on credit from Systems Ltd
  5 Took £250 out of the bank and put it in the cash till
 10 Bought motor van costing £1,750 paying by cheque
 12 Received a loan of £2,000 by cheque from S Ramsden
 15 Returned some of the office equipment costing £56 to Systems Ltd because it was faulty
 20 Bought some machinery costing £250 paying by cheque
 23 Bought some shop fittings costing £175 paying in cash
 26 Paid Systems Ltd the amount owing to them £694 by cheque
 31 Sold some of the shop fittings because they were unsuitable and received £60 in cash

2.7

P Fleming started a new business on 1 December. In your ledger write up the double entry accounts needed to record the following transactions:

Dec 1 Started a new business with £4,000 in cash
  3 Bought motor van costing £2,500 on credit from Ringways Garage
  6 Opened a bank account for the business and paid £3,500 of the cash into the bank account
  9 Bought office furniture costing £275 paying by cheque
 12 Bought some machinery at an auction paying £800 by cheque
 15 Received a loan of £3,000 by cheque from J Gillow
 18 Sold some of the machinery on credit to J Oldridge for £150
 22 Bought more office furniture costing £75, paying in cash
 28 Paid Ringways Garages £2,500 by cheque
 30 Received £150 in cash from J Oldridge

■ ▼   **3** The double entry system for sales and purchases

Usually the aim of a business is to *make a profit*. So far we have seen the double entry accounts for the assets, liabilities and capital of a business. In the same way, all other transactions of the business must be recorded.

Many businesses are involved in buying and selling. So we must now look at the accounts needed when a firm buys goods and sells goods. The firm will not be selling goods at the same price as it buys them because it hopes to make a profit. This is why the words *purchases* and *sales* have a special meaning in accounting. There has to be a separate account for *purchases* and a separate account for *sales*.

When a firm buys goods for resale they are called *purchases*. All goods sold by a firm are called *sales*. It is essential that the purchases and the sales of a business are kept completely separate and are not confused.

Business transactions may be carried out either for cash or on a credit basis. With credit transactions the goods are received immediately but payment is made at a later date. Credit transactions will need personal accounts.

Purchase of goods on credit

When a firm buys goods for resale, they are called *purchases*. They are bought with the intention of being resold at a profit. The purchases account keeps a record of all goods bought for resale.

As we have already seen every transaction must be recorded in two accounts, one account will be *debited* because it *receives* value. The other account will be *credited* because it has *given value*. Always think: '*what value is received?*', this will be the *debit* entry and then '*what value is given?*', this will be the *credit* entry.

A typical example would be: on 1 March goods costing £250 are bought on credit from M Dyson. The firm will *receive* the goods, so the debit entry will be in the purchases account, where a record of all the purchases of goods is kept, like this:

Purchases Account

	£	
Mar 1 M Dyson	250	

The credit entry, the *value given*, is recorded in the account of the person who has supplied the goods, in this example M Dyson, like this:

M Dyson Account

			£
	Mar 1	Purchases	250

Cash purchases

When goods are bought and payment is made immediately, either in cash or by cheque these are called *cash purchases*. The firm will *receive* the goods, so another debit entry will be made in the purchases account, where a record of all the purchases of goods is kept. When payment is made immediately either in cash or by cheque, the credit entry, the *value given*, would be entered in the cash account or the bank account.

A typical example would be: on 4 March the firm bought goods costing £65 paying in cash. The firm *receives* the purchases, so the debit entry is made in the purchases account, like this:

Purchases Account

		£	
Mar 1	M Dyson	250	
Mar 4	Cash	65	

The credit entry will be in the cash account because the firm has *paid out* cash; it would look like this:

Cash Account

			£
	Mar 4	Purchases	65

Another example would be: on 10 March goods costing £95 are bought, a cheque being paid immediately. The double entry accounts would now look like this:

Purchases Account

		£	
Mar 1	M Dyson	250	
Mar 4	Cash	65	
Mar 10	Bank	95	

Bank Account

			£
		Mar 10 Purchases	95

Sales of goods on credit

Only those goods bought with the intention of being resold at a profit are *sales*. In the normal course of business when a firm sells goods, they are called *sales*.

A typical example would be: on 12 March goods priced at £350 are sold on credit to W. Benson. W Benson will *receive the value* of the goods, so the debit entry will be in the personal account of the customer W Benson, like this:

W Benson Account

		£	
Mar 12	Sales	350	

The credit entry will be in the sales account where a record is kept of all *goods sold*; it would look like this:

Sales Account

			£
		Mar 12 W Benson	350

Cash sales

When goods are sold and payment is received immediately, either in cash or by cheque these are called *cash sales*. The firm will *receive* the money, so the debit entry will be in the cash account, if cash is received; or in the bank account if a cheque is received. The credit entry, would be in the sales account where a record of all *sales of goods* is kept.

A typical example would be: on 16 March goods are sold for £50, cash being received immediately. The double entry accounts would now look like this:

Cash Account

		£	
Mar 16	Sales	50	

Sales Account

				£
		Mar 12	W Benson	350
		Mar 16	Cash	50

Another example would be: on 24 March goods are sold for £75, a cheque being received immediately. The double entry accounts would now look like this:

Bank Account

		£	
Mar 24	Sales	75	

Sales Account

				£
		Mar 12	W Benson	350
		Mar 16	Cash	50
		Mar 24	Bank	75

Points to remember

- In accounting, *purchases* are goods bought with the intention of being resold. An example of this could be an electrical business: the firm would buy video recorders and television sets. If a firm buys something else, such as office equipment, this would not be regarded as purchases because the office equipment was bought to be used in the business. Office equipment would have its own separate account because it is an asset of the business and not for resale.
- Sales are the goods in which the firm normally *deals*, such as selling video recorders and television sets for an electrical business; these goods are bought with the intention of selling.
- When entering the transactions in the double entry accounts, *never* write the word '*goods*' in any account. If goods are bought the word '*purchases*' should be written in the personal account of the supplier; and '*purchases*' should appear in the cash account or the bank account for 'cash purchases'.
- Similarly, when goods are sold on credit the word '*sales*' should be written in the personal account of the customer; and '*sales*' should appear in the cash account or the bank account for 'cash sales'.

Worked example

This is a worked example exercise, first showing the transactions and then the completed double entry accounts.

Mar   1   Started a new business with £5,000 in a business bank account
      4   Bought goods costing £550 on credit from D James
      8   Bought machinery costing £350, paying by cheque
     15   Sold goods priced at £200 on credit to W Preston
     20   Bought goods costing £45, paying by cheque
     26   Sold goods priced at £150, a cheque was received immediately

The double entry accounts for these transactions would look like this:

Bank Account

			£				£
Mar	1	Capital	5,000	Mar	8	Machinery	350
	26	Sales	150		20	Purchases	45

Capital Account

				£
		Mar 1	Bank	5,000

Purchases Account

		£			
Mar 4	D James	550			
20	Bank	45			

D James Account

				£
		Mar 4	Purchases	550

Machinery Account

		£		
Mar 8	Bank	350		

W Preston Account

		£		
Mar 15	Sales	200		

Sales Account

				£
		Mar 15	W Preston	200
		26	Bank	150

Assignments

3.1

Look at the following typical business transactions and work out which accounts are involved in each transaction. In every case, think *what* has happened and decide which account has *received value* (the account to be debited) and which account has *given value* (the account to be credited).

Complete the blank spaces by inserting the name of the account to be debited and the name of the account to be credited for each transaction:

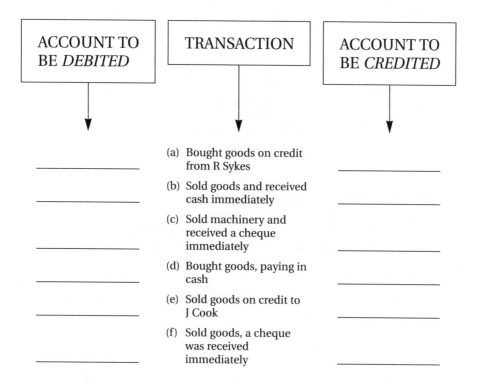

ACCOUNT TO BE *DEBITED*	TRANSACTION	ACCOUNT TO BE *CREDITED*
_____	(a) Bought goods on credit from R Sykes	_____
_____	(b) Sold goods and received cash immediately	_____
_____	(c) Sold machinery and received a cheque immediately	_____
_____	(d) Bought goods, paying in cash	_____
_____	(e) Sold goods on credit to J Cook	_____
_____	(f) Sold goods, a cheque was received immediately	_____

3.2

Look at the following typical business transactions and work out which accounts are involved in each transaction.

Complete the blank spaces by inserting the name of the account to be debited and the name of the account to be credited for each transaction:

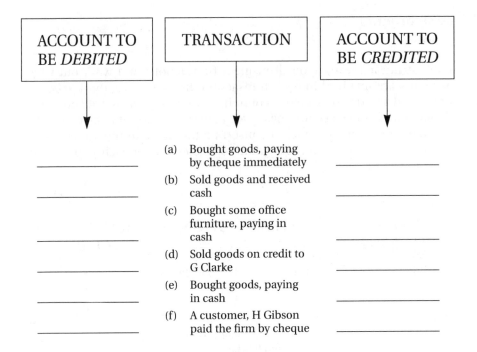

ACCOUNT TO BE *DEBITED*	TRANSACTION	ACCOUNT TO BE *CREDITED*
_____	(a) Bought goods, paying by cheque immediately	_____
_____	(b) Sold goods and received cash	_____
_____	(c) Bought some office furniture, paying in cash	_____
_____	(d) Sold goods on credit to G Clarke	_____
_____	(e) Bought goods, paying in cash	_____
_____	(f) A customer, H Gibson paid the firm by cheque	_____

3.3
Look at the following typical business transactions and work out which accounts are involved in each transaction.

Complete the blank spaces by inserting the name of the account to be debited and the name of the account to be credited for each transaction:

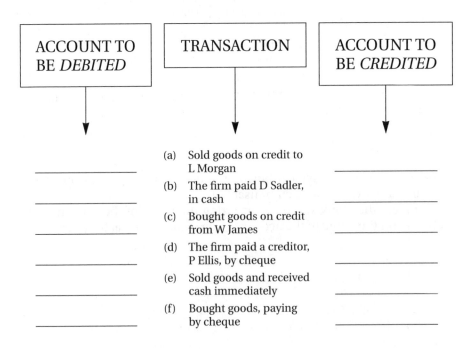

ACCOUNT TO BE *DEBITED*	TRANSACTION	ACCOUNT TO BE *CREDITED*
_____	(a) Sold goods on credit to L Morgan	_____
_____	(b) The firm paid D Sadler, in cash	_____
_____	(c) Bought goods on credit from W James	_____
_____	(d) The firm paid a creditor, P Ellis, by cheque	_____
_____	(e) Sold goods and received cash immediately	_____
_____	(f) Bought goods, paying by cheque	_____

Now use your ledger to work through the following Assignments.

3.4

M Donaldson started a new business on 1 March. In your ledger write up the double entry accounts needed to record the following transactions:

Mar	1	Started a new business with £5,000 in cash
	3	Bought office equipment costing £750, paying in cash
	8	Opened a bank account for the business and paid £4,000 of the cash into the bank account
	10	Bought goods costing £500 on credit from J Lyons
	12	Bought a secondhand motor van costing £1,900, paying by cheque
	15	Sold goods on credit priced at £150 to M Jackson
	18	Bought goods costing £120, paying in cash
	21	Sold goods for £85 and received payment by cheque
	25	Bought goods costing £275 on credit from J Lyons
	30	Received a cheque for £150 from M Jackson

3.5

J Singh started a new business on 1 May. In your ledger write up the double entry accounts needed to record the following transactions:

May	1	Started a new business with £8,000 in cash
	3	Paid £7,000 of the cash into a bank account for the business
	5	Bought goods costing £350 on credit from G Moore
	9	Bought office furniture costing £700, paying by cheque
	14	Sold goods on credit priced at £450 to F Green
	17	Bought motor van costing £5,000 on credit from Newtown Motors
	20	Sold goods priced at £50 for cash
	25	The firm paid G Moore £350 by cheque
	30	Bought goods costing £75, paying in cash

3.6

S Munro started a new business on 1 June. In your ledger write up the double entry accounts needed to record the following transactions:

June	1	Started a new business by placing £5,000 in a business bank account
	3	Bought goods costing £150 on credit from C Clifton
	5	Sold goods priced at £250, receiving payment by cheque
	7	Sold goods priced at £150 for cash
	9	Bought goods costing £50, paying in cash
	11	Bought goods costing £660 on credit from K Ingram
	14	Sold goods priced at £500 on credit to E Mason
	15	Bought motor vehicle costing £2,000, paying by cheque
	20	Received a loan of £1,000 by cheque from T Wilson
	22	The firm paid a creditor C Clifton £150 by cheque
	26	Bought goods costing £70, paying by cheque
	30	Sold goods priced at £90 on credit to G Spink

3.7

C Gulliver started a new business on 1 August. In your ledger write up the double entry accounts needed to record the following transactions:

Aug 1 Started a new business with £10,000 in cash
2 Paid £8,500 of the cash into a bank account for the business
3 Bought goods costing £150, paying in cash
5 Sold goods priced at £100 on credit to F Fieldhouse
7 Bought office equipment costing £250 on credit from Nelsons Ltd
12 Bought goods costing £650 on credit from J Black
15 Sold goods priced at £200 for cash
20 Bought motor van costing £4,000 on credit from Bright Motors
24 Sold goods priced at £150 on credit to J Smith
26 Bought goods costing £450, paying in cash
27 The firm paid Nelsons Ltd £250 in cash
28 A customer, F Fieldhouse, paid the firm £100 by cheque
29 Bought display equipment costing £350, paying by cheque
30 The firm paid J Black £650 by cheque
31 Sold goods priced at £220, receiving payment by cheque

3.8

M Gonzalas started a new business on 1 November. In your ledger write up the double entry accounts needed to record the following transactions:

Nov 1 Started a new business with £5,000 in a business bank account
2 Bought goods costing £490 on credit from W Rycroft
3 Withdrew £250 cash from the bank and placed it in the cash box
4 Bought goods costing £175, paying in cash
5 Sold goods priced at £325 on credit to J Buckley
6 Bought some display equipment costing £550 on credit from Thompson Ltd
7 Sold goods priced at £225 for cash
9 Bought goods on credit from G Stewart £595, and W Rycroft £355
10 Sold surplus display equipment on credit to E Somes for £150
12 Sold goods on credit to F Armitage £220, J Buckley £295
14 M Gonzalas, the owner puts a further £500 cash into the business
16 Bought motor van costing £1,500, paying by cheque
18 Bought goods costing £420, paying in cash
20 Received a cheque for £150 from E Somes
21 Bought some shop fittings costing £150, paying in cash
22 Bought goods costing £225 on credit from G Stewart
24 Sold goods for £190 cash
26 The firm paid W Rycroft £490 by cheque
27 J Buckley paid the firm £325 in cash
28 Bought goods costing £395 on credit from G Stewart
30 F Armitage paid the firm £220 by cheque

◪ 4 The double entry system for returns

In any business where goods are bought and sold it is likely that some will need to be *returned*. Sometimes goods will be returned to the suppliers and sometimes goods will be returned to the firm by its customers.

Goods are returned for many reasons: it may be that the goods supplied were the wrong size or colour, they may be faulty, or they may have been damaged in transit. Whatever the reason, when goods are returned the necessary entries must be made in the accounts. Goods are returned in two ways:

- Goods returned *to the firm* by its customers are called *returns inwards*.
- Goods returned *by the firm* to its suppliers are called *returns outwards*.

Returns inwards

After a sale has been made, any goods returned to the firm by its customers must be recorded in the double entry accounts.

Every transaction must be recorded in two accounts: one account will be *debited* because it *receives value*, the other account will be *credited* because it has *given value*. Always think: '*what value is received*?', this will be the *debit entry* and then '*what value is given*?', this will be the *credit entry*.

A typical example would be: on 18 March goods priced £65 are returned to the firm by W Benson.

The firm *receives* the goods so the debit entry will be in the returns inwards account, where a record of all goods returned to the firm is kept, like this:

Returns Inwards Account

	£	
Mar 18 W Benson	65	

The credit entry, the *value given*, is recorded in the account of the person who has returned the goods, in this example W Benson, like this:

W. Benson Account

			£
	Mar 18	Returns inwards	65

In some firms, goods which are returned to the firm are called *sales returns*: this is because they are sales which have now been received back by the firm. In this case the debit entry will be in a sales returns account, and the credit entry in the customer's account.

Returns outwards

When a firm returns goods to its suppliers they are usually called *returns outwards*.

A typical example would be: on 8 March goods previously purchased from M Dyson, costing £50, are now returned to the supplier.

The supplier, M Dyson, will *receive the goods*, so the debit entry will be in the personal account of M Dyson, like this:

M Dyson Account

		£	
Mar 8	Returns outwards	50	

The credit entry will be in the returns outwards account where a record is kept of all goods *returned to suppliers*, like this:

Returns Outwards Account

			£
	Mar 8	M Dyson	50

In some firms, goods which are returned by the firm to suppliers are called *purchase returns*: this is because they are purchases which have now been returned to the supplier. In this case, the debit entry is in the supplier's account but the credit entry will be in a purchase returns account.

Points to remember

- When entering the transactions in the double entry accounts, **never** write the word *'goods'* in any account. The description of the transaction will usually call the items 'goods', but if goods are returned to a firm, *returns inwards* should be written in the personal account of the customer.
- When goods are returned by a firm to a supplier, *returns outwards* should be written in the personal account of the supplier.
- If a firm returns something else to a supplier, perhaps because it is faulty, such as an office desk, this would **not** be regarded as returns outwards, because the desk was bought to be used in the business. Office furniture would have its own separate account because it is an asset to be used in the business and is not for resale.
- Instead of a returns inwards account, some firms use a *sales returns account*; and instead of a returns outwards account they use a *purchase returns account*. When this happens it is only the name of the account which differs, the double entries are the same.

Worked example

In the following worked example, consider each transaction carefully and then find each double entry in the ledger accounts:

Feb 1   Bought goods costing £150 on credit from M Singer
     4   Sold goods and received £75 in cash
     6   Bought goods costing £450 on credit from V Hood
   10   Returned goods costing £20 to M Singer
   12   Sold goods costing £125 on credit to A Towers
   15   Bought goods costing £50, paying in cash
   20   A Towers returned goods costing £25 to the firm
   22   Bought goods costing £600 on credit from J Davine
   25   Sold goods costing £250 on credit to A Towers
   28   Returned goods costing £150 to J Davine

The double entry accounts would appear as follows:

Purchases Account

		£	
Feb	1 M Singer	150	
	6 V Hood	450	
	15 Cash	50	
	22 J Davine	600	

M Singer Account

		£			£
Feb 10	Returns outwards	20	Feb 1	Purchases	150

Cash Account

		£			£
Feb 4	Sales	75	Feb 15	Purchases	50

Sales Account

					£
			Feb 4	Cash	75
			12	A Towers	125
			25	A Towers	250

V Hood Account

					£
			Feb 6	Purchases	450

Returns Outwards Account

					£
			Feb 10	M Singer	20
			28	J Davine	150

A Towers Account

		£			£
Feb 12	Sales	125	Feb 20	Returns inwards	25
25	Sales	250			

Returns Inwards Account

		£		
Feb 20	A Towers	25		

J Davine Account

	£			£
Feb 28 Returns outwards	150	Feb 22 Purchases		600

Look at the illustration of some typical business transactions in Figure 4.1. Sometimes goods are returned and sometimes assets are returned; it shows which accounts are involved in each transaction:

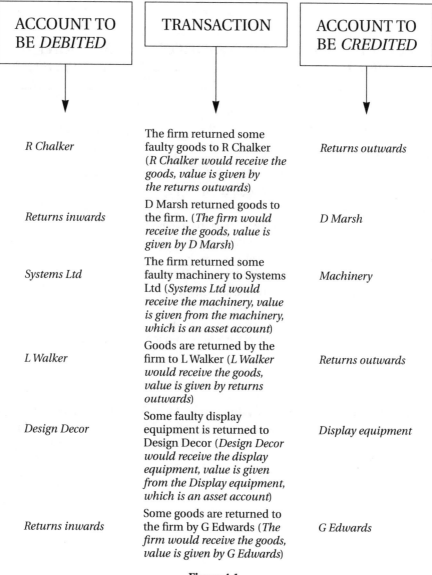

ACCOUNT TO BE *DEBITED*	TRANSACTION	ACCOUNT TO BE *CREDITED*
R Chalker	The firm returned some faulty goods to R Chalker (*R Chalker would receive the goods, value is given by the returns outwards*)	Returns outwards
Returns inwards	D Marsh returned goods to the firm. (*The firm would receive the goods, value is given by D Marsh*)	D Marsh
Systems Ltd	The firm returned some faulty machinery to Systems Ltd (*Systems Ltd would receive the machinery, value is given from the machinery, which is an asset account*)	Machinery
L Walker	Goods are returned by the firm to L Walker (*L Walker would receive the goods, value is given by returns outwards*)	Returns outwards
Design Decor	Some faulty display equipment is returned to Design Decor (*Design Decor would receive the display equipment, value is given from the Display equipment, which is an asset account*)	Display equipment
Returns inwards	Some goods are returned to the firm by G Edwards (*The firm would receive the goods, value is given by G Edwards*)	G Edwards

Figure 4.1

Assignments

4.1

Look at the following typical business transactions and work out which accounts are involved in each transaction. In every case, think what has happened and decide which account has *received value* (the account to be *debited*) and which account has *given value* (the account to be *credited*).

Complete the blank spaces by inserting the name of the account to be debited and the name of the account to be credited for each transaction:

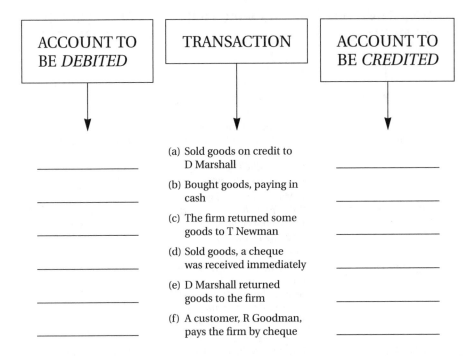

ACCOUNT TO BE *DEBITED*	TRANSACTION	ACCOUNT TO BE *CREDITED*
_____	(a) Sold goods on credit to D Marshall	_____
_____	(b) Bought goods, paying in cash	_____
_____	(c) The firm returned some goods to T Newman	_____
_____	(d) Sold goods, a cheque was received immediately	_____
_____	(e) D Marshall returned goods to the firm	_____
_____	(f) A customer, R Goodman, pays the firm by cheque	_____

4.2

Complete the blank spaces by inserting the name of the account to be debited and the name of the account to be credited for each transaction:

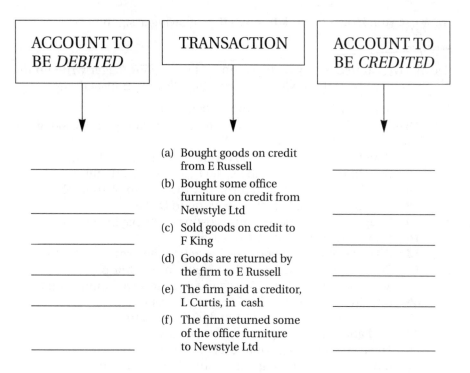

ACCOUNT TO BE *DEBITED*	TRANSACTION	ACCOUNT TO BE *CREDITED*
_____	(a) Bought goods on credit from E Russell	_____
_____	(b) Bought some office furniture on credit from Newstyle Ltd	_____
_____	(c) Sold goods on credit to F King	_____
_____	(d) Goods are returned by the firm to E Russell	_____
_____	(e) The firm paid a creditor, L Curtis, in cash	_____
_____	(f) The firm returned some of the office furniture to Newstyle Ltd	_____

4.3

Complete the blank spaces by inserting the name of the account to be debited and the name of the account to be credited for each transaction:

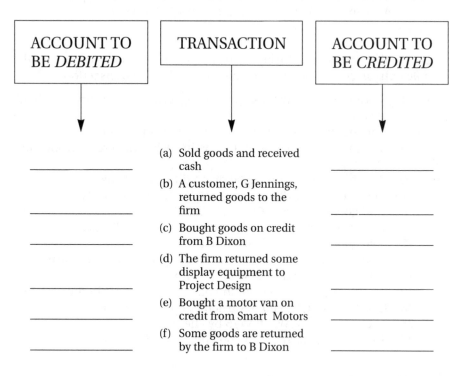

ACCOUNT TO BE *DEBITED*	TRANSACTION	ACCOUNT TO BE *CREDITED*
_____	(a) Sold goods and received cash	_____
_____	(b) A customer, G Jennings, returned goods to the firm	_____
_____	(c) Bought goods on credit from B Dixon	_____
_____	(d) The firm returned some display equipment to Project Design	_____
_____	(e) Bought a motor van on credit from Smart Motors	_____
_____	(f) Some goods are returned by the firm to B Dixon	_____

Now use your ledger to work through the following assignments:

4.4
Dean Sayer started a new business on 1 May. In your ledger write up the double entry accounts needed to record the following transactions:

May **1** Started a new business with £7,000 in cash
   2 Opened a bank account for the business and paid £6,500 of the cash into the bank account
   3 Bought goods costing £500 on credit from M Trenholme
   5 Bought motor van costing £3,000 on credit from Linton Garages
   6 Goods costing £60 are returned by the firm to M Trenholme
   8 Sold goods priced at £250 on credit to D Davey
   9 Bought some office furniture costing £300, paying by cheque
   10 Sold goods priced at £50 for cash
   12 D Davey returned goods costing £40 to the firm
   15 Bought goods costing £750 on credit from R Marples
   18 Sold goods priced at £75, a cheque was received immediately
   20 Bought goods costing £145, paying in cash
   22 Goods costing £80 are returned by the firm to R Marples
   24 Sold goods priced at £221 to K Bradshaw
   26 The firm paid M Trenholme a cheque for £440
   27 K Bradshaw returned goods costing £21 to the firm
   28 Bought goods costing £350 on credit from R Marples
   29 The firm paid Linton Garages £250 by cheque
   30 Goods costing £25 are returned by the firm to R Marples
   31 A customer, D Davey, paid the firm £210 by cheque

4.5
M Daswani started a new business on 1 June. In your ledger write up the double entry accounts needed to record the following transactions:

June **1** Started a new business by placing £10,000 in a business bank account
   2 Bought goods costing £900 on credit from M Webb
   4 Bought display equipment costing £250 on credit from Euro Designs Ltd
   6 Bought goods costing £500 on credit from T Ross
   7 Goods costing £125 are returned by the firm to M Webb
   8 Sold goods priced at £425 to V Reed
   11 The firm returned some goods costing £50 to T Ross
   12 Sold goods priced at £300 for cash
   15 A customer, V Reed, returned goods costing £75 to the firm
   17 Sold goods priced at £350 to F Redman
   20 Withdrew £500 cash from the bank and placed it in the cash box
   22 Goods costing £25 are returned to the firm by F Redman
   25 The firm paid M Webb £775 by cheque
   27 Sold goods priced at £230 on credit to F Redman

28   A customer, V Reed, paid the firm £350 by cheque

30   The firm paid Euro Designs Ltd £250 in cash

4.6

Jill O'Connor started a new business on 1 August. In your ledger write up the double entry accounts needed to record the following transactions:

Aug **1**   Started a new business with £5,000 in cash

     3   Bought goods costing £875 on credit from T Mann

     5   Opened a bank account for the business, and paid £4,500 of the cash into the bank account

     7   Goods costing £75 are returned by the firm to T Mann

     8   Bought office furniture costing £295, paying by cheque

     9   Sold goods priced at £580 on credit to James Seymore

   10   Bought goods costing £420, paying by cheque

   12   Bought motor van costing £4,500 on credit from Greens Garages

   13   James Seymore returned goods costing £40 to the firm

   14   Sold goods costing £165 on credit to T Williams

   15   Bought goods costing £300 on credit from T Mann

   18   Sold goods priced at £124 for cash

   19   T Williams returned goods costing £36 to the firm

   20   The firm received a loan of £3,000 by cheque from J Kelly

   22   Goods costing £30 are returned by the firm to T Mann

   25   The firm paid first instalment of £200 to Greens Garages by cheque

   28   Sold goods priced at £175 on credit to James Seymore

   29   The firm paid T Mann £1,070 by cheque

   30   Bought goods costing £320, paying in cash

   31   A customer, T Williams, paid the firm £129 in cash

▪ ṃ **5** The double entry system for expenses

Expenses

There will always be some *expenses* incurred when running a business. All firms will have to make payments for expenses such as, telephone, gas, electricity, rates, rent, wages, motor expenses and so on. If a business kept only one account called an '*expenses account*' this would give only the overall total of all the expenses. Because a business needs to know exactly how much is spent on each individual expense, separate ledger accounts are opened for each type of expense.

Every transaction must be recorded in two accounts: one account will be debited and another *account* will be credited.

A typical example would be: on 8 March the firm paid wages of £550 in cash. The firm's employees *receive* the wages so the debit entry will be in the wages account, where a record of all payments for wages is kept, like this:

Wages Account

			£		
Mar 8	Cash		550		

The credit entry, the *value given*, is recorded in the cash account like this:

Cash Account

			£
	Mar 8	Wages	550

Another example of an expense account could be motor expenses; these usually include items such as: petrol, oil, servicing and repairs.

On 21 March the firm paid motor expenses of £75 by cheque. The debit entry will be in the motor expenses account, where a record of all *payments for motor expenses* is kept, like this:

Motor Expenses Account

	£		
Mar 21 Bank	75		

The credit entry, the *value given*, is recorded in the bank account, like this:

Bank Account

			£
	Mar 21 Motor expenses		75

The proprietor's drawings account

Sometimes the proprietor, who is the owner of the business, will want to take money or goods out of the business for his private use. Whether he takes cash or goods, these withdrawals are known in book-keeping as *drawings*.

We have already seen that the owner's original investment in the business is recorded in the capital account. This is a very important account, and in order to prevent numerous entries being made in it, any withdrawals from the business by the owner are recorded in a drawings account. At the end of the financial year the total of the drawings account will be transferred to the capital account. Drawings are recorded in the double entry accounts as illustrated in the following examples.

A typical example would be: on 8 March, the proprietor takes £100 cash out of the business for his personal use. The debit entry will be in the drawings account, where a record of all money or goods *taken by the owner* is kept, like this:

Drawings Account

	£		
Mar 8 Cash	100		

The credit entry, the *value given*, is recorded in the cash account like this:

Cash Account

			£
	Mar 8 Drawings		100

Another example would be: on 17 March the proprietor takes £60 of goods out of the business for his own use. The debit entry will be in the drawings account, where a record of all money or goods *taken by the owner* is kept, like this:

Drawings Account

	£	
Mar 8 Cash	100	
Mar 17 Purchases	60	

The credit entry, the *value given*, is recorded in the purchases account like this:

Purchases Account

		£
	Mar 17 Drawings	60

Revenue received accounts

While all businesses will have to pay for various expenses to enable them to operate, some will also *receive income for the services they provide* for others.

Special attention is required when dealing with revenue received accounts. This is revenue (money) which is received by the business. An example of this could be if a firm occupied a large building with three floors and decided to sub-let one complete floor, renting this part of the building to another firm would provide a useful income. To avoid confusion with the rent account, which is an *expense*, a separate account is opened for rent received. This is illustrated in the following example:

A retailer lets the flat above his shop for £145 a month. The rent is received by cheque on the first of each month from the sub-tenant.

Consider the twofold effect: the money is received by cheque so a debit entry is made in the bank account, like this:

Bank Account

	£	
Mar 1 Rent received	145	

The credit entry is recorded in the rent received account, like this:

Rent Received Account

		£
	Mar 1 Bank	145

Another example of revenue received would be *commission received*. One firm may provide a service for another and charge a commission. On 8 March £60 cash is received for commission earned by the firm.

Consider the twofold effect: the money is received in cash so a debit entry is made in the cash account, like this:

Cash Account

	£	
Mar 8 Commission received	60	

The credit entry is recorded in the commission received account, like this:

Commission Received Account

		£
	Mar 8 Cash	60

Points to remember

- Various expenses are incurred in running a business, each type of expense is kept in a *separate account*. This is to enable the business to see exactly how much is spent on each individual expense.
- All withdrawals from a business by the owner, for *private use*, are recorded in a drawings account.
- *Revenue* (*money*) *received transactions* always require careful consideration. They are particularly popular with examiners as they are an excellent test of a student's knowledge of the double entry system.

Assignments

5.1

For each of the following transactions complete the blank spaces by inserting the name of the account to be debited and the name of the account to be credited:

(a) Paid motor expenses in cash

Debit _____ Account   Credit _____ Account

(b) Paid rent by cheque

Debit _____ Account   Credit _____ Account

(c) Proprietor took cash out of the business for personal use

Debit _____ Account   Credit _____ Account

(d) Paid rates by cheque

Debit _____ Account   Credit _____ Account

(e) Received commission in cash

Debit _____ Account   Credit _____ Account

(f) Paid insurance by cheque

Debit _____ Account   Credit _____ Account

5.2

For each of the following transactions complete the blank spaces by inserting the name of the account to be debited and the name of the account to be credited:

(a) Bought goods, paying in cash

Debit _____ Account   Credit _____ Account

(b) Received rent by cheque

Debit _____ Account   Credit _____ Account

(c) Paid motor expenses by cheque

Debit _____ Account   Credit _____ Account

(d) Sold goods on credit to J Kendall

Debit _____ Account   Credit _____ Account

(e) Bought motor van on credit from Leaders Garages

Debit _____ Account   Credit _____ Account

(f) Paid wages in cash

Debit _____ Account   Credit _____ Account

5.3

For each of the following transactions complete the blank spaces by inserting the name of the account to be debited and the name of the account to be credited:

(a) Paid electricity bill by cheque

Debit _____ Account   Credit _____ Account

(b) Sold goods and received cash

Debit _____ Account   Credit _____ Account

(c) Received commission by cheque
     Debit _____ Account   Credit _____ Account
(d) Goods are returned to the firm by J Kilburn
     Debit _____ Account   Credit _____ Account
(e) Bought office furniture, paying by cheque
     Debit _____ Account   Credit _____ Account
(f) Proprietor took cash out of the business for personal use
     Debit _____ Account   Credit _____ Account

5.4
For each of the following transactions complete the blank spaces by inserting the name of the account to be debited and the name of the account to be credited:

(a) Goods are returned to R Bright
     Debit _____ Account   Credit _____ Account
(b) Paid rates by cheque
     Debit _____ Account   Credit _____ Account
(c) Sold goods on credit to K Williams
     Debit _____ Account   Credit _____ Account
(d) Proprietor took goods for personal use
     Debit _____ Account   Credit _____ Account
(e) Goods are returned to the firm by K Williams
     Debit _____ Account   Credit _____ Account
(f) Received a refund of rates in cash
     Debit _____ Account   Credit _____ Account

Now use your ledger to work through the following Assignments:

5.5
A Oldridge started a new business on 1 May 20-7. In your ledger write up the double entry accounts needed to record the following transactions:

May	1	Started business with £5,000 in a business bank account
	2	Bought goods on credit costing £750 from J Richardson
	4	Withdrew £500 cash from the bank
	6	Returned goods costing £40 to J Richardson
	7	Proprietor took £100 cash for personal use
	9	Sold goods costing £250, receiving a cheque immediately
	11	Sold goods on credit to K Stead £150, M Day £229
	12	Paid rent £75 by cheque
	14	K Stead returned goods priced at £24 to the firm
	15	Paid motor expenses in cash £58
	16	Received rent for premises sub-let £30 by cheque
	19	Bought goods on credit costing £950 from S Ramsden
	22	Paid wages £150 in cash
	24	Received £126 by cheque from K Stead

25 Cash sales £88

26 Sold goods on credit to T Barnett £122, M Day £159

27 Returned goods £68 to S Ramsden

28 Bought office furniture costing £200, paying in cash

29 Proprietor took £50 by cheque for his private use

30 Paid J Richardson the amount owing of £710 by cheque

31 Paid rent of £75 in cash

5.6

K Wilson started a new business on 1 June 20-7. In your ledger write up the double entry accounts needed to record the following transactions:

Jun 1 Started business with £10,000 in cash

2 Bought goods costing £500, paying in cash

3 Paid rent of £100 in cash

6 Paid £9,000 of the cash into a business bank account

8 Sold goods on credit to J Stevens £250

9 Received sales commission of £50 in cash

10 Purchased goods on credit from A Dawson £329, C Page £172

12 K Wilson took £75 cash for his own use

14 J Stevens returned goods £25

15 Bought motor van costing £4,000 on credit from Northtown Garages

16 Returned goods £22 to C Page

18 Paid rates by cheque £150

20 Bought goods £750, paying by cheque immediately

22 Bought stationery £18, paying in cash

23 Sold goods on credit to G Blackman £495

24 K Wilson took £120 by cheque for personal use

26 Sold goods and received £265 in cash

27 Received sales commission £28 by cheque

28 J Stevens paid his account of £225 by cheque

29 G Blackman returned goods to the firm £58

30 Paid motor expenses £55 in cash

5.7

D Shelley started a new business on 1 August 20-7. In your ledger write up the double entry accounts needed to record the following transactions:

Aug 1 Started business with £5,000 in a business bank account

2 Purchased goods on credit £359 from Smith & Weston Ltd

4 Bought office furniture costing £460 on credit from Newstylax

5 Bought goods costing £675, paying by cheque

7 Returned goods £29 to Smith & Weston Ltd

9 Sold goods on credit to H Gibson £450

10 Withdrew £300 cash from the bank

12 D Shelley took £50 cash for his private use

14 Paid rent £200 in cash

15 Sold goods £150, receiving a cheque immediately
16 Paid insurance £30 by cheque
18 Received a loan of £2,000 by cheque from R Cawood
19 H Gibson returned goods £40
20 Paid Smith & Weston a cheque of £330
21 Received part of the amount owing from H Gibson £200 in cash.
22 Paid wages in cash £175
23 Paid electricity bill of £68 by cheque
24 Sold goods on credit to J Youngman £278, H Dale £181
26 Paid Newstylax a cheque £460
27 Goods returned to the firm by J Youngman £58
28 Received rent of £50 in cash for part of premises sub-let
29 Cash purchases £45
30 Insurance was overpaid; a refund of £5 is received by cheque
31 Received a cheque of £181 from H Dale

5.8

T Garside started a new business on 1 October 20-8. In your ledger write up the double entry accounts needed to record the following transactions:

Oct 1 Started business with £7,000 in the business bank account and £500 in cash
2 Bought goods on credit from T Richie £750, R Kemp £375 and P Douglas £480
3 Paid rates £75 by cheque
4 Bought motor van costing £2,000 on credit from Abbot Garages
5 Sold goods on credit to D Jenkins £295, A Andrews £190
6 Returned goods to R Kemp £45
7 Paid insurance £150 in cash
8 Cash sales £65
9 Received commission of £75 by cheque
10 Bought goods on credit from R Kemp £267, W Wallace £290
11 A Andrews returned goods to the firm £38
12 Paid motor expenses £35 in cash
13 Sold goods for cash £150
14 Received refund of rates £20 by cheque
15 Paid wages £250 in cash
16 Received a loan of £4,000 by cheque from A Goldman
17 Bought office fixtures costing £195 on credit from Burton Supplies
18 A Andrews paid the firm £152 by cheque
19 Bought goods on credit from R Kemp £360
20 Cash purchases £150
21 Paid T Richie £750 by cheque
22 Returned goods to R Kemp £55
23 Sold goods on credit to D Jenkins £130, R Smythe £276
24 Commission received in cash £95
24 Paid wages £200 in cash

25 Paid R. Kemp the amount owing, £902 by cheque
26 Received a cheque of £425 from D Jenkins
27 Paid motor expenses £22 in cash
28 T Garside took £150 by cheque for his personal use
29 R Smythe returned goods £26
30 Paid first instalment of £150 by cheque to Abbot Garages
31 Sold goods for cash £96

5.9
F Patel started a new business on 1 November 20-8. In your ledger write up the double entry accounts needed to record the following transactions:

Nov 1 Started business with £4,000 in a business bank account and £350 in cash
2 Bought goods on credit from J Dean £650, R Reagan £467 and M Nichols £265
3 Sold goods for cash £150
4 Received a loan of £2,500 by cheque from J Franks
5 Paid rates £212 by cheque
6 Bought motor van costing £1,500 on credit from Websters Garages
7 Sold goods on credit to E Barker £221, J Armitage £357 and S Grey £128
8 Paid motor expenses £35 in cash
9 F Patel took £80 cash for his own use
10 Paid insurance £55 by cheque
11 Bought goods on credit from R Reagan £330, J Dean £125
12 Sold goods for cash £245
13 A refund of rates £25 is received by cheque
14 Paid wages in cash £130
15 Returned goods to R Reagan £45
16 Sold goods on credit to E Barker £325, S Grey £250
17 Paid electricity bill of £124 by cheque
18 Received rent £55 in cash from sub-tenant
19 Bought goods on credit from M Nichols £356, B Harris £95
20 Bought stationery costing £47, paying by cheque
21 Returned goods to M Nichols £38
22 F Patel took £150 by cheque for private use
23 Paid J Dean the amount outstanding £775 by cheque
24 Received a cheque of £378 from S Grey
25 Cash sales £200
25 Bought office fixtures costing £150, paying in cash
26 Received a cheque of £357 from J Armitage
27 Paid wages in cash £75
28 Paid Websters Garages £1,500 by cheque
29 Bought goods on credit from B Harris £450
30 Returned goods to B Harris £65

⏷ 6 Balancing accounts

The term 'balance' is the word used in accounting to describe the difference between the two sides of an account. It is the most important figure in any account because it tells the value of that account.

We will now look at the method used to calculate the balance at a particular time. Accounts can be balanced at any time but in most firms they are balanced at the end of each month. This is how it is done:

1 Add up the side of the account which is *greatest in value*
2 Add up the *other side* of the account
3 Deduct the *smaller total* from the *larger total*: the difference between the two sides is the '*balance*'
4 Now enter the balance on the side which is *smallest in value*; this is described as the *balance c/d*, which means that the balance is to be carried down
5 Enter the totals on *both sides of the account*, making sure that the two totals are level with each other; as the difference between the two sides has been added to the smaller side, both sides will now be equal
6 The *balance* is then brought down, to the opposite side of the account

To illustrate the process, let us look at a typical cash account:

Cash Account

		£				£
Mar 1	Sales	350	Mar	2	Motor expenses	35
				4	Rent	50
				9	Stationery	15
				15	Drawings	100

Cash *received* is entered at the *debit* side of the account, cash *paid out* is entered at the *credit* side:

	£
	£
The debit side is greatest in value, it totals	350
The credit side totals	200
The difference between the two sides is the *balance*	150
(it represents the amount of cash which *remains*)	

This is how the cash account will look after it has been balanced:

Cash Account

		£				£
Mar 1	Sales	350	Mar	2	Motor expenses	35
				4	Rent	50
				9	Stationery	15
				15	Drawings	100
				31	Balance c/d	150
		350				350
Apr 1	Balance b/d	150				

Most firms balance their accounts at the end of each month, so the balance to be carried down, abbreviated as 'c/d', is written in the account on the last day of the current month. The balance is then brought down '(b/d)' on the first day of the next month. These two balancing entries are a *double entry*.

When the balance is brought down to the debit side of an account, it is described as a 'debit balance'. When the balance is brought down to the credit side of an account, it is described as a 'credit balance'.

Balancing debtors' accounts

Every firm will need to know *how much is owed by its customers for goods supplied*.

We can now look at a customer's account for transactions during April 20-6:

B Senior Account

		£				£
Apr 3	Sales	235	Apr	10	Returns inwards	46
15	Sales	350		28	Bank	189
25	Sales	145				

To balance this account, the same principles apply; first total the side which is *greatest in value*:

	£
The debit side is greatest in value, it totals	730
The credit side totals	235
The difference between the two sides is the *balance*	495
(it represents the *amount owed* by B Senior)	

This is how B Senior's account will look after it has been balanced:

B Senior Account

			£				£
Apr	3	Sales	235	Apr	10	Returns inwards	46
	15	Sales	350		28	Bank	189
	25	Sales	145		30	Balance c/d	495
			730				730
May	1	Balance b/d	495				

We can now look at G Palmer's account:

G Palmer Account

			£				£
Apr	2	Sales	120	Apr	26	Bank	280
	8	Sales	160				

This customer owed the firm nothing at the end of April 20-6 because his account was paid in full: both sides are equal so there is no balance, but the account needs to be totalled, like this:

G Palmer Account

			£				£
Apr	2	Sales	120	Apr	26	Bank	280
	8	Sales	160				
			280				280

If accounts contain only one entry **do not** enter a total. A double line ruled under each side will mean that the entry is its own total, the balance is written in and brought down like this:

H Malik Account

			£				£
Apr	18	Sales	250	Apr	30	Balance c/d	250
May	1	Balance b/d	250				

Balancing creditors' accounts

Firms regularly need to know *how much they owe to their suppliers*. Exactly the same principles will apply when balances are brought down to the credit side. We can now look at a supplier's account for transactions during April 20-6:

F Reedman Account

			£				£
Apr	12	Returns outwards	25	Apr	7	Purchases	625
	29	Bank	600		18	Purchases	300

To find the balance on this account, first total the side which is *greatest in value*:

	£
The credit side is greatest in value, it totals	925
The debit side totals	625
The difference between the two sides is the *balance*	300
(it represents the *amount owed to* F Reedman)	

This is how F Reedman's Account will look after it has been balanced:

F Reedman Account

			£				£
Apr	12	Returns outwards	25	Apr	7	Purchases	625
	29	Bank	600		18	Purchases	300
	30	Balance c/d	300				
			925				925
				May	1	Balance b/d	300

If an account contains only one entry on each side which are equal to each other, totals are not entered; a double line is ruled under each side, like this:

T Gordon Account

		£				£
Apr 28	Bank	250	Apr	5	Purchases	250

Personal accounts

Every personal account has the name of a person or firm with which the business deals. These are mainly debtors and creditors who may be sole traders, partnerships or limited companies: their accounts keep a record of the firm's dealings with this person or firm.

From our earlier work we know that the capital account is a very special type of a personal account. The value of the *proprietor's investment* in the business is recorded in this account.

Real accounts

Real accounts keep a record of the assets of a business. They are called 'real' because it is possible to touch them: they are real things, such as buildings, office furniture, motor vehicles, machinery and cash. All asset accounts are real accounts.

Nominal accounts

Nominal accounts contain the records of *income and expenses*. Rent, rates, electricity, wages and insurance are typical examples of expenses, while commission received and rent received are examples of income. *Nominal* means 'in name only'. The wages account keeps a record of money paid out for wages; it may have a balance of £1,500 but the money is not really there, it has been paid in wages to the employees.

It is of vital importance that firms keep records of their income and expenses during the year because at the end of the year this information is used to calculate the *profit or loss of the business.*

Points to remember

- The *balance* of an account is the difference between the two sides. It is the most significant figure in any account because it tells the value of that account.
- When the balance is brought down to the debit side, it is described as a *debit balance.*
- When the balance is brought down to the credit side, it is described as a *credit balance.*
- Accounts can be balanced at any time but generally they are balanced at the end of each month.

Assignments

6.1

Complete the blank spaces by classifying the following accounts as personal, real or nominal; the first one is completed as an example:

(a)	D Wilson	*personal* account
(b)	Display equipment	_____ account
(c)	Telephone	_____ account
(d)	Motor van	_____ account
(e)	Smith & Pearson Ltd	_____ account
(f)	Cash	_____ account

6.2

Complete the blank spaces by classifying the following accounts as personal, real or nominal; the first one is completed as an example:

(a)	Works machinery	*real* account
(b)	Rent received	_____ account
(c)	T Greenwood	_____ account
(d)	Office furniture	_____ account
(e)	Electricity	_____ account
(f)	Stylax Ltd	_____ account

6.3

Enter the following transactions in the *personal* accounts only, do not write up the other accounts. Balance each personal account at the end of the month and bring down the balance:

Jan 1 Bought goods on credit from D Hall £348, L Walker £576, B Hagston £850

4 Purchases on credit from L Walker £125, B Dickson £367

9 Returned goods to B Hagston £50, L Walker £55

16 Bought goods on credit from B Dickson £146, J Dunn £85

18 Returned goods to B Dickson £67

26 Paid D Hall £348 by cheque

30 Paid B Dickson £300 in cash

6.4

Enter the following transactions in the *personal* accounts only, do not write up the other accounts. Balance each personal account at the end of the month and bring down the balance:

Feb 1 Sold goods on credit to M Harding £360, J Johnstone £98, E Briggs £450, T Myers £212

3 Sales on credit to R Godfrey £330, P Ellis £421

6 Goods returned to the firm by J Johnstone £24, E Briggs £50

9 Sold goods on credit to T Myers £152, R Godfrey £135

12 Goods returned to the firm by M Harding £60

15 Received £300 in cash from M Harding

18 Sales on credit to E Briggs £220, T Myers £240

19 P Ellis paid the firm £421 by cheque

20 Goods returned to the firm by T Myers £52

25 Received a cheque of £400 from E Briggs

27 Sales on credit to R Kemp £350, E Briggs £90

28 Received £74 in cash from J Johnstone

6.5

Enter the following transactions in the *personal* accounts only, do not write up the other accounts. Balance each personal account at the end of the month and bring the balance down:

Mar 1 Bought goods on credit from J Radcliffe £525, P Coates £450, W James £695, P Williams £155

    4 Sold goods on credit to J Burns £158, S Daniel £350, D Hall £212, P Harper £90

    6 Returned goods to P Coates £55, P Williams £25

    8 Purchases on credit from W James £152, P Coates £295, J Allen £355

  12 Sold goods on credit to S Daniel £395, D Hall £422, J Nixon £125

  15 Paid J Radcliffe £525 by cheque

  18 Goods returned to the firm by J Nixon £20, S Daniel £45

  21 Received £158 in cash from J Burns

  25 Sold goods on credit to P Harper £155, J Nixon £120

  27 Purchased goods on credit from P Williams £240, J Allen £170

  29 Returned goods to J Allen £28

  30 Paid cheques to P Coates £395, P Williams £130

  31 Received £212 by cheque from D Hall

6.6

Enter the following transactions in the *personal* accounts only, do not write up the other accounts. Balance each personal account at the end of the month and bring down the balance:

Apr 1 Bought goods on credit from R Pearson £459, S Dean £360, L Gregg £126, N Banks £280

    3 Sold goods on credit to P Lodge £240, D Simons £120

    5 Goods returned to S Dean £30, L Gregg £26

    7 Sold goods on credit to J Watson £195, P Lodge £150, R Sutcliffe £95, T Barnsdale £360

  10 Purchased goods on credit from L Gregg £326, R Pearson £231

  11 Sold goods on credit to D Simons £97, J Watson £219

  12 Bought goods on credit from N Banks £350, S Dean £195

  15 Sold goods on credit to J Watson £175, R Sutcliffe £150, F McKay £220, T Barnsdale £155

  18 Returned goods to S Dean £45, N Banks £50

21 Goods returned to the firm by F McKay £20, J Watson £25
23 Paid R Pearson £459 by cheque
25 Received £200 in cash from F McKay
26 Sold goods on credit to R Sutcliffe £235, D Simons £190
27 Bought goods on credit from K Stocks £490, S Dean £280, N Banks £125, J Carlton £175
28 Received £360 by cheque from T Barnsdale
29 Returned goods to K Stocks £35, J Carlton £25
30 Paid L Gregg £426 and N Banks £230, by cheque

6.7
W Peterson started a new business on 1 May 20-8. In your ledger write up the double entry accounts needed to record the following transactions: write up *all* the accounts. Balance the accounts at the end of the month and bring the balances down:

May 1 Started business with £2,500 in a business bank account
3 Bought goods on credit from M Seal £240, J Green £195, S Sutcliffe £280
5 Sold goods on credit to E Phillips £125, W Lodge £178
6 Withdrew £500 cash from the bank
7 Returned goods to J Green £35, S Sutcliffe £20
8 Paid rent in cash £75
9 W Peterson took £50 cash for his private use
12 Received a loan of £1,000 by cheque from G Normanton
14 Sold goods and received £120 in cash
15 Bought office stationery costing £45, paying by cheque
18 Received a cheque £125 from E Phillips
20 Paid insurance £95 in cash
22 Bought goods on credit from J Green £450, M Seal £335
24 Purchased goods costing £250, paying in cash
25 Proprietor took £50 cash for own use
27 Paid rent £75 by cheque
28 Paid by cheque S Sutcliffe £260, M Seal £240
30 Sold goods on credit to W Lodge £258, E Phillips £160

6.8
M Kellerman started a new business on 1 June 20-8. In your ledger write up the double entry accounts needed to record the following transactions: write up *all* the accounts. Balance the accounts at the end of the month and bring the balances down:

Jun 1 Started business with £6,000 in a business bank account and £250 in cash
2 Bought goods on credit from B Lewis £619, E Daley £197
3 Bought stationery costing £24, paying in cash
4 Returned faulty goods to E Daley £29
5 Paid rent £125 by cheque

6   Sold goods on credit to D Mills £136, J Kendall £333, W Barry £85
7   Bought machinery costing £316 on credit from Groves & Bean Ltd
8   Paid wages £65 in cash
9   Goods returned to the firm by J Kendall £23
10   Bought motor vehicle costing £950 on credit from Lockwood Motors
11   Sold some surplus machinery £125 on credit to B Freeman
12   M Kellerman took £50 cash for personal use
13   Purchased goods on credit from D Trent £367, E Daley £522, B Todd £168
14   Paid motor expenses £48 in cash
15   Received rent from sub-tenant £25 by cheque
16   Sold goods and received cash £155
17   Returned goods to D Trent £47, B Todd £18
18   Paid wages £75 in cash
19   Bought goods costing £76, paying in cash
21   Sold goods on credit to W Barry £96, D Mills £134
22   Proprietor took £50 by cheque for own use
23   Received £125 in cash from B Freeman
24   Bought goods on credit from B Lewis £447, E Daley £292
25   Received £181 by cheque from W Barry
26   Goods returned to the firm by D Mills £22
27   Paid D Trent £320 by cheque
28   Goods bought on credit from B Todd £275, B Lewis £196
29   Received £310 in cash from J Kendall
30   Paid Lockwood Motors £950 by cheque

■ ⊻ **7** The trial balance

A trial balance is a simple way of checking that all entries made in the ledger have been completed correctly. When transactions are entered in the ledger accounts every debit entry will have a corresponding credit entry, therefore in principle the *debit balances should equal the credit balances.* Checking that the debit balances do in fact equal the credit balances is done by preparing a trial balance.

A trial balance is a list of *balances only*, arranged in two columns according to whether they are debit balances or credit balances. When there is a debit balance on an account, the balance is entered in the debit column; when there is a credit balance on an account, the balance is entered in the credit column; *accounts which do not have a balance are not entered.* When all the balances are entered, the two columns are totalled and they should agree. When they do, it is a good indication that the transactions have been entered correctly in the ledger accounts.

A trial balance is usually drawn up at the end of each month, its purpose is to test the arithmetical accuracy of the book-keeping. Although useful as a means of checking the accuracy of transactions recorded in the ledger, the agreement of a trial balance does not prove that errors have not been made, it has limitations as there are some errors it will not reveal; these are considered later in Unit 28.

A trial balance is always taken out at a *specific date* and this date should be clearly written as part of the heading. A trial balance is *not* an account and should not be placed in the ledger; the ruling on journal paper, which has two columns on the right-hand side is generally used for preparing a trial balance.

Look at this worked example, all transactions have been entered and the accounts balanced for May 20-8.

Worked example

Bank Account

			£				£
May	1	Capital	15,000	May	10	Motor van	4,950
	4	Sales	125		14	Purchases	295
	21	Sales	50		18	Drawings	100
					26	Insurance	175
					28	D Carter	220
					29	Drawings	85
					31	Balance c/d	9,350
			15,175				15,175
Jun	1	Balance b/d	9,350				

Capital Account

			£				£
May 31		Balance c/d	15,000	May	1	Bank	15,000
				Jun	1	Balance b/d	15,000

Purchases Account

			£				£
May	3	D Carter	270	May 31		Balance c/d	870
	14	Bank	295				
	22	J Hussain	305				
			870				870
Jun	1	Balance b/d	870				

D Carter Account

			£				£
May	8	Returns outwards	50	May	3	Purchases	270
	28	Bank	220				
			270				270

Sales Account

		£				£
May 31	Balance c/d	395	May 4	Bank		125
			12	A Jones		75
			21	Bank		50
			24	A Jones		145
		395				395
			Jun 1	Balance b/d		395

Returns Outwards Account

		£				£
May 31	Balance c/d	80	May 8	D Carter		50
			27	J Hussain		30
		80				80
			Jun 1	Balance b/d		80

Motor Van Account

		£			£
May 10	Bank	4,950	May 31	Balance c/d	4,950
Jun 1	Balance b/d	4,950			

A Jones Account

		£			£
May 12	Sales	75	May 31	Balance c/d	220
24	Sales	145			
		220			220
Jun 1	Balance b/d	220			

Drawings Account

		£			£
May 18	Bank	100	May 31	Balance c/d	185
29	Bank	85			
		185			185
Jun 1	Balance b/d	185			

J Hussain Account

		£			£
May 27	Returns outwards	30	May 22	Purchases	305
31	Balance c/d	275			
		305			305
			Jun 1	Balance b/d	275

Insurance Account

		£			£
May 26	Bank	175	May 31	Balance c/d	175
Jun 1	Balance b/d	175			

We can now draw up a trial balance by making a list of all the balances remaining in the ledger. Take care when listing your balances in a trial balance because things can go wrong. You can make mistakes by entering a balance in the wrong column or copy the figures incorrectly, or you can miss out an entry completely.

The column headings of *debit* and *credit* are usually abbreviated and written as Dr and Cr:

Trial Balance as at 31 May 20-8

	Dr £	Cr £
Bank	9,350	
Capital		15,000
Purchases	870	
Sales		395
Returns outwards		80
Motor van	4,950	
A Jones	220	
Drawings	185	
J Hussain		275
Insurance	175	
	15,750	15,750

When all the balances are entered, the two columns are totalled, and they *should agree*.

What the examiner will look for

Examination questions frequently require candidates to open ledger accounts, post transactions by means of double entries, balance the accounts and take out a trial balance. You need to make sure that all transactions are correctly recorded in the double entry accounts. Write neatly and avoid crossing out as marks will be lost for careless or untidy work.

When a trial balance is required, the accounts **must** be balanced and the balances brought down. Balancing accounts uses more lines on the paper so make sure your accounts are positioned several lines apart to avoid a 'jumbled' appearance.

Frequently in this type of question candidates are first given a list of 'balances', often in the form of a trial balance. These balances must be entered in the appropriate accounts first *before* you begin to record any other transactions. It is also likely that the transactions will not be in date order. When this happens they will appear under several headings, such as: *sales on credit, purchases on credit* and so on, but you will be expected to enter all transactions in the ledger accounts in strict date order. This is not difficult if you follow these guidelines:

1 *Open an account for each of the balances given,* enter the date, balance b/d and the amount stated. (Debit balances are entered at the debit side of the account, credit balances are entered at the credit side.)
2 *Enter each transaction in date order* and open any other accounts which may be required.
3 When all transactions are entered, *balance the accounts* and *bring down the balances.*
4 Extract a trial balance by making a list of all the remaining balances, then *total your trial balance.* (*Accounts which do not have a balance are not entered.*)

Points to remember

- A trial balance is always drawn up at a *specific date*, and this date should be clearly written as part of the heading.
- If your trial balance totals do not agree, the following procedure will very often reveal the errors:
  1 *Re-check the addition of the totals* to make sure the error is not a simple matter of addition.
  2 Check the balances to make sure they have been entered into the *correct column*: has a debit balance in the ledger been incorrectly entered in the credit column of the trial balance or vice versa?
  3 Check for *transposition of figures*: a very common mistake is for figures to be transposed; this means the figures are written down in the wrong order – for example, a balance of £275 written in the trial balance as £257.
  4 Check that you have calculated the balances *on each account accurately*.
- Errors can occur which are *not revealed* by a trial balance. These types of errors are covered in unit 28, which deals with errors not affecting trial balance agreement.

Assignments

7.1

Brian Stones runs a small retail business. In your ledger write up the double entry accounts needed to record the following transactions for the month of March 20-8. At the end of the month balance the accounts and extract a trial balance as at 31 March 20-8:

Mar 1 Commenced business with £6,000 in a business bank account
     2 Bought office fixtures costing £400, paying by cheque
     3 Bought goods on credit from Thompson Ltd £840
     5 Paid rent £420 by cheque
     6 Cash sales £400
     8 Paid insurance £74 by cheque
     9 Paid wages in cash £45
   10 Bought goods costing £200, paying in cash
   11 Bought goods on credit from Thompson Ltd £600
   14 Cash sales £210
   16 Returned goods to Thompson Ltd £45
   18 Paid Thompson Ltd the balance on their account by cheque
   20 Sold goods on credit to S Lawson £440
   26 Paid wages in cash £45

27 S Lawson returned goods £40

28 Withdrew £60 in cash for private use

31 S Lawson settled his account in full by cheque

7.2

Ron Stewart is a wholesaler; on 1 January 20-8 he had the following balances in his ledger:

	Dr	Cr
	£	£
Capital		6,800
A Frazer		880
Motor vehicle	3,800	
A Hodges	1,100	
J Jennings	740	
Bank	2,040	
	7,680	7,680

During the month of January 20-8 the following transactions took place:

Jan 2 Received £740 by cheque from J Jennings

3 Bought goods on credit costing £1,070 from A Frazer

4 Bought office equipment costing £560, paying by cheque

5 Sold goods on credit to A Hodges £930

8 Paid A Frazer £880 by cheque

11 A Hodges returned goods to the firm £37

14 Sold goods on credit to J Jennings £590

17 Drawings of £500 by cheque

20 Purchased goods on credit from A Frazer £760

22 Received £1,100 by cheque from A Hodges

26 Sold goods on credit to A Hodges £710

28 Returned goods to A Frazer £98

31 Paid salaries of £480 by cheque

You are required to:

(a) Open ledger accounts at 1 January 20-8.

(b) Record the transactions during January in the appropriate ledger accounts and open any other accounts which may be required.

(c) Balance the accounts and extract a trial balance on 31 January 20-8.

7.3

The following information refers to a small engineering business owned by Douglas Whitby:

Trial Balance as at 31 October 20-8

	Dr £	Cr £
Capital		9,000
Premises	6,250	
Debtors: P Cave	1,580	
R Webster	1,640	
V Bruce	870	
Loan: G Franks		2,000
Creditors: T Cummings		1,250
G Fenland		730
Bank	2,640	
	12,980	12,980

During the month of November 20-8 his transactions were as follows:

Sales on credit

		£
8 Nov	V Bruce	130
10 Nov	P Cave	810
24 Nov	H Crossley	480

Purchases on credit

		£
2 Nov	T Cummings	855
12 Nov	G Fenland	330
13 Nov	T Cummings	914
18 Nov	I Shaw	295

Purchase returns

6 Nov	T Cummings	115

Payments received by cheque

26 Nov	P Cave	1,580
29 Nov	V Bruce	870

Payments made by cheque

4 Nov	Motor van	2,000
7 Nov	T Cummings	1,250
15 Nov	Rates	600
25 Nov	Motor expenses	90
30 Nov	Drawings	250

You are required to:

(a) Open ledger accounts for all items shown in the trial balance and enter the balances as at 1 November 20-8.
(b) Post the transactions which have taken place during the month of November 20-8 to the appropriate ledger accounts, and open any other accounts which may be necessary.
(c) Balance the accounts and extract a trial balance as at 30 November 20-8.

7.4

The trial balance of Ken Stevens on 30 April 20-4 was as follows:

	Dr £	Cr £
Sales		20,750
Purchases	13,170	
General expenses	4,972	
Fixtures	2,500	
K Gibson	1,130	
T Lowe		700
Bank	1,720	
Drawings	2,800	
Capital		7,228
Stock	2,386	
	28,678	28,678

During the month of May the following transactions took place:

May 1 Bought goods on credit from T Lowe £85
    2 Sold goods on credit to K Gibson £105
   18 Banked cash sales £400
   20 K Gibson paid £680 by cheque in part settlement of his account
   26 Paid general expenses by cheque £97; sent a cheque value £300 to T Lowe in part settlement of his account
   28 Paid general expenses by cheque £275
   30 Withdrew £300 from the bank for his own use

You are required to:

(a) Open the accounts at 1st May 20-4.
(b) Record the transactions directly in the accounts by means of double entries.
(c) Extract a trial balance at 31 May 20-4.

7.5

J Fisher runs a small mail order business. A bank account is kept through which all amounts received and paid are entered. Amounts paid for packing materials and postage are entered into the general expenses account. On 30 September 20-6 the following balances remain in the books:

	Dr £	Cr £
G Rogers	675	
N Fuller	120	
A Lewis		75
Bank	360	
Capital		1,080
	1,155	1,155

You are required to:

(a) Open ledger accounts for the above items and enter the balances as at 1 October 20-6.
(b) Post the transactions indicated direct to the appropriate ledger accounts and open any other accounts which may be required.
(c) Balance the accounts and extract a trial balance at 31 October 20-6.

Purchases on credit

		£
6 Oct	A Lewis	80
13 Oct	A Lewis	40

Sales on credit

		£
15 Oct	G Rogers	50
24 Oct	N Fuller	80
28 Oct	G Rogers	20

Payments received

		£
2 Oct	G Rogers	675
30 Oct	N Fuller	200

Payments made

		£
1 Oct	Packing materials	15
15 Oct	Postage	25
21 Oct	A Lewis	75

7.6
David Williams owns a small manufacturing business which makes superior quality greenhouses and garden sheds.
   On 30 September 20-8 his trial balance was as follows:

	Dr £	Cr £
Capital		8,525
Cash at bank	6,957	
D Morris	3,500	
R Johnson	1,938	
S Desmonds	4,105	
L Morgan		2,760
G Edwards		5,215
	16,500	16,500

During the month of October 20-8 the following transactions took place:

Sales on credit

		£
2 Oct	R Johnson	759
8 Oct	S Desmonds	1,260
20 Oct	R Johnson	306

Purchases on credit

		£
6 Oct	G Edwards	480
15 Oct	L Morgan	850
24 Oct	G Edwards	635

Returns inwards

		£
8 Oct	R Johnson	59

Returns outwards

		£
20 Oct	L Morgan	110

Payments made by cheque

		£
22 Oct	L Morgan	2,760
27 Oct	G Edwards	2,500

Payments received by cheque

		£
3 Oct	S Desmonds	1,805
14 Oct	R Johnson	1,938
26 Oct	D Morris	3,500

You are required to:
(a) Open ledger accounts for all items shown in the trial balance and enter the balances as at 1 October 20-8.
(b) Post the transactions which have taken place during the month of October 20-8 to the appropriate ledger accounts, and open any other accounts which may be necessary.
(c) Balance the accounts at the end of the month and take out a trial balance as at 31 October 20-8.

■ ⍰ 8 Separating the accounts into four main ledgers

So far, we have been thinking of the ledger as one book containing all the accounts. Even in a relatively small business it would be very difficult to keep all the accounts in one ledger, and this would mean that only one person would be able to use it at any given time. It is necessary to divide the ledger into smaller units to enable the work of recording transactions to be shared and carried out more efficiently. The names of the new ledgers are a good indication of the accounts they contain.

The first stage involves removing the debtors' and creditors' accounts. These are now kept in their own separate ledgers.

Purchases ledger

This ledger contains all the *suppliers' personal accounts*. Goods purchased on credit are bought from suppliers who then become *creditors*.

Sales ledger

This ledger contains all the *customers' personal accounts*. Sales on credit are made to customers who then become *debtors*.

Cash book

The next stage is to take out the two accounts which are used most, the cash account and bank account, and place them in a separate book which is called the *cash book*. This book is concerned only with the *receiving and paying out of money*, both in cash and by cheque.

Private ledger

This ledger contains accounts which the owner *wishes to keep private*. The capital account is one example and the drawings account is another. It may also include details of loan accounts. Most owners decide to keep these accounts separate because they contain information which is private and confidential.

General ledger or nominal ledger

All other accounts are kept in the general ledger, including the sales account, purchases account, returns inwards account and the returns outwards account.

Some firms keep a nominal ledger *instead* of a general ledger. Today most large businesses use some kind of computerised book-keeping system and the name '*nominal ledger*' is usually associated with these systems. Before computerised book-keeping methods were introduced this ledger was always known as the *general ledger*.

Points to remember

- *Purchases ledger* contains all the suppliers' personal accounts.
- *Sales ledger* contains all the customers' personal accounts.
- *Cash book* contains the two most used accounts, the cash account and bank account.
- *Private ledger* contains accounts which the owner wishes to keep confidential.
- *General ledger* contains all other accounts. Some businesses use the name 'nominal ledger' instead of 'general ledger'.

Assignments

8.1
Complete the blank spaces by inserting the name of the ledger in which the following accounts would appear:

(a) Purchases account   _____ ledger
(b) B Smith – supplier's personal account   _____ ledger
(c) Returns inwards account   _____ ledger
(d) F Jones – customer's personal account   _____ ledger
(e) Sales account   _____ ledger
(f) Fixtures account   _____ ledger

8.2

Complete the blank spaces by inserting the name of the ledger in which the following accounts would appear:

(a) Returns outwards account   _____ ledger
(b) Brown & Co Ltd – customer's personal account   _____ ledger
(c) Motor vehicle account   _____ ledger
(d) Wages account   _____ ledger
(e) Capital account   _____ ledger
(f) Walsh & Pine Ltd – supplier's personal account   _____ ledger

8.3

Complete the blank spaces by inserting the name of the ledger in which the following accounts would appear:

(a) Rent account   _____ ledger
(b) Drawings account   _____ ledger
(c) Office equipment account   _____ ledger
(d) D Lawrence – customer's personal account   _____ ledger
(e) Stylax Ltd – supplier of display equipment   _____ ledger
(f) J Norbury – supplier's personal account   _____ ledger

8.4

Complete the blank spaces by inserting the name of the book or ledger in which the following accounts would appear:

(a) Rent received account   _____ ledger
(b) Cash account   _____ book
(c) K Chippendale – customer's personal account   _____ ledger
(d) Forbes & Sykes – supplier's personal account   _____ ledger
(e) Insurance account   _____ ledger
(f) Bank account   _____ book

▾◧ 9 Banking

In recent years, both the number of people with bank accounts and the services that banks offer have steadily grown. No other country in the world has a banking system more highly developed than that in the United Kingdom. It is renowned for its stability, its network of branches and services offered.

Banks operate two main types of accounts, *current accounts* and *deposit* or *savings accounts.*

Deposit accounts

Deposit means, 'to put down' or 'leave' so this type of account is normally concerned with saving over a period of time. Interest is given on the balance held in the account. *Interest* is an amount paid by a bank to a customer as a reward for saving the money in the account. The rate of interest at any time, which is stated as a percentage, is always displayed inside the bank. Money placed in a deposit account cannot be drawn upon by cheque and, in some cases, notice may be required before money can be withdrawn.

Current accounts

These are used for *regular payments into and out of a bank account.* When a customer opens a current account the bank will issue a *cheque book* to enable the customer to make payments by cheque. The customer will also be given a *paying-in book* so that money can be paid into the account.

Practically all businesses have current accounts because of the many advantages offered with this type of account.

Advantages of a current account

- Businesses can avoid the risks involved in *holding large quantities of cash* on their premises
- Payments to suppliers by cheque are *more convenient and secure* than cash; they also provide additional *proof* that payment has been made
- Customers may wish to pay their accounts *by cheque*

- Other bank services are available, such as loans or overdrafts, and advice is available on a wide range of business problems.

Bank charges

Banks give advice and offer customers many advantages and services free of charge. However, they do make charges for some of their services and also charge interest on any money borrowed by customers. Special arrangements can be made for customers to 'overdraw' their current accounts. This occurs when the bank pays out more money than has been deposited in the account, and is known as a *bank overdraft*. It is used for temporary or short-term borrowing. When a bank account has been overdrawn the abbreviation 'DR' or 'O/D' is placed after the balance on the bank statement. Customers have to pay an *interest charge* on an overdraft. The amount of interest charged is calculated on a daily basis on the actual amount that is overdrawn.

Standing orders

The standing order service provided by banks is a way of ensuring that specific payments are made to certain people or organisations on the date they are due. It is used by customers who want the bank to make payments for them on a regular basis. Many people use this service for paying fixed amounts which fall due on certain dates – for example: mortgage repayments or insurance premiums. The bank will ensure that the money is taken out of the customer's account and paid into the account of the person or organisation named. As standing order payments are made *automatically through the banking system*, this saves the customer time and expense: there is no need to remember to write cheques or pay postage costs.

Direct debit

This is another way of making regular payments out of a current account. But instead of instructing the bank to make fixed payments, the customer completes a *direct debit mandate* giving a person or an organisation permission to withdraw amounts on a regular basis.

It is a more flexible system than standing orders because the amount of the payment can be easily changed. For this reason, direct debit is particularly suitable when the payments to be made are regular but the amount may change fairly often.

Direct debit payments are arranged by the person or organisation to be paid. They instruct *their* bank to request *your* bank to pay them by transferring the amount due from your account to their account. This can happen only if you have agreed to this method of payment in the first place.

Bank giro credit transfer

Bank giro is a system of transferring money directly from the account of one person to that of another. This system is also known as the *credit transfer service.*

The bank giro credit service provides a convenient way of receiving and paying money through the banking system. Some organisations encourage their customers to use this service by providing tear-off forms on their statements. Many people pay their telephone, gas or electricity bills by this method.

Cheques

To operate a current account, the bank will issue the customer with a cheque book and a paying-in book. A cheque is an order to the bank to pay a stated sum of money to the person named on the cheque. Each cheque is numbered with its own serial number. Most banks personalise their cheques by printing the name of the account holder and the cheque must be signed beneath the printed name. Whether making out a cheque or accepting a cheque in payment, you should always ensure that all of the necessary details are completed correctly. If they are not the bank will refuse to accept it.

There are *three named parties* involved with a cheque (see Figure 9.1):

- the *drawee*   is the name of the bank *holding the money*
               (in this example, Barclays Bank)
- the *payee*   is the person *to whom the cheque is made payable*; this
               person will receive the money
               (in this example, E Wilding)
- the *drawer*   is the *account holder*; this person signs the cheque
               (in this example, J M England).

How to write a cheque

The drawer will normally write *four things* on a cheque:

- the *date*
- the *payee's name*
- the *amount of money* in words and figures
- his or her own *signature* (a specimen of which is held by the bank).

When we make out a cheque we should also copy the details onto the *counterfoil* which is kept in the cheque book and used for reference

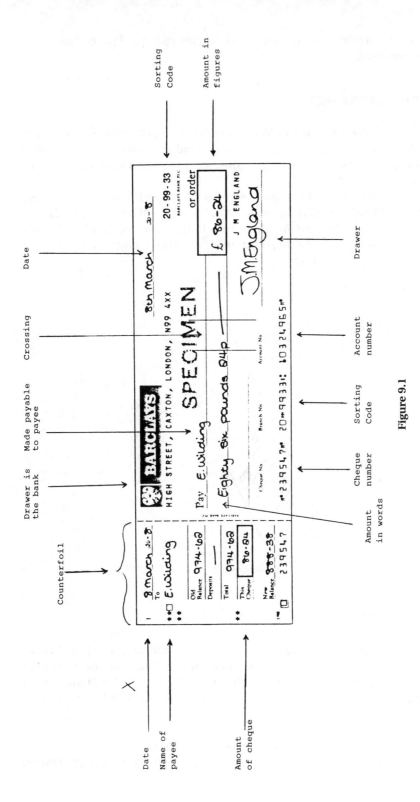

Figure 9.1

purposes. By referring to the counterfoils, we can quickly see how each cheque was used.

Cheque crossings

If two parallel lines are drawn down the cheque, it is a *crossed* cheque and it cannot be exchanged for cash; it **must** be paid into a bank account. Most cheques have a general crossing printed on them as a safeguard against loss, theft and fraud.

Cheques can be further safeguarded by using a *special crossing*, these are specific instructions which are inserted between the lines (Figure 9.2).

- *Account Payee only*   means that the cheque can be paid *only into* the account of *the named payee*, and no one else.

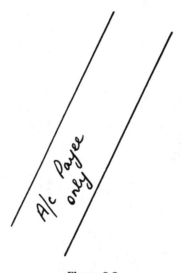

Figure 9.2

'Refer to drawer'

In certain circumstances, the bank will refuse to *honour* (to pay) a cheque. Cheques which are not passed for payment by the drawer's bank are said to have been 'dishonoured'. The drawer's bank will write '*Refer to drawer*' or the abbreviation 'R/D' on a cheque it will not pay. This can be for any one of the following reasons:

- there are *insufficient funds* in the drawer's account
- the amount written in *words* does not agree with the amount in *figures*

- the cheque is *unsigned*
- the cheque has been *stopped* by the drawer (the drawer has instructed the bank not to make payment)
- the cheque is *stale* (it was written more than six months from the current date)
- the cheque is *post-dated* (dated for some time in the future)
- an *alteration* on the cheque has not been initialled by the drawer.

At regular intervals, usually once a month, the bank will provide the customer with a copy of their account, this is known as a *Statement of Account* or a *Bank Statement,* and will give full details of all the *transactions* during the period, and also details of any *bank charges.*

Paying-in slips

Bank credit or paying-in slips are used to pay cash and cheques into a current account (Figure 9.3). They are completed by stating the amount to be paid in and the form it takes. Cash in notes and coins are listed collectively against the appropriate unit of currency. Cheques or money orders should be listed separately and totalled on the reverse side of the paying-in slip. The total of any cheques/money orders is then written in the relevant box on the front of the slip. The paying-in slip counterfoil is completed with the same details. The completed credit slip, together with the cash/cheques, is then handed to the bank cashier. The paying-in slip counterfoil will be date stamped by the bank cashier and returned to the customer.

Reed & Company keep a current account at the Bond Street branch of Barclays Bank. Their account number is 87655678, on 21 May 20-8 the cashier banked the following items:

3	£50 notes
4	£20 notes
7	£10 notes
125	£1 coins
35	50p coins
26	20p coins
15	10p coins
50	2p coins

Cheques made payable to Reed & Company from:

J Green	£161.17
G Moore	£245.15
B Bingley	£ 78.84
H Fellows	£159.95

Figure 9.3 is an illustration of the front and the reverse side of the completed paying-in slip.

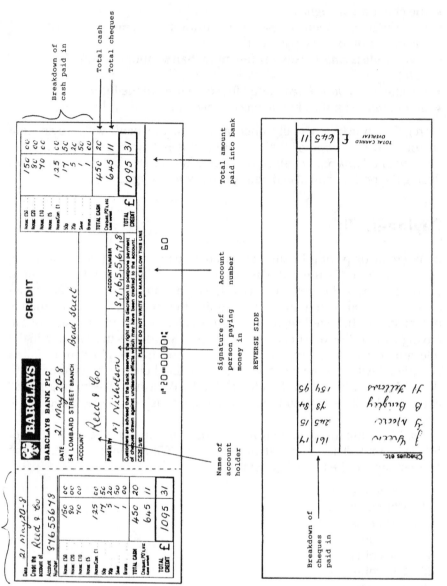

Figure 9.3

Points to remember

- A business bank account offers many advantages and services to a firm, and almost all businesses have a *current account*; this enables them to make payments by cheque and receive payments through the banking system.
- Most banks personalise their cheques by printing the name of the account holder; the cheque *must* be signed beneath the printed name. A crossed cheque cannot be cashed on demand, it must be paid into a *bank account.*
- Cash and cheques received by a business are paid into the bank by completing a *paying-in slip.* Details of notes and coins are listed on the front; cheques/and money orders are listed on the reverse side; this total is then carried forward to the front and added to the total cash. The counterfoil is stamped by the cashier at the bank as a proof of the deposit.

Assignments

The following assignments are taken from past examination papers to enable you to practise completing cheques/counterfoils and paying-in slips.

9.1
You are employed by Office Supplies in Leeds. The firm banks with the Lombard Street branch of Barclays Bank. Their current account number is 76543211. On 8 March 20-8, you pay the following items into the bank:

10	£50 notes
8	£20 notes
6	£10 notes
32	£ 5 notes
35	£ 1 coins
15	50p coins
20	20p coins
100	2p coins

Cheques from:

K Jones	£194.67
A Smith	£218.54
R Hurford	£ 18.50
J Oldridge	£ 37.55

You are required to complete all parts of the paying-in slip in Figure 9.4.

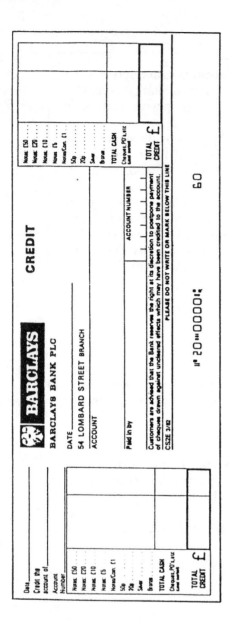

Figure 9.4

9.2

On 7 June 20-3 you received an account from Modern Office Equipment Ltd for the supply of two new electric typewriters. The amount due for payment is £1,890 and is subject to a small discount of 2½ per cent if paid within 28 days. You settle the account on 21 June 20-3. The balance at bank prior to this transaction was £3,113.18.

You are required to:

(a) Complete the cheque in Figure 9.5 settling the account.
(b) Fill in the counterfoil showing clearly the new balance to be carried forward.

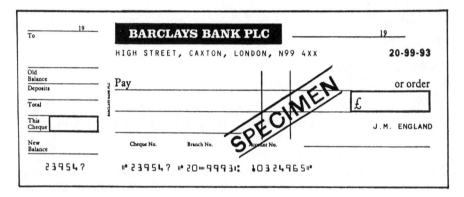

Figure 9.5

9.3

You are employed by White & Co as a cashier at their Westminster Branch. Their bank current account, number 76543211 is maintained at the Lombard Street Branch of Barclays Bank. On 15 May 20-7 you pay the following items into the local branch of Barclays Bank:

5	£50 notes
2	£20 notes
8	£10 notes
130	£1 coins
55	50p coins
24	20p coins
20	10p coins
100	2p coins

Cheques from:

R S Adams	£169.95
T Bromley	£261.14
A Kent	£ 61.24

You are required to complete all parts of the paying-in slip in Figure 9.6.

9.4

On 8 November 20-4 J M England received an invoice from Parkway Garage for motor servicing and repairs. The invoice was for the sum of £358 and was subject to a discount of $2\frac{1}{2}$ per cent for payment within 10 days.

You paid this account on 12 November 20-4. The bank balance immediately prior to this transaction was £925.75.

You are required to complete the cheque and counterfoil, using the form provided in Figure 9.7, with the amount required to settle the account.

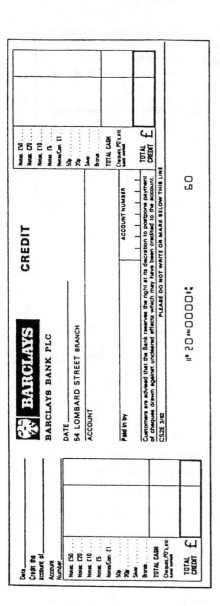

Figure 9.6

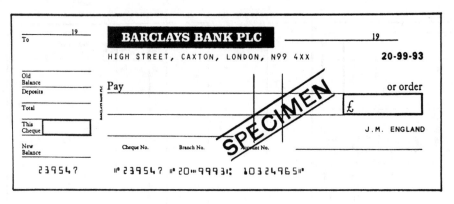

Figure 9.7

9.5   **Diane Glover**
in account with
Northern Joint Bank PLC

Date	Description	Debit	Credit	Balance
20-6		£	£	£
May 1	Balance			125 O/D (a)
2	000344 (b)	220 (c)		345 O/D
3	Sundries		200	145 O/D
4	Standing Order (d)	10		155 O/D
5	Credit Transfer		195	40
6	D Allday (R/D) (e)	85		? (f)

(a) Would Diane Glover have shown the balance as a current asset or a current liability on her balance sheet as at 30 April 20-6? . . . .
. . . .

(b) To what do the numbers 000344 refer? . . . .

(c) Was the item (c) paid in or withdrawn? . . . .

(d) Briefly explain the meaning of the term 'standing order' . . . .
. . . .

(e) (i) What does the abbreviation R/D stand for? . . . .
   (ii) Give a reason why a cheque may be marked R/D . . . .
. . . .

(f) What is the new balance on 6 May? . . . .

■ ☑ **10** Two-column cash books

In our earlier work the cash and bank accounts were kept in the ledger; but because of the considerable number of entries in these two accounts, they were removed from the ledger and brought together in a special book called a *cash book*.

Although the accounts for cash and bank are brought together, they still remain completely *separate* accounts, laid side by side so that both accounts are visible at once. For this reason it is very important to label the columns clearly and you must be careful to make entries in the correct columns. By tradition the cash column *always* appears *to the left* of the bank column.

Only a responsible member of staff, usually the cashier, makes entries in the cash book, since these two accounts deal with money and cheques. The cash book is the book of original entry for all money received and paid out, whether in cash or by cheque.

Student cash books can be purchased from most good stationers and you will need to get one. The first single side is not used because a cash book has the entire left-hand page for the debit side and the entire right hand page for the credit side:

Cash column   As with our earlier cash accounts, the *debit* side is used to record cash *received,* the *credit* side to record cash *paid out*

Bank column   In the same way, the *debit* side is used to record cheques *received,* the *credit* side to record *cheques paid out*

Cash Book

Date	Particulars	F	Cash	Bank	Date	Particulars	F	Cash	Bank

Here is an illustration showing the cash account and the bank account as they would have appeared previously, as two separate accounts:

Cash Account

20-8		£	20-8		£
May 1	Balance b/d	270	May 4	Insurance	58
7	M Fellows	105	11	D Riley	86
10	E Ashby	94	16	Rates	116
18	J Douglas	62	19	Motor expenses	42
29	H Sinclair	75	27	Drawings	90
			31	Balance c/d	214
		606			606
Jun 1	Balance b/d	214			

Bank Account

20-8		£	20-8		£
May 1	Balance b/d	859	May 2	Rent	175
6	J Wiseman	255	13	T Norbury	187
12	D Glover	392	17	A Longdon	422
24	B McCann	576	30	J Lyons	385
			31	Balance c/d	913
		2,082			2,082
Jun 1	Balance b/d	913			

These two accounts are now brought together, side by side, in the cash book:

Cash Book

Date	Particulars	F	Cash	Bank	Date	Particulars	F	Cash	Bank
20-8			£	£	20-8			£	£
May 1	Balances b/d		270	859	May 2	Rent			175
6	J Wiseman			255	4	Insurance		58	
7	M Fellows		105		11	D Riley		86	
10	E Ashby		94		13	T Norbury			187
12	D Glover			392	16	Rates		116	
18	J Douglas		62		17	A Longdon			422
24	E McCann			576	19	Motor exps		42	
29	H Sinclair		75		27	Drawings		90	
					30	J Lyons			385
					31	Balances c/d		214	913
			606	2,082				606	2,082
Jun 1	Balances b/d		214	913					

The cash and the bank accounts are totalled and balanced *separately*, in the same way that we would if they were kept apart.

You should be able to explain each of the entries in the cash book. *Debit* entries are receipts of *cash* or *amounts paid into the bank*. *Credit* entries are payments by *cash* or *amounts paid out of the bank*.

Since it is not possible to spend more cash (notes and coins) than you actually have, the cash account will always have a *debit balance*. This is not the case with the bank account. A business may find it is short of money for a variety of reasons and the bank may be willing to make some of its money available to the business: this is usually in the form of an *overdraft*.

Bank overdraft

When a bank allows an overdraft it means that a customer can draw more money out of a current account than has been paid in, up to an agreed limit.

You will notice when balancing the cash book that an overdraft occurs when the total of the bank column at the *credit* side *exceeds* the total of the bank column at the *debit* side.

Contra entries

Certain entries in the cash book are called *contra* entries. The word 'contra' is the Latin word for 'opposite' and indicates that the two halves of a double entry are opposite one another: one on the debit side of the cash book and the other on the credit side.

In a cash book we have two accounts placed side by side for convenience, when a contra entry occurs it will affect both the cash and bank accounts: one account *receives* money, the other *account* gives it.

Contra entries are transfers of money, they can occur only:

When money is taken out of the cash account and paid into the bank account

or

When money is taken out of the bank account and placed in the cash account

Contra entries can sometimes cause confusion. This is because both the debit and credit entries appear in the same book.

Let us look at a typical example: on 5 June, £200 of the office cash is paid into the bank. The entries in the cash book would look like this:

Cash Book

Date	Particulars	F	Cash	Bank	Date	Particulars	F	Cash	Bank
20-8			£	£	20-8			£	£
Jun 5	Cash	C		200	Jun 5	Bank	C	200	

The credit entry shows that the cash has been reduced by £200, the cash account *gave* the money (*credit* the *giver*). The particulars column always shows where the other entry has been made, so the word *bank* appears at the credit side.

At the debit side, the bank account is increased by £200, the bank *receives* the money (*debit* the *receiver*): the description 'cash' explains how by naming the other account involved in the transaction.

Against each entry, the letter 'C', which is short for 'contra', is placed in the folio (F) column to indicate that these items do not require posting as double entry has taken place in the cash book.

A contra entry can operate the other way, when money is withdrawn from the bank for business use. On 22 June, £350 is withdrawn from the bank for use in the business. The entries in the cash book would look like this:

Cash Book

Date	Particulars	F	Cash	Bank	Date	Particulars	F	Cash	Bank
20-8			£	£	20-8			£	£
Jun 22	Bank	C	350		Jun 22	Cash	C		350

The credit entry shows that the bank account has been reduced by £350; the bank account *gave* the money (*credit* the *giver*). The particulars column always shows where the other entry has been made, so the word *cash* appears at the credit side.

At the debit side, the cash account is increased by £350; the cash account *receives* the money (*debit* the *receiver*): the description *bank* explains how by naming the other account involved in the transaction.

A letter 'C' again appears in the folio columns to indicate that double entry has taken place in the cash book.

Worked example

This is a worked example exercise, first showing the cash and bank transactions for the month of June 20-8, then how they would appear in a two-column cash book.

Jun	1	Balances brought forward from last month: cash £147, bank £850	
	2	Sold goods and received cash £252	
	3	Received a cheque of £368 from F Lewis	
	4	Paid rent in cash £60	
	5	Banked £200 of the office cash	*(Contra entry)*
	8	Paid I Robson £216 by cheque	
	10	Bought goods costing £75, paying in cash	
	12	Sold goods and received cash £93	
	15	Paid telephone bill £58 in cash	
	17	Received a cheque of £498 from C Miles	
	22	Withdrew £350 from the bank for business use	*(Contra entry)*
	25	Paid insurance £74 by cheque	
	29	Bought goods costing £165, paying in cash	

Cash and cheques received are entered on the debit side, the first entry shows the *opening balances*, in both cases a *debit* balance. Since the cash and bank accounts are asset accounts we would expect a debit balance (but it is possible to be *overdrawn* at the bank and consequently have a credit balance on the bank account in the cash book).

On the *credit* side the firm is *paying money*, either in cash or by cheque.

Take each item, in date order, and trace the item to where it appears in the following two-column cash book:

Cash Book

Date		Particulars	F	Cash	Bank	Date		Particulars	F	Cash	Bank
20-8				£	£	20-8				£	£
Jun	1	Balances b/d		147	850	Jun	4	Rent		60	
	2	Sales		252			5	Bank	C	200	
	3	F Lewis			368		8	I Robson			216
	5	Cash	C		200		10	Purchases		75	
	12	Sales		93			15	Telephone		58	
	17	C Miles			498		22	Cash	C		350
	22	Bank	C	350			25	Insurance			74
							29	Purchases		165	
							30	Balances c/d		284	1,276
				842	1,916					842	1,916
Jul	1	Balances b/d		284	1,276						

Points to remember

- Although the cash and bank accounts have been placed side by side in the cash book, they still remain *two completely separate accounts.* It is very important to label the columns clearly and you must be careful to make entries in the correct columns. By tradition the cash column *always* appears to the left of the bank column. Both the cash and bank accounts are ledger accounts and this new arrangement does not alter the fact that they are ledger accounts and form an integral part of the double entry system.
- *Contra* entries are simply transfers, taking money out of one account and putting it in another.
- The cash book is the book of original entry for all money *received and paid out,* whether in cash or by cheque. The cash and bank accounts are totalled and balanced *separately.* An overdraft occurs when the total of the bank column *at the credit side exceeds* the total of the bank column *at the debit side.*
- When there is an overdrawn bank balance either at the beginning or at the end of a period, it is entered at the *credit side* of the cash book.

Assignments

Now use your cash book to work through the following Assignments. Contra entries are not included in the first four Assignments (10.1–10.4), to enable you to gain some initial routine practice.

10.1
Robert Hurford keeps a two-column cash book; during the month of May 20-8 the following transactions took place. Enter each transaction in the cash book, balance at the end of the month, and bring down the balances:

May 1 Balances brought forward from last month:
cash £262, bank £2,756
2 Received £368 by cheque from R Douglas
3 Bought stationery £37, paying in cash
4 Bought new office furniture £560, paying by cheque
5 Cash received from sales £125
8 Paid insurance £48 by cheque
9 Bought goods costing £62, paying in cash
10 M Curtis paid the firm £149 by cheque
11 Cash drawings £100
12 Received £375 in cash from J Singh
15 Paid garage for motor repairs £97 by cheque

17 Cash received from sales £250

19 Received £595 from S Myers by cheque

22 Paid wages £450 in cash

24 Sold goods and received cash £172

25 Paid D Nicholas £368 by cheque

26 Cash drawings £100

30 Bought display equipment £695, paying by cheque

10.2

Donna Lenton keeps a two-column cash book; during the month of June 20-8 the following transactions took place. Enter each transaction in the cash book, balance at the end of the month, and bring down the balances:

June 1 Balances brought forward from last month: cash £435, bank £2,100

2 Received £650 by cheque from L Goodman

3 Paid rates £1,500 by cheque

4 Received rent from sub-tenant £230 in cash

5 Cash received from sales £170

5 Paid insurance by cheque £450

8 Paid Marcus Ltd £106 by cheque

9 Bought office stationery £34, paying in cash

10 Bought goods costing £52, paying in cash

11 Paid C M Lupton £139 by cheque

12 Cash received from sales £96

15 Received £275 by cheque from B Matthews

16 Cash drawings £200

17 Bought office furniture £158, paying by cheque

18 Paid motor expenses £75 in cash

19 Cash received from sales £185

22 M Dixon paid the firm £1,650 by cheque

23 Received rates refund £28 by cheque

24 Cash drawings £100

25 Bought goods costing £65, paying in cash

26 Paid wages by cheque £750

30 Received £45 in cash from J Oldridge

10.3

Peter Colley keeps a two-column cash book; during the month of July 20-8 the following transactions took place. Enter each transaction in the cash book, balance at the end of the month, and bring down the balances:

July 1 Balances brought forward from last month: cash £635, bank £1,600

2 Bought goods costing £125, paying in cash

3 Received rent from sub-tenant £230 in cash

4 Paid J Crossley £345 by cheque

5	Cash drawings £150
8	Cash received from sales £280
9	R Wilson paid the firm £496 by cheque
10	Bought office stationery £76, paying by cheque
14	T Burton paid the firm £2,250 by cheque
15	Cash received from sales £275
16	Cash drawings £100
17	Bought motor van £1,500, paying by cheque
18	Bought goods costing £90, paying in cash
21	Paid motor expenses £100 in cash
22	Received a cheque for £854 from B Sykes
23	Cash received from sales £220
24	Paid R Mills £196 by cheque
25	Cash drawings £150
26	Paid E Williams £525 by cheque
28	Cash received from sales £240
29	Paid wages in cash £650

10.4

Ann Bannister keeps a two-column cash book; during the month of August 20-8 the following transactions took place. Enter each transaction in the cash book, balance at the end of the month, and bring down the balances:

Aug 1	Balances brought forward from last month: cash £515, bank £2,558
2	Cash received from sales £226
3	Paid D Nicholas £492 by cheque
4	Received rent from sub-tenant £230 in cash
5	Paid insurance £48 by cheque
8	Bought office supplies £69, paying in cash
9	M Curtis paid the firm £527 by cheque
10	Paid motor repairs £104 by cheque
11	Cash received from sales £176
12	Bought goods costing £38, paying in cash
15	Received a cheque for £424 from S Myers
16	Cash drawings £250
17	Paid C Linton £750 by cheque
18	Cash received from sales £182
19	Paid R Mills £193 in cash
23	Cash drawings £200
26	J Singh paid the firm £471 in cash
28	Paid motor expenses £98 by cheque
29	Paid wages in cash £550

10.5

Barry Ward keeps a two-column cash book; during the month of April 20-9 the following transactions took place. Enter each transaction in the cash book, balance at the end of the month, and bring down the balances:

April 1 Balances brought forward from last month:
cash £248, bank £3,664
  2 Paid rates by cheque £140
  3 Sold goods and received cash £175
  4 Received £469 by cheque from M Roberts
  5 Banked £150 of the office cash
  8 Paid motor expenses £57 by cheque
  9 Rent received from sub-tenant £50 in cash
  10 Cash sales paid direct into bank £120
  11 Bought goods costing £96, paying in cash
  12 Paid wages in cash £150
  15 Withdrew £200 from the bank for business use
  16 B Stevens paid the firm £655 by cheque
  17 Sold goods and received cash £86
  18 Received a cheque £166 from C Verity
  19 Paid insurance £85 in cash
  22 Paid £250 of the cash into the bank
  25 Paid D Shaw £750 by cheque
  26 Bought office furniture costing £175, paying by cheque
  27 Received £55 in cash from B Lord
  28 Withdrew £200 from the bank for business use
  29 Bought stationery costing £28, paying in cash

10.6
William Dyson keeps a two-column cash book; during the month of June 20-9 the following transactions took place. Enter each transaction in the cash book, balance at the end of the month, and bring down the balances:

June 1 Started business with £6,000 in cash
  2 Paid rent £120 in cash
  3 Bought goods £495, paying in cash
  4 Paid £5,000 cash into the bank
  5 Sold goods and received cash £220
  8 Bought office equipment costing £296, paying by cheque
  9 Received £75 in cash from R Trent
  10 Bought goods costing £298, paying in cash
  11 Paid rates £120 by cheque
  12 Cash drawings £80
  15 Paid wages in cash £150
  16 Withdrew £250 from the bank for business use
  17 Received refund of rates £26 by cheque
  18 Paid M Timpson £45 in cash
  19 Sold goods and received cash £145
  20 Received a loan of £500 by cheque from D Chadwick

23 Paid £200 of the cash into the bank
24 Bought goods costing £141, paying in cash
25 Paid E Robinson £267 by cheque
26 Received £68 in cash from M Castle
27 Paid insurance by cheque £64

10.7

Alison De Klerk keeps a two-column cash book; during the month of October 20-9 the following transactions took place. Enter each transaction in the cash book, balance at the end of the month, and bring down the balances:

Oct 1 Balances brought forward from last month:
cash £269, bank £3,086
2 Paid rent by cheque £75
3 Received £294 by cheque from J Kendall
4 Paid motor expenses in cash £32
5 Paid £200 of the cash into the bank
8 Bought stationery costing £18, paying in cash
9 Received £68 in cash from M Kaye
10 Withdrew £350 from the bank for use in the business
11 Bought goods costing £240, paying in cash
12 Cash drawings £125
13 Bought machinery costing £368, paying by cheque
14 Paid rates £165 by cheque
17 Sold goods and received £175 in cash
18 Paid wages in cash £80
19 Cash sales paid direct into bank £226
20 Paid general expenses £42 in cash
21 Received commission £67 by cheque
24 Received £142 in cash from K Waterman
25 Paid M Hutton £490 by cheque
26 Sold goods and received £160 in cash
27 Banked all the cash except for £50
28 Paid rates by cheque £210
29 Bought office fixtures costing £470, paying by cheque

10.8

Denise Lockwood keeps a two-column cash book; during the month of January 20-9 the following transactions took place. Enter each transaction in the cash book, balance at the end of the month, and bring down the balances:

Jan 1 Balances brought down from previous month:
cash £78, bank £2,649
2 Paid rent by cheque £95
3 Withdrew £350 from the bank for business use
4 Bought goods costing £226, paying in cash

5   Bought motor van costing £1,950, paying by cheque
6   Sold goods for cash £78
7   Cash drawings £50
8   Paid J Carson £165 by cheque
9   Paid motor expenses £25 in cash
10 Sold goods and received £168 in cash
11 Paid £200 of the cash into the bank
12 Sold surplus fixtures and received £165 by cheque
13 Bought goods costing £65, paying in cash
14 Received £798 by cheque from W Powers
15 Paid insurance £69 by cheque
16 Drawings by cheque £50
17 Withdrew £400 from the bank for business use
18 Bought goods costing £195, paying in cash
19 Cash sales paid direct into bank £112
20 Received commission in cash £65
21 Received £268 in cash from L Spencer
22 Paid motor expenses in cash £35
23 Paid £350 cash into the bank
24 Bought display equipment costing £425, paying by cheque
25 Paid wages £150 in cash
26 Bought stationery costing £46, paying by cheque
27 Paid T Norbury £550 by cheque
28 Sold goods and received £158 in cash
29 Cash drawings £100
30 Paid W Freeman £478 by cheque

☑ 11 Three-column cash books and cash discounts

Combining the cash and bank accounts together in one book has increased efficiency, but when accounts are settled the question of *discount* may arise. In many firms payments to suppliers are timed to enable the business to receive a discount. At the same time money will be received from customers who will have *deducted discount allowed* in return for prompt settlement.

The only difference between the traditional two-column cash book we looked at earlier is an extra column at each side. These extra columns are used to record cash discounts: the column for *discount allowed* is on the *debit* side, because a customer who is *paying* is allowed to take a discount. The column for *discount received* from suppliers on the *credit* side. It is important to remember that the discount columns are *not* accounts, they are 'memorandum columns' only, where a note is made of cash discount as it occurs.

Cash discounts

Firms appreciate customers who pay their accounts quickly and cash discount is offered as an incentive to encourage prompt payment. Many firms will accept a smaller amount in full settlement if payment is made within a certain period of time. The rate of cash discount, usually expressed as a percentage, and the period in which payment is to be made are quoted on the invoice. A typical example would be: *subject to 5 per cent cash discount if the account is settled within one month from date of invoice.*

When cash discount is offered, it is not shown as a deduction from the total value of the invoice. A customer deducts the amount of discount if payment is made within the stated time. It is still called *cash discount* if payment is made by cheque.

Look at a typical example: A Thompson, a customer, owes the firm £100. He pays by cheque within the stated time and the firm allows him 5 per cent cash discount. (£100 *less* £5 = £95), so A Thompson will pay £95 in full settlement of his account.

Discounts allowed

On the debit side of the cash book the discount allowed column is used to enter amounts of cash discount on the date they occur. These are cash discounts allowed by a firm to its customers when they pay their accounts within the time limit specified.

Look at a typical example: on 1 October goods valued at £326 were sold on credit to T Gregson, subject to 5 per cent cash discount if payment is received within one month from date of invoice. In the sales ledger, T Gregson's account would look like this:

T Gregson Account

	£
Oct 1 Sales	326.00

On 22 October, T Gregson pays his account by cheque having deducted 5 per cent cash discount. He pays £309.70 in full settlement of his account. (£326 *less* £16.30 cash discount = £309.70). Entries in the firm's cash book would look like this:

Cash Book

Date	Particulars	F	Discount allowed	Cash	Bank	Date	Particulars	F	Discount received	Cash	Bank
			£	£	£				£	£	£
Oct 22	T Gregson		16.30		309.70						

Details of cheque and discount are posted from the cash book to the ledger accounts. T Gregson's account would now look like this:

T Gregson Account

	£			£
Oct 1 Sales	326.00	Oct 22	Bank	309.70
		22	Discount allowed	16.30
	326.00			326.00

When discount is allowed the customer's account *must* be reduced by the full amount of the debt being settled. Although the firm has agreed to accept less money than was originally owed in full settlement of the account, the amount of the discount allowed, in this example £16.30, must also be credited to T Gregson's account to show that the account is fully paid. If the discount was ignored, there would be a balance on T Gregson's account equal to the amount of discount and it would look as though T Gregson still owed £16.30.

This transaction is shown in the three-column cash book for October (Figure 11.1, p. 99).

As we have seen, each time discount is allowed the customer's account must be credited with the payment and discount; to complete the double entry the total of the discount allowed column is posted to the debit side of the discount allowed account in the general ledger, like this:

Discount Allowed Account

		£	
Oct 31 Total for month		51.50	

Discounts received

In the same way as most firms encourage debtors to pay quickly by offering them cash discount, many suppliers will be trying to attract *prompt payment.*

On the credit side of the cash book the discount received column is used to enter amounts of cash discount on the date they occur. These are cash discounts received by a firm when they pay their accounts within the time limit specified.

Look at a typical example: on 3 October goods costing £185 were purchased on credit from S Dyson, subject to 5 per cent cash discount if payment is received within 28 days from date of invoice. In the purchase ledger S Dyson's account would look like this:

S Dyson Account

		£
	Oct 3 Purchases	185.00

On 25 October the firm pays S Dyson's account by cheque, £185 *less* £9.25 cash discount = £175.75 in full settlement of his account.

Entries in the firm's cash book would look like this:

Cash Book

Date	Particulars	F	Discount allowed	Cash	Bank	Date	Particulars	F	Discount received	Cash	Bank
			£	£	£				£	£	£
						Oct 25	S Dyson		9.25		175.75

Details of cheque and discount are posted from the cash book to the ledger accounts. S Dyson's personal account would now look like this:

S Dyson Account

		£				£
Oct 25	Bank	175.75	Oct 3	Purchases		185.00
25	Discount					
	received	9.25				
		185.00				185.00

When discount is received a supplier's account *must* be reduced by the full amount of the debt being settled. Although S Dyson has agreed to accept less money than was originally owed in full settlement of the account, the amount of the discount received, in this example £9.25, must also be debited to S Dyson's account to show that the account is fully paid. If the discount was ignored, there would be a balance on S Dyson's account equal to the amount of discount. It would look as though £9.25 was still owed to S Dyson.

This example is also shown in the three-column cash book for October (Figure 11.1, p. 99).

As we have seen, each time discount is received the supplier's account must be debited with the payment and discount; to complete the double entry the total of the discount received column is posted to the credit side of the discount received account in the general ledger, like this:

Discount Received Account

		£
Oct 31	Total for month	14.25

Points to remember

- The term *'cash discount'* refers to the amount of the reduction given for prompt payment. It is still called 'cash discount' if payment is made by cheque.
- To firms having sufficient funds to pay their accounts promptly cash discount offers an *additional profit*, and during the course of a year's trading could amount to a considerable sum. Details of cash or cheque and discount are posted from the cash book to the respective individual accounts.
- The discount allowed column is at the debit side, the discount received column is at the credit side of the cash book. At the end of the month the discount columns must be totalled but **never** balanced because they are **not** accounts.
- The discount columns are *memorandum columns* only, where a note is made of the discount as it occurs. It reminds whoever is posting entries from the cash book to remember to also post any discount in the personal accounts.
- At the end of the month, the total discount allowed is *debited* in the discount allowed account, the total discount received is *credited* to the discount received account to complete the double entry.
- The discount allowed account and the discount received account are in the general ledger, along with all other revenue and expense accounts. Discount allowed is an *expense* to a business, discount received is *additional revenue*.

Worked example

In the following worked example for the month of October 20-9, consider each transaction carefully and then find each entry in the three-column cash book in Figure 11.1.

Oct   1   Balances brought forward from previous month: cash £137, bank £3,921

      2   Sold goods and received cash £75

      4   Received a cheque of £296.40 from J Dickenson in full settlement of his account of £312

      6   Paid rent in cash £125

      8   Withdrew £250 from the bank for business use   *(contra entry)*

    10   Paid B Armitage's account of £90 in cash *less* £5 cash discount

    12   Purchased goods costing £134, paying in cash

    15   Received £372.40 by cheque from R Rhodes in full settlement of his account of £392.00

    18   Paid insurance by cheque £68

    20   Cash sales £245

22 Received a cheque of £309.70 from T Gregson in full settlement of his account £326

24 Banked £250 of the cash   (*contra entry*)

25 Paid S Dyson's account of £185 *less* 5 per cent cash discount

30 Paid motor expenses of £72 in cash

Figure 11.1 shows how they would appear in a three-column cash book.

Three-Column Cash Book

Date	Particulars	F	Discount Allowed	Cash	Bank	Date	Particulars	F	Discount Received	Cash	Bank
20-9						20-9					
Oct 1	Balances b/d			137.00	3,921.00	Oct 6	Rent			125.00	
2	Sales			75.00		8	Cash	C			250.00
4	J Dickenson		15.60		296.40	10	B Armitage		5.00	85.00	
8	Bank	C		250.00		12	Purchases			134.00	
15	R. Rhodes		19.60		372.40	18	Insurance				68.00
20	Sales			245.00		24	Bank	C		250.00	
22	T Gregson		16.30		309.70	25	S Dyson		9.25		175.75
24	Cash	C			250.00	30	Motor Expenses			72.00	
						31	Balances c/d			41.00	4,655.75
			£51.50	707.00	5,149.50				£14.25	707.00	5,149.50
Nov 1	Balances b/d			41.00	4,655.75						

Figure 11.1

Assignments

11.1

Andrew Fox keeps a three-column cash book; during the month of August 20-9 the following transactions took place. Enter each transaction in the cash book, balance at the end of the month, and bring down the balances:

Aug 1 Balances brought down from last month: cash £168, bank £2,998

3 Sold goods and received cash £160

4 Bought display equipment costing £248, paying by cheque

5 Paid £250 of the cash into the bank

6 Received £357 by cheque from S Driver in full settlement of his account of £375

9 Bought stationery costing £34, paying in cash

10 Withdrew £250 from the bank for use in the business

11 Bought goods costing £128, paying in cash

12 Received a cheque of £146 from J Scott in full settlement of her account of £154

13 Paid wages £90 in cash

17 Received £180 in cash from B Jones

18 Paid £200 cash into the bank

19 Paid B Dixon's account of £60 by cheque *less* 5 per cent cash discount

20 Sold goods and received cash £140

23 Received £196 by cheque from S Ryder in full settlement of his account of £208

26 Paid M Dean £45 in cash

27 Withdrew £150 from the bank for business use

28 Paid B Wilson's account of £80 in cash, *less* $2\frac{1}{2}$ per cent cash discount

29 Bought motor van costing £950, paying by cheque

30 Cash drawings £120

11.2

Madhur Daswani keeps a three-column cash book; during the month of November 20-9 the following transactions took place. Enter each transaction in the cash book, balance at the end of the month, and bring down the balances:

Nov 1 Balances brought forward from last month: cash £76, bank £2,641

2 Received £378 by cheque from D Chadley in full settlement of his account of £394

3 Sold goods and received £150 in cash

4 Withdrew £250 from the bank for business use

5 Paid R Fox's account of £160 by cheque *less* $2\frac{1}{2}$ per cent cash discount

6 Cash drawings £125

7 Received £192 by cheque from M Richardson in full settlement of her account of £204

8 Bought goods costing £72, paying in cash

9 Received £278 by cheque from D Sellers in full settlement of his account of £292

10 Received £198 in cash from D Crofton

11 Paid £250 of the cash into the bank

13 Paid motor expenses £197 by cheque

14 Received £595 by cheque from R Best in full settlement of his account of £603

15 Paid R Keaton's account of £320 by cheque *less* 5 per cent cash discount

16 Sold goods and received £45 in cash

17 Withdrew £200 from the bank for use in the business

18 Bought goods costing £162, paying in cash

20 Paid rates £170 by cheque

21 Received £98 in cash from T Bramley

24 Paid W Temple's account of £200 by cheque *less* $2\frac{1}{2}$ per cent cash discount

26 Received rent £45 by cheque from sub-tenant

28 Paid £200 of the cash into the bank

29 Received £165 by cheque from B Matthews in full settlement of his account of £178

11.3

Joseph Simpson is a trader who keeps a three-column cash book; during the month of March 20-9 the following transactions took place. Enter each transaction in the cash book, balance at the end of the month, bring down the balances and show the discount accounts as they would appear in the general ledger:

Mar 1 Balances brought down from previous month: cash £141, bank £2,894.20
   2 Bought goods costing £78, paying in cash
   3 Received a cheque from G Horsfall £185.20 in full settlement of his account of £190
   5 Withdrew £300 from bank for use in the business
   6 Paid rent £75 in cash
   7 Bought goods costing £152, paying in cash
   9 Paid M Green £275 by cheque
  10 Paid L Moore's account of £478.50 by cheque *less* 5 per cent cash discount
  12 Cash sales £98
  14 Cash drawings £150
  16 Withdrew £350 from the bank for business use
  18 A Thompson pays £121.50 in cash, this was in full settlement of his account of £128.75
  20 Purchased goods costing £55, paying in cash
  22 Paid G Strong's account of £296 by cheque *less* 5 per cent cash discount
  24 Received £386 in cash from J Seymore in full settlement of his account of £403.30
  26 Paid £250 of the cash into the bank
  27 Paid wages £75 in cash
  28 Received £325.25 by cheque from R Lewis in full settlement of her account of £342.75
  30 Paid R Morton's account of £760.80 by cheque, *less* 5 per cent cash discount.

11.4

Harry Bairstow keeps a three-column cash book; during the month of May 20-9 the following transactions took place. Enter each transaction in the cash book, balance at the end of the month, bring down the balances and show the discount accounts as they would appear in the general ledger:

May 1 Balances brought down from last month: cash £176, bank £1,823.33
   2 Sold goods and received £151 by cheque
   3 Paid G Binn's account of £312 by cheque *less* $2\frac{1}{2}$ per cent cash discount
   5 Cash drawings £75
   6 Bought goods costing £92, paying cash

7	Withdrew £200 from the bank for business use
8	Received a cheque from B Thornton in full settlement of his account of £554 *less* 5 per cent cash discount
10	Paid wages in cash £150
12	Bought office equipment costing £365, paying by cheque
13	Sold goods and received £185 in cash
15	Received £209 in cash from S Vickers in full settlement of his account of £220
17	Paid £300 cash into the bank
18	Paid motor expenses of £55 in cash
20	Bought goods costing £416, paying by cheque
21	Drawings of £175 by cheque
22	Received a cheque of £441.75 from T Hunt in full settlement of his account of £465.00
24	Paid in cash R Dobson's account of £94 *less* $2\frac{1}{2}$ per cent cash discount
26	Withdrew £250 from bank for use in the business
27	Paid rates £160 by cheque
28	Cash purchases £126
29	Paid R Bates account of £258 by cheque *less* 5 per cent cash discount
30	Cash sales £225
31	Paid wages in cash £150

11.5

George Singer keeps a three-column cash book; during the month of August 20-9 the following transactions took place. Enter each transaction in the cash book, balance at the end of the month, bring down the balances and show the discount accounts as they would appear in the general ledger:

Aug	1	Balances brought down from previous month: cash £217, bank overdraft £1,295.45
	2	Bought goods costing £76, paying in cash
	3	Withdrew £200 from bank for use in the business
	4	Received a cheque of £927.20 from P Aston in full settlement of his account of £976.00
	6	Sold goods and received £162 in cash
	8	Paid wages in cash £125
	9	Paid rent by cheque £65
	10	Received £182 by cheque from M Miles
	12	Sold goods and received £278 in cash
	14	Cash drawings £50
	15	Paid £300 cash into the bank
	17	Paid Newton Supplies account of £520 by cheque *less* $2\frac{1}{2}$ per cent cash discount
	18	Received £20 in cash rent from sub-tenant

20 Paid insurance by cheque £78
21 Received a cheque of £674.70 from D Lawrence in full settlement of his account of £692.00
22 George Singer drew a cheque of £165 for private use
23 Withdrew £250 from the bank for use in the business
24 Cash purchases £145
25 Paid motor expenses £35 in cash
26 Paid R Tetley's account of £397 by cheque *less* 5 per cent cash discount
28 Sold goods and received £225 in cash
30 Paid £300 cash into the bank
31 Received £76 in cash from R Gill

11.6
Jean Jones opened a greengrocer's shop on 1 April 20-4. She had £1,000 cash, of which she placed £900 into a bank account. Transactions for the shop during the month of April were:

April	3	Purchased goods from T Duke on credit	150.00
	4	Paid half year's rent by cheque	600.00
	7	Cash sales for week	685.40
	7	Cash drawings by J Jones	100.00
	7	Paid cash into bank	500.00
	8	Purchased goods from B Prince on credit	75.50
	8	Purchased goods from R Knight on credit	115.00
	11	Paid T Dukes account by cheque in full settlement	135.00
	14	Cash sales for week	732.80
	14	Paid cash into bank	600.00
	14	Cash drawings by J Jones	100.00
	14	Purchases from B Prince on credit	125.00
	18	Paid B Prince by cheque	75.50
	18	Paid R Knight by cheque on account	50.00
	19	Sales to J Lord on credit	30.00
	21	Cash sales for week	483.70
	21	Paid cash into bank	500.00
	23	Purchases from R Knight on credit	176.30
	25	J Lord settled his account by cheque (*less* 10 per cent cash discount)	?
	28	Cash sales for week	572.50
	28	Paid cash into bank	700.00
	28	Drawings by cheque	200.00

Note: Candidates should calculate the amount of the cheque paid by J Lord on 25 April

From this information you are required to:

(a) Record the appropriate transactions in a three-column cash book, and bring down the balances as at 30 April 20-4.

(b) Write up the ledger accounts of T Duke, B Prince, R Knight and J Lord and bring down the balances as at 30 April 20-4.

11.7

Cash Book (Credit side only)

Date		Discount	Cash	Bank
20-5		£	£	£
May 1	Balance			2,200 (. . .)
10	J Archer	20 (. . .)		380 (. . .)
15	Bank		160 (. . .)	
20	Purchases		95 (. . .)	
27	Fixtures			750 (. . .)
31	Balances		55 (. . .)	440 (. . .)
		20	310	3,770

You are required to choose from the following statements the one which you feel best expresses the meaning of each entry shown in the cash book above. Enter the letter (**A–M**) representing your choice, in the space provided at the side of each entry (. . .)

A Discount allowed to a debtor for prompt payment
B The balance in the firm's bank account
C Discount allowed by a creditor
D Cash paid into bank
E The purchase of fixtures
F The amount of the bank overdraft
G Cash withdrawn from bank for office use
H Value of cheque received from a debtor
J Cash paid for purchase of goods
K The amount of cash held in the firm's office
L Value of cheque paid to a creditor
M The sale of a computer

■ Ṽ **12** Bank cash books

The bank cash book is a modern version of the original three-column cash book and is now used by many businesses. It was designed to control cash and follows the golden rule that '**all** money received, whether in cash or cheques, is paid into the bank intact, and all payments are made by cheque'. This means there are no *contra* entries or cash payments so the cash column is not needed, it is used instead as a *details* column.

Firms who use bank cash books usually make small cash payments out of petty cash. Analysed petty cash books and the imprest system are fully covered in Unit 13.

At the debit side, the particulars column shows the names of each separate ledger account, the *details* column is used to list individual amounts received, only the total amount paid into the bank is entered in the bank column. This amount should always agree with the total shown in the bank paying in book.

Look at a typical example: on 2 March 20–8 the following cash and cheques were received and paid into the bank.

Cash from sales £441.40, a cheque of £34.00 from L Green and a cheque of £146.25 from G Newton in full settlement of his account of £150.

The entries in the firm's bank cash book would look like this:

Bank Cash Book

Date	Particulars	F	Discount allowed	Details	Bank	Date	Particulars	F	Discount received	Details	Bank
			£	£	£				£	£	£
Mar 1	Balance b/d				2,532.18						
2	Sales			441.40							
2	L Green			34.00							
2	G Newton		3.75	146.25	621.65						

Notice that on 2 March the total paid into the bank is the only figure to appear in the bank column. This is very useful since it enables a firm to compare the bank figures very easily when the bank statement arrives from the bank. A line is ruled under the last item to show it is the addition of the day's banking.

At the credit side the details column is used only when one cheque is drawn, to cover two or more payments which will subsequently require posting to separate ledger accounts. All other payments by cheque are entered in the bank column.

This is a typical example of when the details column would be used at the credit side. On 5 March the proprietor needed £150 for personal use and £35.60 was required for petty cash. On these occasions it would be a waste of time writing two cheques, so one cheque is drawn for £185.60. Details of the amounts concerned are entered in the details column, the total amount of the cheque is entered in the bank column. A line is ruled across the details column to show the addition, like this:

Bank Cash Book

Date	Particulars	F	Discount allowed	Details	Bank	Date	Particulars	F	Discount received	Details	Bank
			£	£	£				£	£	£
Mar 1	Balance b/d				2,532.18	Mar 5	Drawings			150.00	
						5	Petty cash			35.60	185.60

Notice that on 5 March the cheque total is the only figure to appear in the bank column. Again, this is very useful since it enables a firm to compare the figures very easily when the bank statement arrives from the bank. (Only the *total amount* of each cheque will appear on the bank statement.)

In all other respects the bank cash book is exactly like a three-column cash book, but as you can see there is only one account to be totalled and balanced in the usual way. The discount allowed and discount received columns are always totalled but **never** balanced.

Points to remember

- Bank cash books are a modern development of the three-column cash book and are now preferred by many firms. They are favoured as a means of preventing discrepancies in cash. It follows the rule that *all money received, whether in cash or cheques, is paid into the bank intact.*
- At the debit side the *details* column is used to list individual amounts received, only the total amount paid into the bank is entered in the bank column. At the credit side the details column is used only when *one* cheque is drawn, to cover two or more payments which will subsequently require posting to separate ledger accounts. (This will usually be when a cheque is drawn for drawings and petty cash.) All other payments by cheque are entered in the bank column.
- Questions relating to bank cash books regularly appear in book-keeping and accounting examinations, sometimes they are combined with a petty cash question. There are several questions taken from recent examination papers included in the Assignments for this unit.

Worked example

This is a worked example of a typical question set in recent examinations. Brian Walsh makes all payments over £20 by cheque and pays all money received into the bank. On 1 March 20–8 the bank column of his bank cash book showed a balance in the bank of £2,532.18. During the week, the following transactions took place:

2 Mar Banked £441.40 cash from sales, a cheque of £34 from L Green and a cheque of £146.25 from G Newton in full settlement of his account of £150

2 Mar Paid rent £100 by cheque

3 Mar Paid S Smythe's account of £450 *less* 5 per cent cash discount

4 Mar Banked £298.20 cash from sales, a cheque of £50 from G Lewis and a cheque of £248.16 from M Hobson in full settlement of her account of £252

4 Mar Paid J Martin's account of £676 *less* 5 per cent cash discount

5 Mar Drew a cheque for £185.60; £150.00 was for personal use, £35.60 was for petty cash

5 Mar Paid B Binn's account of £120 *less* 5 per cent cash discount

6 Mar Banked £98 cash from sales, a cheque of £21 rebate of insurance which had been overpaid and a cheque of £106.57 from R Coleman in full settlement of his account of £109

Now look at the fully worked answer of this question (Figure 12.1). Make sure you take each transaction, in date order, then find the entry in the bank cash book.

Bank Cash Book

Date	Particulars	F	Discount allowed	Details	Bank	Date	Particulars	F	Discount received	Details	Bank
20.8			£	£	£	20.8			£	£	£
Mar 1	Balance b/d				2,532.18	Mar 2	Rent				100.00
2	Sales			441.40		3	S. Smythe		22.50		427.50
2	L. Green			34.00		4	J. Martin		33.80		642.20
2	G. Newton		3.75	146.25	621.65	5	Drawings			150.00	
4	Sales			298.20		5	Petty Cash			35.60	185.60
4	G. Lewis			50.00		5	B. Binns		6.00		114.00
4	M. Hobson		3.84	248.16	596.36	6	Balance c/d				2,506.46
6	Sales			98.00							
6	Insurance			21.00							
6	R. Coleman		2.43	106.57	225.57						
			10.02		3,975.76				62.30		3,975.76
Mar 7	Balance b/d				2,506.46						

Figure 12.1

Assignments

12.1

John Dawson makes all payments over £20 by cheque and pays all money received into the bank. On 1 January 20–9 the bank column of his bank cash book showed a balance in the bank of £2,252.58. During the week the following transactions took place:

2 Jan   Paid D Guy a cheque of £114.40, this was in full settlement of his account of £120

2 Jan   Banked a cheque of £338.20 from S Peters in full settlement of her account of £356, cash from sales of £142 and a cheque of £67 from J Myers

3 Jan   Drew a cheque for £526.80; £350 was for wages, £76.80 for petty cash and the remainder was for personal use

4 Jan   Banked £167.80 cash from sales, a cheque of £137 from D. Adams in full settlement of his account of £150 and a cheque of £48 from M Cliff

4 Jan   Paid S Barnes' account of £127 by cheque

5 Jan   Banked a cheque of £92 from B Groves, a cheque of £30 for commission received and £126.20 cash from sales

5 Jan   Bought office equipment costing £365.20, paying by cheque

6 Jan   Paid rates £125 by cheque

6 Jan   Banked £238.95 cash from sales, a cheque of £750 from G Spink and a cheque of £155.50 from T Denton in full settlement of his account of £160

6 Jan   Paid B Mills' account of £480 *less* 5 per cent cash discount

You are required to write up and balance the bank cash book for the week.

12.2

Graham Dean makes all payments over £20 by cheque and pays all money received into the bank. On 1 March 20–9 the bank column of his bank cash book showed a balance in the bank of £1,376.30. During the week the following transactions took place:

2 Mar   Paid insurance £150 by cheque

2 Mar   Banked £236.65 cash from sales

2 Mar   Paid W Kay's account of £220 *less* 5 per cent cash discount

3 Mar   Banked £276.55 cash from sales, a cheque of £35, rent received from sub-tenant and a cheque of £145 from C Prince in full settlement of her account of £150

3 Mar   Paid E Franks a cheque of £76.60

4 Mar   Banked a cheque of £150 from the sale of an old machine and £122.20 cash from sales

4 Mar   Paid rent £120 by cheque

5 Mar   Paid F Peters' account of £450 *less* 5 per cent cash discount

6 Mar Banked a cheque of £347.50 from P Timms in full settlement of his account of £365.70, cash from sales £178.80 and a cheque of £160.50 from J Jacques in full settlement of his account of £166.76

6 Mar Drew a cheque for £218.65; £68.65 was for petty cash, the remainder was for personal use

You are required to write up and balance the bank cash book for the week.

12.3

James McCann makes all payments over £20 by cheque and pays all money received into the bank. On 5 February 20–9 the bank column of his bank cash book showed a balance in the bank of £1,602.55. During the week the following transactions took place:

6 Feb Paid rent £135 by cheque

6 Feb Banked £138.50 cash from sales

7 Feb Paid D. Spencer's account of £220 by cheque, *less* $2\frac{1}{2}$ per cent cash discount

7 Feb Banked £175.75 cash from sales and a cheque of £209 from B. Moore in full settlement of her account of £220.50

8 Feb Paid insurance £67.50 by cheque

8 Feb Banked £195.80 cash from sales

9 Feb Drew a cheque for £262.90; £75 was for personal use, £150 for wages and £37.90 for petty cash

9 Feb Banked a cheque of £55 from T Warren, £67.75 cash from sales and a cheque of £195.50 from M Munro in full settlement of her account of £209

10 Feb Paid J Black £280.50 by cheque, this was in full settlement of his account of £295

10 Feb Banked £221.55 cash from sales and a cheque of £100 from B Andrews

You are required to write up and balance the bank cash book for the week.

12.4

Charles Hargreaves makes all payments over £20 by cheque and pays all money received into the bank. On 1 June 20–9 the bank column of his bank cash book showed a balance in the bank of £1,870.85. During the week the following transactions took place:

2 Jun Paid W Dyson £244 by cheque, this was in full settlement of his account of £256

2 Jun Banked a cheque of £126.25 from J Larkin in full settlement of his account of £130, cash from sales £235 and a cheque of £150 from D Mawson

2 Jun Paid rent £215 by cheque

3 Jun Banked cash from sales £236.40, a cheque of £68 from S Senior in full settlement of her account of £70.50, a cheque of £15 refund of insurance overpaid and a cheque of £339 from C. Masters in full settlement of his account of £345.50

3 Jun	Paid D Stead £123 by cheque, this was in full settlement of his account of £128.40
3 Jun	Paid rates £58.90 by cheque
4 Jun	Banked £195.80 cash from sales
4 Jun	Paid G Barker's account of £178 *less* 5 per cent cash discount
4 Jun	Paid motor expenses £100 by cheque
5 Jun	Banked a cheque of £40 from George Lewis, a cheque of £49.14 from M Griffin in full settlement of his account of £50.40, cash from sales of £98.90 and a cheque of £136.50 from Joseph Plumb in full settlement of his account of £140
5 Jun	Paid A Paul £66.00 by cheque, this was in full settlement of his account of £68.50
5 Jun	Drew a cheque for £647.60; £47.60 was for petty cash, £450 for wages and the remainder was for personal use
5 Jun	Paid Stylax Ltd £196.50 for a new office desk

You are required to write up and balance the bank cash book for the week.

12.5

Karen Jones makes all payments over £20 by cheque and pays all money received into the bank. On 1 May 20–9 the bank column of her bank cash book showed a balance at the bank of £3,258.

During the month of May the following transactions took place:

2 May	Paid D Fisher £472 by cheque in full settlement of a debt of £500
4 May	Paid Ringways Garage £178 for repairs to van
5 May	Banked £400 cash from sales, a cheque of £325 from B Mills in full settlement of his account of £362 and a cheque of £95 from M Wilson
9 May	Paid Systems Ltd a cheque of £125 for repairs to office printer
12 May	Drew cheque of £250 for personal use
14 May	Banked £550 cash from sales and a cheque of £268 from L Stevens in full settlement of her account of £300
16 May	Bought goods costing £124 paying by cheque
18 May	Paid a trade creditor, T Simpson, a cheque for £325 in full settlement of his account of £350
20 May	Banked £700 cash from sales, a cheque of £359 from B Ellis in full settlement of his account of £384 and a cheque of £50 from J Singh
24 May	Paid electricity bill of £482 by cheque
27 May	Drew a cheque for £400, £120 was for petty cash and the remainder was for personal use
28 May	Banked £550 cash from sales, a cheque of £65 from D Ross in full settlement of his debt of £73 and £250 cash from M Patel
30 May	Paid D Jennings £254 by cheque in full settlement of his account of £270
31 May	Banked cash sales of £650

You are required to write up and balance Karen Jones' bank cash book for the month of May 20–9.

12.6

Gina Howard makes all payments over £20 by cheque and pays all money received into the bank. On 1 June 20–9 the bank cash book showed a balance in the bank of £1,405.

During the month of June the following transactions took place:

3 Jun   Drew a cheque for £450; £105 was for petty cash the remainder was for personal use

4 Jun   Paid D King's account of £120 *less* $2\frac{1}{2}$ per cent cash discount

5 Jun   Banked cash from sales £205, a cheque of £86 from W Kelly in full settlement of his account of £92 and £27 in cash from P Ellison

8 Jun   Paid electricity bill £328 by cheque

12 Jun   Banked cheque of £136 from J Dean in full settlement of her account of £148, a cheque of £28 from H Khan and cash from sales £145

15 Jun   Bought goods costing £299, paying by cheque

18 Jun   Paid telephone bill £384 by cheque

19 Jun   Banked cash from sales £150

25 Jun   Paid M Dyson's account of £480 *less* $2\frac{1}{2}$ per cent cash discount

27 Jun   Bought a new photocopier costing £699 from Copywell

28 Jun   Paid Smart Motors £325 by cheque for servicing and repairs

30 Jun   Banked a cheque of £93 from J Kendall in full settlement of his debt of £98, cash from sales £205 and a cheque of £70 from C Dunn, who purchased a photocopier which was no longer required

You are required to write up and balance Gina Howard's bank cash book for the month of June 20–9.

■ ⊻ **13** Analysed petty cash book and the imprest system

When a firm pays *all* money received into the bank intact (see Unit 12 on bank cash books) they normally use a *petty cash book* to keep a record of small cash payments.

'Petty cash' is the name given to money that can be used to pay for small cash purchases. The word '*petty*' means small. If someone was asked to buy a new plant for the reception area, the money spent would be repaid out of petty cash. A receipt should be obtained for all transactions involving cash. Petty cash is often used to pay for small items of stationery, postage stamps, refreshments, petrol and travelling expenses such as taxi, bus and train fares. The rules for entering petty cash transactions are the same as for any other cash account: that is, debit receipts of cash and credit payments.

In an office the person responsible for petty cash is known as the *petty cashier*. This person will usually carry out these duties as well as their other work.

Petty cash vouchers

Whenever anyone needs to claim money out of petty cash they must fill in a petty cash voucher showing exactly what the payment was for. Staff are usually expected to obtain a receipt for the item purchased, the receipt is then attached to the voucher (Figure 13.1). Each completed voucher is then signed by the person receiving the money to verify that they have been paid by the petty cashier. Vouchers are dated and numbered *in the order they are received*, each voucher is given the next higher number.

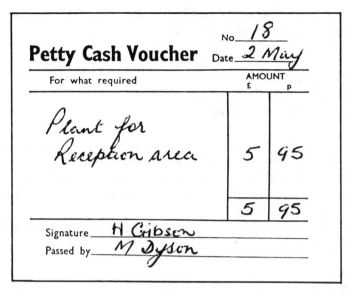

Figure 13.1

Rules for dealing with cash

- Cash is valuable. When you are receiving or paying out cash *always* count it carefully
- Petty cash should be paid out only in return for a *completed voucher and receipt*
- *Never leave cash unattended,* even for a few minutes
- Always keep cash in a *lockable box* and store it in a safe place
- Be careful with *keys.*

The imprest system

Under the imprest system of keeping petty cash an agreed sum of money is given to the petty cashier as a *float,* this is known as the *imprest.* It is used to make petty cash payments over a period of time, this could be a week or a month. At the end of the period, the petty cashier is repaid the *amount that has been spent;* this will bring the float back to its starting level. Each new period begins with the original amount. This is known as *restoring the imprest.*

   If the petty cashier started the week with £100, and during the week paid out £85.50. There should be £14.50 in the petty cash box. This £14.50 is known as the *balance.* A senior clerk will check that the amount of cash left (the balance) agrees with the amount shown in the petty cash book, then the petty cashier would receive £85.50, *the amount spent.* This would restore the petty cash to the original amount of £100. Each new period starts with the *full amount* of the imprest:

	£ p
Imprest (float) at start of week was	100.00
Total paid out during the week was	85.50
Balance of cash at end of week	14.50

A petty cashier should regularly check the contents of the petty cash box. This is done by counting the cash in the petty cash box and then adding the amounts shown on the vouchers. The total cash in the petty cash box, *plus* the total of the vouchers, should equal the amount of the float (imprest) at any time during the period.

Now test yourself on these important points by completing this Assignment.

Assignment

13.1

(a) The imprest (float) to start the week was £50.00. You have petty cash vouchers to the value of £35.20. How much should be in your petty cash box?

(b) The imprest at the start of the week was £75.00. If £64.30 is spent during the week, how much will you receive at the end of the week?

(c) To start the month the imprest was £100.00. Your petty cash box now contains:
$4 \times £5$ notes, $2 \times £1$ coins, $5 \times 50p$ coins, $1 \times 10p$ coin, $2 \times 2p$ coins and $1 \times 1p$ coin.
How much has been spent during the month?

(d) The imprest to start the week was £100.00. You have petty cash vouchers to the value of £79.25. How much should be in your petty cash box?

(e) You have petty cash vouchers to the value of £42.45.
Your petty cash box contains:
$4 \times £1$ coins, $3 \times 50p$ coins, $6 \times 20p$ coins, $7 \times 10p$ coins and $3 \times 5p$ coins.
How much was the imprest?

Analysis columns

In the analysed petty cash book the types of expenditure which occur most frequently will be given an analysis column of their own. The word '*analysis*' means to break up into smaller parts, so various items of expense can be arranged under a suitable column heading. It is then possible to see how much is being spent on certain items.

Obviously the number of analysis columns used will depend on what each firm finds useful. At the end of the period, all the analysis columns are totalled to show the amount spent under each heading.

Various types of payments are made through petty cash, but generally they will fit under one of the following column headings:

Travelling	Postage	Stationery	Sundry expenses	Cleaning	Ledger

Most firms use a *sundry expenses* column for items which will not easily fit under any of the other column headings.

Sometimes one of the columns is chosen as a *ledger* column. It is used only for items paid out of petty cash which need posting to a ledger other than the general ledger – for example, when a creditor is paid out of petty cash.

The total of each individual analysis column will be posted to the ledger account for that expense. For example, the stationery paid for out of petty cash will be posted to the stationery account in the general ledger.

Filling in the petty cash book

Each new period begins with the amount of the imprest (float). This is entered in the *receipts column.* Very often this will consist of two amounts:

- *balance of cash* which is brought down from the previous week
- amount of cash received to *restore the imprest to the original amount.*

In this example the imprest amount is £100. To illustrate the process, let us look at a typical petty cash book:

Petty Cash Book

Receipts	Date	Details	Voucher number	Total payments	Sundry expenses	Cleaning	Postage and stationery	Ledger
£				£	£	£	£	£
15.50	1 May	Balance brought down						
84.50	1 May	Cash received to restore imprest						

- All payments are entered in the petty cash book in *date order*
- Each amount spent is entered *twice*, once in the *total payments column* and again in one of the analysis columns.

The vouchers in Figure 13.2 are shown entered in the petty cash book in Figure 13.3.

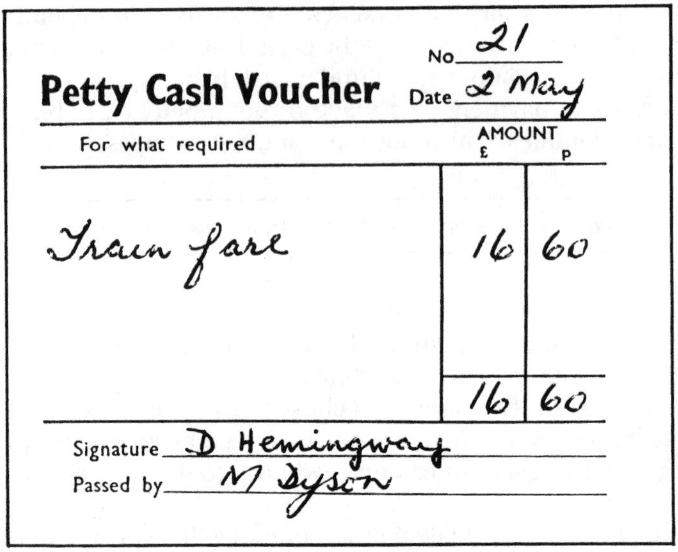

Petty Cash Voucher

No. 21
Date 2 May

For what required	AMOUNT £	p
Train fare	16	60
	16	60

Signature D Hemingway
Passed by M Dyson

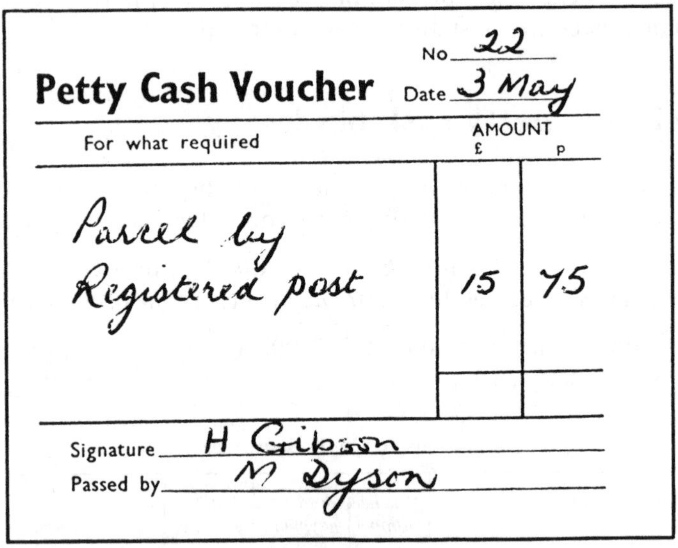

Petty Cash Voucher

No. 22
Date 3 May

For what required	AMOUNT £	p
Parcel by Registered post	15	75

Signature H Gibson
Passed by M Dyson

Figure 13.2

Petty Cash Book

Receipts	Date	Details	Voucher number	Total payments	Sundry expenses	Cleaning	Postage and stationery	Ledger
£				£	£	£	£	£
15.50	1 May	Balance brought down						
84.50	1 May	Cash received						
	2 May	Train fare	21	16.60	16.60			
	3 May	Registered post	22	15.75			15.75	

Figure 13.3

Balancing the petty cash book

When all payments during the period have been entered (this could be a week or a month), all the columns are totalled separately.

The total of all the analysis columns should *always* equal the addition of the *total payments column*. This method of checking is known as *cross-casting* and will usually reveal any mistakes; either in the *addition* of the columns or if an item has been entered in the total payments column but not *extended into one of the analysis columns*.

This is the procedure to balance the petty cash book:

- Add up *all* the columns
- Then cross-cast analysis columns, this figure should equal the *total payments*
- *Calculate the balance* by deducting the total payments from the imprest (float)
- This amount is entered as the balance to carry down, generally abbreviated to *balance c/d* (this is the amount of *cash in hand*)
- Enter the totals, in the *receipts column* and *total payments column*, make sure the two totals are written on the same line, parallel with each other
- The balance is then brought down into the *receipts column* to start the next period.

When the petty cash book has been checked, the amount of cash spent – that is, the amount of the total payments – is then handed to the petty cashier to restore the imprest to the original amount.

To illustrate this process let us now look at a typical petty cash book, balanced for the week ending 5 May (Figure 13.4):

Petty Cash Book

Receipts	Date	Details	Voucher number	Total payments	Sundry expenses	Cleaning	Postage and stationery	Ledger
£				£	£	£	£	£
15.50	1 May	Balance brought down						
84.50	1 May	Cash						
	2 May	Train fare	21	16.60	16.60			
	3 May	Registered post	22	15.75			15.75	
	3 May	Window cleaner	23	12.50		12.50		
	4 May	Torch and batteries	24	7.65	7.65			
	5 May	Large envelopes	25	4.25			4.25	
	5 May	Coffee and tea bags	26	8.38	8.38			
	5 May	G Morgan (creditor)	27	19.95				19.95
				85.08	32.63	12.50	20.00	19.95
	5 May	Balance c/d		14.92				
100.00				100.00				
14.92	5 May	Balance b/d						

Figure 13.4

At the end of the period, each individual analysis column *total* will be posted to the ledger account for that expense, like this:

General Ledger

Sundry Expenses Account

		£	
5 May	Petty cash	32.63	

Cleaning Account

		£	
5 May	Petty cash	12.50	

Postage and Stationery Account

		£	
5 May	Petty cash	20.00	

Purchase Ledger

G Morgan Account

		£			£
5 May	Petty cash	19.95	1 May	Balance b/d	19.95

Assignment

13.2 Look carefully at the illustration of the completed petty cash book for the week ending 5 May (Figure 13.4) and answer the following questions:
   (a) What is the amount of the imprest?
   (b) How much was spent on postage and stationery during the week?
   (c) Was there any petty cash left at the end of the week? If so, how much?
   (d) What was the total of all the analysis columns?
   (e) How much was needed to restore the imprest on 1 May?
   (f) What was the total amount spent during the week?
   (g) How much is needed to restore the imprest on 5 May?

Value Added Tax

Most of the goods and services we buy in shops are subject to Value Added Tax; this is generally abbreviated and known as VAT. It is a type of *sales tax* which is charged as a percentage and added to the price of certain goods and services. The percentage rate is set by the government and is changed from time to time by the Chancellor of the Exchequer. H M Customs and Excise Department is responsible for administering VAT.

Some petty cash payments may be subject to VAT; when they are, the amount of VAT should be shown on the petty cash voucher. This is because firms who are registered for VAT can reclaim the amount of VAT paid on business expenses from Customs and Excise. Firms who wish to reclaim VAT must keep a separate VAT column in their petty cash book to enter amounts of VAT.

When petty cash expenses are subject to VAT, the amount of VAT is shown separately on the voucher (Figure 13.5).

Petty Cash Voucher	No. 28 Date 8 May		
For what required		AMOUNT £	p
Petrol		14	30
VAT		2	50
		16	80
Signature D Jennings			
Passed by M Dyson			

Figure 13.5

When this voucher is recorded in the petty cash book, there will be *three* amounts to enter: £16.80 in the *total payments column*, £14.30 in *motor expenses* and £2.50 in the *VAT* column (Figure 13.6).

Petty Cash Book

Receipts	*Date*	*Details*	*Voucher number*	*Total payments*	*Sundry expenses*	*Cleaning*	*Motor expenses*	*Postage and stationery*	*VAT*
£				£	£	£	£	£	£
15.02	5 May	Balance brought down							
84.98	6 May	Cash							
	8 May	Petrol	28	16.80			14.30		2.50

Figure 13.6

During the week the petty cash payments shown in Figure 13.7 were made:

Petty Cash Voucher No. 29 Date 9 May

For what required	AMOUNT £	p
Magazines for Reception	6	20
	6	20

Signature H Gibson
Passed by M Dyson

Petty Cash Voucher No. 30 Date 9 May

For what required	AMOUNT £	p
Cleaning materials	7	99
VAT	1	40
	9	39

Signature K Jones
Passed by M Dyson

Petty Cash Voucher No. 31 Date 10 May

For what required	AMOUNT £	p
Parcel tape	3	37
VAT		58
	3	95

Signature S Millburn
Passed by M Dyson

Petty Cash Voucher No. 32 Date 10 May

For what required	AMOUNT £	p
Parcel by Registered post	15	75
	15	75

Signature H Gibson
Passed by M Dyson

Petty Cash Voucher No. 33 Date 11 May

For what required	AMOUNT £	p
Locking petrol cap for delivery van	11	06
VAT	1	93
	12	99

Signature T Wilson
Passed by M Dyson

Petty Cash Voucher No. 34 Date 12 May

For what required	AMOUNT £	p
Self-adhesive labels	2	13
VAT		37
	2	50

Signature A Patel
Passed by M Dyson

Figure 13.7

These vouchers are now entered in the petty cash book: *remember* that when payments are subject to VAT, the amount of VAT *must* be shown separately:

Petty Cash Book

Receipts	Date	Details	Voucher number	Total payments	Sundry expenses	Cleaning	Motor expenses	Postage and stationery	VAT
£				£	£	£	£	£	£
15.02	5 May	Balance brought down							
84.98	6 May	Cash							
	8 May	Petrol	28	16.80			14.30		2.50
	9 May	Magazines	29	6.20	6.20				
	9 May	Cleaning materials	30	9.39		7.99			1.40
	10 May	Parcel tape	31	3.95				3.37	58
	10 May	Registered post	32	15.75				15.75	
	11 May	Locking petrol cap	33	12.99			11.06		1.93
	12 May	Self-adhesive labels	34	2.50				2.13	37
				67.58	6.20	7.99	25.36	21.25	6.78
	12 May	Balance c/d		32.42					
100.00				100.00					
32.42	12 May	Balance b/d							

Points to remember

- The rules for entering petty cash transactions are the same as for any other cash account – that is, debit receipts of cash and credit payments. Only the *receipts column* represents the *debit* side of the petty cash book. *Total payments and analysis columns* are the *credit* side.
- Each item of expense is entered in the *total payments column* and again in the *appropriate analysis column*. Voucher numbers are placed alongside each entry.
- When petty cash payments are subject to VAT, the amount of VAT *must be shown separately* in the petty cash book:
  total amount spent is entered in the *total payments column*
  cost (excluding VAT) is entered in the relevant *analysis column*
  the amount of VAT is entered in the *VAT column*.
- The totals of the combined analysis columns should *always* agree with the addition of the total payments column; this is called *cross-casting* and will usually locate any errors.
- Deduct the total payments from the original imprest to find the *balance of petty cash in hand.*
- At the end of the week or month, the total of each analysis column is posted to the *debit side* of the relevant expense account in the ledger.

Assignments

13.3

Mark Alexander is a sole trader who keeps his petty cash on the imprest system. The imprest of £100 is restored at the beginning of each month.

During the month of February 20-8 the following transactions took place:

			Voucher number
Feb	**1**	Petty cash in hand £15.62	
	1	Petty cash restored to imprest amount	
	2	Paid wages £16.10	18
	4	Bought postage stamps £3.44	19
	8	Paid a creditor, G Newman £12.40	20
	10	Car sponge and car polish £5.65	21
	12	Paid cleaner's wages £18.20	22
	15	Envelopes £2.25	23
	17	Bought rear light reflector for van £14.55	24
	18	Postage on parcel £1.70	25
	21	Paid wages £12.50	26
	24	Packet of A4 paper £3.45	27

You are required to draw up a petty cash book to record the above transactions and also give the entry on 1 March 20-8 restoring the petty cash to the imprest amount.

Your analysis columns will be for Wages, Postage, Stationery, Motor expenses and Ledger.

13.4

John Beaumont keeps a petty cash book with analysis columns for Travelling, Motor expenses, Postage and stationery and Ledger accounts. At the close of business on 31 March 20-8 his cash in hand stood at the imprest amount of £200.

You are required to write up the petty cash book for the month of April 20-8:

			Voucher number
Apr	**1**	Petrol £14.50	34
	2	Postage stamps £6.90	35
	3	Van tyre £18.30	36
	4	Envelopes £2.50	37
	5	Train fares £7.20	38
	8	Paper clips £1.35	39
	9	Car polish £2.80	40
	10	Petrol and oil £16.90	41
	11	Bus fares £1.40	42
	12	George Seal, a creditor, £18.50	43
	15	Stapler and staples £5.30	44

16	Postage on parcel £2.60	45
17	Train fares £6.50	46
18	Petrol £14.00	47
19	Postage stamps £5.80	48
22	Alan Smith, a creditor, £15.40	49
24	Typing paper £2.30	50
25	Van seat covers £12.60	51
26	Bus fares £1.20	52
29	James Jones, a creditor, £8.50	53
30	Taxi fare £4.00	54

13.5

Jennifer Peterson is a florist who keeps her petty cash on the imprest system. The imprest of £150 is restored at the beginning of each month. Her petty cash transactions for the month of August 20-8 were:

		Voucher number
Aug 1	Petty cash in hand £12.60	
1	Petty cash restored to imprest amount	
2	Bus fares £4.20	71
3	Window cleaner £12.50	72
4	F Harrison, a creditor, £19.70	73
5	Postage stamps £8.60	74
6	Petrol and oil £15.00	75
8	Train fare £3.40	76
9	Cleaning materials £4.75	77
10	Self-adhesive labels £2.25	78
11	Air mail postage £2.60	79
12	Window cleaner £12.50	80
14	Taxi fare £6.50	81
15	Large envelopes £1.75	82
16	Andrew Ford, a creditor, £6.20	83
17	Petrol £12.00	84
18	Cleaning lady £14.00	85
21	Locking petrol cap £5.95	86
22	Felt tip pens £2.20	87
24	Train fare £4.60	88
28	Eric Morgan, a creditor, £4.80	89
30	Postage stamps £2.65	90

You are required to write up her petty cash book to record the above transactions and also give the entry on 1 September to restore the imprest. Use analysis columns for: Cleaning, Motor expenses, Travelling, Postage and stationery, Ledger accounts.

13.6

Robert Groves keeps his petty cash on the imprest system. The imprest of £100 is restored at the beginning of each week. His petty cash transactions were:

		Voucher number
Jun 16	Petty cash in hand £15.74	
16	Petty cash restored to imprest amount	
17	Batteries for wall clock £2.77 (*plus* VAT 48p)	12
18	Postage stamps £12.50	13
18	Window cleaner £15.00	14
19	Scissors £4.05 (*plus* VAT 70p)	15
20	Petrol for delivery van £12.77 (*plus* VAT £2.23)	16
20	Box file £2.98 (*plus* VAT 52p)	17
21	Cleaner's wages £18.00	18
21	Seat cover for van £6.77 (*plus* VAT £1.18)	19

You are required to write up and balance his petty cash book. Use analysis columns for: Sundry expenses, Cleaning, Motor expenses, Postage and stationery, VAT.

13.7

Hazar Khan keeps his petty cash on the imprest system. On 1 July there was £21.35 balance in hand and the first available petty cash voucher was number 28. The imprest of £150 is restored at the beginning of each week. His petty cash transactions were:

Jul 1	Petty cash restored to imprest amount
2	Milkman £3.74
2	Envelopes and sellotape £6.25 (*plus* VAT £1.09)
3	Taxi fare £6.50
4	Printer ribbon £6.80 (*plus* VAT £1.19)
4	Tea bags and coffee £8.26
5	Train fare £14.30
5	Cleaning materials £9.82 (*plus* VAT £1.72)
5	Airmail parcel £12.75
6	Electric kettle £16.98 (*plus* VAT £2.97)
6	Cleaners wages £18.00
6	Computer disks £7.65 (*plus* VAT £1.34)

You are required to write up and balance his petty cash book. Use analysis columns for: Sundry expenses, Travel, Cleaning, Postage and stationery, VAT.

13.8

Denise Fielding keeps her petty cash on the imprest system. On 1 August there was £35.28 balance in hand and the first available petty cash voucher was number 62. The imprest of £200 is restored at the beginning of each month. Her petty cash transactions during the month of August were:

Aug 1 Petty cash restored to imprest amount
2 Hole punch £8.94 (*plus* VAT £1.56)
3 Petrol £12.54 (*plus* VAT £2.19)
4 Computer cleaning kit £14.99 (*plus* VAT £2.62)
5 Box of pencils £2.53 (*plus* VAT 44p)
8 Tea bags £3.84
10 Petrol £13.20 (*plus* VAT £2.31)
12 Stapler and staples £8.74 (*plus* VAT £1.52)
15 Window cleaner £12.50
17 Step stool £9.68 (*plus* VAT £1.69)
19 Postage stamps £15.00
21 Correction fluid £1.05 (*plus* VAT 18p)
22 Petrol £16.00 (*plus* VAT £2.80)
25 Copier paper £5.99 (*plus* VAT £1.05)
26 Torch and batteries £8.62 (*plus* VAT £1.50)
29 Window cleaner £12.50
30 Petrol £11.83 (*plus* VAT £2.07)
31 Milkman £14.86

You are required to write up and balance her petty cash book. Use analysis columns for: Sundry expenses, Cleaning, Motor expenses, Postage and stationery, VAT.

On recent examination papers petty cash questions have been combined with a bank cash book question. To enable candidates to gain valuable practice working these type of questions, the assignments which follow require a petty cash book and a bank cash book.

13.9

George Mainwaring maintains a petty cash book for all payments less than £20. The imprest of £100 is restored at the end of each week. Other payments are made by cheque, and all receipts are paid into the bank. At the start of business on Monday 3 March 20-6 his bank cash book showed a balance in hand of £1,468.12.

For the week which followed his bank paying-in book counterfoils showed the following:

4 Mar Cash from sales £280.80, a cheque for £97.50 from C Godfrey in full settlement of a £100 debt and a cheque for £24.25 from M Square

6 Mar Cash sales £488.30 and a cheque for £15 from H Blewitt who had bought Mainwaring's old typewriter

7 Mar Cash from sales £272.90

During the same week Mainwaring drew the following cheques:

		£
4 Mar	For personal use	250.00
6 Mar	Warmington Council (rates)	315.30
6 Mar	M Fox (in full settlement of his account of £800.00)	780.00
7 Mar	Petty cash	?

Payments out of petty cash were:

		Voucher number	£
3 Mar	Petrol	501	16.80
3 Mar	A Yeatman, a creditor	502	18.10
4 Mar	Cleaning lady	503	11.40
5 Mar	Box file	504	4.30
5 Mar	Train fares	505	10.10
6 Mar	Postage stamps	506	15.20
7 Mar	Window cleaner	507	5.50

You are required to:

(a) Write up and balance the petty cash book. Use analysis columns for: Travelling, Cleaning, Postage and stationery, Ledger accounts.

(b) Write up and balance the bank cash book.

13z.10

Doug Wigby pays all receipts into his bank account and makes all payments greater than £15 by cheque. All other payments are made out of petty cash, at the end of each week the petty cash is restored to the imprest amount of £50.

On 5 January 20-7 Doug Wigby's bank cash book showed a balance in the bank of £620.78 and there was £50 in his petty cash.

Paying-in book counterfoils showed:

Jan 5 Cheque of £106.39 from Ian Tait
    6 Cash from sales £195.72 and a cheque from Martin Quantrill for £97.50 in settlement of a debt of £100
    8 Cash from sales £160.58
    9 Cash from sales £248.03 and a cheque for £135 from Bridget Rogers

Cheque book counterfoils showed:

Jan 5 West Loamshire County Council for rates £350
    7 £114 to David Hunter in settlement of £120 owing to him
    8 Drawings £75
    9 Petty cash £29
    9 Midland Motors Ltd £1,500 for second-hand delivery van

Petty cash payments were as follows, the first available petty cash voucher is number 42:

		£
Jan 5	Postage stamps	5.80
6	Travelling expenses	4.70
7	George Lingard, a creditor	12.00
8	Stationery	6.50

Doug Wigby was informed on 9 January that the cheque from Ian Tait for £106.39 paid in on 5 January had been returned marked R/D (refer to drawer).

You are required to:

(a) Write up the bank cash book.
(b) Write up the petty cash book. Use analysis columns for Postage and stationery, Travelling expenses and Ledger accounts. Balance both books on 9 January 20-7.
(c) Open ledger accounts and complete the double entry for each of the petty cash analysis columns.

13.11

Penny Wheelwright runs a small retail business. She makes all payments over £20 by cheque and pays all money received into the bank. On 1 April 20-9 her bank cash book showed a balance in the bank of £304.28 and there was £28.96 petty cash in hand.

Penny keeps her petty cash book on the imprest system. The imprest of £150 is restored at the beginning of each month.

During the month of April the following transactions took place:

2 Apr   Bought goods costing £164.52
        Received an amount from the bank, in cash to restore petty cash to imprest amount
        Received a cheque of £278.00 from G Roberts in full settlement of his account of £306.30

4 Apr   Paid postage on parcel £14.96
        Cash sales £152
        Paid E Mellor, a creditor, £18.78

8 Apr   Penny Wheelwright withdrew £200 for personal use
        Paid B Dixon's account of £252.00 *less* $2\frac{1}{2}$ per cent cash discount
        Bought large envelopes £5.95

15 Apr   Received £584.50 from James Fox in full settlement of his account of £608.00
        Bought coffee and tea bags £7.84

22 Apr   Paid Parkway's account of £195.20 *less* 5 per cent cash discount
        Paid taxi fare £8.50
        Received £78 in cash from B Myers in full settlement of her account of £92.65

25 Apr   Bought new electric kettle £19.95
        Paid M Dyson's account of £524.80 *less* $2\frac{1}{2}$ per cent cash discount

29 Apr   Received a cheque of £106.40 from R Williams in full settlement of his account of £115.25
        Paid D Mills' account of £380.60 *less* 5 per cent cash discount

You are required to:

(a) Enter each of the above transactions in either a bank cash book or a petty cash book. Use analysis columns for Sundry expenses, Travel, Postage and stationery and Ledger accounts. (The first available petty cash voucher is number 34.)
(b) Balance both the bank cash book and the petty cash book and bring down the balances as at 1 May 20-9.

13.12

James Rogers operates a small electrical business. He makes all payments over £25 by cheque and pays all money received into the bank. On 1 May 20-9 his bank cash book showed an overdrawn bank balance of £726.85 and there was £14.30 petty cash in hand.

James Rogers keeps his petty cash book on the imprest system. The imprest of £200 is restored at the beginning of each month.

During the month of May the following transactions took place:

1 May Paid rates £450
Received an amount from the bank, in cash to restore petty cash to imprest amount
Bought new plant for reception costing £7.95

3 May Cash sales £385
Paid L Millar, a creditor, £22.50
Bought postage stamps £9.20

8 May Received a cheque of £145.80 from W King in full settlement of his account of £153.48
Paid window cleaner £8.50
Bought goods costing £76.99

12 May Banked cash from sales £295.28, a cheque of £62.74 from R. Patel and a cheque of £204.96 from B Groves in full settlement of his account of £215.20

16 May Paid P Temple's account of £164.80 *less* $2\frac{1}{2}$ per cent cash discount
Bought coffee £3.99
James Rogers withdrew £150 for personal use

23 May Received £73.75 from K Williamson in full settlement of her account of £76.80

25 May Paid cleaner's wages £24.50
Cash sales £194.36
Paid Crossroads Garage bill of £181.77 *less* 5 per cent cash discount

28 May Bought a packet of felt tip pens £2.75
Paid F Moore's account of £407.20 *less* 5 per cent cash discount
Paid A Newton, a creditor, £18.62

30 May Banked cash from sales £73.95, a cheque of £28.40 from J Marsh and a cheque of £36.15 from B Lewis in full settlement of his account of £41.28
Paid milk bill £16.96

You are required to:

(a) Enter each of the above transactions in either a bank cash book or a petty cash book. Use analysis columns for Sundry expenses, Cleaning, Postage and stationery and Ledger accounts. (The first available petty cash voucher is number 58.)

(b) Balance both the bank cash book and the petty cash book and bring down the balances as at 1 June 20-9.

▮▼ 14 Bank reconciliation statements

If you have a current account with a bank you may receive a statement showing a balance in the bank quite different to what you expected it to be. When this happens you will need to find out why. If you keep a record of payments into your account and your spending, then explaining the difference should not be too difficult. If we can show that the difference in the balances is due to genuine reasons – for example, a time lapse: a cheque written yesterday would not appear on your bank statement today, because it would not have had time to pass through the Bankers' Clearing System (BACS). Explaining the differences between your records and those of your bank is called *reconciling* the two balances.

In a business where there have been numerous entries to record money received and paid out it may take a little longer, but the principles are the same. On the same date, when we look at the closing balance in our cash book, and then compare it with the balance on the bank statement we will usually find that the two balances are different. We will need to draw up a *bank reconciliation statement* to discover the reasons for the difference in the balances. This will show if errors have been made or that there are logical reasons which will explain why this may have happened.

At any particular date, there are several reasons why the bank balance in the cash book may not agree with the balance on the bank statement, and in practice the two accounts rarely show the same balance.

(a) The most common example of this surrounds the *writing of cheques*. We enter cheques in the cash book on the day they are written, but our bank will learn of this only when a cheque is presented for payment. This will take a few days even if the receiver pays it into his bank immediately. If he keeps it for a while, this increases the time our bank balance will be out of step with our cash book. Inevitable delays also occur through the Bankers' Clearing System, so it is very likely there will be some cheques which have not yet been presented for payment at the firm's bank. (These are known as *unpresented cheques.*)

(b) Cheques and/or cash paid into the bank will have been entered in the firm's cash book on the date the money was banked, but this may have been late in the afternoon and when the statement was issued the bank did not know the money had been paid in. Such items will *not yet appear on the bank statement.*

(c) Banks receive money on behalf of their customers. These often include interest from investments and money received by bank giro credit transfer from customers. Money received in this way will appear on the bank statement on the date it is received by the bank, but these items are not entered in the cash book until the bank statement arrives. When such items are discovered on a bank statement, they should be entered at the *debit side* of the cash book.

(d) Banks also make payments for their customers by direct debit and standing orders; such items will appear on the bank statement on the date the payment is made but these items are not entered in the cash book until the bank statement arrives. When such items are discovered on a bank statement, they should be entered at the *credit side* of the cash book.

(e) Banks make charges for some of their services; they do not send a bill, they simply take money out by debiting the account with the amount of bank charges, interest on overdrafts or loans. When this happens, these amounts must be entered at the *credit side* of the cash book.

(f) *Dishonoured cheques*: there are several reasons why a bank may refuse to *honour* (to pay) a cheque (see Unit 9). Such a cheque is returned to the person who paid it in with the words '*refer to drawer*' written on it. This invites the person who paid it in to contact the person who drew the cheque and ask for an explanation. There may be a good reason, but whether there is or not the book-keeping entry for the dishonoured cheque is the same: *the debt must be restored.*

Let us consider a typical example: on 1 May a debtor, Nicholas Davidson, owed the firm £250. His account would look like this:

Nicholas Davidson Account

		£	
1 May	Balance b/d	250	

On 21 May we receive a cheque of £250 from Nicholas Davidson. This would be entered at the *debit* side of the bank account, like this:

Bank Account

		£	
21 May	Nicholas Davidson	250	

and to complete double entry it is posted to the *credit* side of Nicholas Davidson's account, like this:

Nicholas Davidson Account

	£			£
1 May Balance b/d	250	21 May Bank		250

Nicholas Davidson's account was cleared when the cheque was received. However, a few days later it may be found that his bank will not honour the cheque (pay it), this is called a *dishonoured cheque*.

Now the procedure *must* be reversed.

A *credit* entry is made in the bank account, like this:

Bank Account

	£			£
		26 May Nicholas		
		Davidson R/D	250

Nicholas Davidson still owes the firm £250, this debt is restored to his account with a *debit* entry, like this:

Nicholas Davidson Account

	£		£
1 May Balance b/d	250	21 May Bank	250
26 May Bank (cheque dishonoured)	250		

Purpose of the bank reconciliation statement

The word *reconcile* means '*to make friendly again*'. It often happens in business that two sets of figures should agree, but for some reason they do not; this is when we need to reconcile – that is, make the two sets of figures agree, by examining and explaining the reasons for the difference. A bank reconciliation statement, as its name suggests, is a written statement, at a particular date, which explains why there is a difference between the balance shown on the bank statement and the bank balance in the cash book.

A neat copy of the bank reconciliation statement is usually placed in the cash book or filed with the bank statement for future reference.

Worked example

Let us now look at a worked example. Here is a copy of our cash book (bank columns only) and of our bank statement:

Dr		£		Cash Book (bank columns only)		Cr £
20-8			**20.8**			
1 Mar	Balance b/d	810.00	8 Mar	H Ryder		132.00
6	Cash	96.00	16	A Jackson		57.00
13	C Fox	324.00	28	E Tyler		249.00
31	B Smith	148.00	31	Balance c/d		940.00
		1,378.00				1,378.00
1 Apr	Balance b/d	940.00				

On 31 March 20-8 the following bank statement was received from the bank:

Date	Details	Debit	Credit	Balance
1 Mar	Brought forward			810.00
6 Mar	Cash		96.00	906.00
10 Mar	H Ryder	132.00		774.00
13 Mar	C Fox		324.00	1,098.00
15 Mar	J Tyson (giro credit transfer)		460.00	1,558.00
18 Mar	A Jackson	57.00		1,501.00
30 Mar	Bank charges	15.00		1,486.00

1 To illustrate the best procedure, we must first *compare each item in the cash book with the bank statement.* It is useful to tick each entry in the cash book that is also on the bank statement and each entry on the statement that is also in the cash book, like this:

Dr			£	Cash Book (bank columns only)			Cr £
20-8				**20-8**			
1 Mar	Balance b/d	✓	810.00	8 Mar	H Ryder	✓	132.00
6	Cash	✓	96.00	16	A Jackson	✓	57.00
13	C Fox	✓	324.00	28	E Tyler		249.00
31	B Smith		148.00	31	Balance c/d		940.00
			1,378.00				1,378.00
1 Apr	Balance b/d		940.00				

Date	Details	Debit	Credit	Balance
1 Mar	Brought forward			✓ 810.00
6 Mar	Cash		✓ 96.00	906.00
10 Mar	H Ryder	✓ 132.00		774.00
13 Mar	C Fox		✓ 324.00	1,098.00
15 Mar	J Tyson (giro credit transfer)		460.00	1,558.00
18 Mar	A Jackson	✓ 57.00		1,501.00
30 Mar	Bank charges	15.00		1,486.00

It is the *unticked entries* that will help to explain why the balances are different. Unticked items on the bank statement normally represent money received or payments made by the bank, these items have not yet been entered in the cash book.

There are two unticked items on the statement; the first is on 15 March J Tyson (giro credit transfer). It is likely that J Tyson is a customer who has paid his account by instructing his bank to pay direct through the banking system instead of sending a cheque. This money has been received into our account but we have not been informed.

The second unticked item is on 30 March for bank charges; this means the bank has made a charge for its services. This amount has been taken out of our account but we have not been notified of the bank's actions.

2 The next step is to *bring* the cash book *up to date* by entering both these items in the cash book and re-calculating the balance. J Tyson's giro credit transfer is entered at the *debit* side because this was money *received* and the bank charges are entered at the *credit* side because this was *paid out*, like this:

Dr   **Cash Book**   Cr
(bank columns only)

20-8			£	20-8			£
1 Mar	Balance b/d	✓	810.00	8 Mar	H Ryder	✓	132.00
6	Cash	✓	96.00	16	A Jackson	✓	57.00
13	C Fox	✓	324.00	28	E Tyler		249.00
31	B Smith		148.00	31	Balance c/d		940.00
			1,378.00				1,378.00
31 Mar	Balance b/d		940.00	31 Mar	Bank charges		15.00
31 Mar	J Tyson C/T		460.00	31 Mar	Balance c/d		1,385.00
			1,400.00				1,400.00
1 Apr	Balance b/d		1,385.00				

There are two items entered in the cash book that are not on the bank statement. First, the unticked item at the credit side on 28 March represents a cheque sent to E Tyler which has not yet been presented to the bank for payment. This item is an *unpresented cheque* which will be adjusted on the bank reconciliation statement: unpresented cheques are *added back* to the cash book balance, since the bank thinks we still have this money.

The second unticked item at the debit side of the cash book represents a cheque received from B Smith which was paid into the bank on 31 March, the last day of the month. Clearly the bank has not yet increased the account with the value of this cheque because it has not yet appeared on the bank statement. This item is known as a *bank lodgement* (money paid into the bank) and must be explained on the bank reconciliation statement.

3 The final step is to draw up a brief statement to *reconcile the differences which remain*, like this:

Bank Reconciliation Statement as at 31 March 20-8

	£
Balance as per cash book	1,385
Add unpresented cheque (E Tyler)	249
	1,634
Less bank lodgement, not yet entered on bank statement	148
Balance as per bank statement:	1,486

Sometimes, these type of questions are presented in an alternative way. Several points of interest will be given and you will be asked to update the cash book by entering such items as need to be entered, to balance the cash book and then, using this new balance, prepare a bank reconciliation statement. This is a typical example:

On 30 June 20-9, Brian Green's cash book showed a balance at the bank of £420.18, but at the same date the monthly statement from his bank showed a balance of £624.83.

The difference between the two balances was found to be due to the following:

(a) On 15 June a standing order for insurance of £95 had been paid by the bank but this had not been entered in the cash book

(b) On 20 June an investment dividend of £250 had been paid into the bank by giro credit transfer; Brian Green was not aware that this money had been paid into his account until the bank statement arrived and no entry had been made in the cash book

(c) On 30 June the bank deducted £25.50 bank charges from Brian Green's account; no entry had been made in the cash book

(d) Cheques for £184.20 and £173.95 drawn in favour of A Jones and S Millburn had not been presented for payment

(e) On 30 June Brian Green had paid cheques amounting to £283 into the bank but the bank statement did not include this item

You are asked to:

(i) Open Brian Green's cash book on the 30 June with the balance of £420.18, to enter such items as have been omitted and to find the new balance that results.

(ii) Using this new balance prepare a bank reconciliation statement as at 30 June 20-9.

Worked solution

The first thing to do is to bring the cash book up to date by entering items (a), (b) and (c), then find the new balance, like this:

Dr			**Cash Book** (bank columns only)				Cr
20-9		£		20-9			£
30 Jun	Balance b/d	420.18		30 Jun	Insurance S/O (a)		95.00
30	Investment			30	Bank charges (c)		25.50
	Dividend C/T (b)	250.00			D/D		
				30	Balance c/d		549.68
		670.18					670.18
1 Jul	Balance b/d	549.68					

We are now ready to draw up the bank reconciliation statement. We start with the new updated cash book balance of £549.68, then *add back* the cheques drawn but not yet presented for payment (item (d)) and *deduct* the bank lodgement (item (e)) – this money was paid into the bank but has not been included on the bank statement:

Bank Reconciliation Statement as at 30 June 20-9

			£
Balance as per cash book			549.68
Add unpresented cheques	A Jones	184.20	
	S Millburn	173.95	358.15
			907.83
Less bank lodgement, not yet entered on bank statement			283.00
Balance as per bank statement:			624.83

Bank overdrafts

Take care if there is a bank overdraft – that is, a credit balance in the cash book (*a debit balance on the bank statement*). When a bank account is overdrawn any amounts drawn out of the bank will cause the overdraft to *rise*, while amounts paid in will cause the overdraft to *decrease* and the adjustments needed to reconcile will be opposite.

When a bank account is overdrawn the abbreviation DR or O/D is usually placed after the balance on the bank statement.

Points to remember

- When comparing the cash book with the bank statement you must realise that in the cash book all receipts are shown as debit entries and all payments as credit entries; on a bank statement the entries are shown exactly the *opposite way around*. This is because the bank statement is kept from the bank's point of view.
- You may be asked to write up the cash book for the month or you may be given an extract of the cash book and the bank statement. Always compare the cash book with the bank statement and *tick each entry that appears on both*. It is only the remaining *unticked items* which will require attention.
- Unticked items on the bank statement will usually need to be entered in the cash book. Unticked items at the *debit* side of the cash book will usually be money paid into the bank which has not been entered on the bank statement (*bank lodgements*). Unticked items at the *credit* side of the cash book will usually be cheques drawn but not yet presented for payment (*unpresented cheques*).
- A *bank reconciliation statement* is a brief report drawn up to explain any differences which remain. Its purpose is to prove that although there may be a difference between the balance in the cash book and the balance shown on the bank statement, there are logical reasons why this may have happened.

Assignments

14.1

Christine Groves' cash book for the month of May 20-4 is shown below:

Cash Book
(bank columns only)

20-4		£	20-4		£
May 1	Balance b/d	900.00	May 2	T Rogers	175.00
9	C Briggs	465.00	8	YEB	368.00
18	Sales	575.00	19	L Gibson	112.00
25	A Ridgeway	750.00	28	Rates	125.00
30	Sales	590.00	31	Balance c/d	2,500.00
		3,280.00			3,280.00
May 31	Balance b/d	2,500.00			

On 31 May the following bank statement was received:

Bank Statement

		Debit	Credit	Balance
		£	£	£
May 1	Brought forward			900.00
6	T Rogers	175.00		725.00
10	Cheque		465.00	1,190.00
15	Standing order (Insurance)	135.00		1,055.00
19	Cash and cheques		575.00	1,630.00
14	YEB	368.00		1,262.00
25	Credit transfer			
	(investment dividend)		250.00	1,512.00
26	Cheque		750.00	2,262.00
28	L Gibson	112.00		2,150.00
30	Annual subscription	50.00		2,100.00

You are required to:

(a) Make the necessary entries to update the cash book on the 31 May 20-4.

(b) Prepare a bank reconciliation statement as at 31 May 20-4.

14.2
Here is Andrew Garcia's cash book for the month of June 20-4:

Cash Book
(bank columns only)

20-4		£	20-4		£
Jun 1	Balance b/d	750.00	Jun 3	R Moore	298.00
4	Sales	455.00	8	B Ramsden	324.00
9	B Sinclair	250.00	12	Insurance	450.00
13	Sales	625.00	14	S Franks	675.00
19	R Patel	170.00	30	Rent	150.00
30	L Greenwood	230.00	30	Balance c/d	583.00
		2,480.00			2,480.00
Jun 30	Balance b/d	583.00			

On 1 July the following bank statement was received:

Bank Statement

		Debit	Credit	Balance
		£	£	£
June 1	Brought forward			750.00
5	Cash and cheques		455.00	1,205.00
6	R Moore	298.00		907.00
10	Cheque		250.00	1,157.00
15	Insurance	450.00		707.00
16	Cash and cheques		625.00	1,332.00
17	Standing order	175.00		1,157.00
	(business rates)			
20	Cheque		170.00	1,327.00
21	S Franks	675.00		652.00
25	Credit transfer (B. Groves)		985.00	1,637.00
26	B Ramsden	324.00		1,313.00
30	Charges	68.00		1,245.00

You are required to:

(a) Make the necessary entries to update the cash book on the 30 June 20-4.

(b) Prepare a bank reconciliation statement as at 30 June 20-4.

14.3

On 31 October 20-4 David Alexander's cash book showed a bank balance of £2,750; on the same date his bank statement showed a balance of £2,290. The difference between the two balances was found to be due to the following:

(a) On 15 October a payment of £25 for a trade subscription had been made by the bank; this had not been entered in David Alexander's cash book

(b) A direct debit payment for business insurance of £175 had been made by the bank on 20 October, but no entry had been made in the cash book

(c) Bank charges amounting to £60 had been charged on the bank statement but not yet entered in the cash book

(d) A payment from W Jones of £462 by giro credit transfer had not been entered in the cash book

(e) Cheques for £238 and £376 drawn by David Alexander had not been presented for payment

(f) A cheque for £442 from K Williams paid into the bank on 3 October had been returned by the bank marked 'refer to drawer'; No entry of this dishonoured cheque had been made in the cash book

(g) On 30 October David Alexander had paid cash and cheques amounting to £834 into the bank, but this item had not yet appeared on the bank statement

You are required to:

(a) Make the necessary entries to update the cash book on the 31 October 20-4.

(b) Prepare a bank reconciliation statement as at 31 October 20-4.

14.4

Carol Sanderson's cash book for the month of Mar 20-4 is shown below:

Cash Book
(bank columns only)

20-4		£	20-4		£
Mar 1	Balance b/d	2,500.00	Mar 3	Drawings	150.00
8	T Oliver	365.00	6	R Kemp	263.00
15	L McQuade	186.00	14	Rates	500.00
23	M Singh	470.00	28	B Dixon	128.00
31	D Warner	259.00	30	F Readman	364.00
			31	Balance c/d	2,375.00
		3,780.00			3,780.00
Mar 31	Balance b/d	2,375.00			

On 1 April the following bank statement was received:

Bank Statement

		Debit	Credit	Balance
		£	£	£
Mar 1	Brought forward			2,750.00
4	Cash	150.00		2,600.00
6	G Sanderson	250.00		2,350.00
8	Cheque		365.00	2,715.00
10	R Kemp	263.00		2,452.00
16	Cheque		186.00	2,638.00
20	City Council	500.00		2,138.00
22	Credit Transfer		575.00	2,713.00
	(A Richmond)			
24	Cheque		470.00	3,183.00
25	Standing order			
	(Business Insurance)	275.00		2,908.00
31	Charges	24.00		2,884.00

You are required to:

(a) Make the necessary entries to update the cash book on the 31 March 20-4.
(b) Prepare a bank reconciliation statement as at 31 March 20-4.

14.5

On 2 May 20-9 Jenny Ashcroft received her bank statement for the month of April 20-9. On 30 April her cash book showed a balance in hand of £1,975. On checking her records the following information was revealed:

(a) The bank had paid a standing order of £195 for Rent and a direct debit of £368 for Insurance
(b) Jenny Ashcroft had made out a cheque payable to R Cox for £268, this had been entered in her cash book as £286
(c) Two cheques drawn in favour of S Bowes £492 and F Wilson £580 had not yet been presented at the bank
(d) Bank charges of £65 were recorded on the bank statement but had not been entered in the cash book
(e) Cash and cheques of £278 had been entered in the cash book but had not been credited by the bank
(f) The bank statement showed the sum of £593 had been received from T Mason by giro credit transfer

You are required to:

(i) Correct any errors and bring Jenny Ashcroft's cash book up to date as at 30 April 20-9.
(ii) Prepare a bank reconciliation statement as at 30 April 20-9, commencing with the revised cash book balance.

14.6

The bank columns of Robert Williams' cash book for the month of April 20-5 are shown below:

Cash Book

20-5		£	20-5		Cheque number	£
1 Apr	Balance b/d	765	3 Apr	Rent	59635	170
5 Apr	F Mills	250	7 Apr	Smart Motors	59636	108
10 Apr	J Kingsway	590	8 Apr	L Summers	59637	325
17 Apr	M Fieldhouse	186	20 Apr	Rates	59638	380
24 Apr	K Jones	485	27 Apr	Drawings	59639	150
27 Apr	C Bradshaw	74	28 Apr	T Pearson	59640	242
			30 Apr	Balance c/d		975
		2,350				2,350

Robert Williams received the following bank statement for the month of April 20-5:

Date	Details	Debit	Credit	Balance
1 Apr	Brought Forward			900
4 Apr	59634	135		765
5 Apr	Cheque		250	1,015
7 Apr	59635	170		845
10 Apr	Cheque		590	1,435
12 Apr	59637	325		1,110
17 Apr	Cheque		186	1,296
18 Apr	59636	108		1,188
20 Apr	Direct Debit (Insurance)	200		988
24 Apr	Cheque		485	1,473
28 Apr	59639	150		1,323
28 Apr	Interest on shares		125	1,448

You are required to:

(a) Make the necessary entries in the cash book in order to show the revised cash book balance at 30 April 20-5.
(b) Prepare a bank reconciliation statement as at 30 April 20-5, commencing with the revised cash book balance.

14.7
Jill Chippendale makes all payments over £20 by cheque and pays all money received into the bank. On 1 May 20-9 the bank column of her cash book showed a balance at the bank of £2,780.

During the month of May the following transactions took place:

3 May Paid M Hudson a cheque of £285 (cheque number 61623) in full settlement of a debt of £300

4 May Paid Insurance for delivery van £475 (cheque number 61624)

6 May Banked £600 cash from sales, a cheque of £225 from J Conway in full settlement of his account of £250 and a cheque of £75 from Martin Lewis, a sub-tenant

9 May Paid Crossroads Garage £185 (cheque number 61625) for repairs to delivery van

10 May Drew cheque £200 (cheque number 61626) for own use

13 May Banked £750 cash from sales and a cheque of £194 from Alison King in full settlement of her debt of £200

18 May Paid a cheque of £175 (cheque number 61627) to Systems Ltd for a new desk for the office

23 May Paid a trade creditor, E Mellor, a cheque for £425 (cheque number 61628) in full settlement of her account of £450

29 May   Banked £900 cash from sales, a cheque of £240 from J Kershaw in full settlement of his debt of £254 and a cheque of £30 from L Hussain

29 May   Paid telephone bill of £358 by cheque (cheque number 61629)

31 May   Drew a cheque for £500 (cheque number 61630), £140 was for petty cash and the remainder was for own use

On 3 June she received her bank statement which contained the following information:

Date	Details	Debit	Credit	Balance
1 May	Brought forward			2,780
6 May	61624	475		2,305
9 May	Cash and cheques		900	3,205
10 May	61623	285		2,920
11 May	61626	200		2,720
13 May	Cash and cheques		944	3,664
14 May	61625	185		3,479
16 May	Direct Debit (Business rates)	750		2,729
20 May	61628	425		2,304
22 May	61627	175		2,129
31 May	Investment interest		500	2,629

You are required to:

(a) Write up and balance the bank cash book for the month of May 20-9.

(b) Make the entries necessary to update the bank cash book after receiving the bank statement on 3 June 20-9.

(c) Prepare a bank reconciliation statement as at 31 May 20-9.

14.8

Denise Hemingway makes all payments over £20 by cheque and pays all money received into the bank. On 2 October 20-9 her bank cash book showed a balance in the bank of £2,304.

During the month of October the following transactions took place:

4 Oct   Drew a cheque for £450 (cheque number 60619), £105 was for petty cash, the remainder was for own use

5 Oct   Banked cash from sales £265, a cheque of £158 from K Williams in full settlement of his account of £165 and a cheque of £205 from B Myers

5 Oct   Paid fire insurance £392 (cheque number 60620)

6 Oct   Paid D Fox's account of £320 *less* 5 per cent cash discount (cheque number 60621)

12 Oct   Banked a cheque of £123 from K Stocks in full settlement of his debt of £132, a cheque of £75 from L Young and cash from sales of £498

16 Oct Bought goods costing £186 (cheque number 60622)
18 Oct Paid telephone bill £378 (cheque number 60623)
20 Oct Banked cash from sales £250
23 Oct Bought new photocopier costing £599 (cheque number 60624)
24 Oct Paid Alison Kirk's account of £280 *less* 2½ per cent cash discount
(cheque number 60625)
27 Oct Paid Parkside Garage £434 (cheque number 60626)
30 Oct Banked a cheque of £292 from J Kendal in full settlement of his
account of £308, a cheque of £120 from T Malik and cash from
sales £306

On 2 November 20-9 Denise Hemingway received her bank statement
which contained the following information:

Date	Details	Debit	Credit	Balance
1 Oct	Brought forward			2,479
2 Oct	60618	175		2,304
5 Oct	Cash and cheques		628	2,932
6 Oct	60619	450		2,482
10 Oct	60621	304		2,178
13 Oct	Cash and cheques		696	2,874
16 Oct	60620	392		2,482
17 Oct	Shares dividend		250	2,732
19 Oct	60622	186		2,546
21 Oct	Cash and cheques		250	2,796
27 Oct	60625	273		2,523
30 Oct	Direct debit (rates)	142		2,381
31 Oct	60623	378		2,003

You are required to:

(a) Write up and balance the bank cash book for the month of October
20-9.
(b) Make the entries necessary to update the bank cash book after
receiving the bank statement on 2 November 20-9.
(c) Prepare a bank reconciliation statement as at 31 October 20-9.

14.9
Gina Howard makes all payments over £20 by cheque and pays all money
received into the bank. On 1 May 20-5 the bank cash book showed a
balance in the bank of £1,405.

During the month of May the following transactions took place:

3 May Drew a cheque for £450 (cheque number 20609), £105 was for
petty cash the remainder was for personal use
4 May Paid D King's account of £120 *less* 2½ per cent cash discount
(cheque number 20610)

5 May	Banked cash from sales £205, a cheque of £86 from W Kelly in full settlement of his account of £92 and £27 in cash from P Ellis
8 May	Paid electricity bill £328 (cheque number 20611)
12 May	Banked cheque of £136 from J Dean in full settlement of her debt of £148, a cheque of £28 from H Khan and cash from sales £145
15 May	Bought goods costing £299 (cheque number 20612)
18 May	Paid telephone bill £384 (cheque number 20613)
19 May	Banked cash from sales £150
25 May	Paid M Dyson's account of £480 *less* $2\frac{1}{2}$ per cent cash discount (cheque number 20614)
27 May	Bought a new photocopier costing £699 from Copywell (cheque number 20615)
28 May	Paid Smart Motors £325 for servicing and repairs (cheque number 20616)
30 May	Banked a cheque of £93 from J Kendall in full settlement of his debt of £98, cash from sales £205 and a cheque of £70 from C Dunn who purchased a photocopier which was no longer required

On 2 June Gina Howard received her bank statement which contained the following information:

Date	Details	Debit	Credit	Balance
1 May	Brought forward			1,405
4 May	20609	450		955
5 May	Cash and cheques		318	1,273
10 May	20611	328		945
13 May	Cash and cheques		309	1,254
18 May	20612	299		955
20 May	Cash		150	1,105
22 May	20610	117		988
24 May	Investment dividend		256	1,244
28 May	20614	468		776
29 May	Insurance (direct debit)	191		585
30 May	Michells (giro credit)		502	1,087
30 May	20616	325		762

You are required to:

(a) Write up and balance Gina Howard's bank cash book for the month of May 20-5.
(b) Make the entries necessary to update the bank cash book after receiving the bank statement on 2 June 20-5.
(c) Prepare a bank reconciliation statement as at 31 May 20-5.

15 Business documents – sales day book

Almost every business transaction begins with a *document*. We have already looked at some documents, such as: cheque counterfoils, bank paying in slips and petty cash vouchers.

So far, we have emphasised the importance of the double entry system of book-keeping and for each transaction we have considered the double entry involved. This important principle will always remain true, but when transactions become very numerous posting each separate transaction as a double entry would be very time consuming and some accounts would be extremely overloaded with entries.

In business there are many transactions of a similar nature – for example, there are usually numerous sales on credit. The purpose of day books is to group together all like transactions and so reduce the number of entries that need to be made in the ledger.

Because all business activities really start with a document, day books are known as '*books of original entry*'.

Sales invoice

In many businesses most of the sales will be made on a *credit basis* (to be paid for at a future date) rather than for immediate cash. There are some businesses which consist entirely of credit sales.

When goods are sold on credit the seller will send a document to the buyer giving full details of the goods sold and the prices of the goods. This document is called an *invoice* and to the firm selling the goods it is known as a *sales invoice*. It is the original document which provides the financial information which will subsequently be recorded in the ledger. Invoices will differ in appearance, as each business will have its own individual design.

For convenience, invoices are frequently prepared in sets, with each copy being used for a specific purpose. This enables a firm to properly organise sending the goods and ensures they can confirm they are safely received. The exact number of copies will vary from one firm to another but the seller will keep at least one copy of each sales invoice for his own records. Extra copies may be used as:

- **Advice note**
  This will be sent to the customer *before the goods are despatched.* Its purpose is to notify the customer that the goods are on the way, it states the method of transport and when they are expected to arrive. If the goods do not arrive within a reasonable time then the customer will notify the seller, so that enquiries can be made to establish what has happened to the goods.
- **Delivery note**
  This is sent *with the goods* so that the customer can check immediately that all the items listed are being received.

Trade discount

Trade discount is a *reduction,* usually quoted as a percentage of the selling price, which is given by a supplier to customers in the same trade. For example, Lawnswood Timber Merchants sell to two different kinds of customers:

(a) builders and joiners in the trade who regularly buy from them, and
(b) direct to the general public.

To avoid having two separate price lists all goods are shown at the same price but a reduction called *trade discount* is given to trade customers.

As far as the accounts are concerned trade discount is **never** recorded in the books of a business, it is simply a convenient way of calculating prices and is shown *only* as a deduction on an invoice.

Example

Use your calculator to work out, £500 *less* 15 per cent trade discount:

- make sure your calculator is on and clear
- enter 500 into your calculator
- now press the key marked **X**
- enter 15   (*this is the percentage*)
- now press the key marked **%**
- the display should show 75   (*this is the amount of trade discount*)
- now press the key marked –
- now press the key marked =
- the display should show 425   (*this is the answer*)

Assignments

15.1
Your firm has decided to buy an Amastar Computer. Three different suppliers were asked for prices and delivery dates and the following quotations have now been received:

(a) Use your calculator to work out all three prices
(b) State which supplier is offering the best price.

Suppliers	Price £	Discount
Micro Electronics	800	*less* 15 per cent
Hitech (UK) Ltd	835	*less* 20 per cent
Systems Unlimited	750	*less* 10 per cent

You will find that all invoices have some features in common; they are always dated and usually numbered, but basically an invoice is a *bill sent by the seller to the purchaser requesting payment.*

Figure 15.1 is an illustration of a typical invoice.

DEMLAND SUPPLIES
Sandmore Lane
LEEDS

Telephone 0113 7771941
Fax   0113 7609345

LS11 5EA

INVOICE

To	Grove & Sons
	Woodside Lane
	LEEDS
	LS16 8ER

Invoice Number	DS/7876
Date	1 November 20-
Your Order Number	3842

VAT Registration Number 98765432

Qty	Description	Cat Number	Unit price	£	p
			£		
6	Electric kettles	EK10	19.50	117	00
3	Electric toasters	ET16	18.75	56	25
				173	25
	Less trade discount 20%			34	65
TERMS NET MONTHLY E & O E				138	60

Figure 15.1

Sales day book

Day books are often referred to as books of *original entry*. Sales on credit begin with an *invoice*; this document is the original accounting record of the transaction. When the sales invoices have been made out the top copy is sent to the customer. The firm selling the goods will keep copies of all sales invoices and it is from the copies the seller enters up his sales day book. Day books are also known as *journals* (the word journal is simply the French word for '*day book*'.

Cash sales are *never* entered in the sales day book: when goods are paid for immediately by cash, the original entry is made in the cash book (*debit cash account* and *credit sales account*).

A modern sales day book (Figure 15.2) is simply a list, in date order, of all sales on credit, showing:

- date
- name of customer
- invoice number
- final amount of invoice.

Sales Day Book

Date	Name	Invoice Number	F	£	p
1 Nov	Grove & Sons	7876	SL	138	60
9 Nov	M Dean	7877	SL	120	20
18 Nov	G Parkinson	7878	SL	176	80
25 Nov	J Spencer	7879	SL	237	10
30 Nov	T Gill	7880	SL	142	20
	Transferred to Sales Account		GL	814	90

Figure 15.2

Entries are made for a certain period, usually a week or a month. But the important rule of the sales day book is that *each customer's account is debited* and the *sales account is credited from this original source*. At the end of the period the credit sales are posted, one by one, to the debit side of each customer's personal account in the sales ledger, like this:

Sales Ledger

Grove & Sons Account

	£		
1 Nov Sales	138. 60		

M Dean Account

		£		
9 Nov	Sales	120. 20		

G Parkinson Account

		£		
18 Nov	Sales	176. 80		

J Spencer Account

		£		
25 Nov	Sales	237. 10		

T Gill Account

		£		
30 Nov	Sales	142. 20		

Instead of making a double entry for each invoice in the sales account, *one single entry is made to correspond with the total for the period*, like this:

General Ledger

Sales Account

			£
	30 Nov	Total for month	814.90

It is immediately evident that this procedure is more efficient and considerably reduces the number of entries in the sales account. To save space only a few examples have been used, but the real value is seen when the number of entries is very large. Only five invoices were used in the illustration, but during a month, for some firms this could easily be 500.

As each item is posted, the folio column is completed to show that the entry has been made. *Posting to the ledger* is a phrase used to describe the process of making entries in the ledger accounts.

In practice, you may find a variety of methods in use for dealing with numerous credit sale transactions, but all will result eventually in the same ledger entries – a *debit entry in the customer's account* and an *accumulated total to be credited to the sales account.*

Slip system

This is an alternative method of dealing with credit sales. Instead of entering copy invoices into a sales day book, the copy invoices are kept together, in date order, usually in a lever arch file. At the end of the period (this may be a week or a month), they are added together and the *accumulated total* is entered at the *credit* side of the sales account. As its name suggests, they are added together by slipping through and listing each copy invoice. Entries to the debit side of each customer's account are made direct from the copy invoices.

Credit control

In many firms most of the sales will be made on a credit basis. This means the goods are received immediately but payment is made at a later date. Any firm which sells goods on credit should ensure that customers pay their accounts on time. If this is not done properly outstanding debts can quickly grow to an amount that will seriously damage or even ruin a business. Credit control means checking and monitoring the volume of credit allowed to customers.

Unfortunately, the risk of some customers not paying their debts will always exist, so it is extremely important to be cautious with new customers and to act quickly when a slow payer is identified.

The following procedures should be carried out:

- A *maximum credit limit* should be set for each customer. This will depend on the firm's previous dealings with this customer and his ability to pay debts promptly within the period of time allowed. Failure to pay on time may mean refusing to supply further goods unless payment is made immediately.
- In some circumstances, where payment is not forthcoming it may be necessary to take *legal action* to recover the debt.
- With new customers, caution should always be observed. It is vital to determine a potential customer's *credit worthiness* and his or her *ability to pay debts promptly.*
- New customers should be asked to provide *trade references*; that is, the names and addresses of firms with whom they have previously conducted business and a bank reference.
- Some organisations also require a new customer to sign a '*customer undertaking*'. This document sets out the terms and conditions under which credit facilities will be granted.

Points to remember

- An *invoice* is a document made out whenever goods or services are supplied *on credit*. There are usually at least four copies. Of these, the top copy is sent to the customer; the second copy is kept by the seller and becomes the basis of his book-keeping records; the third and fourth copies are often used as advice notes and delivery notes.
- Invoices will vary in appearance, as each business will have its *own individual design*.
- *Trade discount* is simply a way of calculating sales prices; no entry for trade discount should be made in the double entry records, or in the sales day book. Trade discount **NEVER** enters any ledger account.
- Details of the goods sold are *not* entered in a sales day book. Alternative names for the sales day book are: sales journal and sales book.
- Cash sales are *never* entered in the sales day book: the book of original entry for all cash sales is the cash book.
- Slip system is an alternative method of dealing with copies of sales invoices.

Assignments

15.2

James Dickson of 34 Kingsway, Leeds LS16 8ER is the proprietor of a small business. His sales on credit for the month of May 20-7 were as follows:

2 May   G A Coleman, 2 Parkfield, Nottingham, Invoice number 3481
6 Garden chairs at £4.50 each
10 Deck chairs at £3.75 each
6 Patio furniture sets at £26 each
All *less* trade discount 15 per cent

9 May   Kota Supplies, 2 Deansgate, Bradford, Invoice number 3482
10 Deck chairs at £3.75 each
10 Patio furniture sets at £26 each
10 Luxury garden chairs at £12.50 each
All *less* trade discount 20 per cent

15 May   B Newton, 66 Cross Green Road, Bridlington, Invoice number 3483
3 Garden chairs at £4.50 each
3 Patio furniture sets at £26 each
6 Deck chairs at £3.75 each
All *less* trade discount 15 per cent

22 May   Moss Linton, 46 Ridgeway, Castleford, Invoice number 3484
             6 Luxury garden chairs at £12.50 each
             6 Patio furniture sets at £26 each
             6 Sun loungers at £7.50 each
             All *less* trade discount 25 per cent

30 May   L Gibson & Son, 58 The Causeway. Scarborough, Invoice number 3485
             25 Deck chairs at £3.75 each
             20 Luxury garden chairs at £12.50 each
             15 Sun loungers at £7.50 each
             All *less* trade discount $33\frac{1}{3}$ per cent

You are required to:

(a) draw up a sales invoice for each of the above sales.
(b) enter up the sales day book for the month of May.
(c) post to the personal accounts in the sales ledger and transfer the total to the sales account in the general ledger.

15.3
Speed Electrics of 2 High Street, Huddersfield is a wholesale electrical business. During the month of June 20-7 they make the following sales:

1 June   James McMillan, 2 Spring Lane, Bradford, Invoice number 5724
             3 Electric kettles at £19.50 each
             10 Electric toasters at £18.75 each
             3 Electric knives at £15.50 each
             All *less* trade discount 25 per cent

5 June   J Sanderson, 34 Knights Court, York, Invoice number 5725
             6 Electric coffee makers at £14.95 each
             6 Electric knives at £15.50 each
             All *less* trade discount 20 per cent

12 June   B Sinclair, 67 Beech Terrace, Denby Dale, Invoice number 5726
             10 Electric kettles at £19.50 each
             4 Electric coffee makers at £14.95 each
             All *less* trade discount 15 per cent

19 June   T Matthews, 1 Kingsway, Nottingham, Invoice number 5727
             5 Electric toasters at £18.75 each
             5 Electric knives at £15.50 each
             5 Electric coffee makers at £14.95 each
             All *less* trade Discount $33\frac{1}{3}$ per cent

30 June   L Booth, 4 Richmond Lane, Manchester, Invoice number 5728
             2 Electric kettles at £19.50 each
             6 Electric knives at £15.50 each
             6 Electric can openers at £6 each
             3 Electric toasters at £18.75 each
             All *less* trade discount 20 per cent

You are required to:

(a) Show your calculations for each of the above sales.
(b) Write up the sales day book for the month of June.
(c) Post to the personal and nominal accounts in the ledger.

15.4
Martin Greendale, 8 Parkside, Darlington is the owner of a garden accessories business. During the month of August 20-7 his sales on credit were:

1 Aug   Adel Garden Shop, Heathway, Adel, Leeds, Invoice number 395
        3 Lawn mowers at £55 each
        6 Garden forks at £6.50 each
        3 Garden spades at £7.50 each
        4 Ornamental garden gnomes at £3.50 each
        All *less* trade discount 15 per cent

4 Aug   George Riley, High Ash Croft, Mansfield, Invoice number 396
        6 Lawn mowers at £55 each
        6 Rotary mowers at £95 each
        6 Garden shears at £9.50 each
        6 Garden spades at £7.50 each
        All *less* trade discount 25 per cent

8 Aug   T Newbury, 8 Longdon Close, Nuneaton, Invoice number 397
        15 Garden forks at £6.50 each
        10 Ornamental garden gnomes at £3.50 each
        6 Garden shears at £9.50 each
        5 Lawn sprinklers at £5.50 each
        All *less* trade discount 20 per cent

14 Aug   B J Lacey, 2 Crosby Court, Chester, Invoice number 398
        2 Rotary mowers at £95 each
        5 Lawn mowers at £55 each
        6 Garden spades at £7.50 each
        5 Garden tool sets at £8 per set
        All *less* trade discount 15 per cent

20 Aug   S Stocks, 57 Dunbar Lane, Beverley, Invoice number 399
        5 Garden shears at £9.50 each
        10 Garden spades at £7.50 each
        6 Ornamental garden gnomes at £3.50 each
        10 Garden tool sets at £8 per set
        All *less* trade discount 25 per cent

25 Aug   H Crossley, 34 High Street, Dewsbury, Invoice number 400
        5 Rotary mowers at £95 each
        4 Lawn mowers at £55 each
        20 Garden forks at £6.50 each
        15 Garden spades at £7.50 each
        All *less* trade discount $33\frac{1}{3}$ per cent

31 Aug Thornton Supplies, 33 Main Street, Birmingham, Invoice number
401

        15 Garden spades at £7.50 each
        10 Ornamental garden gnomes at £3.50 each
        4 Garden shears at £9.50 each
        6 Garden tool sets at £8 per set
        5 Lawn sprinklers at £5.50 each
        All *less* trade discount 20 per cent

You are required to:

(a) Show your calculations for each of the above sales.
(b) Write up the sales day book for the month of August 20–7.
(c) Post to the personal accounts and show the transfer to the sales account in the general ledger.

15.5
James Sellars, 34 High Street Bradford, is a textile wholesaler.

Price list
White cotton pillow cases 45p each
White cotton sheets £2.50 each
Grey mixture blankets £5.75 each
White wool blankets £7.50 each

During the month of September 20-8 he made the following sales:

1 Sep   G Miller
        10 White cotton pillow cases
         6 Grey mixture blankets
        15 White wool blankets
        All *less* trade discount 25 per cent

5 Sep   T Bennett
        10 White cotton sheets
        10 Grey mixture blankets
        5 White wool blankets
        All *less* trade discount 20 per cent

8 Sep   B Watkinson
        20 White cotton pillow cases
        10 White cotton sheets
        All *less* trade discount 10 per cent

14 Sep L Roberts
        15 Grey mixture blankets
        20 White wool blankets
        20 White cotton sheets
        All *less* trade discount 25 per cent

22 Sep   A Dixon
               30 White cotton pillow cases
               25 White cotton sheets
               20 White wool blankets
               All *less* trade discount 15 per cent

30 Sep   D Hewitt
               25 White cotton pillow cases
               6 Grey mixture blankets
               6 White wool blankets
               All *less* trade discount 20 per cent

You are required to:

(a) Show your calculations for each of the above sales.
(b) Enter up the sales day book and post to the personal and nominal accounts in the ledger.

▶ 16 Business documents – purchases day book

In business there are many transactions of a similar nature: for example, there are usually numerous purchases on credit. The purpose of day books is to *group together all like transactions* and so reduce the number of entries that need to be made in the ledger.

Because all business activities really start with a document, day books are also known as '*books of original entry*'.

Purchase invoice

In many businesses most of the purchases will be made on a *credit basis* (to be paid for at a future date) rather than for immediate cash.

When a business buys goods on credit an *invoice* will be made out by the supplier showing full details of the goods, prices and any trade discount. This is known as a *purchase invoice*. It is the original document which provides the financial information which will subsequently be recorded in the ledger.

In practice, you will find that invoices will differ in appearance, each business having its own individual design.

When invoices are received from suppliers they should always be checked to ensure that they are *genuine and accurate*. These procedures should be carried out:

- Check the goods were *ordered*
  (Invoices are sometimes received for goods which have never been ordered)
- Check all goods have been *received in good condition* and *details correspond* with order
  (It may be only part of the order has been received)
- Check *prices charged* on the invoice are correct
- Check all *calculations* are accurate.

Purchases day book

Only when the checking procedures have been carried out should the purchase invoices be entered in the purchases day book. This book contains details of all credit purchases of goods for resale. When a purchase invoice is received this document is the original accounting record of the transaction. Day books are also known as *journals* (the word 'journal' is simply the French word for '*day book*'.

Cash purchases are **never** entered in the purchases day book, when goods are bought and payment is made immediately in cash, the original entry is in the cash book (*credit cash account* and *debit purchases account*).

A modern purchases day book (Figure 16.1) is simply a list, in date order, of all purchases on credit, showing:

- date
- name of supplier
- invoice number
- final amount of invoice.

Purchases Day Book

Date	Name	Invoice Number	F	£	p
2 May	F Craig	79801	PL	380	50
6 May	B Johnson	J/1025	PL	252	65
12 May	V Porter & Son	P/9041	PL	465	30
18 May	Grice Bros	93372	PL	184	90
24 May	W Nelson	517683	PL	519	40
	Transferred to Purchases Account		GL	1,802	75

Figure 16.1

Entries are made for a certain period, usually a week or a month. But the important rule of the purchases day book is that each supplier's account is credited and the purchases account is debited from this original source. At the end of the period the credit purchases are posted, one by one, to the credit side of each supplier's personal account in the ledger, like this:

Purchase Ledger

F Craig Account

		£
	2 May Purchases	380. 50

B Johnson Account

			£
	6 May	Purchases	252. 65

V Porter & Son Account

			£
	12 May	Purchases	465. 30

Grice Bros Account

			£
	18 May	Purchases	184. 90

W Nelson Account

			£
	24 May	Purchases	519. 40

Instead of making a double entry for each invoice in the purchases account, *one single entry is made to correspond with the total for the period,* like this:

General Ledger

Purchases Account

		£	
31 May	Total for		
	month	1,802. 75	

It is immediately evident that this procedure is more efficient and considerably reduces the number of entries in the purchases account. To save space only a few examples have been used, but the real value is seen when the number of entries is very large. Only five invoices are shown in the illustration, but for some firms, during a month this could easily be 500.

As each item is posted the folio column is completed to show that the entry has been made. *Posting to the ledger* is a phrase used to describe the process of making entries in the ledger accounts.

In practice, you may find a variety of methods in use for dealing with numerous credit purchase transactions, but all will result eventually in the same ledger entries: a *credit entry in the supplier's account* and an *accumulated total to be debited to the purchases account.*

Slip system

This is an alternative method of dealing with credit purchases. Instead of entering invoices into a purchases day book, the suppliers' invoices are kept together, in date order, usually in a lever arch file. At the end of the period (this may be a week or a month), they are added together and the *accumulated total* is entered at the *debit* side of the purchases account. As its name suggests, they are added together by slipping through and listing each invoice. Entries to the credit side of each supplier's account are made direct from the invoices.

Points to remember

- An *invoice* is a document made out whenever goods or services are supplied *on credit.*
- In accounting terms, *purchases* are goods bought for resale. For example: an electrical business would buy various electrical appliances for resale. If this firm buys something else – for instance, some office equipment – this will not be regarded as purchases. Office equipment is bought for use within the business, it would be an asset and not for resale so it would *not* be entered in the purchases day book. Assets will always have their own accounts.
- Similarly, *sales* in accounting terms applies to the goods in which a firm normally deals, as described in the example of an electrical business. If some old office furniture was sold it would *not* be entered in the sales day book.
- Purchase invoices will vary in appearance, because each supplier will have its *own particular design.*
- *Trade discount* is simply a way of calculating prices and no entry for trade discount should be made in the double entry records, or in the purchases day book. Trade discount *never* enters any ledger account.
- Alternative names for the purchases day book are: purchases journal and purchases book.
- Cash purchases are *never* entered in the purchases day book: the book of original entry for all cash purchases is the cash book.
- The slip system can also be used for purchase invoices.

Assignments

<hr/>

16.1

Bryan Forbes is the owner of a small electrical business. During the month of February 20-9 he has the following purchases on credit:

2 Feb General Supplies Ltd, Invoice number G9054
        12 electric razors at £19.70 each
        5 electric wall clocks at £7.50 each
        All *less* trade discount 10 per cent

7 Feb Jones Manufacturing Ltd, Invoice number 37516
        100 lamps 100w at 65p each
        50 lamps 75w at 55p each
        25 lamps 60w at 45p each
        15 lamps 40w at 35p each
        10 lamps 15w at 30p each
        All *less* trade discount 20 per cent

15 Feb General Supplies Ltd, Invoice number G9168
        10 electric wall clocks at £7.50 each
        15 hairdryers at £9.90 each
        All *less* trade discount 10 per cent

22 Feb Thomas Dean Ltd, Invoice number 5073
        25 battery torches B.65 at £1.75 each
        20 battery torches B.50 at £1.50 each
        10 battery torches B.45 at £1.25 each
        All *less* trade discount 25 per cent

28 Feb Peter Simmonds, Invoice number 06814
        5 electric heaters Model S107 at £22.50 each
        6 electric heaters Model S227 at £35 each
        All *less* trade discount 15 per cent

You are required to:

(a) Show your calculations of the net amount to be invoiced by each supplier.
(b) Enter each invoice in the purchases day book for the month of February 20-9.
(c) Post to the suppliers' personal accounts and transfer the total to the purchases account in the general ledger.

16.2

John Haines is the proprietor of a retail business. His purchases on credit during the month of March 20-8 were as follows:

2 Mar Kenneth Ingram, Invoice number 67413
        20 cassette tapes C120 at £1.30 each
        50 cassette tapes C90 at 95p each
        30 cassette tapes C60 at 75p each
        All *less* trade discount 15 per cent

4 Mar   Graham Clifton, Invoice number 49216
        6 hand blenders at £9.90 each
        10 food processors at £35.50 each
        6 food mixers at £22.50 each
        5 liquidisers at £10.25 each
        6 electric knives at £12.00 each
        All *less* trade discount 20 per cent

8 Mar   Stewart Brothers, Invoice number 2963
        20 packs HP16 batteries at £1.20 per pack
        50 packs EP12 batteries at £1.50 per pack
        25 packs HP18 batteries at £1.75 per pack
        All *less* trade discount 25 per cent

16 Mar   Frederick Rycroft, Invoice number F/5087
        10 mens' digital watches at £5.90 each
        5 ladies' digital watches at £4.90 each
        All *less* trade discount 10 per cent

24 Mar   Robert Linton, Invoice number 38525
        10 cassette recorders at £12.50 each
        6 radio/cassette recorders at £27.25 each
        6 pocket radios at £3.50 each
        15 stereo radios at £15.80 each
        All *less* trade discount $33\frac{1}{3}$ per cent

30 Mar   Vincent Hood, Invoice number 2416
        20 steam irons at £18.20 each
        15 steam/spray irons at £22.50 each
        10 travel irons at £7.70 each
        All *less* trade discount 20 per cent

You are required to:

(a) Clearly show your calculations of the net amount to be invoiced by each supplier.

(b) Write up the purchases day book for the month and post to the personal and nominal accounts in the ledger.

16.3

William Giles owns a retail store. During the month of May 20-8 the following transactions took place:

2 May   Sold goods £282 on credit to F Spencer
4 May   Sold goods £247 on credit to R Gordon
5 May   Purchased stock on credit from Harold Tyler, list price £340 subject to trade discount of 20 per cent
9 May   Sold goods £225 on credit to E Nelson
10 May   Sold goods £190 on credit to J Stokes
12 May   Purchased stock on credit from B Hobson, list price £360 *less* trade discount of 15 per cent
13 May   Sold goods £414 on credit to T Marshall

15 May	Purchases on credit from Harold Tyler, list price £220 subject to trade discount 20 per cent
17 May	Sales on credit £350 to F Spencer
18 May	Purchased stock on credit from J Douglas, list price £570 subject to trade discount of $33\frac{1}{3}$ per cent
20 May	Sold goods £174 on credit to J Marple
22 May	Sold goods £195 on credit to R Gordon
24 May	Purchases on credit from B Hobson, list price £290 subject to trade discount of 15 per cent
25 May	Purchased stock on credit from A Sylvester, list price £416 *less* trade discount of 25 per cent
26 May	Sales on credit £255 to C Barnes
28 May	Purchases on credit from J Douglas, list price £318 *less* trade discount of $33\frac{1}{3}$ per cent
30 May	Sales on credit £124 to F Spencer
31 May	Purchased stock on credit from T Norman, list price £280 *less* trade discount of 10 per cent

You are required to:

(a) Write up the sales day book and the purchases day book for the month of May 20-8.
(b) Post to the personal and nominal accounts as they would appear in the ledgers of William Giles.

■Ⅴ 17 Business documents – returns day books

In business there are many transactions of a similar nature. The purpose of day books is to group together all like transactions and so reduce the number of entries that need to be made in the ledger. Sometimes customers will *return goods* if they are not completely satisfied; this might be for any of the following reasons:

- goods were *damaged*
- goods were *faulty*
- goods were the *wrong size*
- goods were *wrong colour*
- goods were the *wrong type*.

In such cases it will be necessary to *reduce the amount owed* by the customer.

Credit note

As we have already seen, almost every business transaction begins with a *document*. A credit note is another important original document which relates to goods which have been returned. They are made out by the seller showing full details of the goods returned, prices and any trade discount. The top copy is sent to the customer and the seller keeps copies of all credit notes for his own records. It is the original document which provides the financial information which will subsequently be recorded in the ledger. It is called a 'credit note' because the customer's account will be *credited* with the value of the goods he has returned, to show a reduction in the amount owed.

Credit notes will differ in appearance, as each business will have its own individual design; they are often printed in red to distinguish them from invoices.

Figure 17.1 is an illustration of a typical credit note.

CREDIT NOTE

DEMLAND SUPPLIES
Sandmore Lane
LEEDS

Telephone 0113 7771941

Fax 0113 7609345

LS11 5EA

CREDIT NOTE

To	Grove & Sons	Credit Note	CN/3741
	Woodside Lane		
	LEEDS	Date	10 November 20-
	LS16 8ER		

VAT Registration Number 98765432

Qty	Description	Cat Number	Unit price	£	p
1	Electric kettle	EK10	£ 19.50	19	50

		£	p
		19	50
Less trade discount 20%		3	90
Total		15	60

Figure 17.1

This credit note has been sent by Demland Supplies to Grove & Sons because one of the electric kettles sold to them on 1 November was returned because it was faulty. Now look at the original invoice (Figure 15.1, p. 147) and work out the cost of one electric kettle.

Because trade discount was allowed on the original invoice it *must* now be *deducted on the credit note for the item returned.* It is vital to understand this important principle. When goods are sold *less* a trade discount it reduces the price of the goods; if it is not deducted on a credit note the customer will receive a higher price for the returned goods than was first paid. It would be quite wrong to give a customer a credit note for the full price if trade discount was allowed on the original invoice; he would actually be making a profit on the returned goods. We must be careful to make the credit note out only for the amount charged in the first place. This concept is often a pitfall for students and is frequently tested in examination questions.

Returns inwards day book

Day books are often referred to as *books of original entry*. When goods have been returned a credit note is made out and the top copy is sent to the customer. Firms keep copies of all credit notes and it is from the copies the seller enters up his returns inwards day book. Day books are also known as *journals* (the word 'journal' is simply the French word for '*day book*'.

A modern returns inwards day book (Figure 17.2) is simply a list, in date order, of all credit notes showing:

- date
- name of customer
- credit note number
- final amount of allowance.

Returns Inwards Day Book

Date	Name	Credit Note Number	F	£	p
10 Nov	Grove & Sons	CN/3741	SL	15	60
15 Nov	M Dean	CN/3742	SL	22	70
28 Nov	G Parkinson	CN/3743	SL	26	20
	Transferred to Returns Inwards Account		GL	64	50

Figure 17.2

Entries are made for a certain period (usually a week or a month). But the important rule of the returns inwards day book is that each customer's account is credited and the returns inwards account is debited from this original source. At the end of the period they are posted, one by one, to the credit side of each customer's personal account in the sales ledger thus reducing the amount owed. The original sales to the customers have been inserted so that the entries you need to consider are meaningful; it would be unrealistic to show returns if we had not sold goods in the first place:

Sales Ledger

Grove & Sons Account

		£			£
1 Nov	Sales	138.60	10 Nov	Returns inwards	15.60

M Dean Account

		£			£
9 Nov	Sales	120.20	15 Nov	Returns inwards	22.70

G Parkinson Account

		£			£
18 Nov	Sales	176.80	28 Nov	Returns inwards	26.20

Instead of making a double entry for each credit note in the returns inwards account, one single entry is made to correspond with the total for the period, like this:

General Ledger

Returns Inwards Account

		£	
30 Nov	Total for month	64.50	

It is immediately evident that this procedure is more efficient and considerably reduces the number of entries in the returns inwards account. To save space only a few examples have been used, but the real value is seen when the number of entries is very large.

As each item is posted the folio column is completed to show that the entry has been made. *Posting to the ledger* is a phrase used to describe the process of making entries in the ledger accounts.

Alternative names for the returns inwards day book are: returns inwards journal and sales returns book.

Debit notes

A debit note is another important original document which relates to goods which have been returned. When a purchaser returns goods, a debit note is made out giving details of the goods and the reason for their return. It is used for advice purposes only.

The purchaser keeps copies of all debit notes for his own records. It is the original document which provides the financial information which will subsequently be recorded in the ledger. It is called a 'debit note' because the customer wants to *debit the supplier's account with the value of the goods he is receiving back.*

A debit note could also be used if a buyer has been *undercharged*: it will be issued to claim the extra money outstanding. (Another invoice would not be appropriate since no goods are being delivered.)

Debit notes will differ in appearance, as each business will have its own individual design.

Returns outwards day book

Day books are often referred to as *books of original entry*. Firms keep copies of all debit notes and these are entered in the returns outwards day book. Day books are also known as *journals* (the word 'journal' is simply the French word for '*day book*'.

A modern returns outwards day book (Figure 17.3) is simply a list, in date order, of all debit notes showing:

- date
- name of supplier
- debit note number
- value of goods returned.

Returns Outwards Day Book

Date	Name	Debit Note Number	F	£	p
8 May	F Craig	DN/1922	PL	36	70
15 May	V Porter & Son	DN/1923	PL	25	60
29 May	W Nelson	DN/1924	PL	46	20
	Transferred to Returns Outwards Account		GL	108	50

Figure 17.3

Entries are made for a certain period (usually a week or a month). But the important rule of the returns outwards day book is that each supplier's account is debited and the returns outwards account is credited from this original source. At the end of the period they are posted, one by one, to the debit side of each supplier's personal account in the purchase ledger, thus reducing the amount owed. The original purchases from the suppliers have been inserted so that the entries you need to consider are meaningful; it would be unrealistic to show returns if we had not bought goods in the first place:

Purchase Ledger

F Craig Account

		£			£
8 May	Returns outwards	36.70	2 May	Purchases	380.50

V Porter & Son Account

		£			£
15 May	Returns outwards	25.60	12 May	Purchases	465.30

W Nelson Account

		£			£
29 May	Returns outwards	46.20	24 May	Purchases	519.40

Instead of making a double entry for each debit note in the returns outwards account, one single entry is made to correspond with the total for the period, like this:

General Ledger

Returns Outwards Account

			£
	31 May	Total for month	108.50

This procedure is more efficient and considerably reduces the number of entries in the returns outwards account. To save space only a few examples have been used, but the real value is seen when the number of entries is very large.

As each item is posted the folio column is completed to show that the entry has been made. *Posting to the ledger* is a phrase used to describe the process of making entries in the ledger accounts.

Alternative names for the returns outwards day book are: returns outwards journal and purchase returns book.

Statements

At the end of each month a statement should be sent to each customer. It lists, in date order, all the transactions which have taken place during the month. It should show:

- *amount owing* (if any) by customer *at start of month*
- *amount of each sales invoice* sent to customer during month
- *amount of each credit note* sent during month
- *cash and cheques received* from customer during month
- finally, the amount owing by customer at *end of month*.

A monthly statement also reminds the customer that *payment is due,* and will show the date by which *payment should be made.*

Points to remember

- Both credit notes and debit notes relate to goods which have been *returned*. Trade discount is simply a way of calculating prices and no entry for trade discount should be made in the double entry records, or in the returns day books. Trade discount **never** enters any ledger account.
- When trade discount is allowed on the original invoice it **must** be deducted for item(s) being returned. It is vital to understand this important principle. When goods are sold *less* a trade discount it reduces the price of the goods: it would be quite wrong if a customer received a higher price for any returned goods than they originally cost.
- The *slip system* can also be used for returns; copies of the credit and debit notes would be kept, in date order, in a lever arch file.
- Statements are sent to customers at the end of each month giving details of *all the transactions which have taken place* during the month.

Assignments

17.1

John Mortimer has a small business manufacturing a wide range of travel goods. During the month of June 20-8 the following transactions took place:

1 Jun Sold goods on credit to G Spink £218, J Goodall £127, Scott Bros £92

5 Jun Sales on credit to B Moss £117, L Gibson £138, P Andrews £242, F Benn £189

8 Jun Goods were returned by J Goodall £21, Scott Bros £17

11 Jun Sold goods on credit to F Myers £233, B Moss £186

14 Jun Goods were returned by L Gibson £28, P Andrews £32

20 Jun Sales on credit to J Goodall £149, F Benn £256

23 Jun Sales on credit to K Williams £212, G Spink £306

27 Jun Goods were returned by F Benn £37

30 Jun Sales on credit to B Moss £290, E Nelson £135

You are required to:

(a) Write up John Mortimer's sales day book and returns inwards day book for the month of June 20-8.
(b) Post to the personal accounts in the sales ledger and show the transfers to the general ledger.

17.2

Owen Pritchard owns an electrical business. During the month of August 20-8 the following transactions took place:

1 Aug   Purchased goods on credit from W Lawrence £258

4 Aug   Purchases on credit from the following: J Barrymore £316, T Groves £192, H Roper £257, D Passmore £168

8 Aug   Goods were returned to W Lawrence £17

10 Aug   Purchased goods on credit from T Groves £388, P Armstrong £219, H Roper £242, W Jones £312

12 Aug   Goods were returned to the following: J Barrymore £56, D Passmore £35

18 Aug   Purchases on credit from W Lawrence £280, M Hardy £116

20 Aug   Goods were returned to T Groves £28

24 Aug   Purchased goods on credit from J Barrymore £185

28 Aug   Goods were returned to M Hardy £15

30 Aug   Purchased goods on credit from F King £395

You are required to:

(a) Write up the purchases day book and returns outwards day book for the month of August 20-8.
(b) Post to the personal and nominal accounts in the ledger.

17.3

Elaine Rowe has a small business which produces a wide range of educational toys and games. During the month of October 20-9 the following transactions took place:

1 Oct   Purchased goods on credit from E Smythe £326 *less* 20 per cent trade discount

3 Oct   Sold goods on credit to B Marsh £126, L Young £65 and D Davey £38

5 Oct   Purchases on credit from R Chalker £543, subject to 25 per cent trade discount

9 Oct   Goods were returned by L Young £14

14 Oct   Sales on credit to W Preston £124, M Dyson £273

16 Oct   Returned goods to R Chalker with a list price of £48

18 Oct   M Dyson returned goods £36

20 Oct   Purchased goods on credit from M Trenholme £450, subject to 15 per cent trade discount

22 Oct   Sold goods on credit to B Marsh £212

24 Oct   Returned goods to M Trenholme with a list price of £50

26 Oct   Sales on credit to V Reedman £173

28 Oct   Goods were returned by B Marsh £28

29 Oct   Purchases on credit from C Hemingway £398 *less* 10 per cent trade discount

30 Oct   Sold goods on credit to W Preston £78, J Jackson £132

You are required to:

(a) Write up the sales, purchases, sales returns and purchase returns day books for the month of October 20-9.
(b) Post to the personal and nominal accounts in the ledger.

17.4
The following account appears in the ledger of Dawn Gwinnett:

Denise Hathersmith Account

20-6		£	20-6		£
1 Jan	Balance b/d	500.00	7 Jan	Bank	475.00
12 Jan	Goods	1,800.00	7 Jan	Discount	25.00
			20 Jan	Returns	40.00
			31 Jan	Balance c/d	1,760.00
		2,300.00			2,300.00
Feb 1	Balance b/d	1,760.00			

Answer the following questions relating to the above account:

(a) On 1 January was Denise Hathersmith a debtor or a creditor of Dawn Gwinnett?
(b) On 12 January did Denise Hathersmith purchase or sell goods?
(c) Who received the cheque on 7 January?
(d) What rate per cent of discount was allowed on 7 January?
(e) Was the discount on 7 January trade or cash?
(f) Does Denise Hathersmith regard the returns on 20 January as returns inwards or returns outwards?
(g) If the debt owing on 1 February was settled on 9 February, *less* 2½ per cent discount:
   (i) What was the amount of discount?
   (ii) What was the amount of the cheque?

17.5
State briefly the checking procedures you would follow before authorising payment of an invoice received from a supplier.

17.6

```
┌─────────────────────────────────────────────────────────────────────┐
│                                                                       │
│                         Statement                                     │
│                         J Hunt                                        │
│                         24 Coventry Road                              │
│                         NUNEATON                                      │
│                         NC4 2MN                                       │
│                                                                       │
│   R J Cook                                                            │
│   14 Thorn Street                                                     │
│   DERBY                                                               │
│   DE3 5XH                                                             │
│                                                                       │
│                                           31 March 20-4               │
│                                     £           £            £        │
│    1 Feb      Balance                                      130.42     │
│    6          Invoice 512         140.64                   271.06     │
│    8          Cheque                        127.16                    │
│               Discount                        3.26         140.64     │
│    12         Returns                        16.30         124.34     │
│    26         Invoice 540         184.42                   308.76     │
│    28         Undercharge           3.60                   312.36     │
│                                                                       │
└─────────────────────────────────────────────────────────────────────┘
```

Study the statement above:

(a) Name the person who is supplying goods.
(b) Explain in simple terms the meaning of each item on the statement from 1–26 February.
(c) State the document used for the item on 28 February and the names of the sender and the receiver.
(d) Give the names of the debtor and the creditor and the amount owed on 28 February 20-4.

17.7
You have been newly appointed as a clerk in your company's credit control department and an order from an old established customer has been passed to you for clearance.

(a) What procedure would you follow before passing the order to the sales department for completion?
(b) In what way would the procedure be different if the order was from a new customer?

■ M **18** Value Added Tax

Value Added Tax (VAT) is a tax charged on the supply of most goods and services in the United Kingdom. The percentage rate is set by the government and is changed from time to time, usually on Budget day. VAT is added at every stage of production and it is the *responsibility of the firm making the sale to charge and collect VAT from the customer.* The government authority which deals with VAT is the Customs and Excise Department. Most goods and services are subject to VAT but there are some exceptions:

- Some services and certain classes of goods are completely *exempt* from VAT. Examples of these are: postal services, food and children's clothes.
- Some classes of goods are *not taxed* and are said to be *zero rated.* In effect this means that, at the present time, these goods or services are not subject to VAT. However, changes may take place in the future and VAT could be applicable.
- There are some traders or providers of services whose taxable turnover (sales) is under a certain amount. This figure is referred to as the *taxable threshold.* The taxable threshold limit is usually reviewed and increased each year. Firms with a turnover of less than the threshold limit do not have to register for VAT. However, firms who are not registered for VAT cannot charge VAT to their customers, nor can they recover the amount of VAT paid on their purchases.

Registration for VAT is compulsory for firms whose turnover is above the threshold limit.

Note: Because the VAT percentage rate set by the government changes from time to time, most examination boards set questions assuming a rate of 10 per cent. For this reason, all examples shown in this book will be at a rate of 10 per cent.

Value Added Tax and sales invoices

A taxable firm will have to add VAT to the value of its sales invoices. This is known as *output tax* and is based on the amount of the invoice *after* any trade discount has been deducted.

Figure 18.1 is an illustration of a typical tax invoice.

DEMLAND SUPPLIES
Sandmore Lane
LEEDS

Telephone 0113 7771941

Fax   0113 7609345

LS11 5EA

INVOICE

To Grove & Sons
Woodside Lane
LEEDS
LS16 8ER

Invoice Number   DS/4362

Date   1 March 20-

Your Order Number   7492

VAT Registration Number 98765432

Qty	Description	Cat number	Unit price	£	p
			£		
10	Electric kettles	EK10	19.50	195	00
20	Electric toasters	ET16	18.75	375	00
	Less trade discount 20%			570	00
				114	00
TERMS NET	*Add* VAT at 10%			456	00
MONTHLY				45	60
				501	60

Figure 18.1

Sales day book

When the sales invoices have been made out the top copy is sent to the customer. Copies are kept of all sales invoices and it is from the copies the seller enters up his sales day book. VAT fits into the accounting system by adding extra columns to the sales day book.

Cash sales are *never* entered in the sales day book; when goods are paid for immediately, the original entry is in the cash book.

Recording tax invoices is very important for a business because these documents act as evidence and are subject to inspection by Customs and

Excise. A modern sales day book is now illustrated (Figure 18.2), beginning with the example invoice.

Sales Day Book

Date	Name	Invoice number	F	Total £	Goods £	VAT £
1 Mar	Grove & Sons	DS/4362	SL	501.60	456.00	45.60
8 Mar	G Parker	DS/4363	SL	173.80	158.00	15.80
18 Mar	J Oliver	DS/4364	SL	376.20	342.00	34.20
23 Mar	M Spencer	DS/4365	SL	298.65	271.50	27.15
29 Mar	B Conway	DS/4366	SL	479.60	436.00	43.60
				1,829.85	1,663.50	166.35
					GL	GL

Figure 18.2

Entries are made for a certain period, usually a week or a month. But the important rule of the sales day book is that each customer's account is debited with the *total* amount of each invoice, *including* VAT, and the sales and VAT accounts are credited from this original source. At the end of the period the credit sales are posted, one by one, to the debit side of each customer's personal account in the sales ledger, like this:

Sales Ledger

Grove & Sons Account

	£	
1 Mar Sales	501.60	

G Parker Account

	£	
8 Mar Sales	173.80	

J Oliver Account

	£	
18 Mar Sales	376.20	

M Spencer Account

		£	
23 Mar	Sales	298.65	

B Conway Account

		£	
29 Mar	Sales	479.60	

All the personal accounts have been debited with the total value of each invoice *including* VAT; this is the amount the customers will have to pay. Instead of making a double entry for each invoice in the sales account, one single entry is made to correspond with the total *sales value* for the period, like this:

Nominal Ledger

Sales Account

		£
	31 Mar Total for month	1,663.50

The Value Added Tax account fits easily into the double entry system; it is just another account we have to deal with. Instead of making a double entry for every amount of VAT charged on each invoice, one single entry is made to correspond with the total for the period, like this:

Value Added Tax Account

		£
	31 Mar Total for month	166.35

If you check the totals you will find out that the debit entries exactly equal the credit entries, so our double entry is correct.

This procedure is more efficient and considerably reduces the number of entries in the sales and VAT accounts. To save space only five examples have been used, but the real benefit is seen when the number of entries is very large. During a month, for some firms this could easily be 500.

As each item is posted the folio column is completed to show that the entry has been made. *Posting to the ledger* is a phrase used to describe the process of making entries in the ledger accounts.

Value Added Tax and purchases

A taxable firm will be able to get a *refund* of the VAT which it pays on its purchases. This is known as *input tax* and is based on the amount of the invoice *after* any trade discount has been deducted.

When a taxable firm buys goods on credit an invoice will be made out by the supplier showing full details of the goods, prices, any trade discount and the amount of VAT. This is known as a *purchase invoice*. It is the original document which provides the financial information which will subsequently be recorded in the ledger.

When invoices are received from suppliers they should always be checked to ensure that they are genuine and accurate.

Purchases day book

Only when the checking procedures have been carried out should the purchase invoices be entered in the purchases day book. This book contains details of all credit purchases of goods for resale. When a purchase invoice is received, this document is the original accounting record of the transaction. Day books are also known as *journals* (the word 'journal' is simply the French word for *day book*).

Cash purchases are **never** entered in the purchases day book; when goods are bought and payment is made immediately, the original entry is in the cash book.

Recording tax invoices is very important for a business because these documents act as evidence and are subject to inspection by Customs and Excise. A modern purchases day book is now illustrated (Figure 18.3).

Purchases Day Book

Date	Name	Invoice number	F	Total £	Goods £	VAT £
2 Mar	S Ramsden	R/6109	PL	275.00	250.00	25.00
6 Mar	B Johnson	10892	PL	214.50	195.00	19.50
17 Mar	Grice Bros	90514	PL	187.55	170.50	17.05
25 Mar	J Silverwood	S/4618	PL	260.15	236.50	23.65
30 Mar	V Porter & Son	43176	PL	132.00	120.00	12.00
				1,069.20	972.00	97.20
					GL	GL

Figure 18.3

Entries are made for a certain period (usually a week or a month). But the important rule of the purchases day book is that each supplier's account is credited with the *total* amount of each invoice, *including* VAT and the purchases and VAT accounts are *debited* from this original source.

At the end of the period the credit purchases are posted, one by one, to the credit side of each supplier's personal account in the purchase ledger, like this:

Purchase Ledger

S Ramsden Account

		£
	2 Mar Purchases	275.00

B Johnson Account

		£
	6 Mar Purchases	214.50

Grice Bros Account

		£
	17 Mar Purchases	187.55

J Silverwood Account

		£
	25 Mar Purchases	260.15

V Porter & Son Account

		£
	30 Mar Purchases	132.00

You will see that the personal accounts have been credited with the total value of each invoice *including* VAT; this is the amount the firm will have to pay its suppliers.

Instead of making a double entry for each invoice in the purchases account, one single entry is made to correspond with the *actual cost of the purchases* for *the* period, like this:

Nominal Ledger

Purchases Account

		£	
31 Mar	Total for month	972.00	

Instead of making a double entry for every single amount of VAT charged on each invoice, one entry is made, at the *debit* side, to correspond with the total for the period; the same VAT account has been used so that the entries you need to consider are meaningful:

Value Added Tax Account

		£			£
31 Mar	PDB total for month	97.20	31 Mar	SDB total for month	166.35

Returns inwards day book

When goods have been returned a *credit note* is issued and the top copy is sent to the customer. Firms keep copies of all credit notes and it is from the copies the seller enters up his returns inwards day book.

A modern returns inwards day book is illustrated in Figure 18.4.

Returns Inwards Day Book

Date	Name	Credit note	F	Total £	Goods £	VAT £
9 Mar	Grove & Sons	CN/2513	SL	64.02	58.20	5.82
27 Mar	J Oliver	CN/2514	SL	39.60	36.00	3.60
				103.62	94.20	9.42
					GL	GL

Figure 18.4

Entries are made for a certain period (usually a week or a month). But the important rule of the returns inwards day book is that each customer's account is credited with the total amount, *including* VAT and the returns inwards and VAT accounts are debited from this original source.

Now look at the postings: each customer's personal account has been credited; the original sales have been inserted so that the entries you need to consider are meaningful. It would be unrealistic to show returns if we have not recorded any sales in the first place:

Sales Ledger

Grove & Sons Account

		£			£
1 Mar	Sales	501.60	9 Mar	Returns inwards	64.02

J Oliver Account

		£			£
18 Mar	Sales	376.20	27 Mar	Returns inwards	39.60

Nominal Ledger

Returns Inwards Account

		£	
31 Mar	Total for month	94.20	

Instead of making a double entry for every amount of VAT charged on each credit note, one entry is made, at the *debit* side, to correspond with the total for the period. The VAT is *debited* because these customers will pay *less* tax to us because of these returns. It is useful to show the same VAT account so that the entries you need to consider are meaningful:

Value Added Tax Account

		£			£
31 Mar	PDB total for month	97.20	31 Mar	SDB total for month	166.35
31 Mar	RIB total for month	9.42			

Returns outwards day book

A *debit note* is another important original document which relates to goods which have been returned. When a purchaser returns goods, a debit note is made out giving details of the goods and the reason for their return. It is used for advice purposes only.

Firms keep copies of all debit notes and it is from the copies the purchaser enters up his returns outwards day book.

A modern returns outwards day book is illustrated in Figure 18.5.

Returns Outwards Day Book

Date	Name	Debit note	F	Total £	Goods £	VAT £
7 Mar	S Ramsden	DN/3841	PL	68.20	62.00	6.20
26 Mar	Grice Bros	DN/3842	PL	44.00	40.00	4.00
				112.20	102.00	10.20
					GL	GL

Figure 18.5

Entries are made for a certain period (usually a week or a month). But the important rule of the returns outwards day book is that each supplier's account is debited with the *total* amount *including* VAT and the returns outwards and VAT accounts are credited from this original source.

Now look at the postings: each supplier's personal account has been debited; the original purchases have been inserted so that the entries you need to consider are meaningful. It would be unrealistic to show returns if we had not recorded any purchases in the first place:

Purchase Ledger

S Ramsden Account

		£			£
7 Mar	Returns outwards	68.20	2 Mar	Purchases	275.00

Grice Bros Account

		£			£
26 Mar	Returns outwards	44.00	17 Mar	Purchases	187.55

Nominal Ledger

Returns Outwards Account

		£
	31 Mar Total for month	102.00

Instead of making a double entry for every amount of VAT, one entry is made at the *credit* side, to correspond with the total for the period. The VAT is credited because the firm will now pay *less tax* on their purchases because of these returns. It is useful to show the same VAT account so that the entries you need to consider are meaningful:

Value Added Tax Account

		£			£
31 Mar	PDB total for month	97.20	31 Mar	SDB total for month	166.35
31 Mar	RIB total for month	9.42	31 Mar	ROB total for month	10.20

Just like all other accounts, the VAT account is balanced at the end of each month, like this:

Value Added Tax Account

		£			£
31 Mar	PDB total for month	97.20	31 Mar	SDB total for month	166.35
31 Mar	RIB total for month	9.42	31 Mar	ROB total for month	10.20
31 Mar	Balance c/d	69.93			
		176.55			176.55
			1 Apr	Balance b/d	69.93

At the end of every three months, instead of paying the VAT charged on its sales invoices (*output tax*) to Customs and Excise and then claiming a refund of the VAT on its purchases (*input tax*), only the *difference at the end of the quarter* has to be settled, with a *payment* to Customs and Excise when there is a *credit* balance, or a *refund* from Customs and Excise when there is a *debit* balance.

Because firms always add a profit margin to cost prices to find their selling prices, most firms owe money to Customs and Excise at the end of each quarter.

VAT on expenses and assets

VAT is also charged on many items of expense and on the purchase of fixed assets. Expenses will include such things as: petrol, telephone and stationery. Fixed assets are items purchased for long-term use in the business such as: plant, machinery, office furniture and computers. Because such items are used in running a business a taxable firm can recover the amount of VAT paid on some business expenses and on fixed assets.

For example, if a taxable firm bought a computer for office use they would receive an invoice showing the price of the computer and the amount of VAT, similar to that in Figure 18.6.

It is important to remember that in accounting, the term '*purchases*' is used to describe goods which are bought with the *intention of being resold*. When a firm buys a computer for use in the business this would be a fixed asset and this invoice would **not** be entered in the purchases day book or in the purchases account.

As we have already seen, assets have their own accounts; computers are usually entered in an office equipment account. The general rule is:

- The *actual cost* of the asset should be shown in the *asset account*
- The *amount of VAT to be reclaimed* should be entered at the *debit* side of the *VAT account*,

like this:

Office Equipment Account

		£	
3 Apr	Atlantis Systems	1,500.00	

Value Added Tax Account

		£	
3 Apr	Asset VAT content	150.00	

INVOICE

ATLANTIS SYSTEMS
Dewsbury Road
LEEDS

Telephone 0113 250231

Fax   0113 271692

LS12 7MN

To Demland Supplies	Invoice Number	38219
Sandmore Lane		
LEEDS	Date	3 April 20-
LS11 5EA		
	Your Order Number	2613

VAT Registration Number 21234567

Qty	Description	Cat number	Unit price	£	p
1	Intel Epcon computer	IE686	£ 1,500	1,500	00

TERMS NET MONTHLY		1,500	00
Add VAT at 10%		150	00
		1,650	00

Figure 18.6

You will see that the personal account has been credited with the total value of the invoice *including* VAT, this is the amount the firm will have to pay:

Atlantis Systems Account

		£
3 Apr	Office equipment	1,650.00

VAT and the balance sheet

At the end of the financial year when the final accounts of a business are prepared any VAT *owing to Customs and Excise* would appear as a *creditor* on the balance sheet; any VAT *owing to the business* would appear as a *debtor* on the balance sheet.

Points to remember

- The main problems associated with VAT are understanding the rules. Like other taxes, VAT is simply another way the government raises money and the VAT account acts as a *special account for the government.*
- Firms who are registered for VAT must *charge and collect VAT from their customers.* The government authority which deals with VAT is the Customs and Excise Department.
- VAT fits into the accounting process by *adding extra columns in the day books* and inserting the Value Added Tax account into the double entry system.
- '*Posting to the ledger*' is a phrase used to describe the process of making entries in the ledger accounts from the day books. As each item is posted, the folio column is completed to show that the entry has been made. All personal accounts of customers and suppliers are posted with the total value *including* VAT. To complete the double entry the *goods value only* is entered in the sales, purchases and returns accounts; all VAT is collected together in the Value Added Tax account.
- Because the VAT percentage rate set by the government changes from time to time, most examination boards set questions assuming a rate of 10 per cent.

Assignments

18.1

Joseph Stephenson is a trader. During the month of April 20-8 sales on credit were made to the following:

		£
2 Apr	Sales to J Wilson	250
5 Apr	Sales to K Allen	178
10 Apr	Sales to F Stones	490
15 Apr	Sales to R Lockwood	155
22 Apr	Sales to B McKenzie	212
30 Apr	Sales to M Newman	364

All transactions are subject to VAT at 10 per cent.
   You are required to:

(a) Write up the sales day book for the month of April 20-8.
(b) Post to the personal and nominal accounts in the ledgers to complete the double entry.

18.2

During the month of May 20-8 Cyril Sanderson's purchases on credit were as follows:

1 May   Purchases from M Booth £296, *less* 20 per cent trade discount
4 May   Purchases from J Price £492, *less* 25 per cent trade discount
8 May   Purchases from B Ramsden £184, *less* 15 per cent trade discount
14 May Purchases from L Nelson £273, *less* 20 per cent trade discount
20 May Purchases from M Senior £158, *less* 15 per cent trade discount
25 May Purchases from D Rawdon £332, *less* 25 per cent trade discount

All the above transactions are subject to VAT at 10 per cent.
   You are required to:

(a) Write up the purchases day book for the month of May 20-8.
(b) Post to the personal and nominal accounts in the ledgers.

18.3

You are employed by Anderson and Littlewood, 22 Grange Street HULL, HN5 7BZ, suppliers of office equipment and materials. On 29 February your firm had supplied the following goods to T Woodward of 44 Market Cross, Driffield, North Humberside YO16 4NL; the Invoice number is 66161, VAT Registration number 23456789:

   100 reams of A4 paper at £4 per ream
   200 bottles of correction fluid at 48p per bottle
   150 boxes of address labels at 80p per box
   1 four-drawer metal filing cabinet at £120
   VAT is charged at 10 per cent on all items.

You are required to prepare the invoice to be sent to T Woodward.

18.4

Adel Enterprises is a small business buying and selling goods on credit. During the month of May 20-9 the following transactions took place:

3 May   Bought goods from A Lucas £258, D Nicholas £326, V Cummings £302, all *less* trade discount 25 per cent
8 May   Sold goods to M Dyson £172, B Dixon £95
12 May Returned goods to D Nicholas £48
18 May Bought goods from S Milner £135, R Sykes £148, all *less* trade discount 20 per cent
20 May Goods were returned to the firm by M Dyson £32
22 May Sold goods to A Bannister £196, E Rowe £269, B Dixon £138
24 May Returned goods to S Milner £25
28 May Sold goods to M Dyson £172, A Bannister £84
30 May Goods were returned to the firm by E Rowe £43

All transactions are subject to VAT at a rate of 10 per cent.
  You are required to:

(a) Enter the above transactions in the appropriate day books.
(b) Close the day books at the end of the month.
(c) Post to the personal and nominal accounts in the ledger and balance only the VAT account at the end of the month.

18.5

SuLing Textiles imports and sells oriental items. During the month of October 20-9 the following transactions took place:

2 Oct   Bought goods from Hongtay Supplies £508, T Ambala £364, Jade Cane £290, all *less* trade discount 15 per cent
4 Oct   Sold goods to S Khan £193, Lotus Grove £250, J Kamran £138
7 Oct   Returned goods to T Ambala £38 and Jade Cane £46
13 Oct Bought goods from Ali Raj £208, Hong Van £192, all *less* trade discount $12\frac{1}{2}$ per cent
14 Oct J Kamran returned goods £26
15 Oct Sold goods to B Patel £175, S Khan £283
18 Oct Lotus Grove returned goods £65
20 Oct Bought goods from T Ambala £186, Hongtay Supplies £416, all *less* trade discount 15 per cent
25 Oct Returned goods £52 to Ali Raj
29 Oct Sold goods to J Kamran £98, B Patel £165

All items are subject to VAT at a rate of 10 per cent.
  You are required to:

(a) Enter the above transactions in the appropriate day books.
(b) Close the day books at the end of the month.

(c) Post to the personal and nominal accounts in the ledger and balance only the VAT account at the end of the month.

18.6

D Withers is a wholesaler. The *credit* transactions listed below took place during the month of May 20-2. Enter each transaction in the appropriate book of original entry, total for the month and post to the purchases, sales, returns and value added tax accounts in the ledger.

All amounts given are before the addition of VAT, which is to be taken at 10 per cent.

All trade purchases are allowed a trade discount of 20 per cent, not yet taken into account in the figures given below. Trade discount is not allowed on any sales.

20-2		£
1 May	Purchased stock from T Smithers Ltd	400
3 May	Sold stock to W Wilkin	350
4 May	Sold stock to T Wilson	300
11 May	Returned stock bought on 1 May to T Smithers Ltd	50
12 May	Purchased stock from J Williams	270
20 May	T Wilson returned stock	20
22 May	Returned stock bought on 12 May to J Williams	45
29 May	Sold stock to W Wilkin	170
30 May	Purchased stock from T Smithers Ltd	150

18.7

During the month of September 20-5 Oliver Stanley's *credit* transactions were as follows:

2 Sep	Sales to E Cowan £182
4 Sep	Sales to R Douglas £357
5 Sep	Purchases from H Pearce £440 *less* 20 per cent trade discount
10 Sep	Sales to N Eddie £225
12 Sep	Returns from E Cowan £14
13 Sep	Purchases from P Stokes £360 *less* 25 per cent trade discount
17 Sep	Sales to T Galloway £412
23 Sep	Purchases from P Stokes £250 *less* 30 per cent trade discount
24 Sep	Received credit note from H Pearce in respect of goods with list price of £50
26 Sep	Sales to R Douglas £383
30 Sep	Returns from T Galloway £33

All transactions are subject to VAT at a rate of 10 per cent.

You are required to write up Oliver Stanley's sales, purchases, sales returns and purchases returns day books for the month of September 20-5.

18.8

The following sales and purchases were made by Smithers during the month of May 20-6:

5 May   Sold on credit to Ace Furnishings, 3 desks list price £150 each, *less* trade discount of $33\frac{1}{3}$ per cent

10 May   Sold on credit to Comfy Chair Co, 2 dining suites list price £360 each, *less* trade discount of 25 per cent

18 May   Purchased the following goods on credit from The Top Woodworkers

24 kitchen chairs list price £12.00 each, *less* trade discount of 25 per cent

12 wall cupboards list price £10 each, *less* trade discount of 20 per cent

All transactions are subject to VAT at a rate of 10 per cent.

In addition to the above, Smithers received an invoice for £110 on 20 May from Jones. This was for shop fittings supplied for use within the business and included VAT at 10 per cent.

You are required to:

(a) Calculate the net value of the invoice in each of the four instances mentioned above.

(b) Write up the sales account, purchases account, shop fittings account, VAT account and relevant personal accounts for the month of May. Your VAT account should show the amount owing to/by Customs and Excise as at 31 May 20-6.

▪ ⩗ 19 Sales and purchases analysed day books

A firm may deal in a variety of different products or may be divided into several departments. In many cases, just to know the total credit sales or credit purchases is simply not enough. They may want to know which lines sell best or which department is most profitable.

Today many retail stores and supermarkets use electronic tills and computerised accounting systems to obtain this useful information as it is processed. This reveals which are the most popular lines and deserve most shelf space, while less popular items are given less space.

When a business is divided into several departments floor space is allocated according to the greatest volume of sales. An easy way to discover which product sells best or which department is most profitable, is to add extra columns to the day books to collect this information. Such books are called *analysed day books*.

There will be a total column in which the total amount of each document is entered and a column for each product or department and VAT. At the end of the week or month *all* the columns are totalled. The totals of the combined analysis columns should agree with the addition of the main total column. This is called *cross-checking* or *cross casting* and will usually help you find any mistakes.

Examination questions often require candidates to work out trade discount, and calculate invoices and credit notes; *all* calculations should be completed before entering any details in the analysed day books.

Note: As most examination boards set questions assuming a VAT percentage rate of 10 per cent, all examples shown are calculated at this rate.

An analysed sales day book is illustrated in Figure 19.1.

Analysed Sales Day Book

Date 20-9	Details	F	Total invoice	Televisions	Video recorders	Personal computers	VAT
			£	£	£	£	£
1 Mar	F Briggs	SL	935.00	850.00			85.00
6	M King	SL	1,870.00		650.00	1,050.00	170.00
9	B Franks	SL	1,699.50	795.00	750.00		154.50
15	D Grice	SL	2,618.00	480.00	650.00	1,250.00	238.00
23	W Newton	SL	1,265.00			1,150.00	115.00
31	M Dyson	SL	1,749.00	630.00		960.00	159.00
			10,136.50	2,755.00	2,050.00	4,410.00	921.50
				NL	NL	NL	NL

Figure 19.1

Posting the analysed sales day book

Entries are made for a certain period, usually a week or a month but the personal accounts are not affected by the analysis. Each customer's account in the sales ledger is debited with the *total* amount of each invoice, *including* VAT, like this:

Sales Ledger

F Briggs Account

		£		
1 Mar	Sales	935.00		

M King Account

		£		
6 Mar	Sales	1,870.00		

B Franks Account

		£		
9 Mar	Sales	1,699.50		

D Grice Account

		£		
15 Mar	Sales	2,618.00		

W Newton Account

		£		
23 Mar	Sales	1,265.00		

M Dyson Account

		£		
31 Mar	Sales	1,749.00		

All the personal accounts have been debited with the total value of each invoice *including VAT* because this is the amount the customers will have to pay.

We can now see how the information given in the analysis columns provides the figures which are posted to the nominal ledger. This is achieved by having separate sales accounts, one for each product or department. One entry is made to correspond with the total *sales value* for each product, like this:

Sales Account – Televisions

				£
		31 Mar	Total for month	2,755.00

Sales Account – Video Recorders

				£
		31 Mar	Total for month	2,050.00

Sales Account – Personal Computers

				£
		31 Mar	Total for month	4,410.00

Value Added Tax Account

		£
	31 Mar SDB total for month	921.50

If you check the totals you will discover that the debit entries exactly equal the credit entries, so our double entry is correct. As each item is posted the folio column is completed to show that the entry has been made.

Alternatively, one analysed sales account could be used, with separate columns for each product or department. However, where there are several products or departments it is difficult to have sufficient columns without causing the ledger to be exceedingly cumbersome in size. Generally separate accounts for each product or department are preferred.

Similar analysed day books would be kept for returns. An analysed returns inwards day book (sometimes called a sales returns day book) is illustrated in Figure 19.2.

Analysed Returns Inwards Day Book

Date 20-9	Details	F	Total invoice	Televisions	Video recorders	Personal computers	VAT
			£	£	£	£	£
14 Mar	M King	SL	416.90			379.00	37.90
25	D Grice	SL	203.50		185.00		18.50
			620.40		185.00	379.00	56.40
					NL	NL	NL

Figure 19.2

Posting the analysed returns inwards day book

Entries are made for a certain period, usually a week or a month but the personal accounts are not affected by the analysis. Each customer's account in the sales ledger is credited with the total amount, *including* VAT. Now look at the postings, each customer's account has been credited; the original sales have been inserted so that the entries you need to consider are meaningful. It would be unrealistic to show returns if we have not recorded any sales in the first place:

Sales Ledger

M King Account

		£			£
6 Mar	Sales	1,870.00	14 Mar	Returns inwards	416.90

D Grice Account

		£			£
15 Mar	Sales	2,618.00	25 Mar	Returns inwards	203.50

We can now see how the information given in the analysis columns provides the figures which are posted to the nominal ledger. This is achieved by having separate returns inwards accounts for each product or department. One entry is made to correspond with the total *returns inwards value* for each product, like this:

Nominal Ledger

Returns Inwards Account – Video Recorders

		£	
31 Mar	Total for month	185.00	

Returns Inwards Account – Personal Computers

		£	
31 Mar	Total for month	379.00	

It is useful to show the same VAT account so that the entries you need to consider are meaningful:

Value Added Tax Account

		£			£
31 Mar	RIDB total for month	56.40	31 Mar	SDB total for month	921.50

Similar analysed day books would be kept for purchases, and returns outwards. An analysed purchases day book for a firm which has divided its business into three departments is illustrated in Figure 19.3.

Analysed Purchases Day Book

Date 20-9	Details	F	Total invoice	Carpet department	Furniture department	Electrical department	VAT
			£	£	£	£	£
1 Apr	D Smythe	PL	638.00		580.00		58.00
5	H Benson	PL	1,073.60	630.00	346.00		97.60
12	F Parker	PL	1,295.80	458.00	720.00		117.80
19	P Ellis	PL	935.00			850.00	85.00
25	G Wilson	PL	1,622.50	850.00	625.00		147.50
30	A Jones	PL	1,028.50			935.00	93.50
			6,593.40	1,938.00	2,271.00	1,785.00	599.40
				NL	NL	NL	NL

Figure 19.3

Posting the analysed purchases day book

Entries are made for a certain period (usually a week or a month), but the personal accounts are not affected by the analysis. Each supplier's account in the purchase ledger is credited with the *total* amount of each invoice, *including* VAT, like this:

Purchase ledger

D Smythe Account

		£
	1 Apr Purchases	638.00

H Benson Account

		£
	5 Apr Purchases	1,073.60

F Parker Account

		£
	12 Apr Purchases	1,295.80

P Ellis Account

			£
	19 Apr	Purchases	935.00

G Wilson Account

			£
	25 Apr	Purchases	1,622.50

A Jones Account

			£
	30 Apr	Purchases	1,028.50

All the personal accounts have been credited with the total value of each invoice *including VAT* because this is the amount the firm will have to pay its suppliers.

We can now see how the information given in the analysis columns provides the figures which are posted to the nominal ledger. This is achieved by having separate purchases accounts for each department. One entry is made to correspond with the total *purchases value* for each department, like this:

Nominal Ledger

Purchases Account – Carpet Department

		£	
30 Apr	Total for month	1,938.00	

Purchases Account – Furniture Department

		£	
30 Apr	Total for month	2,271.00	

Purchases Account – Electrical Department

		£	
30 Apr	Total for month	1,785.00	

Value Added Tax Account

		£	
30 Apr	PDB total for month	599.40	

If you check the totals you will find out that the debit entries exactly equal the credit entries, so our double entry is correct. As each item is posted, the folio column is completed to show that the entry has been made.

Similar analysed day books would be kept for returns. An analysed returns outwards day book (sometimes called a purchase returns day book) is illustrated in Figure 19.4.

Analysed Returns Outwards Day Book

Date 20-9	Details	F	Total invoice	Carpet department	Furniture department	Electrical department	VAT
			£	£	£	£	£
14 Apr	H Benson	PL	71.50	65.00			6.50
20	F Parker	PL	115.50		105.00		10.50
29	P Ellis	PL	62.70			57.00	5.70
			249.70	65.00	105.00	57.00	22.70
				NL	NL	NL	NL

Figure 19.4

Posting the analysed returns outwards day book

Entries are made for a certain period, usually a week or a month but the personal accounts are not affected by the analysis. Each supplier's account in the purchase ledger is debited with the total amount *including* VAT.

Now look at the postings: each customer's account has been debited; the original purchases have been inserted so that the entries you need to consider are meaningful. It would be unrealistic to show returns if we had not recorded any purchases in the first place:

H Benson Account

		£			£
14 Apr	Returns outwards	71.50	5 Apr	Purchases	1,073.60

F Parker Account

		£			£
20 Apr	Returns outwards	115.50	12 Apr	Purchases	1,295.80

P Ellis Account

		£			£
29 Apr	Returns outwards	62.70	19 Apr	Purchases	935.00

We can now see how the information given in the analysis columns provides the figures which are posted to the nominal ledger. This is achieved by having separate returns outwards accounts for each department. One entry is made to correspond with the total *returns outwards value* for each department, like this:

Nominal Ledger

Returns Outwards Account – Carpet Department

			£
	30 Apr	Total for month	65.00

Returns Outwards Account – Furniture Department

			£
	30 Apr	Total for month	105.00

Returns Outwards Account – Electrical Department

			£
	30 Apr	Total for month	57.00

It is useful to show the same VAT account so that the entries you need to consider are meaningful:

Value Added Tax Account

	£			£
30 Apr PDB total for month	599.40	30 Apr RODB total for month		22.70

If you check the totals, you will discover that the debit entries exactly equal the credit entries, so our double entry is correct. As each item is posted, the folio column is completed to show that the entry has been made.

Points to remember

- Analysed day books provide firms with useful information regarding which products *sell best* or which department is *most profitable.*
- All personal accounts of customers and suppliers are posted with the total value *including* VAT. To complete the double entry the *goods value only* is entered in the sales, purchases and returns accounts (for each product or department). All VAT is collected together in the VAT account.
- Some firms prefer to call the 'returns inwards day book' the '*sales returns day book*'; and 'returns outwards day book' the '*purchase returns day book*'.
- *Trade discount* is simply a way of calculating prices and no entry for trade discount should be made in the analysed day books or in any ledger account.

To help you gain valuable practice, all the following Assignments are taken from past examination papers.

Assignments

19.1

'Handyman' is a local 'Do it Yourself' store which divides its purchases of stock into two main departments: General Household and Garden Accessories. Purchases on credit during the month of April 20-9 were:

2 Apr Self Paste Ltd
Wallpaper supplies at list price £1,040, *less* trade discount 20 per cent
Emulsion paint at list price £1,600, *less* trade discount 15 per cent

15 Apr   Green Fingers Ltd

12 patio furniture sets at list price £20 each, *less* trade discount 20 per cent

10 lawn mowers at list price £90 each, *less* trade discount 10 per cent

20 Apr   G A Coleman & Son

Plasterboard supplies at list price £220, *less* trade discount 10 per cent

All transactions are subject to VAT at a rate of 10 per cent.

You are required to:

(a) Show clearly your calculations of the net amount to be invoiced by each supplier.

(b) Write up the purchases day book for the month and post the relevant totals to the personal and nominal accounts.

19.2

John Dickenson is the proprietor of a retail business which he has divided into two departments: Furniture and Electrical goods. His purchases on credit during the month of May 20-9 were:

5 May   Overland Furniture Co Ltd

3 dining suites, list price £250 each, *less* trade discount 20 per cent

4 double beds, list price £150 each, *less* trade discount $33\frac{1}{3}$ per cent

13 May   Pelican Co Ltd

25 electric kettles, list price £20 each

5 electric toasters, list price £15 each

5 electric knives, list price £15 each

all these purchases *less* trade discount 20 per cent

25 May   Overland Furniture Co Ltd

24 dining chairs, list price £20 each, *less* trade discount 25 per cent

All transactions are subject to VAT at a rate of 10 per cent.

You are required to:

(a) Show your calculations of the net amount to be invoiced by each supplier.

(b) Rule up a purchases day book with the following columns:

Date	Name of supplier	Total	Furniture department	Electrical department	VAT

(c) Write up the purchases day book for the month of May and post to the personal and nominal accounts in the ledger.

19.3

The Great Outdoors Centre manufacturers a wide range of camping and leisure products at competitive prices. The business is divided into two main departments: Garden Furniture and Camping Equipment. Sales on credit during the month of May were:

Sales

5 May   Dalesman Products
15 Explorer rucksacks at list price £22.70 each,
all *less* trade discount 20 per cent

8 May   Parkway Garden Centre
3 Rialto patio furniture sets at list price £65 each,
10 Luxury garden chairs at list price £15.50 each,
all *less* trade discount 15 per cent.

16 May   Sun Valley Campers
10 Trekker camping stoves at list price £29.00 each,
all *less* trade discount 25 per cent

20 May   Woodland Supplies
5 deck chairs at list price £9.00 each,
2 Challenger ridge tents at list price £49.50 each,
all *less* trade discount at 15 per cent

Sales returns

27 May   Dalesman Products
1 Explorer rucksack invoiced on 5 May was returned because it was damaged; a credit note was issued

Note: VAT at a rate of 10 per cent is to be included on all transactions

You are required to:

(a) Show your calculations for each transaction.
(b) Rule up a sales day book and sales returns day book for the month of May; enter the date, name of customer and amounts of money into the appropriate columns.
(c) Post to the personal and nominal accounts in the ledger.

19.4

M & P Harris have divided their retail business into two departments: China and Cutlery. All items of stock are bought on credit. Their purchases and purchase returns for October were:

6 Oct   Coghlin Supplies
10 china tea sets, list price £12 each, *less* trade discount 20 per cent

14 Oct   Simmonds Services
6 canteens cutlery, list price £30 each, *less* trade discount 25 per cent

16 Oct   Jenson Ltd
6 bone china dinner services, list price £25 each, *less* trade discount 15 per cent

18 Oct   Coghlin Supplies
1 china tea set, invoiced on 6 October, was returned damaged and a credit note was issued

Note: VAT at a rate of 10 per cent is to be included on all transactions.

You are required to:

(a) Rule up appropriate day books to record the above transactions with columns headed:

Date   *Name of supplier*   *Total*   *China*   *Cutlery*   *VAT*

(b) Write up the day books and post to the personal and nominal accounts in the ledger.

19.5

Leisuretime Products are Yorkshire's leading outdoor pursuits specialists. The business is divided into two main departments: Sports Goods and Camping Equipment.

Sales on credit during the month of October were:

Sales

3 Oct   Aire Valley Campers
4 Premier ridge tents at £69.75 each
12 Antler camping stoves at £24.95 each
All *less* trade discount 15 per cent

12 Oct   Arena Centre
6 Glider golf trolleys at £39.95 each,
less trade discount 20 per cent
10 Polywarm sleeping bags at £12.50 each
8 Wanderer camping stoves at £19.25 each
All *less* trade discount 15 per cent

18 Oct   Lakeside Golf Club
3 Masters golf trolleys at £25 each
6 boxes of Elite golf balls at £5.50 a box
All *less* trade discount 20 per cent

Sales returns

24 Oct   Arena Centre
1 Polywarm sleeping bag invoiced on 12 October was returned because it was faulty; a credit note was issued

Note: VAT at a rate of 10 per cent is to be included on all transactions.

You are required to:

(a) Show your calculations for each transaction.
(b) Rule up a sales day book and sales returns day book for the month of October; enter the date, name of customer and amounts of money into the appropriate columns.
(c) Post to the personal and nominal accounts in the ledger.

19.6

City Catering Company supplies the catering trade with a variety of products.

Credit sales during May were as follows:

4 May   Bridge House Motel
         20 sets of wine glasses at £7.50 per set
         4 electric food processors at £90 each
         All *less* 20 per cent trade discount

10 May   Cosy Cafe
         18 china teasets at £12 per set
         less 25 per cent trade discount
         1 microwave oven at £150
         less 10 per cent trade discount
         4 sets of assorted kitchen utensils at £8 per set
         less 20 per cent trade discount

15 May   Sidlow Grange
         100 dinner plates at £1.50 each
         100 side plates at 75p each
         All *less* 20 per cent trade discount

17 May   Bridge House Motel
         4 non-stick frying pans at £15 each
         2 pressure cookers (non-electric) at £25 each
         All *less* 15 per cent trade discount

26 May   Riverside Hotel
         8 Electric toasters at £30 each
         less $33\frac{1}{3}$ per cent trade discount

On 8 May Bridge House Motel returned 2 sets of glasses purchased on 4 May as they were found to be damaged and a full credit was given.

Note: VAT at a rate of 10 per cent is to be included on all transactions.

You are required to:

(a) Rule up appropriate day books to record the above transactions with columns headed:

Date	Customer	Total	Kitchen utensils	Crockery and glass	Electrical appliances	VAT

(b) Write up the day books and post to the personal and nominal accounts in the ledger.

20 Trading and profit and loss accounts and balance sheets

What is the purpose of the trading and profit and loss account?

People set up in business to try and make a profit but if they are not successful they may lose money. To calculate how much profit or loss has been made a *trading and profit and loss account* is prepared. Usually, all businesses prepare trading and profit and loss accounts once a year, although they could be prepared for six months or any other time period required. Their main purpose is to see how profitably the business is being run and to enable the owners to compare the results achieved with those of previous years. They are often referred to as the *final accounts* of a business.

To enable two types of profit to be calculated a trading and profit and loss account is divided into two sections: the trading account (top section) is where we work out the *gross profit*; the profit and loss account (lower section) is where we work out the *net profit*.

Trading account

This is the first of the two *final accounts*, which are normally made out once a year to discover the gross profit of a business.

Gross profit is what the business has gained from the trading activity of buying and selling: it is the difference between *sales* and the *cost of goods sold*. The best explanation of gross profit is:

Sales *less* cost of goods sold = Gross Profit

The trading account, like every other account, must follow the rules of double entry. We cannot debit the trading account unless we credit some other account and we cannot credit the trading account unless we debit another account.

To illustrate this, we will now gradually build up a trading account observing the rules of double entry; to do this we will need the information in the ledger account balances. In business all our sales during the year are collected together in the sales account, the last entry would look like this:

Sales Account

		20-8	£
		31 Dec Balance b/d	24,000

At the end of the accounting period it is closed (leaving it ready to start a new financial year) and the total sales figure is transferred to the trading account, by making a debit entry in the sales account, like this:

Sales Account

20-8		£	20-8		£
31 Dec	Transfer to				
	trading A/c	24,000	31 Dec	Balance b/d	24,000

The corresponding credit entry will be in the trading account, like this:

Trading Account for the year ended 31 December 20-8

		£
	Sales	24,000

All our purchases during the year are collected together in the purchases account, the last entry would look like this:

Purchases Account

20-8		£	
31 Dec	Balance b/d	15,250	

At the end of the accounting period it is closed (leaving it ready to start a new financial year) and the total purchases figure is transferred to the trading account, by making a credit entry in the purchases account, like this:

Purchases Account

20-8		£	20-8		£
			31 Dec	Transfer to	
31 Dec	Balance b/d	15,250		trading A/c	15,250

The corresponding debit entry will be in the Trading Account, like this:

Trading Account for the year ended 31 December 20-8

	£		£
Purchases	15,250	Sales	24,000

We have not yet arrived at the *cost of goods sold*. This is because in real life it would be almost impossible to have sold everything that we had purchased during the year; we would still have some stock remaining at the end of the year. Therefore we must deduct the value of the unsold stock from our purchases to arrive at the *cost of goods sold* figure. To find the value of the unsold goods a stocktaking is carried out at the end of the financial year. 'Stocktaking' means counting every item in stock and then finding its value. Accountants follow certain rules to value stock: in normal circumstances it is valued at cost – that is, the price paid for it. The value of the unsold goods is called the *closing stock* and is deducted from the purchases in the trading account, like this:

Trading Account for the year ended 31 December 20-8

	£		£
Purchases	15,250	Sales	24,000
Less closing stock	2,000		
Cost of goods sold	13,250		

We are now ready to calculate the gross profit – that is: sales £24,000 *less* cost of goods sold £13,250, making a gross profit of: £10,750, the trading account is then completed like this:

Trading Account for the year ended 31 December 20-8

	£		£
Purchases	15,250	Sales	24,000
Less closing stock	2,000		
Cost of goods sold	13,250		
Gross profit c/d	10,750		
	24,000		24,000
		Gross profit b/d	10,750

At this point a stock account is opened and the value of the unsold goods, is placed at the *debit* side, like this:

Stock Account

20-8		£			
31 Dec	Balance b/d	2,000			

The debit balance remains on the stock account until the end of the next trading period. Clearly the *closing stock* at the end of this trading period will become the *opening stock* for the next trading period.

Profit and loss account

Gross profit shows what the business has gained from the buying and selling activity. However, in carrying out this activity many expenses are incurred: such as wages, rent, rates, insurance, telephone, electricity and so on. The profit when all expenses have been taken into consideration is the *net profit*. A good explanation of net profit is:

Gross profit *less* expenses = net profit

As the main source of income comes from trading (buying and selling) the profit and loss account begins with the balance of gross profit from the trading account, like this:

Profit and Loss Account for the year ended 31 December 20-8

Expenses		£
	Gross profit b/d	10,750

Like every other account, the profit and loss account must follow the rules of double entry. In every transfer to the profit and loss account we shall be doing the same sort of closing entry as we did in the trading account, to transfer the balances on the accounts we use.

To illustrate this, we will now gradually build up a profit and loss account observing the rules of double entry; to do this we will need the information in the ledger account balances. In business all expenses incurred during the year are recorded in separate accounts; using a typical wages account as an example, the last entry would look like this:

Wages Account

20-8		£		
31 Dec	Balance b/d	3,200		

At the end of the accounting period it is closed (leaving it ready to start a new financial year) and the total wages figure is transferred to the profit and loss account, by making a credit entry in the wages account, like this:

Wages Account

20-8		£	20-8		£
31 Dec	Balance b/d	3,200	31 Dec	Profit and loss	3,200

The corresponding debit entry will be in the profit and loss account, like this:

Profit and Loss Account for the year ended 31 December 20-8

Expenses	£		£
Wages	3,200	Gross profit b/d	10,750

In the same way, all the remaining expense accounts are closed, leaving them ready to start a new financial year. Each balance is transferred to the profit and loss account by making a credit entry in each expense account, like this:

Rent Account

20-8		£	20-8		£
31 Dec	Balance b/d	850	31 Dec	Profit and loss	850

Telephone Account

20-8		£	20-8		£
31 Dec	Balance b/d	500	31 Dec	Profit and loss	500

Motor Expenses Account

20-8		£	20-8		£
31 Dec	Balance b/d	300	31 Dec	Profit and loss	300

Electricity Account

20-8		£	20-8		£
31 Dec	Balance b/d	650	31 Dec	Profit and loss	650

The corresponding *debit* entry for each expense account will appear in the profit and loss account, like this:

Profit and loss Account for the year ended 31 December 20-8

Expenses	£		£
Wages	3,200	Gross profit b/d	10,750
Rent	850		
Telephone	500		
Motor expenses	300		
Electricity	650		

We are now ready to discover the *net profit*. To calculate the amount of net profit we need to *deduct the total expenses from the gross profit* – that is: gross profit £10,750 *less* total expenses £5,500 making a net profit of £5,250; the profit and loss account is then completed like this:

Profit and loss Account for the year ended 31 December 20-8

Expenses	£		£
Wages	3,200	Gross profit b/d	10,750
Rent	850		
Telephone	500		
Motor expenses	300		
Electricity	650		
Net profit	5,250		
	10,750		10,750

The expenses incurred in running a business are often referred to as the *overheads*. As we have seen, the surplus when the overhead expenses are deducted is called *net* profit. 'Net' means *clear*, and is the true profit after *all* expenses have been met. If the expenses are greater than the gross profit a *net loss* will occur.

Final accounts are always dated for the particular period of time for which profit is being calculated. Normally it is one year, as shown in the examples, but there is nothing to prevent profit being calculated for six months or any other time period.

Because a trading account is always immediately followed by a profit and loss account they are usually shown under one combined heading, like this:

Trading and Profit and Loss Account for the year ended 31 December 20-8

	£		£
Purchases	15,250	Sales	24,000
Less closing stock	2,000		
Cost of goods sold	13,250		
Gross profit c/d	10,750		
	24,000		24,000
Wages	3,200	Gross profit b/d	10,750
Rent	850		
Telephone	500		
Motor expenses	300		
Electricity	650		
Net profit	5,250		
	10,750		10,750

When we have discovered the net profit of the business (shown as a *debit entry* in the profit and loss account) the profit belongs to the owner so a corresponding entry must be made in the owner's capital account. As we have already seen, in Unit 2, the first entry in the capital account is made when the owner introduces capital into the business; on 1 January the capital account would look like this:

Capital Account

		20-8	£
		1 Jan Bank	5,000

At the end of the accounting period the net profit is transferred by making a credit entry in the capital account, like this:

Capital Account

		20-8			£
		1 Jan	Bank		5,000
		31 Dec	Net profit		5,250

Net profit increases capital, but if a loss had been made a debit entry would be needed in the capital account to reduce it. We are now ready to complete the account; to do this we must transfer any drawings to the capital account. Sometimes the owner of a business will take money or goods out of the business for his private use. Whether he takes money or goods, these withdrawals are known in book-keeping as *drawings*. During the year, a record is kept in the drawings account, of all money or goods taken by the owner for personal use. At the end of the financial year the drawings account is totalled and transferred to the capital account. ('Drawings' means 'withdrawals of capital'.) The drawings account would show all the separate amounts drawn by the owner, week by week during the year, but the last entry would look like this:

Drawings Account

20-8		£	
31 Dec	Balance b/d	800	

At the end of the year the drawings account is closed (leaving it ready for next year's entries). The total drawings are transferred to the capital account by making a credit entry in the drawings account, like this:

Drawings Account

20-8		£	20-8		£
31 Dec	Balance b/d	800	31 Dec	Capital account	800

The corresponding debit entry is in the capital account, like this:

Capital Account

20-8		£	20-8		£
31 Dec	Drawings	800	1 Jan	Bank	5,000
			31 Dec	Net profit	5,250

The capital account can now be completed and balanced ready to start a new year, like this:

Capital Account

20-8		£	20-8		£
31 Dec	Drawings	800	1 Jan	Bank	5,000
31 Dec	Balance c/d	9,450	31 Dec	Net profit	5,250
		10,250			10,250
			20-9		
			1 Jan	Balance b/d	9,450

Balance sheet

After the trading and profit and loss account has been prepared some accounts will still remain. These accounts cannot be closed because they must be carried forward into the next trading period. All balances remaining have to be assets, capital or liabilities. All other balances should have been closed off when the trading and profit and loss account was completed. It is the *balances which remain* that are used to prepare a balance sheet. This is usually done on the last day of the trading period to show the financial position at that moment in time.

Balance sheets are **not** part of the double entry system. It is useful to remember that if you see the word *'account'* you will know that it is part of the double entry system and will involve debit and credit entries. If the word *'account'* is not used it is **not** part of the double entry system. For example:

- *Trial Balance* – a list of balances to check if the *records are correct*
- *Balance Sheet* – a list of balances arranged according to whether they are *assets, capital* or *liabilities*.

We will learn the most common method used for small businesses, which is the *traditional style balance sheet* arranged in the *order of permanence*.

Generally before starting to prepare the final accounts, the balances on the accounts are shown in a trial balance. We can now look at William Dyson's trial balance (Figure 20.1) which was drawn up after his first year of trading. His trial balance has been used in the examples shown in this chapter.

Each balance listed in the trial balance is used only once. To illustrate this important rule, the balances already used to prepare the trading and profit and loss account have been ticked.

Trial Balance as at 31 December 20-8

		Dr £	Cr £
✓	Sales		24,000
✓	Purchases	15,250	
✓	Wages	3,200	
✓	Rent	850	
✓	Telephone	500	
✓	Motor expenses	300	
✓	Electricity	650	
	Fixtures and fittings	550	
	Office equipment	1,200	
	Motor vehicle	5,000	
	Debtors	1,050	
	Creditors		850
	Bank	425	
	Cash	75	
	Capital		5,000
	Drawings	800	
		29,850	29,850

Figure 20.1

We can now prepare a balance sheet using the balances that remain and the closing stock (Figure 20.2). The value the of closing stock is **never** included in a trial balance, because the actual amount is not known until after the close of business at the end of the financial year, when the stock of unsold goods must be counted and valued. The closing stock of a business is available to sell in the following year, so we must include this figure as an asset on the balance sheet.

Balance Sheet as at 31 December 20-8

	£	£		£	£
Fixed Assets			Capital at start	5,000	
Fixtures and fittings	550		*Add* net profit	5,250	
Office equipment	1,200			10,250	
Motor vehicle	5,000	6,750	*Less* drawings	800	9,450
Current Assets			*Current Liabilities*		
Closing Stock	2,000		Creditors		850
Debtors	1,050				
Bank	425				
Cash	75	3,550			
		10,300			10,300

Figure 20.2

It is a rule of accounting that balance sheets should be arranged in such a way that anyone reading them can immediately appreciate the important features of a business. For this reason a *traditional style* balance sheet shows items grouped together under various headings. Assets are divided into two sections: *fixed assets* and *current assets*.

Fixed assets

These assets are for continuing use in a business and will be retained over a long period of time. Examples are: land, premises, buildings, plant and machinery, fixtures and fittings, furniture, office equipment and motor vehicles. On a balance sheet fixed assets are listed in order of permanence, with the *longest lasting placed first*. Motor vehicles are placed last because they are usually kept only a few years.

The general rule for a fixed asset is that it would be kept for *more than one year*.

Current assets

Current assets consist of cash and things which the firm intends to turn into cash within a short period of time, including bank balances. The general rule for a current asset is that it will be kept for *less than one year*. Examples are: stock (closing stock at the end of the trading period because it has been bought for resale), debtors (customers who are due to pay their accounts in the near future), cash at bank and cash. On a balance sheet they are listed in *order of permanence for realisation into cash*. Stock is listed first because it is considered to be the most difficult to convert into cash. Debtors are next, as they have promised to pay within one month, cash at bank can easily be obtained by drawing it out, cash is already in cash form.

Liabilities

Liabilities are *debts owed by a business that must be paid sooner or later*. Just as the assets are arranged into two groups it is useful to show the liabilities under three separate headings: capital, long-term liabilities and current liabilities.

Capital

This is the owner's *original investment in the business*. To show how the capital was calculated, full details of the capital account are displayed on the balance sheet, commencing with the capital at the start of a trading period, *adding* the net profit and *deducting* the drawings. This enables anyone looking at the balance sheet to see the *profits* earned in that trading period.

Long-term liabilities

These are usually *formal loans which may be repayable over many years.* Good examples are: loans from a bank, building society, private investor or a finance company. A legal contract is made with the owner of the business stating: the amount of the loan, the terms of repayment and the period of time (number of years). Loans represent amounts of money which do not have to be repaid in the near future. The general rule is: *payable more than twelve months after the balance sheet date.*

Current liabilities

These are debts which will *need to be paid in the near future.* Creditors are a good example as they are due to be paid within one month. Another example would be a bank overdraft as they are intended to be only a short-term facility. Overdrafts are a way of helping a firm to overcome a temporary shortage of cash.

Points to remember

- Trading and profit and loss accounts are prepared to discover the profit or loss of a business during a trading period. Like every other account they follow the rules of double entry. Headings are essential and must clearly state the period of time concerned, it is usually 'for the year ending . . .'.
- Stocks can sometimes present a problem. *Closing stock* at the end of one trading period will clearly be the *opening stock* for the next trading period. When opening stock appears in a trial balance it must be included in the calculation of the *cost of goods sold.*
- Look at it like this: what last year hands over, starts the new year, we then buy more stock which are purchases, then at the end of the year we must carry out a stocktaking to find the value of our closing stock. A trading account which included both stock figures would look like this:

	£
Opening stock	2,500
Add purchases	18,500
	21,000
Less closing stock	1,750
= Cost of goods sold	19,250

- Opening stock will be listed in a trial balance and dated for the first day of the new trading period; closing stock is always given as additional information and **never** included in a trial balance.

Continued

- The surplus when all expenses are deducted from the gross profit is called *net profit*, this means clear profit. A *net loss* will occur if the total expenses are greater than the gross profit.
- A balance sheet is **not** an account. It is a financial statement which lists a firm's assets, capital and liabilities at a given moment in time, usually the end of its trading year. It is prepared after the trading and profit and loss account has been completed, using the balances that remain and the closing stock.
- On a balance sheet, a bank overdraft would be listed under *current liabilities* because money is owing to the bank.
- A balance sheet has five main sections, items in each group are listed, then *totalled.*

There are still many things to learn about final accounts, but we must first practise using our present knowledge by preparing a number of final accounts.

Assignments

20.1

From the following trial balance of Sandra Ramsden, who has been trading for one year, you are required to draw up a trading and profit and loss account and balance sheet for the year ended 31 December 20-6.

Trial Balance as at 31 December 20-6

	Dr £	Cr £
Sales		20,662
Purchases	15,269	
Rent	650	
Insurance	155	
Motor expenses	545	
Wages	2,568	
Equipment	2,850	
Motor Vehicle	1,100	
Debtors	2,350	
Creditors		1,682
Cash at bank	1,864	
Cash in hand	68	
Drawings	925	
Capital at 1 January 20-6		6,000
	28,344	28,344

Closing Stock at 31 December 20-6 was £2,868

20.2

The following trial balance was taken from the books of Michael Seymour after one year's trading. You are required to prepare a trading and profit and loss account and balance sheet for the year ending 31 December 20-7.

Trial Balance as at 31 December 20-7

	Dr	Cr
	£	£
Purchases	14,650	
Sales		18,874
Rates	720	
General expenses	490	
Wages and salaries	3,105	
Motor expenses	382	
Insurance	220	
Premises	7,700	
Fixtures and fittings	1,750	
Motor vehicle	3,900	
Debtors	2,865	
Creditors		1,926
Cash at bank	1,646	
Cash in hand	122	
Drawings	1,250	
Capital at 1 January 20-7		18,000
	38,800	38,800

Stock at 31 December 20-7 was £3,235

20.3

From the following trial balance of Pauline Ellis you are required to prepare a trading and profit and loss account for the year ended 31 May 20-7 and a balance sheet as at that date.

Trial Balance as at 31 May 20-7

	Dr £	Cr £
Capital on 1 June 20-6		20,508
Purchases	23,308	
Sales		27,974
Debtors	3,670	
Creditors		2,018
Stock at 1 June 20-6	2,342	
Rent	760	
Lighting and heating expenses	520	
Salaries and wages	2,950	
Fixtures and fittings	2,500	
Cash at bank	4,438	
Cash in hand	170	
Insurance	280	
Motor vehicles	6,750	
Motor expenses	612	
Drawings	2,200	
	50,500	50,500

Stock at 31 May 20-7 was £5,995

20.4

From the following trial balance of Frederick Allen, you are required to draw up a trading and profit and loss account for the year ending 31 October 20-7 and a balance sheet as at that date.

Trial Balance as at 31 October 20-7

	Dr £	Cr £
Sales		35,650
Purchases	28,452	
Stock at 1 November 20-6	5,425	
Premises	15,000	
Fixtures and fittings	5,600	
Motor vehicles	8,800	
Loan – T Wiseman		6,000
Debtors	4,926	
Creditors		4,124
Rates	970	
Electricity	644	
General expenses	933	
Salaries and wages	3,850	
Insurance	617	
Drawings	2,450	
Bank overdraft		2,326
Cash in hand	338	
Motor expenses	795	
Capital on 1 November 20-6		30,700
	78,800	78,800

Stock at 31 October 20-7 was £4,965

20.5

On 31 March 20-8 the following trial balance was taken from the books of James Conway:

Trial Balance as at 31 March 20-8

	Dr £	Cr £
Capital on 1 April 20-7		38,200
Cash at bank	13,326	
Cash in hand	234	
Debtors	15,808	
Creditors		13,864
Stock at 1 April 20-7	16,940	
Motor van	7,000	
Sales		45,736
Purchases	28,435	
Telephone	672	
Insurance	593	
Premises	12,000	
Rates	764	
Loan – J Graham		5,000
General expenses	316	
Wages	4,800	
Motor expenses	412	
Drawings	1,500	
	102,800	2,800

Stock at 31 March 20-8 was £15,420

You are required to prepare a trading and profit and loss account for the year ended 31 March 20-8 and a balance sheet as at that date.

20.6

David Nicholson is the owner of a textile business. He has completed his trading and profit and loss account for the year ended 31 December 20-2. The following balances remain in his ledger:

	£
Net profit	18,500
Capital at 1 January 20-2	25,750
Drawings	5,000
Debtors	3,475
Creditors	1,025
Motor vehicles	16,500
Office equipment	5,650
Furniture and fittings	3,800
Bank	5,380
Cash	520
Stock at 31 December 20-2	4,950

You are required to:

(a) Prepare a balance sheet as at 31 December 20-2 clearly showing all the items under the appropriate headings.
(b) David Nicholson had taken drawings in 4 equal instalments, by cheque, at the end of each quarter.
   You are required to:
   Write up the drawings account and the capital account, including all relevant dates and transfers, and balance the accounts for the year ended 31 December 20-2.

20.7

Anne Parfitt owns a retail carpet business. After her trading and profit and loss account for the year ended 31 May 20-5 was completed, the following balances remain in her ledger:

	£
Net profit	29,720
Premises	48,000
Motor vehicles	12,750
Equipment	7,500
Debtors	4,318
Creditors	3,804
Cash	572
Loan – Northern Bank	5,000
Capital at 1 June 20-4	45,250
Drawings	7,000
Bank overdraft	1,726
Stock at 31 May 20-5	5,360

You are required to:

(a) Prepare a balance sheet as at 31 May 20-5 clearly showing all the items under the appropriate headings.
(b) Anne Parfitt had taken drawings in 4 equal instalments, by cheque, at the end of each quarter.
   You are required to:
   Write up the drawings account and the capital account, including all relevant dates and transfers, and balance the accounts for the year ended 31 May 20-5.

▪ ⅴ **21** Further trading and profit and loss accounts

In any business where goods are bought and sold it is likely that some will need to be *returned*. Sometimes goods will be returned to suppliers (*returns outwards*) and sometimes goods will be returned to the firm by its customers (*returns inwards*). In our first look at the trading account in Unit 20 returns were not included. This was quite deliberate so that our first set of final accounts would be straightforward.

So that the entries you need to consider are meaningful, William Dyson has continued his business for another year. In Unit 20 we prepared his final accounts after his first year of trading; he started without any stock, so there was closing stock only. For his second year of trading, to 31 December 20-9, both opening and closing stock figures will be used in the calculations. As you will see, last year's closing stock is now included in his trial balance (Figure 21.1).

Remember this important rule: *each balance listed in a trial balance is used once only*. To illustrate this process, look back to the trial balance in Figure 21.1 and tick each item when it is used to prepare the trading and profit and loss account for his second year of trading, to 31 December 20-9.

William Dyson
Trial Balance as at 31 December 20-9

	Dr £	Cr £
Sales		36,000
Purchases	21,500	
Returns inwards	650	
Returns outwards		980
Stock at 1 January 20-9	2,000	
Carriage inwards	320	
Carriage outwards	760	
Discount received		250
Discount allowed	240	
Wages	5,450	
Rent	900	
Telephone	680	
Motor expenses	490	
Electricity	750	
Fixtures and fittings	2,500	
Office equipment	1,350	
Motor vehicle	7,000	
Debtors	3,480	
Creditors		1,602
Bank overdraft		518
Loan from City Bank		2,000
Cash	230	
Capital at 1 January 20-9		9,450
Drawings	2,500	
	50,800	50,800

On 31 December 20-9 closing stock was valued at £3,240

Figure 21.1

Returns inwards

One of the most vital figures in any business is the *net sales*, often referred to as, the *turnover*. The word 'net' means 'clear' and indicates that any returns have been deducted from the sales figure to obtain the *correct turnover*.

Good style presentation of final accounts is essential so that important figures can be seen instantly. To do this, the value of any returns inwards (goods which have been returned by customers) are *deducted* from the sales, in the trading account, like this:

Trading and Profit and Loss Account for the year ended 31 December 20-9

	£
Sales	36,000
Less returns inwards	650
	35,350

Returns outwards

We must now find the accurate *purchases figure* by *deducting* the value of any returns outwards (goods which have been returned to suppliers) from our purchases, in the trading account, like this:

Trading and Profit and Loss Account for the year ended 31 December 20-9

	£		£
Opening stock	2,000	Sales	36,000
Add purchases	21,500	*Less* returns inwards	650
	23,500		35,350
Less returns outwards	980		
	22,520		

Carriage inwards

When goods are bought the cost of transport may be included in the purchase price, or there may be an additional charge. When an extra charge is made for delivery, it increases the cost of the goods being purchased. Although most of the business expenses are included in the profit and loss account, *carriage inwards* is dealt with in the trading account. This is because it is a direct expense incurred bringing goods into the firm and consequently increases the cost of the purchases.

Whenever carriage inwards is charged on goods purchased, a separate record is kept of these costs in the *carriage inwards account*. Because these additional costs have increased the price of the goods purchased, carriage inwards is added in the trading account, like this:

Trading and Profit and Loss Account for the year ended 31 December 20-9

	£		£
Opening stock	2,000	Sales	36,000
Add purchases	21,500	*Less* returns inwards	650
	23,500		35,350
Less returns outwards	980		
	22,520		
Add carriage inwards	320		
	22,840		
Less closing stock	3,240		
Cost of goods sold	19,600		
Gross profit c/d	15,750		
	35,350		35,350
		Gross profit b/d	15,750

Carriage outwards

Carriage outwards are the costs incurred in transporting goods sold to customers. A separate record is kept in the *carriage outwards account* of these expenses. Because these costs are directly related to selling they are *always* entered with the other expenses in the profit and loss account.

Discount allowed

Discount allowed to customers for prompt payment means a firm has agreed to accept less money than was originally owed. This is another *expense* and a record is kept of these expenses in the discount allowed account. Because these costs are directly related to selling they are *always* entered with the other expenses in the profit and loss account.

Discount received

Discount received from suppliers makes more profit. It is added to the gross profit in the profit and loss account along with any other items of income, such as rent received and commission received.

All incomes received are positioned immediately below the gross profit.

We are now ready to discover the *net profit*. As you will see, discount received has been added to the gross profit, then we deduct the total of all expenses to find the amount of net profit, the calculation is:

£16,000 *less* total expenses of £9,270 = a net profit of £6,730.

The profit and loss account is then completed like this:

Trading and Profit and Loss Account for the year ended 31 December 20-9

	£		£
Opening stock	2,000	Sales	36,000
Add purchases	21,500	*Less* returns inwards	650
	23,500		35,350
Less returns outwards	980		
	22,520		
Add carriage inwards	320		
	22,840		
Less closing stock	3,240		
Cost of goods sold	19,600		
Gross profit c/d	15,750		
	35,350		35,350
Carriage outwards	760	Gross profit b/d	15,750
Discount allowed	240	Discount received	250
Wages	5,450		
Rent	900		
Telephone	680		
Motor expenses	490		
Electricity	750		
Net profit	6,730		
	16,000		16,000

The expenses incurred in running a business are often referred to as the *overheads*. As we have seen, the surplus when the overhead expenses are deducted is called *net profit*. This is the true profit after all expenses have been met. A *net loss* will occur if the expenses are greater than the income received.

Final accounts are always dated for the particular period of time for which profit is being calculated. Normally it is one year, but there is nothing to prevent profit being calculated for six months or any other time period.

If you have clearly marked each item on the trial balance when it was used to prepare the trading and profit and loss account, you will see that all the remaining balances are *assets, capital* or *liabilities*. We can now prepare a balance sheet (Figure 21.2) using these balances and the closing stock.

You may need to look back to Unit 20 to see what happens to the accounts which appear in the trading and profit and loss account. At the end

William Dyson
Balance Sheet as at 31 December 20-9

	£	£		£	£
Fixed Assets			Capital at 1 Jan 20-9	9,450	
Fixtures and fittings	2,500		*Add* net profit	6,730	
Office equipment	1,350			16,180	
Motor vehicle	7,000	10,850	*Less* drawings	2,500	13,680
			Long-term liabilities		
Current Assets			Loan from City Bank		2,000
Closing stock	3,240		*Current Liabilities*		
Debtors	3,480		Creditors	1,602	
Cash	230	6,950	Bank overdraft	518	2,120
		17,800			17,800

Figure 21.2

of the financial year all balances on the accounts which are needed to calculate profit are transferred to the trading and profit and loss account. This process of closing accounts (leaving them ready to start a new year) and transferring the balances always follows the rules of double entry.

Other trading account expenses

As we have seen, the cost of *carriage inwards* is an additional expense which increases the cost of the goods purchased. Similarly any costs in incurred in *bringing goods into a saleable condition* may be charged to the trading account. Such costs may include: warehousing, packing, labour or wages costs.

Normally all expenses (except carriage inwards) will appear in the profit and loss section. However, in examination questions you may be required to add part of the cost of any expense to the trading section. This is a typical example:

> *One-quarter of the wages costs are to be charged to the trading account and three-quarters to the profit and loss account.*

To do this, you will need to divide the wages figure by four, to obtain one-quarter. This amount should then be *added* in the trading account, immediately before deducting the closing stock. The remaining three-quarters would be listed with all other expenses in the profit and loss section. A specific instruction will be given in the question if any expense item is to be included in the trading account.

Final accounts in the services sector

So far we have looked at the final accounts for people who are traders, buying and selling goods. However, many firms do not deal in goods, but instead provide services, such as: accountants, doctors, solicitors, hairdressers, insurance brokers and business consultants.

When final accounts are prepared for people who provide services there will not be a trading account, because goods are not bought and sold. Instead a profit and loss account and a balance sheet will be drawn up.

Points to remember

- Carriage inwards and carriage outwards often cause confusion and are frequently included in examination questions. They are both *expenses* and will appear as *debit balances* in their ledger accounts and a trial balance.
- Carriage inwards is the expense of paying for transport when goods are purchased and it *increases the cost of goods*. Although most expenses are included in the profit and loss account, *carriage inwards* is always added to the purchases in the trading account.
- Carriage outwards are the costs involved in *transporting goods sold to customers*; they are always entered with the other expenses in the profit and loss account.
- *Discounts received from suppliers* are shown as income in the profit and loss account along with any other income, such as rent received and commission received. Such incomes *increase profit* and are positioned immediately below the gross profit. Discounts allowed to customers for prompt payment are entered with the other expenses in the profit and loss account.
- *Net profit* is the true profit after all expenses have been met. A *net loss* will occur if the expenses are greater than the income received.
- Many firms do not deal in goods, but instead supply services, such as: accountants and, business consultants. When final accounts are prepared for people who provide services there will not be a trading account, because goods are not bought and sold. Instead a *profit and loss account* and a *balance sheet* will be drawn up.

Assignments

21.1

Ann Bannister extracted the following trial balance from her books on 31 December 20-7:

Trial Balance as at 31 December 20-7

	Dr £	Cr £
Capital on 1 January 20-7		30,200
Debtors	14,950	
Creditors		10,735
Returns inwards	562	
Returns outwards		415
Bank	4,620	
Cash	513	
Stock at 1 January 20-7	21,190	
Rent	1,855	
Wages and salaries	9,890	
Carriage outwards	251	
Insurance	365	
Carriage inwards	204	
Sales		98,650
Purchases	76,990	
Motor vehicle	5,500	
Motor expenses	932	
Furniture and fittings	4,420	
Drawings	2,330	
Loan – D Conway		5,000
General expenses	428	
	145,000	145,000

Stock at 31 December 20-7 was £22,560

You are required to prepare a trading and profit and loss account and balance sheet for the year ended 31 December 20-7.

21.2

David Allen is the owner of an electrical business. On 30 September 20-7 the following trial balance was taken from his books:

Trial Balance as at 30 September 20-7

	Dr £	Cr £
Sales		69,480
Purchases	45,612	
Stock at 1 October 20-6	9,842	
Salaries and wages	7,838	
Insurance	556	
Returns inwards	872	
Returns outwards		684
Rent and rates	740	
Carriage inwards	485	
Carriage outwards	414	
Motor expenses	526	
Discount received		452
Discount allowed	322	
Motor vehicles	7,500	
Fixtures and fittings	2,900	
Drawings	2,500	
Debtors	10,765	
Creditors		8,984
Bank	5,628	
Capital on 1 October 20-6		16,900
	96,500	96,500

Stock at 30 September 20-7 was £8,975

You are required to prepare a trading and profit and loss account for the year ended 30 September 20-7, together with a balance sheet as at that date.

21.3

John Roberts is a retail trader. On 30 April 20-5 the following trial balance was taken from his books:

Trial Balance as at 30 April 20-5

	Dr £	Cr £
Capital on 1 May 20-4		24,640
Furniture and equipment	9,400	
Sales		46,800
Postage and stationery	1,680	
Returns inwards	1,320	
Rates	760	
Insurance	450	
Wages and salaries	7,480	
Purchases	27,510	
Drawings	5,000	
Trade creditors		2,580
Carriage inwards	270	
Cash	180	
Bank overdraft		3,480
Sundry expenses	430	
Stock at 1 May 20-4	6,560	
Loan from City Bank		3,000
Freehold premises	16,500	
Trade debtors	2,960	
	80,500	80,500

Stock at 30 April 20-5 was valued at £6,740

You are required to prepare a trading and profit and loss account for the year ended 30 April 20-5, together with a balance sheet as at that date.

21.4

On 31 December 20-6 the following trial balance was taken from the books of James Giles:

Trial Balance as at 31 December 20-6

	Dr £	Cr £
Capital on 1 January 20-6		25,090
Equipment	6,000	
Furniture and fittings	3,700	
Sales		36,000
Purchases	27,500	
Drawings	4,800	
Carriage outwards	490	
Creditors		5,980
Sundry expenses	322	
Cash	170	
Bank	3,792	
Returns outwards		1,250
Carriage inwards	430	
Wages	5,880	
Printing and stationery	390	
Debtors	9,700	
Rent	550	
Insurance	226	
Commissions received		480
Stock at 1 January 20-6	4,850	
	68,800	68,800

Stock on 31 December 20-6 was valued at £6,500

You are required to prepare a trading and profit and loss account for the year ended 31 December 20-6, and a balance sheet as at that date.

21.5

Nicholas Davidson owns a small business. On 30 September 20-7 the following trial balance was taken from his books:

Trial Balance as at 30 September 20-7

	Dr £	Cr £
Salaries	8,250	
Rent and rates	1,500	
Cash	120	
Bank overdraft		2,890
Debtors	8,810	
Creditors		5,650
Returns inwards	580	
Sundry expenses	256	
Stock at 1 October 20-6	5,995	
Carriage outwards	397	
Discounts received		842
Motor vehicles	9,400	
Insurance	564	
Telephone	290	
Sales		38,800
Purchases	28,640	
Capital on 1 October 20-6		25,218
Vehicle expenses	768	
Fixtures and fittings	8,500	
Drawings	4,330	
Loan from City Bank		5,000
	78,400	78,400

Stock at 30 September 20-7 was £6,870

You are required to prepare a trading and profit and loss account for the year ended 30 September 20-7, and a balance sheet as at that date.

21.6

Brian Stone, a sole trader, extracted the following trial balance from his books at the close of business on 31 October 20-7:

Trial Balance as at 31 October 20-7

	Dr £	Cr £
Freehold land and buildings	25,000	
Motor van	3,500	
Purchases	62,880	
Sales		84,600
Bank	2,990	
Cash	520	
Stock at 1 November 20-6	4,740	
Debtors	7,500	
Creditors		4,950
Carriage inwards	675	
Carriage outwards	890	
Motor expenses	465	
Rates	750	
Sundry expenses	390	
Sales returns	820	
Drawings	3,500	
Stationery and printing	376	
Purchase returns		982
Discounts allowed	246	
Discounts received		378
Wages and salaries	9,058	
Capital at 1 November 20-6		33,390
	124,300	124,300

Stock at 31 October 20-7 was valued at £7,650

You are required to prepare a trading and profit and loss account for the year ended 31 October 20-7, and a balance sheet as at that date.

☑ **22** Calculating depreciation for fixed assets

What is depreciation?

Everyone knows how quickly motor vehicles decrease in value; this loss in value is known as *depreciation.*

Fixed assets are those held for long-term use in a business, but that does not mean they are kept forever. Some fixed assets, such as buildings, may have very long lives, while others such as motor vehicles, are regularly replaced.

Most fixed assets will decrease in value over their useful lifetime. *Depreciation* is the name given to this loss in value.

Causes of depreciation

- *Physical deterioration*   Caused by *wear and tear* when in normal use
- *Obsolescence*   Caused by the asset becoming *obsolete* or *out of date* owing to new technology or improved methods
- *Inadequacy*   Caused by growth or changes in the size of a business which makes the asset *incapable of achieving increased productivity.*

Balance sheet value of fixed assets

Some fixed assets, such as machinery, equipment and motor vehicles, are in constant use over a period of time and consequently their value will decrease. The balance sheet of a business summarises its financial position and must show assets at their *actual value.* In order to determine the correct value of a fixed asset any reduction in value should be taken into consideration, otherwise the balance sheet would not show the true financial position.

For example, a new motor van bought this year may cost £14,000. By next year it will be worth less, probably around £12,000 and in five years' time it will be worth a fraction of its original cost. We cannot keep the motor van on our books valued at £14,000 down the years. Every year we *depreciate it by a fair amount* depending on our estimate of its fall in value.

Depreciation can be defined as part of the cost of a fixed asset which is *used up* during its period of use. By calculating and deducting an estimated amount for depreciation each year, a business can effectively spread the cost of a fixed asset over its expected useful life.

Depreciation is an *expense of production* and is charged to the profit and loss account in the same way as such items as wages, rent, insurance and so on.

Calculating depreciation involves three important factors:

(1) *cost* of the asset
(2) anticipated *life*
(3) *disposal value.*

The *cost* of the asset is the price paid at the time it is purchased. The *anticipated* life is an estimate of the number of years it will be kept by the business. The *disposal value* is an estimate of its value at the end of its useful life to the business. *Disposal value* is also known as *residual value.* This forecast of its useful life is usually based upon a firm's previous experience of similar types of fixed assets.

Methods of calculating depreciation

There are several ways of calculating depreciation, and the method chosen will normally depend upon the type of fixed asset. The two main methods are: the *straight line method* and the *reducing balance method.*

Straight line method

With this method the cost of the fixed asset, *less* any estimated disposal value, is divided equally by the number of years' use.

$$\text{Amount of annual depreciation} = \frac{\text{original cost} - \text{disposal value}}{\text{number of years' use}}$$

Suppose a motor vehicle cost £15,000; it is anticipated it will be kept for three years and at the end of that time it will have an estimated disposal value of £6,000.

This would be expressed as:

Cost £15,000 *less* £6,000 (disposal value) = £9,000 divided by 3 = £3,000

this is the depreciation charge for each of the 3 years.

Or, expressed as a fraction:

$$\text{Annual depreciation} = \frac{£15,000 - £6,000}{3} = £3,000$$

The calculations would be like this:

	£
Cost	15,000
First year depreciation	3,000
	12,000
Second year depreciation	3,000
	9,000
Third year depreciation	3,000
Disposal value	6,000

With this method, the *depreciation charge is the same each year*. It is also known as the *equal instalment method*, because it results in the same amount of depreciation being charged each year.

Reducing balance method

By this method a *fixed percentage rate for depreciation* is deducted from the cost in the first year. In the second and later years the same percentage is taken, but of the reduced balance (cost *less* depreciation already charged). This method is also known as the *diminishing balance method*.

Suppose a machine is bought costing £10,000 and depreciation is to be charged at 20 per cent per annum; the calculations for the first three years would be:

	£
Cost	10,000
First year: depreciation (20 per cent of £10,000)	2,000
	8,000
Second year: depreciation (20 per cent of £8,000)	1,600
	6,400
Third year: depreciation (20 per cent of £6,400)	1,280
	5,120

Using this method, much larger amounts are charged in the early years of the assets life, and much less during the later years. This is often considered to be an advantage because a business enjoys greater efficiency from an asset in its early years. *Repair and maintenance costs* are greater in the later years and these higher costs are then offset by a lower depreciation charge.

It is important to realise that depreciation has nothing to do with putting aside money to replace an asset: it is merely a way of *spreading the cost* over a period of time.

Depreciation charge for part of a year

Until now we have been concerned only with calculations of depreciation on fixed assets which have been in a business for a complete financial year. In practice, assets may be bought or sold at any time during the year. When an asset is purchased or sold during a business's financial year, we must consider how much depreciation is to be charged for the year in which it is purchased or sold. The normal procedure is to provide for a *full year's depreciation in the year of purchase*, and make *no charge for depreciation in the year of sale*.

In examinations you should read the question carefully because you may be expected to calculate the depreciation charge for part of a year. For example, any of the following may happen:

(1) No depreciation is charged during year of purchase or sale
(2) Depreciation is to be calculated according to number of months owned by business.

Worked examination question

This is a typical question:

A business which prepares its accounts annually to 31 December purchased a new motor van on 1 July 20-4 costing £15,000.

It is anticipated that the van will be kept for four years and depreciation is to be calculated at 40 per cent on the reducing balance method. In the first year, depreciation is to be calculated according to the number of months owned.

You are required to show the calculations for depreciation for each year, from the year of purchase to the year ending 31 December 20-7.

Solution
The motor van was purchased on 1 July 20-4. The charge for depreciation for the year ending 31 December 20-4 should be for six months (number of months of ownership). This is calculated as follows:

40 per cent of £15,000 is £6,000, divided by 12 = £500 per month

This figure is then multiplied by six (the number of months owned)

$$6 \times £500 = £3,000$$

This is the depreciation charge for the first year, 20-4:

	£
Cost	15,000
20-4 depreciation (40 per cent for six months)	3,000
	12,000
20-5 depreciation (40 per cent of £12,000)	4,800
	7,200
20-6 depreciation (40 per cent of £7,200)	2,880
	4,320
20-7 depreciation (40 per cent of £4,320)	1,728
	2,592

Points to remember

- Depreciation means a *reduction in value*, due usually to normal wear and tear. The purpose of depreciation is to spread the cost of the asset over its expected useful life. By calculating an amount for depreciation each year these losses are spread over the lifetime of the asset. It is also important to recognise that assets must be correctly valued on a balance sheet; if we do otherwise the balance sheet will not give a true and fair view of the assets. On a balance sheet the assets are shown at cost *less* amounts of depreciation charged to date.
- *Straight line method* of depreciation reduces the original cost of the asset by the same amount each year. This is expressed as: the original cost, *less* any disposal value, divided by the number of years use.
- *Reducing balance method* is calculated by a fixed percentage rate each year. This percentage rate is deducted from the cost in the first year. In the second and later years the same percentage is taken, but of the reduced balance (cost *less* depreciation already charged). This method is also known as the diminishing balance method. This method gives a higher depreciation charge in the early years of the asset's life, and less in the later years. This is sometimes an advantage, as the cost of repairs often increases towards the end of an asset's expected working life.

Assignments

All calculations to the nearest pound

22.1
A packing machine was purchased for £20,000. The business plans to use it for five years, and it is estimated that at the end of that time it will have a disposal value of £5,000. Depreciation is to be calculated by the straight line method.

You are required to calculate the amount of depreciation for each of the five years.

22.2
John Preston purchased a delivery van on 1 January 20-7 costing £8,000. He anticipated he would keep it for three years, it would then be sold for an estimated figure of £2,744. He decided to calculate depreciation at the rate of 30 per cent per annum, by the reducing balance method.

You are required to calculate the depreciation charges for each of the three years.

22.3

Michael Johnson purchased a new fork-lift machine costing £10,500. He expects to keep it for four years and at the end of that time its residual value is estimated to be £2,520.

You are required to show your calculations for depreciation for each of the four years using:

(a) Straight line method.
(b) Reducing balance method at a rate of 30 per cent.

22.4

Ross Brothers purchased a new machine in July 20-7 costing £3,000. It is estimated it will have a useful life of five years, and a disposal value at the end of this time of £712. Accounts are prepared to 31 December each year and a full year's depreciation is provided in the year of purchase.

You are required to show your calculations for depreciation for each of the five years using:

(a) Straight line method.
(b) Reducing balance method at a rate of 25 per cent.

22.5

D Armstrong's accounts are prepared to 31 December each year. He provides depreciation for his motor vehicles at a rate of 20 per cent per annum using the diminishing balance method.

On 1 January 20-5 Armstrong bought a motor van costing £6,500. On 1 April 20-6 Armstrong purchased a further delivery van costing £7,500. In the year of purchase depreciation is to be calculated according to the number of months owned.

You are required to show your calculations for depreciation, for each vehicle, for the years to 31 December 20-7.

22.6

K Gillow prepares his accounts annually to 30 June. He depreciates all his machinery at a rate of 30 per cent per annum on the reducing balance method. Details of the machines and the dates of purchase are as follows:

Machine type	Date of purchase	Cost-(£)
'M'	1 August 20-5	3,000
'D'	1 January 20-6	4,000
'W'	1 June 20-6	5,000
'B'	1 March 20-7	6,000

In the year of purchase depreciation is to be calculated according to the number of months owned.

You are required to show your calculations of depreciation, for each machine, for each year, from the year of purchase to the year ending 30 June 20-8.

☑ **23** Double entry system for depreciation

The accounting records are exactly the same for both the straight line method and the reducing balance method of calculating depreciation. It is the *amounts* which vary according to the method chosen.

It was illustrated in Unit 22 that as an asset decreases in value we reduce its book valuation to correspond with our estimate of its loss in value. Assets must be shown on a balance sheet at a true and fair value and the loss suffered must be charged against the profits. The depreciation charged each year is an expense and is set against the profits earned by the business at the end of the financial year. There are two methods of recording depreciation in the double entry accounts.

Method 1 – direct depreciation

With this method, the depreciation is shown in the fixed asset account reducing its value each year and in a depreciation expense account.

This is a typical example: on 1 January 20-6 a firm bought a new motor van costing £16,000 paying by cheque. It is to be depreciated at a rate of 25 per cent per annum using the reducing balance method. The double entry accounts for the year ending 31 December 20-6 would appear like this, a credit entry in the motor van account:

Motor Van Account

20-6		£	20-6		£
1 Jan	Bank	16,000.00	31 Dec	Depreciation	4,000.00
			31 Dec	Balance c/d	12,000.00
		16,000.00			16,000.00
20-7					
1 Jan	Balance b/d	12,000.00			

A corresponding debit entry will be made in the depreciation account, like this:

Depreciation Account

20-6	£	
31 Dec Motor van	4,000.00	

Because depreciation is an *expense* it will need to be charged to the profit and loss account. At the end of the accounting period the depreciation account is closed (leaving it ready to start a new financial year) and the amount of depreciation is transferred to the profit and loss account by making a *credit* entry, like this:

Depreciation Account

20-6	£	20-6	£
31 Dec Motor van	4,000.00	31 Dec Profit and loss	4,000.00

A corresponding debit entry will appear in the profit and loss account, like this:

Profit and Loss Account for the year ended 31 December 20-6

Expenses	£	
Depreciation – motor van	4,000.00	

On the balance sheet the fixed asset is shown at its original cost, *less* the depreciation charge, like this:

Balance Sheet as at 31 December 20-6

		£	
Fixed Assets			
Motor van	16,000		
Less depreciation	4,000	12,000.00	

In subsequent years the value of the asset continues to decrease in the ledger account and appears on the balance sheet at the *reduced* figure.

Using the same example, the entries you need to consider are now completed in the ledger accounts for the first three years:

Motor Van Account

20-6		£	20-6		£
1 Jan	Bank	16,000.00	31 Dec	Depreciation	4,000.00
			31 Dec	Balance c/d	12,000.00
		16,000.00			16,000.00
20-7			20-7		
1 Jan	Balance b/d	12,000.00	31 Dec	Depreciation	3,000.00
			31 Dec	Balance c/d	9,000.00
		12,000.00			12,000.00
20-8			20-8		
1 Jan	Balance b/d	9,000.00	31 Dec	Depreciation	2,250.00
			31 Dec	Balance c/d	6,750.00
		9,000.00			9,000.00
20-9					
1 Jan	Balance b/d	6,750.00			

Depreciation Account

20-6		£	20-6		£
31 Dec	Motor van	4,000.00	31 Dec	Profit and loss	4,000.00
20-7			20-7		
31 Dec	Motor van	3,000.00	31 Dec	Profit and loss	3,000.00
20-8			20-8		
31 Dec	Motor van	2,250.00	31 Dec	Profit and loss	2,250.00

The entries in the profit and loss accounts for the three years would look like this:

Profit and Loss Account for the year ended 31 December 20-6

Expenses	£	
Depreciation – motor van	4,000.00	

Profit and Loss Account for the year ended 31 December 20-7

Expenses	£	
Depreciation – motor van	3,000.00	

Profit and Loss Account for the year ended 31 December 20-8

Expenses	£	
Depreciation – motor van	2,250.00	

It is important to remember that with this method, the motor van is shown at its original cost on the balance sheet in the *first year only*, and in later years at its *reduced* value, as shown in the ledger account, like this:

Balance Sheet as at 31 December 20-6

		£	
Fixed Assets			
Motor van	16,000		
Less			
depreciation	4,000	12,000.00	

Balance Sheet as at 31 December 20-7

		£	
Fixed Assets			
Motor van	12,000		
Less			
depreciation	3,000	9,000.00	

Balance Sheet as at 31 December 20-8

		£	
Fixed Assets			
Motor van	9,000		
Less			
depreciation	2,250	6,750.00	

Method 2 – providing for depreciation (modern method)

With this method, the asset account remains at its original cost and no entries for depreciation are made in the asset account. Instead the amount of depreciation is accumulated in a separate *provision for depreciation account*. As each annual charge is credited to the provision for depreciation account, the balance on that account increases to equal the accumulated depreciation which is shown on the balance sheet each year.

This method has been used by most limited companies for many years. This is because company balance sheets show fixed assets at cost *less* total depreciation to date. The double entry is:

> *Debit* the profit and loss account
> *Credit* the provision for depreciation account.

Using the same example, we can show the double entry accounts using the now preferred modern method.

On 1 January 20-6 a firm bought a new motor van costing £16,000. It is to be depreciated at a rate of 25 per cent per annum using the reducing balance method. The double entry accounts for the year ending 31 December 20-6 would appear like this:

Motor Van Account

20-6		£			
1 Jan	Bank	16,000.00			

Provision for Depreciation Account – Motor Van

20-6		£	20-6		£
31 Dec	Balance c/d	4,000.00	31 Dec	Profit and loss	4,000.00
20-7			20-7		
31 Dec	Balance c/d	7,000.00	1 Jan	Balance b/d	4,000.00
			31 Dec	Profit and loss	3,000.00
		7,000.00			7,000.00
20-8			20-8		
31 Dec	Balance c/d	9,250.00	1 Jan	Balance b/d	7,000.00
			31 Dec	Profit and loss	2,250.00
		9,250.00			9,250.00
20-9			20-9		
			1 Jan	Balance b/d	9,250.00

Entries in the relevant profit and loss accounts for the three years would look like this:

Profit and Loss Account for the year ended 31 December 20-6

Expenses	£		
Depreciation (motor van)	4,000.00		

Profit and Loss Account for the year ended 31 December 20-7

Expenses	£	
Depreciation (motor van)	3,000.00	

Profit and Loss Account for the year ended 31 December 20-8

Expenses	£	
Depreciation (motor van)	2,250.00	

It is important to remember that, with this method, the motor van is shown on the balance sheet each year at its *original cost less depreciation to date,* like this:

Balance Sheet as at 31 December 20-6

		£	
Fixed Assets			
Motor van	16,000		
Less			
depreciation	4,000	12,000.00	

Balance Sheet as at 31 December 20-7

		£	
Fixed Assets			
Motor van	16,000		
Less			
depreciation			
to date . . .	7,000	9,000.00	

Balance Sheet as at 31 December 20-8

		£	
Fixed Assets			
Motor van	16,000		
Less			
depreciation			
to date . . .	9,250	6,750.00	

A balance sheet should always represent a true and fair view; with this method, the fixed asset is shown at its realistic value. This value is called its *net book value*. It is usual to keep a separate provision account for each type of fixed asset.

One aspect of this method of accounting for depreciation that often causes problems to students is the name '*provision for depreciation account*'. It gives an impression that money has actually been set aside which can be used to purchase a replacement for the fixed asset when its working life is over. This is a mistaken impression. The provision for depreciation account is simply an account in which the *amount of depreciation written off an asset is accumulated each year*. The actual value of the asset at any given moment is found by *deducting* the depreciation to date from the original cost.

Disposal of fixed assets

When a fixed asset is sold it is unlikely that it will realise a figure exactly equal to its value in the accounts. The annual charge made for depreciation is an *estimate* of its fall in value during each year's use by a business. Only when a fixed asset is scrapped or sold will the true accuracy of the estimates be determined.

If an asset is sold for more than its net book value, we say there is a *profit on disposal*. Similarly an asset may be sold for less than its net book value, in which case we say there is a *loss on disposal*. In fact, a profit on disposal is not really a profit, it simply means we have overestimated the amount of depreciation to be written off. A loss on disposal simply means we have underestimated the amount of depreciation to be written off.

Look at this example: on 1 February 20-9 the motor van was sold for £7,000. The net book value of the motor van is £6,750, this would result in a profit on the sale of £250. On the sale of the motor van the following entries are needed:

(1) Open a motor van disposals account, make *a debit* entry with the original cost price of the asset, namely £16,000:

Disposal Account – Motor Van

20-9		£		
1 Feb	Motor van	16,000.00		

The corresponding *credit* entry is in the original motor van account which was opened when the vehicle was purchased:

Motor Van Account

20-6		£	20-9		£
1 Jan	Bank	16,000.00	1 Feb	Disposal a/c	16,000.00

(2) Next we need a *debit* entry in the provision for depreciation account to transfer the accumulated depreciation to the disposal account:

Provision for Depreciation Account – Motor Van

20-9		£	20-9		£
1 Feb	Disposal a/c	9,250.00	1 Jan	Balance b/d	9,250.00

The corresponding *credit* entry is in the disposal account:

Disposal Account – Motor Van

20-9		£	20-9		£
1 Feb	Motor van	16,000.00	1 Feb	Prov depreciation	9,250.00

(3) Next we need a *debit* entry in the bank account for the amount received from the sale of the vehicle:

Cash Book – (Bank column)

20-9		£			
1 Feb	Motor van	7,000.00			

The corresponding *credit* entry for the remittance is in the disposal account:

Disposal Account – Motor Van

20-9		£	20-9		£
1 Feb	Motor van	16,000.00	1 Feb	Prov depreciation	9,250.00
			1 Feb	Bank	7,000.00

When a fixed asset is *overdepreciated* and sold for more than the estimated disposal value, this profit will be transferred, at the end of the financial year, to the profit and loss account.

Now we can look at the completed entries, showing the transfer at the end of the financial year:

(4) A *debit* entry in the disposal account, like this:

Disposal Account – Motor Van

20-9		£	20-9		£
1 Feb	Motor van	16,000.00	1 Feb	Prov	
31 Dec	Profit and loss	250.00		depreciation	9,250.00
			1 Feb	Bank	7,000.00
		16,250.00			16,250.00

The corresponding *credit* entry will appear in the profit and loss account, like this:

Profit and Loss Account for the year ended 31 December 20-9

	£
Profit on sale of van	250.00

Now we can look at an example of a fixed asset which is *underdepreciated* and sold for less than the estimated disposal value. Using the same example if, instead of being sold at a profit, the motor van had been sold for £6,000, this would result in a loss on the sale of £750. Now look at the accounting entries:

A *credit* entry in the disposal account, like this:

Disposal Account – Motor Van

20-9		£	20-9		£
1 Feb	Motor van	16,000.00	1 Feb	Prov	
				depreciation	9,250.00
			1 Feb	Bank	6,000.00
			31 Dec	Profit and loss	750.00
		16,000.00			16,000.00

A corresponding *debit* entry in the profit and loss account, like this:

Profit and Loss Account for the year ended 31 December 20-9

Expenses	£	
Loss on sale of van	750.00	

A disposal account is a *collecting together* account, which effectively brings together all the information relevant to the disposal of a fixed asset.

Points to remember

- The two main ways of calculating depreciation are: *straight line method* and *reducing balance method.* Whichever method is used, or requested in examinations, the double entry records are the same, it being the *amounts* which vary according to the method used.
- Depreciation is an *expense* and is charged to the profit and loss account. The cost of fixed assets is debited to the relevant ledger accounts. The annual depreciation is credited, either to the same account, or – as is now more likely – to a separate *provision for depreciation account.* It is usual to keep a separate provision account for each fixed asset.
- As each annual charge is credited to the provision account, the balance on that account increases to equal the accumulated depreciation. On each year's balance sheet the fixed asset is shown at *cost price, less* the accumulated depreciation to date.
- When a fixed asset is sold, both its cost and its accumulated depreciation are removed from their respective ledger accounts and transferred into a *fixed asset disposals account.*

Assignments

23.1
Graham Dyson purchased machinery for £3,000 in April 20-4. It is expected to have an effective working life of five years and its estimated disposal value at the end of this period is £712.

You are required to show the machinery and the provision for depreciation accounts for the five years. Depreciation is to be calculated at a rate of 25 per cent per annum on the reducing balance method. Accounts are prepared annually to 31 December and a full year's depreciation is provided in the year of purchase.

23.2

David Allen purchased a vehicle costing £23,000 on 1 January 20-3. Its useful life is anticipated to be five years. At the end of this time it is estimated to be worth £3,000. A provision for depreciation is to be established and depreciation charges calculated on the fixed instalment method. Accounts are prepared to 31 December each year.

You are required to:

(a) Prepare the vehicle account and the provision for depreciation account for the five years to 31 December 20-7.
(b) Show the balance sheet entry at the end of each year.

23.3

Brian Tate purchased machinery costing £25,000 in March 20-5. It is the firm's policy to depreciate machinery by direct depreciation on the machinery account, using the reducing balance method at a rate of 20 per cent per annum. A full year's depreciation is charged in the year of purchase and the financial year ends on 30 September.

Your are required to:

(a) Show the entries for three years, 20-5, 20-6 and 20-7, on the machinery account and the depreciation account.
(b) Show the entries for three years, 20-5, 20-6 and 20-7, in the profit and loss account and the balance sheet.

23.4

James Clayton purchased a motor van on 1 June 20-5 costing £10,800, paying by cheque. It was estimated he would keep it for three years, providing depreciation at a rate of $33\frac{1}{3}$ per cent per annum by the diminishing balance method. On 1 June 20-8 the van was sold for £3,000 cash. Final accounts are prepared to 31 May each year.

(a) You are required to write up for the years 20-5, 20-6, 20-7, 20-8 and 20-9:
    (i) Motor van account.
    (ii) Provision for depreciation account.
    (iii) Disposal account.
(b) Show the relevant extract entries in the profit and loss accounts.
(c) Show the relevant extract entries of the balance sheets.

23.5

William Evans is a sole trader. His financial year ends on 31 December each year. On 4 January 20-5 he purchased machinery costing £15,500, paying by cheque. Evans plans to use the machinery for four years and estimates that at the end of that time its residual value will be £3,000.

A provision for depreciation was established and depreciation was calculated on the fixed instalment method. On 3 January 20-9 the machinery was sold for £3,250.

You are required to draw up for the years 20-5, 20-6, 20-7, 20-8 and 20-9:

(a) Machinery account.
(b) Provision for depreciation account.
(c) Disposal account.
(d) The relevant extracts for each year in the profit and loss account and the balance sheet.

23.6
(i) What is meant by depreciation and why is it important for a business to provide for depreciation?
(ii) A Swain is a haulage contractor. On 1 January 20-6 he purchased three tipper lorries for £4,800 each. Mr Swain estimated that his lorries would have an effective working life of five years with a disposal value of £300 each. The straight line method of depreciation is to be used. The financial year ends on 31 December. One of the lorries kept breaking down and was sold on 1 January 20-8 for £2,500.

You are required to show the relevant entries for the years 20-6, 20-7 and 20-8 in the following ledger accounts:

(a) Lorries.
(b) Lorries disposal.
(c) Provision for depreciation on lorries.

23.7
The financial year end of Hodgson (Builders Merchants) Ltd is 31 December. The company's policy is to depreciate its motor vans at 20 per cent per annum, using the straight line method, and to calculate a full year's depreciation on the assets in existence at the end of the financial year, regardless of when they were purchased or sold. The company's vans were purchased and sold as follows:

			£
1 January 19-9	Purchased	AB 101 T	2,500
1 July 20-0	Purchased	CD 202 V	3,000
31 March 20-1	Purchased	EF 303 W	2,000
31 March 20-1	Sold	AB 101 T	1,000
1 April 20-2	Purchased	GH 404 X	3,500
31 August 20-2	Sold	CD 202 V	2,000

(a) You are required to draw up for the years 19-9, 20-0, 20-1 and 20-2:
    (i) Motor van account.
    (ii) Provision for depreciation of motor vans account.
    (iii) Disposal of motor vans account.
(b) Extracts of the profit and loss accounts.
(c) Extracts of the balance sheets.

■ ⊻ **24** Bad debts and provision for bad and doubtful debts

In business, most transactions are on a *credit basis*. This means that the goods or services are received immediately but payment is made at a later date. Credit is not usually given to customers until references from other suppliers have been obtained regarding their ability to pay their debts promptly.

Bad debts

A debtor is a person who *owes a firm money*. A debtor who cannot or will not pay his debts is known as a *bad debtor* and the amount owing is referred to as a *bad debt*. Once it is discovered that a debt is never going to be collected, the account can no longer be regarded as an asset to the business.

Usually many attempts will have been made in an effort to recover the outstanding amount. However, regardless of the circumstances, if a debtor cannot pay what is owed it is a *business loss*, and must be treated in the same way as other losses and expenses. There are three possibilities:

(1) a debt may be entirely bad
(2) a debt may be partially bad (some part payment is received)
(3) a debt written off may eventually be recovered.

A debt which is entirely bad

Consider a typical example. Edward Hemingway is a debtor for the sum of £95. On 8 July 20–7 he is declared bankrupt and we are informed the amount owing will not be paid. It is decided to write off the amount owing as a bad debt. At the beginning of July, Edward Hemingway's account in the sales ledger would look like this:

Edward Hemingway Account

20-7		£		
1 Jul	Balance b/d	95.00		

To write off this debt, two entries are required. A *debit* entry in a bad debts account, like this:

Bad Debts Account

20-7		£			
8 Jul	E. Hemingway	95.00			

A corresponding *credit* entry to close Edward Hemingway's account, like this:

Edward Hemingway Account

20-7		£	20–7		£
1 Jul	Balance b/d	95.00	8 Jul	Bad debts a/c	95.00

Note that the debtor's account would be ruled off and clearly marked in red pen **BAD DEBTOR** to prevent any further credit being made available.

A bad debts account is a *collecting together* account which brings together all bad debts incurred during a financial year. Only at the end of the financial year is the bad debts account totalled and the balance transferred to the profit and loss account.

At the end of the accounting period the bad debts account is closed (leaving it ready to start a new financial year) and the balance is transferred to the profit and loss account by making a *credit entry*, like this:

Bad Debts Account

20-7		£	20-7		£
8 Jul	E. Hemingway	95.00	31 Dec	Profit and loss	95.00

A corresponding *debit* entry will appear in the profit and loss account, like this:

Profit and Loss Account for the year ended 31 December 20-7

Expenses	£		
Bad debts	95.00		

A debt which is partially bad

Occasionally a debtor comes to an arrangement to repay only part of the debt. This type of voluntary agreement to settle a debt by paying only a portion of the amount owed is called a '*composition with the creditors*'. Sometimes a debtor may go into voluntary liquidation or be declared bankrupt and his assets sold for the benefit of the creditors. In these circumstances the money received would be debited in the bank or cash account, the unpaid portion would be written off to the bad debts account. This is a typical example of a debt which is partially bad. Brian Forbes who owes the firm £268 has been declared bankrupt. On 20 August 20-7 a cheque for 50 pence in the pound is received in full settlement of the debt. At the beginning of August, Brian Forbes' account in the sales ledger would look like this:

Brian Forbes Account

20-7		£			
1 Aug	Balance b/d	268.00			

On 20 August a cheque for £134 is received. This would need a *debit* entry in the bank account, like this:

Bank Account

20-7		£			
20 Aug	Brian Forbes	134.00			

The *credit* entry would be in Brian Forbes' account, like this:

Brian Forbes Account

20-7		£	20-7		£
1 Aug	Balance b/d	268.00	20 Aug	Bank	134.00

Only the balance remaining on Brian Forbes' account of £134 is to be written off as a bad debt. A *debit* entry is made in the bad debts account, like this:

Bad Debts Account

20-7		£			
20 Aug	Brian Forbes	134.00			

A corresponding *credit* entry is made to close Brian Forbes' account, like this:

Brian Forbes Account

20-7		£	20-7		£
1 Aug	Balance b/d	268.00	20 Aug	Bank	134.00
			20 Aug	Bad debts	134.00
		268.00			268.00

Bad debts recovered

When a debtor's account has been closed it is eventually removed from the ledger and stored in a file of *dead* accounts. Because of the bankruptcy laws and the limitations imposed, some debtors do their best to repay their debts. Sometimes bad debts are recovered, often many years later, when this happens it is a pleasant surprise and an unexpected profit of the business.

This is a typical example of a bad debt recovered. Suppose we receive a cheque for £187 from A Slowman with a letter saying that he is now in a position to repay his debt. Because A Slowman's account was written off several years ago it no longer exists in the ledger. In this situation, a *debit* entry would be made in the bank account for the money received, like this:

Bank Account

20-9		£		
8 Mar	A Slowman	187.00		

A corresponding *credit* entry is made in the bad debts account, where it will offset any bad debts that occur during the current financial year:

Bad Debts Account

			20-9		£
			8 Mar	Bank	
				(A Slowman)	187.00

Note that no entries are made in the debtor's *dead* account.

Provision for bad and doubtful debts

Even when bad debtors have been removed, the accounts do not represent a *true and fair view* of the debtors. Accountants know from experience that there will always be some debtors who will be unable to pay their debts. On a balance sheet the total debtors appears as an asset, and this figure should be as accurate as possible.

Practically every business suffers from bad debts, but a good business will know, from experience, approximately what percentage of debts will eventually prove to be bad debts. With this in mind, most firms set aside a certain sum of money to guard against the *likelihood of future bad debts*. A *provision* is the name given to the sum of money which is set aside. This is usually quoted as a *percentage of the total debtors*. Here is a typical example. On 31 December 20-6 the total debtors amounted to £15,000. It is estimated that 4 per cent of debts (that is, £600) would eventually prove to be bad debts, and it is decided to make a provision for these out of the profits for the year. The ledger entries needed to start a provision for bad debts are: a *debit* entry in the profit and loss account, like this:

Profit and Loss Account for the year ended 31 December 20-6

Expenses	£	
Provision for bad debts	600.00	

A corresponding *credit* entry in a provision for bad debts account, like this:

Provision for Bad Debts Account

	20-6	£
	31 Dec Profit and loss	600.00

The provision for bad debts account is totalled and balanced at the end of each financial year. Any adjustment to the provision, increase or decrease is then made on this account.

On the balance sheet, in order to show a true and fair view of debtors, the amount of the provision for bad debts is *deducted* from the total debtors, like this:

Balance Sheet as at 31 December 20-6 (extract)

	£		
Current Assets			
Debtors	15,000		
Less provision			
for bad debts	600	14,400	

Increasing the provision

Usually the provision for bad debts is reviewed each year, and any change since last year is then adjusted. Using the same firm as an example, suppose that at the end of the following year, 31 December 20-7, the bad debts provision needed to be increased. This is because the provision is to be kept at 4 per cent, but debtors have risen to £18,000. A provision of £600 had been brought forward from the previous year, but now a total provision of £720 (that is, 4 per cent of £18,000) is required, an increase of £120. To make this adjustment, the provision for bad debts account is *credited* with the *extra* £120, like this:

Provision for Bad Debts Account

20-6		£	20-6		£
31 Dec	Balance c/d	600.00	31 Dec	Profit and loss	600.00
			20-7		
			1 Jan	Balance b/d	600.00
			31 Dec	Profit and loss	120.00

A corresponding *debit* entry is made in the profit and loss account, like this:

Profit and Loss Account for the year ended 31 December 20-7

Expenses	£	
Provision for bad debts	120.00	

The balance sheet now shows debtors at a more realistic value with the amount of the provision for bad debts *deducted* from the total debtors, like this:

Balance Sheet as at 31 December 20-7 (extract)

		£	
Current Assets			
Debtors	18,000		
Less provision			
for bad debts	720	17,280	

Decreasing the provision

When the provision is reviewed at the end of the next year it is very likely that it will need to be adjusted. Using the same firm as an example, suppose that at the end of the following year, 31 December 20-8, the bad debts provision needed to be reduced. This is because the provision is to be kept at 4 per cent, but debtors had fallen to £16,000. A provision of £720 had been brought forward from the previous year, but now a total provision of £640 (that is, 4 per cent of £16,000) is required, a reduction of £80. To make this adjustment, a *debit* entry in the provision for bad debts account of £80 to is needed *reduce* it, like this:

Provision for Bad Debts Account

20-6		£	20-6		£
31 Dec	Balance c/d	600.00	31 Dec	Profit and loss	600.00
20-7			20-7		
31 Dec	Balance c/d	720.00	1 Jan	Balance b/d	600.00
			31 Dec	Profit and loss	120.00
		720.00			720.00
20-8			20-8		
31 Dec	Profit and loss	80.00	1 Jan	Balance b/d	720.00

A corresponding *credit* entry is made in the profit and loss account, like this:

Profit and Loss Account for the year ended 31 December 20-8

Expenses	£		£
		Reduction in provision	80.00

On the balance sheet the amount of the revised provision is *deducted* from the total debtors, like this:

Balance Sheet as at 31 December 20-8 (extract)

	£	
Current Assets		
Debtors	16,000	
Less provision		
for bad debts	640	15,360

Look carefully at Figure 24.1, showing all the entries in the provision for bad debts account for the three years 20-6, 20-7 and 20-8:

Provision for Bad Debts Account

20-6		£	20-6		£
31 Dec	Balance c/d	600.00	31 Dec	Profit and loss	600.00
20-7			20-7		
31 Dec	Balance c/d	720.00	1 Jan	Balance b/d	600.00
			31 Dec	Profit and loss	120.00
		720.00			720.00
20-8			20-8		
31 Dec	Profit and loss	80.00	1 Jan	Balance b/d	720.00
31 Dec	Balance c/d	640.00			
		720.00			720.00
			20-9		
			1 Jan	Balance b/d	640.00

Figure 24.1

Points to remember

- A debtor who cannot pay his debts is known as a *bad debtor* and the amount owing is referred to as a *bad debt*. When a bad debt occurs, the bad debts account is debited with the relevant amount, the debtor's account is credited with the same amount. A bad debts account is a *collecting together* account which brings together all bad debts incurred during a financial year. Only at the end of the financial year is the bad debts account totalled and the balance transferred to the profit and loss account.
- Many firms make a *provision* for debts which may eventually prove to be bad debts. This is an estimate, usually taken as a percentage of the total debtors. The provision is reviewed each year. Any change since last year (increase or decrease) is then adjusted by making the appropriate entries in the provision for bad debts account and the profit and loss account. An *increase* is treated as an expense in the profit and loss account, while a *decrease* is treated as revenue. On a balance sheet the amount of provision is *deducted* from the total debtors in order to show a true and fair view of debtors.

Assignments

24.1

On 1 March 20-7 D Nelson owes your firm £76.50. He is declared bankrupt and it is reluctantly decided to write off the debt as a bad debt on 30 March

20-7. You are required to prepare: D Nelson's account and a bad debts account.

24.2
Alan Senior is a debtor who owes your firm £350. Because of serious financial difficulties he is unable to pay and asks you to agree to a payment of 50 per cent in full settlement of the debt. After consideration, you agree and he pays by cheque on 30 November 20-7. You are required to prepare: Alan Senior's account and a bad debts account.

24.3
A Baxter is declared bankrupt owing your firm £175. On 15 April 20-7 you receive a final settlement payment of 45 pence in the pound, in cash. You are required to prepare: A Baxter's account and a bad debts account.

24.4
John London's debt of £220 was written off some years ago. On 3 August 20–7 you receive a cheque and a note saying he is now in a position to repay his debt. You are required to open the necessary ledger accounts to show how this matter would be dealt with.

24.5
Every business which sells goods on credit wishes to avoid bad debts. You are required to:

(i) Describe the steps you would take before a new customer is allowed credit.
(ii) Say how you would deal with this customer if his credit worthiness is doubtful.

24.6
(a) What are bad debts? Why is it necessary to write off bad debts?
(b) From the information below write up the bad debts account in the books of Jean Wilder for the year 20-7. Debts written off as irrecoverable were:

		£
30 June	A Noble	160
31 August	P Jones	120
31 October	R Scott	250
30 November	L Skirrow	130

On 1 December 20-7 a final dividend of five pence in the pound was unexpectedly received in respect of the debt due from P Jones. Close off the bad debts account as on 31 December 20-7 and show the amount to be transferred to the profit and loss account.

24.7

Paul Simpson is a sole trader. During the year ended 31 March 20-8 the following customers were declared bankrupt:

Date	Customer	Amount of debt	Rate received in final settlement
20-7		£	
31 July	J Brown	275.50	20p in the pound
30 September	K Lawson	350.00	55p in the pound
31 December	B Nicholas	190.50	40p in the pound
20-8			
28 February	M Swan	164.00	25p in the pound

You are required to write up the bad debts account in the ledger of Paul Simpson for the year ended 31 March 20-8. Include all relevant dates and clearly show the amount to be transferred to the appropriate final account.

24.8

Nigel Barker runs a small business. He decided to make a provision for bad debts equal to 5 per cent of the total debtors outstanding at the end of each financial year:

	Total debtors
	£
31 December 20-5	9,000
31 December 20-6	10,000

You are required to:

(a) Prepare the provision for bad debts account for the years ended 31 December 20-5 and 20-6.
(b) Show the entries in the profit and loss account for the years 20-5 and 20-6.
(c) Show the balance sheet entries (extracts) for the years 20-5 and 20-6.

24.9

H Crawford had a business which adjusted its provision for bad debts at the end of the financial year, at a given percentage of the total debtors. The percentage varied each year, depending on the economic situation. Irrecoverable debts were written off during the year to a bad debts account, as and when they occurred. On 1 January 20-1 the balance on the provision for bad debts account was £500.

	Bad debts written off during year to bad debts account	Total debtors at year end	Rate of percentage for provision of doubtful debts
	£	£	%
31 December 20-1	750	14,000	5
31 December 20-2	4,085	10,000	10
31 December 20-3	2,900	15,000	5

From the above information you are required to:

(a) Prepare the bad debts account clearly showing the transfer to the final accounts, for the financial years 31 December 20-1, 20-2 and 20-3.
(b) Prepare the provision for bad debts account for the years 31 December 20-1, 20-2 and 20-3 clearly showing the balance brought forward each year.
(c) An extract from the balance sheets showing how the provision would affect the total debtors, as at 31 December 20-1, 20-2 and 20-3.

24.10
On 20 September 20-7 Brian Fox's debtors totalled £12,000. He decided to write off the following as bad debts:

	£
G Green	60
H Wilson	80

He further decided to make a provision for doubtful debts of 10 per cent on the remaining debtors. On 30 September 20–8 his debtors totalled £10,000 when Brian Fox decided to maintain the provision at 10 per cent. You are required to show for each of the years ended 30 September 20-7 and 20-8:

(a) Provision for doubtful debts account.
(b) The appropriate entries in the profit and loss account.
(c) The necessary balance sheet entries.

24.11
(a) What are the differences between bad debts written off and provision for bad debts?
(b) Give **two** reasons for creating a provision for bad debts.
(c) What is meant by bad debts recovered? How are such items entered in the profit and loss account of a business?
(d) On 1 January 20–4 there was a balance of £500 in the provision for bad debts account, and it was decided to maintain the provision at 5 per cent of the debtors at each year end.
The debtors on 31 December each year were as follows:

	£
20-4	8,000
20-5	8,000
20-6	11,000

You are required to show the necessary entries for the years ended 31 December 20-4, 20-5 and 20-6 in:

 (i) The provision for bad debts account.
(ii) The profit and loss account.

■ ⋎ **25** Adjustments for final accounts: prepayments and accruals – ledger accounts

In the accounts which we have looked at so far, we have assumed that the expenses and income related exactly to the accounting period for which we were preparing the profit and loss account. At this point in our studies we must now consider what are called *adjustments*. In the preparation of final accounts there are *two main principles*:

(i) Every trading, profit and loss account must be prepared accurately so that the *correct profit or loss for the period* is obtained.
(ii) Every balance sheet must give a *true and fair view* of the business, showing the assets and liabilities at their genuine values.

To achieve these aims, the accounts must be prepared in such a way that all the profit that belongs to the accounting period under consideration is included, *whether it has actually been received or not*. Set against this profit should be all expenses incurred during that period, even if they have *not actually been paid*. This principle is known as the *matching rule* because the incomes and expenditures are matched with one another.

Expense accounts and revenue received accounts may be prepaid at the end of a financial year: that is to say, a business may have paid for something or received revenue in advance of *using up* that item. Alternatively, expenses and revenue received may be accrued at the end of a financial year (accrued is the accounting term for 'owing'); this means a business would have outstanding debts, either owed to it, or owed by it. The purpose of adjustments is to produce an accurate set of final accounts.

The main adjustments are:

1 Payments made in advance by the firm
2 Payments made in advance to a firm
3 Expenses owed by the firm
4 Expenses owed to a firm
5 Unused stocks.

Payments made in advance by the firm

A *prepayment* means that a business has paid in advance for something before fully using up that item. Some payments are always made in advance. For example, insurance cover does not begin until the premium is paid. Similarly rent and rates are frequently paid in advance. These accounts often have an unused portion remaining at the end of the accounting period. This unused portion will require a year end adjustment in respect of the unexpired part of the year.

This is a typical example: Nicholas Davidson is a sole trader. His accounting period runs from 1 January to 31 December each year. Rates of £1,500 per annum are payable by instalments. During the year ended 31 December 20-7 the following payments were made for rates, by cheque:

3 January 20-7   £375 for the three months to 31 March 20-7
1 April 20-7   £750 for the six months to 30 September 20-7
1 October 20-7   £750 for the six months to 31 March 20-8

Each time a payment is made the details are entered (*credit* side of the bank account) and *debit* side of the rates account, like this:

Rates Account

20-7		£		
3 Jan	Bank	375.00		
1 Apr	Bank	750.00		
1 Oct	Bank	750.00		

As the payment made on 1 October was for the six months to 31 March 20-8 only three months (half of £750) will be used up in this financial year, (£375) will be prepaid. The amount transferred to the profit and loss account must be the actual cost of rates for this accounting period to 31 December 20-7, which is £1,500. We need to adjust the figures to get only this year's expenses in the accounts. To make this adjustment the amount of the prepayment is entered at the *credit* side of the rates account, like this:

Rates Account

20-7		£	20-7		£
3 Jan	Bank	375.00			
1 Apr	Bank	750.00	31 Dec	Prepaid c/d	375.00
1 Oct	Bank	750.00			

This will create a balance equal to the amount that has been paid in advance. The amount transferred to the profit and loss account is the difference between the two sides of the account; the completed rates account would look like this:

Rates Account

20-7		£	20-7		£
3 Jan	Bank	375.00	31 Dec	Profit and loss	1,500.00
1 Apr	Bank	750.00	31 Dec	Prepaid c/d	375.00
1 Oct	Bank	750.00			
		1,875.00			1,875.00
20-8					
1 Jan	Prepaid b/d	375.00			

This leaves a balance on the rates account to be carried down to next year. Since this balance is passed on from this year to next year it is one of the *assets* of the business. On the balance sheet for the year ending 31 December 20-7 the prepayment is shown under *Current assets*, as *Rates prepaid £375*.

This is another example: A new business whose financial year is 1 January to 31 December 20-7 decided to take out fire insurance. The annual premium of £480 was paid, by cheque on 1 February 20-7, the details are entered (*credit* side of the bank account) and *debit* side of the insurance account, like this:

Insurance Account

20-7		£			
1 Feb	Bank	480.00			

At the end of the financial year on 31 December 20-7 the business still has one months' value of insurance unexpired: this is a benefit paid for but *not used up* – it is an asset and needs to be carried forward to next year. A year end adjustment is required for the unexpired portion that is prepaid. It is calculated like this: cost for the year is £480, this is divided by 12 to give the cost of one month (£480 divided by 12 = £40). Eleven months have been *used up*, one month is prepaid (£40). To make this adjustment the amount of the prepayment is entered at the *credit* side of the insurance account, like this:

Insurance Account

20-7		£	20-7		£
1 Feb	Bank	480.00			
			31 Dec	Prepaid c/d	40.00

This will create a balance equal to the amount that has been paid in advance. The amount transferred to the profit and loss account is the difference between the two sides of the account; the completed account would look like this:

Insurance Account

20-7		£	20-7		£
1 Feb	Bank	480.00	31 Dec	Profit and loss	440.00
			31 Dec	Prepaid c/d	40.00
		480.00			480.00
20-8					
1 Jan	Prepaid b/d	40.00			

This leaves a balance on the insurance account to be carried down to next year. Since this balance is passed on from this year to next year it is one of the *assets* of the business. On the balance sheet for the year ending 31 December 20-7 the prepayment is shown under *Current assets*, as *Insurance prepaid £40*.

Payments made in advance to the firm

This is income received in advance for services or benefit which have not yet been given. The final accounts should reflect the *true and accurate* figures of the income actually earned during the financial year under review. Special attention is always required when dealing with revenue received. This usually causes problems for students because they forget that *revenue received* will be a *debit* entry in the cash book and a *credit* entry in the revenue received account. This is a typical example: suppose a business has larger premises than they need. On 1 March 20-7 they decide to rent part of it to another firm for £1,200 per annum. During the year ended 31 December 20-7 the following amounts were received from the sub-tenant, by cheque:

1 March	£300 for the three months to 31 May 20-7
2 June	£300 for the three months to 31 August 20-7
1 September	£300 for the three months to 30 November 20-7
2 December	£300 for the three months to 28 February 20-8

Each time a payment is received the details are entered (*debit* side of the bank account) and *credit* side of the rent received account, like this:

Rent Received Account

			£
	20-7		
	1 Mar	Bank	300.00
	2 Jun	Bank	300.00
	1 Sep	Bank	300.00
	2 Dec	Bank	300.00

During the current financial year the sub-tenant has paid £1,200 but has received only 10 months, benefit: 2 months has been paid in advance. The amount transferred to the profit and loss account must be the *actual amount earned during this financial year*, which is 10 months. We have to adjust the figures to get only this year's income in the accounts. It is calculated like this: cost for the year is £1,200; this is divided by 12 to give the cost of one month (£1,200 divided by 12 = £100). Ten months have been *used up*, two months are prepaid (£200). To make this adjustment the amount of the prepayment is entered at the *debit* side of the rent received account, like this:

Rent Received Account

20-7		£	20-7			£
			1 Mar	Bank		300.00
31 Dec	Prepaid c/d	200.00	2 Jun	Bank		300.00
			1 Sep	Bank		300.00
			2 Dec	Bank		300.00

This will create a balance equal to the amount that has been paid in advance. The amount transferred to the profit and loss account is the difference between the two sides of the account; the completed rent received account would look like this:

Rent Received Account

20-7		£	20-7			£
31 Dec	Profit and loss	1,000.00	1 Mar	Bank		300.00
31 Dec	Prepaid c/d	200.00	2 Jun	Bank		300.00
			1 Sep	Bank		300.00
			2 Dec	Bank		300.00
		1,200.00				1,200.00
			20-8			
			1 Jan	Prepaid b/d		200.00

This leaves a balance on the rent received account to be carried down to next year. Since this balance is passed on from this year to next year it is one of the *liabilities* of the business: this is because the firm has the responsibility to provide accommodation for the sub-tenant for which he has already paid. On the balance sheet for the year ending 31 December 20-7 this is shown under *Current liabilities,* as *Rent received in advance £200.*

Expenses owed by the firm

Invariably at the end of the financial year there will be some expenses outstanding which will not be paid until the next financial year. These are called *accrued expenses:* 'accrued' simply means 'owing', 'outstanding' or 'in arrears'. Typical examples are: telephone, wages, rent, electricity and advertising. These are expenses which have been incurred during the current financial year, but full payment has not yet been made. Any expenses which are still outstanding at the end of the financial year will require an adjustment. Suppose that rent of £1,800 a year is payable at the end of every three months. During the year 1 January to 31 December 20-7 the following payments were made for rent, by cheque:

	£
1 April	450
3 July	450
2 October	450

Each time a payment is made the details are entered (*credit* side of the bank account) and *debit* side of the rent account, like this:

Rent Account

20-7		£		
1 Apr	Bank	450.00		
3 Jul	Bank	450.00		
2 Oct	Bank	450.00		

On 31 December 20-7 three months' rent was still owing, this will not be paid until 3 January 20-8. Clearly the actual cost of rent for the year 20-7 is £1,800. We need to adjust the figures to get all of this year's expenses in the accounts. To make this adjustment the amount owing of £450 is entered at the *debit* side of the rent account, like this:

Rent Account

20-7		£			
1 Apr	Bank	450.00			
3 Jul	Bank	450.00			
2 Oct	Bank	450.00			
31 Dec	Accrued c/d	450.00			

This will create a balance equal to the amount owing. The amount transferred to the profit and loss account must be the *actual cost of rent for this accounting period* to 31 December 20-7 which is £1,800. The completed rent account would look like this:

Rent Account

20-7		£	20-7		£
1 Apr	Bank	450.00	31 Dec	Profit and loss	1,800.00
3 Jul	Bank	450.00			
2 Oct	Bank	450.00			
31 Dec	Accrued c/d	450.00			
		1,800.00			1,800.00
			20-8		
			1 Jan	Accrued b/d	450.00

On the balance sheet for the year ending 31 December 20-7 this is shown under *Current liabilities*, as *Rent accrued £450*.

Expenses owed to the firm

It is also possible that there may be revenue owing to the firm. Sometimes a business will not have received all the income to which it is entitled by the end of its financial year. This would be income that had been earned during the current year, but at the end of the year was still outstanding. When this happens, the amount owing must be added to what has been received to show the true income for the year.

Common examples of these are:

(1) *Rent received*, a sub-tenant may be late paying his rent
(2) *Commission received*, the firm may have earned commission which has not yet been received.

Here is a typical example: Anthea Jones is a business consultant, she receives commission on a quarterly basis. During the year 1 January to 31 December 20-7 she received the following amounts by cheque:

	£
1 Apr	650
4 Jul	730
3 Oct	690

On 31 December 20-7 there was commission due of £780 that had not been received. Each time a payment is received the details are entered (*debit* side of the bank account) and *credit* side of the commission received account, like this:

Commission Received Account

			20-7		£
			1 Apr	Bank	650.00
			4 Jul	Bank	730.00
			3 Oct	Bank	690.00

The amount transferred to the profit and loss account must be the *actual amount earned during this financial year*, which is £2,850. We need to adjust the figures to show all this year's income in the accounts. To make this adjustment the amount still owing of £780 is entered at the *credit* side of the commission received account, like this:

Commission Received Account

			20-7		£
			1 Apr	Bank	650.00
			4 Jul	Bank	730.00
			3 Oct	Bank	690.00
			31 Dec	Owing c/d	780.00

This will create a balance equal to the amount still outstanding. The amount transferred to the profit and loss account must be the *actual amount earned during this financial year* to 31 December 20-7 which is £2,850. The completed commission received account would look like this:

Commission Received Account

20-7		£	20-7		£
31 Dec	Profit and loss	2,850.00	1 Apr	Bank	650.00
			4 Jul	Bank	730.00
			3 Oct	Bank	690.00
			31 Dec	Owing c/d	780.00
		2,850.00			2,850.00
20-8					
1 Jan	Owing b/d	780.00			

On the balance sheet for the year ended 31 December 20-7 this is shown under *Current assets, Commission due £780.*

Unused stocks

When items such as packing materials and stationery are bought for use in a business there are often unused stocks remaining at the end of the financial year. This stock is a form of *prepayment* and needs carrying down to the following year in which it will be used. It is only the actual cost of the materials used during the current year which is transferred to the profit and loss account. This is a typical example: during the financial year ended 31 December 20-7 the following amounts were paid, by cheque for packing materials:

	£
10 Mar	386
3 Sep	464

On 31 December 20-7 there was a stock of packing materials valued at £200. Each time a payment is made the details are entered (*credit* side of the bank account) and *debit* side of the packing materials account, like this:

Packing Materials Account

20-7		£	
10 Mar	Bank	386.00	
3 Sep	Bank	464.00	

The amount transferred to the profit and loss account must be the *actual cost of packing materials used during this financial year.* We need to adjust the figures to get only this year's expenses in the accounts. To make this adjustment the value of the unused stock of £200 is entered at the *credit* side of the packing materials account, like this:

Packing Materials Account

20-7		£	20-7		£
10 Mar	Bank	386.00			
3 Sep	Bank	464.00	31 Dec	Stock c/d	200.00

This will create a balance equal to the value of the unused stock. The amount transferred to the profit and loss account is the difference between the two sides of the account; the completed packing materials account would look like this:

Packing Materials Account

20-7		£	20-7		£
10 Mar	Bank	386.00	31 Dec	Profit and loss	650.00
3 Sep	Bank	464.00	31 Dec	Stock c/d	200.00
		850.00			850.00
20-8					
1 Jan	Stock b/d	200.00			

The stock of packing materials is *not* added to the stock of unsold goods on the balance sheet; it is shown separately, under *Current assets*, as *Packing materials stock £200.*

Examination questions are frequently set which require adjustments for prepayments and accruals at *both* the beginning *and* end of the year. Students are often apprehensive when they are asked to prepare these accounts, so we can now see how this is done.

Worked questions

Here are some typical questions with illustrated solutions.

Example 1
The following information refers to the electricity account in the ledger of John Woodstock. On 1 January 20-7 there was an unpaid bill for electricity of £246. During the year the following payments were made for electricity, by cheque:

	£
15 Jan	246
19 Apr	356
16 Jul	242
18 Oct	274

On 31 December 20-7 there was an electricity account, outstanding of £382.

You are required to prepare the electricity account, clearly showing the amount to be transferred to the profit and loss account for the year ended 31 December 20-7 and the amount to be carried forward to the next financial year.

This is a fully illustrated solution; numbers refer to sequence of order entries are made in accounts

(1) Enter amount owing at the beginning of the year (*credit* side).
(2) Enter, in date order, details of the amounts paid during the current year (*debit* side).
(3) Enter details of the electricity account outstanding at the end of the year (*debit* side).

At this point the electricity account would look like this:

Electricity Account

20-7			£	20-7			£
15 Jan	Bank		246.00	1 Jan	Accrued b/d (1)	246.00
19 Apr	Bank	(2)	356.00			
16 Jul	Bank		242.00			
18 Oct	Bank		274.00			
31 Dec	Accrued c/d (3)		382.00			

Once the dates and details of all the information given in the question are entered in the account, the amount transferred to the profit and loss account is the difference between the two sides of the account; the completed electricity account would look like this:

Electricity Account

20-7			£	20-7			£
15 Jan	Bank		246.00	1 Jan	Accrued b/d (1)	246.00
19 Apr	Bank	(2)	356.00	31 Dec	Profit and loss	1,254.00
16 Jul	Bank		242.00			
18 Oct	Bank		274.00			
31 Dec	Accrued c/d (3)		382.00			
			1,500.00			1,500.00
				20-8		
				1 Jan	Accrued b/d	382.00

Example 2

From the following information you are required to write up the rates account in the ledger of E Mellor.

On 1 July 20-2 the rates prepaid were £725. During the year the following amounts were paid for rates, by cheque:

£

8 October 20-2   1,450 for the six months ending 31 March 20-3
5 April 20-3   1,650 for the six months ending 30 September 20-3

Your rates account should clearly show the amount to be transferred to the profit and loss account for the year ended 30 June 20-3 and the amount to be carried forward to the next financial year.

This is a fully illustrated solution; numbers refer to sequence of order entries are made in accounts

(1) Enter amount prepaid at the beginning of the year (*debit* side).
(2) Enter, in date order, details of the amounts paid during the current year (*debit* side).
(3) Enter details of prepayment at the end of the year (*credit* side)

(£1,650 divided by 6 = £275 per month, 3 months are prepaid,
$3 \times £275 = £825$)

At this point the rates account would look like this:

Rates Account

20-2			£	20-3				£
1 Jul	Prepaid b/d (1)		725.00					
8 Oct	Bank ⎤		1,450.00	30 Jun	Prepaid c/d	(3)		825.00
20-3	⎬ (2)							
5 Apr	Bank ⎦		1,650.00					

Once the dates and details of all the information given in the question are entered in the account, the amount transferred to the profit and loss account is the difference between the two sides of the account; the completed rates account would look like this:

Rates Account

20-2			£	20-3			£
1 Jul	Prepaid b/d (1)		725.00	30 Jun	Profit and loss		3,000.00
8 Oct	Bank		1,450.00	30 Jun	Prepaid c/d	(3)	825.00
20-3		(2)					
5 Apr	Bank		1,650.00				
			3,825.00				3,825.00
1 Jul	Prepaid b/d		825.00				

Example 3

The following information refers to the stationery account in the ledger of M Whiteley. On 1 May 20-5 there was a stock of stationery valued at £158, during the year the following amounts were paid for stationery, by cheque:

	£
8 August 20-5	136
4 December 20-5	204
9 March 20-6	192

On 30 April 20-6 there was a stock of stationery valued at £85.

You are required to write up and balance the stationery account for the year ended 30 April 20-6, clearly showing the amount to be transferred to the final accounts and the amount to be carried forward to the next financial year.

This is a fully illustrated solution; numbers refer to sequence of order entries are made in accounts

(1) Enter amount of prepaid stock at the beginning of the year (*debit* side).
(2) Enter, in date order, details of the amounts paid during the current year (*debit* side).
(3) Enter details of stock prepaid at the end of the year (*credit* side).

At this point the stationery account would look like this:

Stationery Account

20-5			£	20-6			£
1 May	Balance b/d	(1)	158.00				
8 Aug	Bank		136.00	30 Apr	Balance c/d	(3)	85.00
4 Dec	Bank		204.00				
		(2)					
20-6							
9 Mar	Bank		192.00				

Once the dates and details of all the information given in the question are entered in the account, the amount transferred to the profit and loss account is the difference between the two sides of the account; the completed stationery account would look like this:

Stationery Account

20-5			£	20-6			£
1 May	Balance b/d	(1)	158.00	30 Apr	Profit and loss		605.00
8 Aug	Bank		136.00	30 Apr	Balance c/d	(3)	85.00
4 Dec	Bank	(2)	204.00				
20-6							
9 Mar	Bank		192.00				
			690.00				690.00
1 May	Balance b/d		85.00				

Points to remember

- An *accounting period* is the length of time from one set of final accounts to the next. It is normally one year.
- An important rule in accounting is that revenue earned must be *matched* with the expenses which have been incurred during the same accounting period. Adjustments are necessary in order to produce an accurate set of final accounts.
- A *prepayment* means that a business has paid in advance for something before fully using up that item, or has received payment before providing the benefit.
- An *accrual* is the accounting term for 'owing'; this means a business would have outstanding debts, either owed to it, or owed by it.
- As well as ensuring that income and expenses are correctly calculated in the profit and loss account, all assets and liabilities must be shown on the balance sheet.
- In examination questions all details should be entered in *date order*. When an annual cost is stated in the question, for example '*a firm occupies premises at annual rental of £2,000*', the amount transferred to the profit and loss account is *always* the cost *for the year.*

Assignments

25.1

James Grant runs a small mail order business. On 1 January 20-7 there was £500 owing for rent in respect of the business premises. During the year the following payments were made for rent, by cheque:

	£
4 January	500
3 April	500
5 July	500
8 October	500

On 31 December 20-7 there was £500 owing for rent.

You are required to write up James Grant's rent account for the year ended 31 December 20-7, clearly showing the amount to be transferred to the profit and loss account and the amount to be carried forward to the next financial year.

25.2

The following information refers to the rates account in the ledger of K. Parker. On 1 January 20-7 the rates prepaid were £525. During the year the following payments were made for rates, by cheque:

30 April   £1,150 for the six months ending 30 September 20-7
5 October   £1,150 for the six months ending 31 March 20-8

You are required to prepare K. Parker's rates account for the year ending 31 December 20-7, clearly showing the amount to be transferred to the profit and loss account and the amount to be carried forward to the next financial year.

25.3

The following information is available in respect of the electricity account in the ledger of M. Summers. On 1 July 20-6 there was an unpaid bill for electricity of £287. During the year the following payments were made for electricity, by cheque:

20-6	£
15 July	287
8 October	320
20-7	
10 January	543
6 April	590

On 30 June 20-7 there was an electricity account outstanding of £350.
You are required to prepare M. Summers' electricity account for the year ending 30 June 20-7, clearly showing the amount to be transferred to the profit and loss account and the amount to be carried forward to the next financial year.

25.4

The following information refers to the packing materials account in the ledger of David Dyson:

	£
On 1 June 20-4 there was a stock of packing materials valued at:	350
Packing materials purchased by cheque, during the year were:	1,275
On 31 May 20-5 stocks of packing materials were valued at:	580

You are required to write up and balance the packing materials account for the year ended 31 May 20-5, clearly showing the amount to be transferred to the final accounts and the amount to be carried forward to the next financial year.

25.5

During the year ended 31 December 20-4 Nigel Giffard paid the following amounts for rent:

18 January   £686 for the half year ended 31 March 20-4
10 July   £890 for the half year ended 30 September 20-4
 5 December   £890 for the half year ended 31 March 20-5

You are required to:

(a) Enter the above information in the rent account of Nigel Giffard.
(b) Balance the rent account at 31 December 20-4, clearly showing the amount to be transferred to the final accounts.

25.6

James Conway commenced trading on 1 January 20-7, on which date he acquired premises at an annual rental of £2,700. On 1 May 20-7 he sub-let a section of the premises at an annual rental of £900.

During the year ended 31 December 20-7 the following *payments had been made* in respect of rent, by cheque:

	£
30 March	675
29 June	675
28 September	675

and the following amounts *had been received* by cheque, from the sub-tenant:

	£
3 May	225
1 August	225
4 November	225

You are required to write up separate accounts for rent payable and rent received for the financial year ending 31 December 20-7. Balance the accounts, and show the relevant transfers to the profit and loss account.

25.7
(i) L George rents his premises at an annual rental of £1,200. On 1 June 20-3 George had paid his rent up to the end of July, and during the year ended 31 May 20-4 he made the following payments for rent, by cheque:

20-3	£
1 August	300
5 November	300
20-4	
1 February	300

(ii) L George sub-lets part of his premises to S Broke at a rent of £480 per annum; on 1 June 20-3 Broke's rent was one month in arrears. During the year ended 31 May 20-4 George received the following amounts in cash from Broke:

20-3	£
25 July	40
18 August	120
4 December	150
20-4	
9 April	60

(iii) On 1 June 20-3 L George owed £74 for electricity supplies up to that date. During the year he made the following payments by cheque:

20-3	£
1 June	74
10 September	82
5 December	104
20-4	
7 April	81

On 31 May 20-4 there was an unpaid bill for electricity of £96.

You are required to:
(a) Write up L George's rent payable account, rent received account and electricity account for the year ended 31 May 20-4, clearly showing the amounts to be transferred to the profit and loss account.
(b) Show how the balances brought down would appear in the balance sheet on 31 May 20-4.

25.8

(i) Kite Sportswear rent their premises at an annual rental of £5,712. On 1 May 20-6 they had paid rent up to the end of June 20-6. During the year ended 30 April 20-7 the following payments were made for rent, by cheque:

	£
3 July for the three months ended 30 September 20-6	1,428
2 October for the three months ended 31 December 20-6	1,428
4 January for the three months ended 31 March 20-7	1,428

(ii) On 1 May 20-6 £498 was owing for sundry expenses. During the year, a total of £2,706 was paid by cheque and on 30 April 20-7 £148 was owing for sundry expenses.

(iii) On 1 May 20-6 the rates prepaid were £1,050. During the year the following payments were made for rates, by cheque:

	£
2 October for the six months ended 31 March 20-7	1,248
3 April for the six months ended 30 September 20-7	1,380

(iv) Kite Sportswear have larger premises than they require and on 1 July 20-6 part of their premises were sub-let to Moorland Textiles for an annual rental of £2,976. During the year ended 30 April 20-7 the following amounts were received from Moorland Textiles, by cheque:

	£
3 July for the six months ended 31 December 20-6	1,488
4 January for the six months ended 30 June 20-7	1,488

You are required to:

(a) Write up the ledger accounts, for rent, sundry expenses, rates and rent received for the year ended 30 April 20-7.

(b) Balance the accounts, showing clearly the relevant transfers to the final accounts and any amounts to be carried forward to the next financial year.

◼ ⅴ 26 Adjustments in trading, profit and loss account and balance sheet

At the end of a financial year before the final accounts are prepared a *trial balance* is taken out. A trial balance (as we saw in Unit 7) is a list of all balances remaining in the ledger accounts, including the cash and bank balances from the cash book.

It is normal accounting practice, as illustrated in Unit 25, for any year end adjustments to be made in the relevant ledger accounts *before* a trial balance is taken out.

Examination questions often ask for final accounts – that is, a trading, profit and loss account and a balance sheet to be prepared from a given trial balance with notes as to the adjustments. These notes give details of the adjustments which need to be made to the figures *before* the final accounts are prepared. Each adjustment will have *two* effects: one may be in the trading or profit and loss account, the other on the balance sheet.

This unit works through a typical examination question with a comprehensive range of adjustments.

Example question

On 31 December 20-7 the following trial balance was extracted from the books of Michael Silverwood:

	Dr	Cr
	£	£
Debtors	6,480	
Creditors		2,360
Stock (1 January 20-7)	4,340	
Motor vehicle	11,500	
Equipment	6,350	
Rent	2,180	
Wages	9,178	
Rates	565	
Purchases	19,200	
Sales		36,840
Returns inwards	450	
Returns outwards		750
Bad debts	142	
Cash at bank	6,250	
Insurance	458	
Sundry expenses	907	
Capital (1 January 20-7)		31,300
Drawings	3,250	
	71,250	71,250

Notes: at 31 December 20-7 the following adjustments had not been made:

(i)   Rates prepaid were £126
(ii) Included in *Sundry expenses* is the cost of stationery; there was a stock of stationery valued at £72
(iii) Wages accrued were £450
(iv) Stock at 31 December 20-7 was valued at £5,328.

You are required to:

(a) Prepare a trading, profit and loss account for the year ended 31 December 20-7.
(b) Prepare a balance sheet as at 31 December 20-7.

Remember, each of the additional notes will have *two* effects – one may be in the trading or profit and loss account, the other on the balance sheet. At this point most students find it useful to look down the trial balance and label each item with **T**, **P & L** or **BS** (trading account, profit and loss account or balance sheet), according to its destination.

The next stage is to prepare a set of *workings* to assist you. We can now look at each adjustment, in turn:

(i)   *Rates prepaid were £126*
      This needs to be deducted from the rates figure given in the trial balance because it represents a *payment made in advance*, to be used in the next financial year. The amount shown in the profit and loss account should be the actual cost of rates for the current financial

year. The amount prepaid is an *asset* and must be included on the balance sheet.

Your *workings* would look like this:

Profit and loss account entry		**Balance sheet entry**
Rates	565	under *Current assets*
Less prepaid	126	Rates prepaid £126
	439	

(ii) *Included in* sundry expenses is *the cost of stationery*; *on 31* December 20-7 there was a stock of stationery valued at £72

This needs to be *deducted* from the Sundry expenses figure given in the trial balance because it is a form of *prepayment*; this stationery stock will be used in the next financial year. It is an *asset* and must be included on the balance sheet.

Your *workings* would look like this:

Profit and loss account entry		**Balance sheet entry**
Sundry expenses	907	under *Current assets*
Less prepaid	72	Stationery stock £72
	835	

(iii) *Wages accrued were £450*

This needs to be *added* to the wages figure given in the trial balance because the expense was incurred during the current financial year but it *will not be paid until next year*.

Your *workings* would look like this:

Profit and loss account entry		**Balance sheet entry**
Wages	9,178	under *Current liabilities*
Add accrued	450	Wages accrued £450
	9,628	

(iv) *Stock at 31 December 20-7 was valued at £5,328*

No calculations are needed here but it is useful to include the closing stock on your preparation list; it is used in the trading account and shown on the balance sheet.

Trading account entry	**Balance sheet entry**
Closing stock £5,328	under *Current assets*
	Closing stock £5,328

Now we can see the completed trading, profit and loss account and balance sheet for the year ended 31 December 20-7 (Figure 26.1).

Your *workings* for all adjustments should be clearly shown (it is usually an examination requirement). They are also of considerable assistance if difficulties arise in making the balance sheet totals agree; this is often owing to an adjusted item being omitted.

When there are several items prepaid, these are usually added together and shown as one figure on the balance sheet, as *Prepaid expenses*. Similarly, when there are several items accrued, these are usually added

Michael Silverwood
Trading, Profit and Loss Account for the year ended 31 December 20-7

	£		£
Stock	4,340	Sales	36,840
Purchases	19,200	*Less* returns inwards	450
	23,540		36,390
Less returns outwards	750		
	22,790		
Less closing stock	5,328		
Cost of goods sold	17,462		
Gross profit c/d	18,928		
	36,390		36,390
Rent	2,180	Gross profit b/d	18,928
Wages (9,178 + 450)	9,628		
Rates (565 – 126)	439		
Bad debts	142		
Insurance	458		
Sundry expenses (907 – 72)	835		
Net profit	5,246		
	18,928		18,928

Balance Sheet as at 31 December 20-7

	£	£		£	£
Fixed Assets			Capital	31,300	
Equipment	6,350		*Add* net profit	5,246	
Motor vehicle	11,500	17,850		36,546	
			Less drawings	3,250	33,296
Current Assets			*Current Liabilities*		
Stock	5,328		Creditors	2,360	
Debtors	6,480		Wages accrued	450	2,810
Rates prepaid	126				
Stationery stock	72				
Bank	6,250	18,256			
		36,106			36,106

Figure 26.1

together and shown as one figure on the balance sheet, as *Accrued expenses.*

We can now look at other types of year end adjustments.

Depreciation of fixed assets

Adjustments usually have to be made regarding the decrease in value of fixed assets. In Unit 23 we established that the amount of depreciation charged to the profit and loss account is an *expense.* On the balance sheet the value of a fixed asset is usually shown at its original cost, *less* the total amount of depreciation to date.

This is a typical example of a year end adjustment note:

(i) Depreciate fixtures and fittings at 20 per cent per annum, at cost. (Assume the figure given in the trial balance for fixtures and fittings at cost is £4,000.)

First a calculation is required: 20 per cent of £4,000 is £800. The amount charged for depreciation is an *expense* and is set against the profits of the business in the profit and loss account. The fixed asset is reduced in value by the amount of depreciation charged in each financial year.

Your *workings* would look like this:

Profit and loss account entry	**Balance sheet entry**		
Debit entry	under *Fixed assets*		
Depreciation £800	Fixtures and Fittings	4,000	
	Less depreciation	800	3,200

Bad debts

These are another type of year end adjustment. This is a typical example:

(ii) A debtor has been declared bankrupt, the amount owing of £250 is to be written off as a bad debt. (Assume the figure given in the trial balance for debtors is £6,750.)

A debtor who cannot pay his debt is called a *bad debtor,* and the amount owing is referred to as a *bad debt.* A bad debt is a *business loss,* and must be treated in the same way as other losses and expenses by charging the amount of the bad debt against the profits of the business. On the balance sheet, in order to show a true and fair view of debtors, the amount of the bad debt is deducted from the total debtors.

Your *workings* would look like this:

Profit and loss account entry	**Balance sheet entry**		
Debit entry	under *Current assets*		
Bad debts £250	Debtors	6,750	
	Less bad debt	250	6,500

Provision for bad debts

Increasing the provision

Some businesses set aside a certain sum of money to guard against the likelihood of future bad debts. A *provision* is the name given to the sum of money which is set aside. Usually the provision for bad debts is reviewed each year, any change since last year is then adjusted.

Frequently year end adjustments are required relating to the provision for bad debts. This is a typical example where the provision for bad debts is to be *increased*:

(iii) The provision for bad debts is to be increased to 10 per cent of debtors. (Assume the following figures are given in the trial balance: provision for bad and doubtful debts £250, and debtors £4,500.)

The amount of the provision which already exists is given in the trial balance: in this example, it is £250. The adjustment requires this figure to be increased to 10 per cent of the total debtors. Calculations are now required:

	£
10 per cent of £4,500 is	450
Less the existing provision of	250
Making an increase of	200

The profit and loss account should be debited with the amount of the *increase*. On the balance sheet the amount of the provision for bad debts is *deducted* from the total debtors.

Your *workings* would look like this:

Profit and loss account entry	**Balance sheet entry**		
Debit entry	under *Current assets*		
Provision for bad and	Debtors	4,500	
doubtful debts £200	*Less* provision	450	£4,050

Decreasing the provision

This is a typical example where the provision for bad debts is to be *decreased*:

(iv) The provision for bad debts is to be adjusted to 10 per cent of total debtors. (Assume the following amounts are given in the trial balance: provision for bad debts £500, debtors £4,000.)

The amount of the provision which already exists is given in the trial balance: in this example it is £500. The adjustment requires this figure to be decreased to 10 per cent of the total debtors. Calculations are now required:

	£
Existing provision is	500
10 per cent of £4,000 is	400
Making a decrease of	100

When the provision for bad debts is decreased the profit and loss account should be *credited* with the amount of the *difference* between the existing provision and the new provision. On the balance sheet the amount of the provision for bad debts is *deducted* from the total debtors.

Your *workings* would look like this:

Profit and loss account entry	**Balance sheet entry**		
Credit entry	under *Current assets*		
Reduction in provision for	Debtors	4,000	
bad and doubtful debts £100	*Less* provision	400	£3,600

Drawings

Frequently year end adjustments are required concerning the proprietor (owner of the business), and these can be stated in various ways. You will need to study the information given and consider the twofold effect. This is a typical example:

(v) One-third of motor expenses for the year is to be regarded as private use. (Assume the following figures are given in the trial balance, motor expenses £1,050, drawings £2,500.)

Calculations are now required:

£1,050 divided by 3 equals £350 (one-third). Motor expenses will need to be reduced by £350 and drawings will need to be increased by £350.

Your *workings* would look like this:

Profit and loss account entry		**Balance sheet entry**	
	£		£
Motor expenses	1,050	Drawings	2,500
Less private use	350	*Add* private use	350
Motor expenses adjusted	700	Drawings adjusted	2,850

Labour or wages

Under normal circumstances wages and salaries will appear in the profit and loss account. However, a year end adjustment may require the cost of wages to be *apportioned*, perhaps one-quarter to the trading account and three-quarters to the profit and loss account. In this situation, calculate the respective amounts, then one-quarter should be debited in the trading account, the remaining three-quarters should be debited in the profit and loss account. *A specific instruction will be given* if any element of labour, wages or any other item of expense is to be apportioned.

Final accounts of non-traders

When final accounts are being prepared for people who are not trading in goods as such – for example, accountants, hairdressers, business consultants and other providers of services – there *will not* be a trading account. This is because goods are not bought and sold. The final accounts for providers of services will consist of a profit and loss account and balance sheet. The profit and loss account will contain all items of *revenue received* at the *credit* side and all items of *revenue expense* at the *debit* side. The balance sheet will be exactly the same as for traders.

Most of the Assignments which follow are taken from past examination papers; they contain many variations of the different types of year end adjustments. Practice is essential if you are to gain skill and confidence in these important techniques.

Points to remember

- Trading, profit and loss accounts are usually prepared annually at the end of the financial year. Their purpose is to calculate the *profit* or *loss of a business*:
  - *Trading account* calculates *gross profit*
  - *Profit and loss account* calculates *net profit* or *net loss*.
- *Headings* are essential and must clearly state the *period of time* concerned – it is usually 'Trading, Profit and Loss Account for the year ending . . .'.
- A Balance sheet is a financial statement which lists a firm's *assets*, *capital* and *liabilities* at a given moment in time, usually the end of its financial year. It is prepared after the trading, profit and loss account, using the balances that remain.
- Examination questions generally give a series of *year end notes* which will usually include prepaid or accrued items.

  These notes give details of the adjustments which need to be made to the figures *before* the final accounts are prepared. Each adjustment will have *two* effects – one may be in the trading or profit and loss account, the other on the balance sheet.
- Always take care when making calculations for adjustments and clearly set out your *workings*.

Assignments

26.1

B Stanley is a sole trader. The following trial balance was extracted from his books on 31 December 20-5:

	£	£
Capital (at 1 January 20-5)		31,660
Drawings	4,500	
Freehold land and buildings	28,000	
Motor van	2,200	
Purchases	60,000	
Sales		82,000
Salaries	9,100	
Discount allowed	820	
Discount received		640
Debtors	2,400	
Creditors		1,800
Cash in hand	600	
Cash at bank	1,980	
Stock at 1 January 20-5	3,800	
Rates	650	
Insurances	150	
Telephone	100	
Fixtures and fittings	1,800	
	116,100	116,100

On 31 December 20-5 the following adjustments had not been made:

(i)   At 31 December 20-5 stock in trade was valued at £4,000
(ii) A telephone bill for £30 was outstanding
(iii) Insurances of £25 were prepaid

You are required to:

(a) Prepare a trading and profit and loss account for the year ended 31 December 20-5.
(b) Prepare a balance sheet as at 31 December 20-5.

26.2

The following trial balance was taken from the books of Robert Witham at 31 December 20-6:

	£	£
Capital (1 January 20-6)		11,700
Drawings	2,100	
Rent and rates	1,340	
Wages and salaries	2,711	
Purchases	23,821	
Sales		32,484
Bad debts	88	
Trade debtors	3,840	
Trade creditors		1,535
Stock (1 January 20-6)	3,112	
Cash at bank	247	
Carriage inwards	138	
Motor vehicles	7,037	
Office expenses	488	
Sundry expenses	797	
	45,719	45,719

Notes:
(i)   Stock at 31 December 20-6 was valued at £2,477
(ii) Office expenses includes the cost of stationery, of which there remained stock worth £56 at 31 December 20-6
(iii) Wages in arrears at 31 December 20-6 were £42

You are required to:

(a) Prepare the trading and profit and loss account of Robert Witham for the year ended 31 December 20-6.
(b) Prepare a balance sheet as at 31 December 20-6.

26.3

Julie Bright is a business consultant. On 30 June 20-3 the following trial balance was extracted from her books:

	£	£
Freehold premises	27,000	
Office equipment	3,500	
Cash in hand	390	
Fixtures and fittings	1,100	
Advertising	6,680	
Cash at bank	4,980	
Repairs to equipment	410	
Rates	1,100	
Rent received from sub-letting		1,248
Telephone	602	
Stationery	180	
General expenses	1,034	
Drawings	9,070	
Wages	3,980	
Insurances	970	
Loan from Loamshire Bank (over five years)		4,000
Loan interest	300	
Commissions received for Professional services		28,847
Capital, 1 January 20-3		27,201
	61,296	61,296

On 30 June 20-3 the following adjustments had not been made:

(i)   Rates prepaid were £325
(ii) A telephone bill of £415 has not been paid
(iii) There was a small stock of stationery in hand valued at £24
(iv) A bill for cleaning expenses of £35 was outstanding – these should be charged to General expenses
(v)   Wages due to staff were £120

You are required to:

(a) Prepare a profit and loss account for the six months ending 30 June 20-3.
(b) Prepare a balance sheet as at 30 June 20-3.

26.4

On 31 May 20-6 the following trial balance was extracted from the books of R. Colebrook:

	Dr £	Cr £
Capital		29,250
Drawings	4,600	
Bank and cash	9,200	
Salaries and wages	23,000	
Purchases and sales	35,000	68,000
Debtors and creditors	12,350	18,000
Office expenses	2,500	
Light and heat	1,700	
Rates	1,400	
Premises	15,000	
Fixtures and fittings	2,300	
Vehicles	4,200	
Stock at 1 June 20-5	4,100	
Sales and Purchase returns	400	500
	115,750	115,750

On 31 May 20-6 the following information is also available:

(i) Stock on 31 May 20-6 was £3,900
(ii) Wages owing but not yet paid £100
(iii) Light, heat and rates are to be apportioned:
$\frac{1}{4}$ to trading account
$\frac{3}{4}$ to profit and loss account
(iv) Included in the office expenses is an insurance prepayment of £50

You are required to:

(a) Prepare R. Colebrook's trading and profit and loss account for the year ended 31 May 20-6.
(b) Prepare a balance sheet as at 31 May 20-6.

26.5

On 30 April 20-5 the following trial balance was extracted from the books of Robert Owen:

	£	£
Capital 1 May 20-4		30,640
Furniture and equipment	10,500	
Sales		46,800
Postage and stationery	1,750	
Returns inwards	1,320	
Rates and insurance	1,200	
Wages and salaries	8,440	
Purchases	27,560	
Drawings	6,000	
Trade creditors		2,830
Petty cash	80	
Bank balance		4,600
Sundry expenses	8,570	
Stock at 1 May 20-4	6,500	
Loan from Mercantile Bank		5,000
Interest on loan	750	
Freehold premises	15,000	
Trade debtors	2,200	
	89,870	89,870

On 30 April 20-5 the following information is also available:

(i)   Stock on 30 April 20-5 was valued at £7,640
(ii) Provide for carriage on purchases owing of £140
(iii) The annual fire insurance premium of £240 was paid on the due date, 1 February 20-5; make the necessary adjustment for the unexpired portion at 30 April 20-5

You are required to:

(a) Prepare a trading and profit and loss account for the year ended 30 April 20-5.
(b) Prepare a balance sheet as at 30 April 20-5.

26.6

W Sims is self-employed as a painter and decorator. On 31 May 20-7 the following trial balance was extracted from his books:

	£	£
Income from decorating		29,000
Commissions received		
from builders		950
Cost of paint and wallpapers	4,750	
Equipment	1,675	
Vehicles	4,700	
Rent and rates	2,250	
Wages	6,900	
Drawings	7,000	
Stationery	1,750	
Vehicle expenses	2,700	
Insurance	650	
Sundry expenses	1,800	
Customer's unpaid account	790	
Trade creditors		840
Telephone	190	
Cash at bank and in hand	126	
Capital 1 June 20-6		4,491
	35,281	35,281

Notes:
(i)   There were no opening or closing stocks of paint and wallpapers
(ii) Vehicle expenses includes £100 road tax for the year ending 31 May 20-8
(iii) There is an unpaid telephone bill of £36 on 31 May 20-7
(iv) Rates prepaid at 31 May 20-7 are £90
(v)   On 31 May 20-7 there was an unused stock of stationery amounting to £300

You are required to:

(a) Prepare a profit and loss account for the year ended 31 May 20-7.
(b) Prepare a balance sheet as at 31 May 20-7.

26.7

David Courtman is a business consultant. On 31 May 20-8 the following balances remain in his ledger:

	£	£
Freehold premises	65,950	
Office equipment	14,600	
Petty cash	324	
Rates	7,216	
Loan – City Bank		25,000
General expenses	5,924	
Insurance	1,896	
Printing and stationery	1,250	
Loan interest	2,748	
Bank		2,728
Vehicles	12,550	
Wages	26,462	
Rent received		6,800
Drawings	10,050	
Bad debts	1,220	
Clients' unpaid accounts	4,590	
Commissions received for professional services		56,782
Capital at 1 June 20–7		63,470
	154,780	154,780

On 31 May 20-8 the following information is also available:

(i) David Courtman insured his premises against fire for the first time on 1 February 20-8 with an annual premium of £1,896
(ii) There was an outstanding bill of £260 for printing and a stock of stationery valued at £378
(iii) Rates of £3,936 were paid on 1 April for the year ending 31 March 20-9
(iv) Rent received in advance from the sub-tenant was £650

You are required to:

(a) Prepare a profit and loss account for the year ended 31 May 20-8.
(b) Prepare a balance sheet as at 31 May 20-8.

26.8

E Sweet is a confectionery wholesaler. On 31 March 20-2 the following trial balance was extracted from his books:

	Dr £	Cr £
Capital at 1 April 20-1		20,000
Fixtures and fittings	5,000	
Debtors and creditors	26,200	13,400
Discount allowed	1,300	
Discount received		1,700
Stock at 1 April 20-1	11,700	
Rent	1,100	
Rates	600	
Purchases and sales	39,300	54,500
Electricity	400	
Salaries	1,500	
Repairs and maintenance	300	
Purchase returns		600
Loan from Finance Co.		6,000
Bad debts	300	
Drawings	2,400	
Hire of motor van	700	
Cash in hand	800	
Cash at bank	4,600	
	96,200	96,200

Notes:
(i)   Stock at 31 March 20-2 amounted to £13,300
(ii) Salaries due but not paid £200
(iii) Fixtures and fittings should be depreciated by 10 per cent
(iv) A provision of £1,400 for doubtful debts should be created
(v)   Rates paid in advance amounted to £100
(vi) Interest of £800 was due on loan

You are required to:

(a) Prepare a trading and profit and loss account for the year ended 31 March 20-2.
(b) Prepare a balance sheet as at 31 March 20-2.

26.9

Elaine Mellor is a toy wholesaler. At the close of business on 31 March 20-9 she extracted the following trial balance from her books:

	Dr £	Cr £
Purchases and sales	17,620	38,330
Stock 1 April 20-8	6,740	
Bank balance		2,450
Cash	480	
Discount allowed and received	380	490
Returns inwards and outwards	670	890
Carriage outwards	1,050	
Rent	1,530	
Rates and insurance	960	
Provision for bad and doubtful debts		520
Fixtures and fittings	5,200	
Delivery van	7,000	
Debtors and creditors	13,790	8,030
Drawings	3,960	
Wages and salaries	7,980	
General expenses	640	
Capital 1 April 20-8		17,290
	68,000	68,000

Notes:
(i)   Stock at 31 March 20-9 was valued at £5,430
(ii) Wages and salaries accrued at 31 March 20-9 were £700
(iii) Rates prepaid were £160 at 31 March 20-9
(iv) Increase the provision for bad and doubtful debts by £270 to £790
(v) Provide for depreciation as follows: fixtures and fittings £200, delivery van £500

You are required to:

(a) Prepare Elaine Mellor's trading and profit and loss account for the year ended 31 March 20-9.
(b) Prepare a balance sheet as at 31 March 20-9.

■ ⊻ **27** The journal

This is often known as the '*journal proper*', the word *journal* is the French word for 'day book'. As we have already seen in earlier units, most transactions are first entered in one of the following *books of original entry*, before being posted to the ledger:

- Sales day book
- Purchases day book
- Returns inwards day book
- Returns outwards day book
- Cash book.

These books have grouped together all similar transactions to reduce the number of entries that need to be made in the ledger. The cash book is also considered to be a book of original entry because entries are made in it directly from documents such as cheques.

At one time all business transactions were first entered in the journal proper before being entered in the ledger. Today the journal is used only to record transactions which cannot be entered into any of the other books of original entry. Each entry in the journal will contain:

- The date
- The name of the account(s) to be debited and the amount(s)
- The name of the account(s) to be credited and the amount(s)
- A description of the transaction (this is called the *narration* or *narrative*).

Figure 27.1 is an illustration of the standard layout of the journal proper:

The Journal

Date	Details	F	Dr	Cr
	Name of account to be debited Name of account to be credited The narration			

Figure 27.1

These are some of the main uses of the journal proper:

- The purchase and sale of fixed assets *on credit*
- The correction of *errors*
- *Opening entries* – these are needed to open a new set of books
- *Transfers* between accounts
- *Writing off bad debts.*

It is important to remember that the journal is *not* a double entry account. It is a type of 'diary' where a record is kept of special transactions that are not everyday occurrences and which require an explanation. Details are recorded in the journal *before* being posted to the double entry accounts. All that is necessary to do a journal entry is to think of the *double entry*: you must determine what entries need to be made on the basis of the information provided. When you have considered the information and decided which accounts to debit and credit you record them in the journal and write a short explanation called a *narration*. We can now look at some uses of the journal.

Purchase and sale of fixed assets on credit

This is a typical example: on 1 March 20-9 Daniel Mason purchased new office furniture costing £680 on credit from Jenkins Supplies.

What will the journal entry be? Clearly the account that has *received value* is the office furniture account (*debit* the receiver). Jenkins Supplies, who has not yet been paid, will be credited (*credit* the giver); the journal entry would look like this:

The Journal

Date	Details	F	Dr	Cr
1 Mar	Office furniture account	GL1	680.00	
	Jenkins Supplies account	PL8		680.00
	Purchase on credit of new office furniture			

Journal entries cover many different types of transactions; to separate each entry, a line is drawn underneath. When we post this entry to the ledger accounts we use the folio numbers as a reminder where to find the entry if we need to check it. The double entry accounts would look like this:

Office Furniture Account   GL1

20-9			£	
1 Mar	Jenkins Supplies	J1	680.00	

Jenkins Supplies Account

PL8

				£
	20-9			
	1 Mar	Office furniture	J1	680.00

We can now look at the sale of a fixed asset on credit. On 15 May 20-9 a delivery van was sold for £2,200 on credit to B Robson.

What will the journal entry be? Clearly B Robson has *received the value* (*debit* the receiver). The delivery van account will be credited (*credit* the giver); the journal entry would look like this:

The Journal

Date	Details	F	Dr	Cr
15 May	B Robson account		2,200.00	
	Delivery van account			2,200.00
	Sale on credit of used Delivery van. Registration No EUM 34			

As part of the narration, it is good practice to record *identification numbers*, such as the serial number or registration number; this additional information is very useful for reference purposes.

Correction of errors

It is inevitable that errors will occur. Alterations and erasures should not be made in the ledger. When an error is discovered the correction is made, first by preparing a journal entry, then by posting to the double entry accounts. When correcting errors there is no simple rule, you will need to consider the error and then decide what action is required to make the correction. Let us look at some typical examples:

On 1 June 20-9 we discover that goods sold on credit to M Cook costing £236.50 had been entered in M Cookson's account.

To correct this error we must remove the £236.50 from M Cookson's account and enter it where it really belongs, in M Cook's account. The journal entry and the ledger accounts would look like this:

Date	Details	F	Dr	Cr
1 Jun	M Cook account M Cookson account Correction of error, posted to wrong personal account		236.50	236.50

M Cook Account

20-9 1 Jun Sales	J1	£ 236.50	

M Cookson Account

20-9 1 Jun Sales		£ 236.50	20-9 1 Jun M Cook	J1	£ 236.50

Now look at another example of an error in posting:

On 15 June 20-9 a payment of £250 for rent had been entered in the rates account.

To correct this error we must remove the £250.00 from the rates account and enter it where it really belongs, in the rent account. The journal entry would look like this:

The Journal

Date	Details	F	Dr	Cr
15 Jun	Rent account Rates account Correction of error, posted to wrong expense account		250.00	250.00

Opening entries

An opening journal entry is required when a business is first established or when opening a new set of books using the double entry system. This is a typical example:

John Clayton has been in business for some time without keeping proper records. On 1 March 20-7 he establishes that his assets and liabilities are as follows:

Assets	Cash in hand £325, Cash at bank £3,862, Office equipment £750, Motor van £4,600, stock of goods £3,500 Debtors: J Lister £763, K Turner £450
Liabilities:	Creditors: B Freeman £670, F Brooks £580

To prepare an opening journal entry we must always *calculate the capital*; the formula is:

$$assets\ less\ liabilities = capital$$

Assets:	£325 + £3,862 + £750 + £4,600 + £3,500 + £763 + £450 = £14,250
Liabilities:	£670 + £580 = £1,250

	£
Assets total	14,250
Less Liabilities	1,250
Capital =	13,000

We can now prepare the opening journal entry:

The Journal

Date	Details		F	Dr	Cr
				£	£
1 Mar	Cash in hand		CB	325.00	
	Cash at bank		CB	3,862.00	
	Office equipment		GL	750.00	
	Motor van		GL	4,600.00	
	Stock		GL	3,500.00	
	Debtors:	J Lister	SL	763.00	
		K Turner	SL	450.00	
	Creditors:	B Freeman	PL		670.00
		F Brooks	PL		580.00
	Capital		GL		13,000.00
				14,250.00	14,250.00
	Being the Assets and Liabilities at this date entered to open the books				

An *opening journal entry* is a summary of the financial position; it is a permanent record to which reference can be made at any time. The next stage is to open the *double entry accounts* in the ledgers. Each asset is shown as a *debit* balance, each liability and capital is shown as a *credit* balance. When the opening journal entry is posted, the ledger accounts would look like this:

Cash Book

Date 20-7	Particulars	F	Cash £	Bank £	Date 20-7	Particulars	F	Cash £	Bank £
1 Mar	Balance	J	325						
1 Mar	Balance	J		3,862					

General Ledger

Office Equipment Account

20-7			£		
1 Mar	Balance	J	750.00		

Motor Van Account

20-7			£		
1 Mar	Balance	J	4,600.00		

Stock Account

20-7			£		
1 Mar	Balance	J	3,500.00		

Capital Account

				20-7			£
				1 Mar	Balance	J	13,000.00

Sales Ledger

J Lister Account

20-7			£		
1 Mar	Balance	J	763.00		

K Turner Account

20-7			£		
1 Mar	Balance	J	450.00		

Purchase Ledger

B Freeman Account

				20-7		J	£
				1 Mar	Balance	J	670.00

F Brooks Account

				20-7		J	£
				1 Mar	Balance	J	580.00

As each item is entered in the ledger, the folio column is completed. All the accounts are then ready for future transactions to be recorded.

Transfers between accounts

There are many types of transfers between accounts and it is impossible to give a complete list. Whenever a transfer is necessary, a *preliminary record* is first made in the journal, with a narration explaining the reasons and then posted to the ledger accounts. This is a typical example: on 17 June 20-7 it was discovered that a garage bill of £250 for stereo equipment fitted to the owner's private car had been entered in the motor expenses account; this should have been charged to drawings.

What will the journal entry be? Clearly we must make a *debit* entry of £250.00 in the drawings account, where it really belongs and remove £250.00 from the motor expenses account by making a *credit* entry. The journal entry would look like this:

The Journal

Date	Details	F	Dr	Cr
17 Jun	Drawings account Motor expenses account Owner's private motor expenses transferred to Drawings account		250.00	250.00

Bad debts written off

A debtor who cannot or will not pay his debts is known as a *bad debtor,* and the amount owing is referred to as a *bad debt.* Once it is discovered that a debt is never going to be collected, the account can no longer be regarded as an asset to the business.

Usually many attempts will have been made in an effort to recover the outstanding amount; however, regardless of the circumstances, if a debtor cannot pay what is owed it is treated as a *business loss*.

This is a typical example:

Charles Bentley is a debtor for the sum of £295. On 31 July 20-7 he is declared bankrupt and the amount owing is written off as a bad debt. To write off this debt, a *debit* entry is made in the bad debts account, a *credit* entry in Charles Bentley's account. A preliminary record is first made in the journal, like this:

The Journal

Date	Details	F	Dr	Cr
31 Jul	Bad Debts account Charles Bentley account Irrecoverable debt written off		295.00	295.00

A debt which is partially bad

Sometimes a debtor comes to an arrangement to repay only part of the debt. In these circumstances the *money received* would be *debited* in the bank or cash account; the *unpaid portion* would be *written off* to the bad debts account. This is a typical example of a debt which is partially bad:

Brian Forbes, who owes the firm £268, has been declared bankrupt. On 20 August 20-7 a cheque for 50 pence in the pound, of the amount owed, is received in full settlement of the debt. The remainder is to be written off as a bad debt.

A *preliminary record* is first made in the journal, like this:

The Journal

Date	Details	F	Dr	Cr
20 Aug	Bank account Bad debts account Brian Forbes account 50 pence in the pound received in final settlement of debt, balance irrecoverable		134.00 134.00	268.00

Points to remember

- Today the journal proper is used only to record transactions which cannot be entered into any of the other books of original entry. Details are recorded in the journal *before* being posted to the double entry accounts.
- To prepare a journal entry you need to think of the *double entry*. First decide what entries need to be made on the basis of the information provided; then make the journal entry and write a short explanation called a *narration*.

Assignments

27.1

A Teagle owns a hardware shop. During February 20-3 the following transactions took place:

4 Feb Teagle purchased some new shop fittings costing £8,600 on credit from Arthur Blake

15 Feb Peter Payne bought some old shop fittings from A Teagle at an agreed price of £400, payable on 1 April 20-3

18 Feb Simon Bates owed A Teagle £51; the debt had been outstanding for over a year and Teagle decided to treat this as a bad debt

29 Feb Goods purchased on credit from Henry Jones costing £210 had been incorrectly posted to the account of Harry Albert Jones

You are required to prepare journal entries, including narrations, to record the above items.

27.2

Elaine Patterson owns a small business. During the month of June 20-3 the following transactions took place:

3 Jun Purchased on credit new office furniture costing £4,500 from Crescent Furniture Ltd

7 Jun Philip Richards' account of £470 was written off as a bad debt

9 Jun Goods sold on credit to John Belling costing £150 had been posted to John Bell's account

10 Jun Sold old motor van for £70 on credit to Car Trader

You are required to prepare journal entries, including narrations, to record the above items.

27.3

(a) Percy Green had been in business for several years and had not kept proper records. His new financial year began on 1 May 20-7 and he decided to convert his accounts to a full double entry system; he establishes that his assets and liabilities are as follows:

	£
Freehold premises	32,000
Motor van	2,600
Fixtures	1,800
Stock	6,400
Bank and cash	2,965
Debtors: T Ross	90
A Baker	64
T Bone	128
Long-term loan at 10 per cent per annum	10,000
Creditors: T Black	271
D Bacon	194
Rates prepaid	42
Interest on loan outstanding	1,100

You are required to prepare the journal entry necessary to open the books, clearly showing the amount of his capital.

(b) During the month of May 20-7 the following transactions took place:

6 May Purchased on credit new fixtures costing £950 from Micawber & Sons

8 May Some of the fittings, costing £60 were returned to Micawber & Son because they were unsuitable

12 May Green was notified that Baker had been declared bankrupt; his account of £64 was written off as a bad debt

22 May Some of the fixtures which had been purchased from Micawber & Son, costing £90, were found to be surplus to requirements and were sold to Gatt & Co on credit

29 May Goods sold on credit to T Davies costing £130 had been posted to T Davis' account

You are required to prepare journal entries, with narrations, to record the above transactions.

27.4

George Jones is the owner of a small business. During the month of May 20-6 the following transactions took place:

7 May £40 paid for rent had been entered in error in the rates account

16 May A motor van costing £2,400 bought for use in the business had been entered into the purchases account

18 May An amount of £250 received from John Boon had been credited to Tom Boon's account

22 May Cash sales of £205 had been entered in the cash book and posted to the ledger as £250

You are required to prepare journal entries, with narrations, to record the above transactions.

27.5

(a) David Robson runs a small business. He has not kept a correct set of books but now wishes to start a double entry system from 1 February 20-7.

On 1 February 20-7 he had the following assets and liabilities:

	£
Stock	5,950
Equipment	7,350
Bank overdraft	2,738
Insurance prepaid	962
Motor vehicles	18,500
Rent owing	358
Debtors	6,898
Creditors	3,094
Cash	160

You are required to write up David Robson's opening journal entry, showing clearly the amount of his capital.

(b) At the end of February the following matters were discovered:

(i) Goods costing £350 purchased on credit from T Marsland had been posted to T Marsden's account

(ii) F Ryder, who owes the firm £475, has been declared bankrupt; a cheque for 20 per cent of the amount owed has been received in full and final settlement of the debt, the remainder is to be written off as a bad debt

(iii) David Robson had taken goods costing £176 and £150 in cash for his own use, but no entry had been made in the books

(iv) B Clifton had taken £65 cash discount to which he was not entitled; this had been entered in both the customer's and the discount account

(v) A payment made to D Anderson of £395 had been entered at the debit side of the bank account and the credit side of D Anderson's account

You are required to draft the journal entries, including narrations, to record items (i–v).

27.6

(a) On 1 May 20-7 John Drake had the following assets and liabilities:

	£
Freehold land and buildings	25,000
Fixtures and fittings	1,250
Vehicle	2,000
Stock	2,600
Bank and cash	1,580
Debtors	1,500
Long-term loan	1,200
Creditors	1,300
Electricity account outstanding	30

You are required to prepare an opening Journal entry for Drake, showing his capital as at that date.

(b) During the month of May the following transactions took place:

7 May   Drake purchased a new van costing £4,750 from Better Motors, paying £1,000 cash and being given credit for the remainder

14 May   Drake sold on credit to A Baker fixtures and fittings which the business no longer required, value £250

18 May   Notification was received by Drake that J Smith, a debtor for £100, had been declared bankrupt; it was decided to write off this account as a bad debt

21 May   It was discovered that a purchase of goods on credit from T Murphy, value £25, had been debited to Murphy's account and credited to sales

You are required to prepare journal entries, including narrations, to record the above transactions.

27.7

(a) John Jennings is the owner of a small engineering firm. During October the following transactions took place:

3 Oct   New office equipment was purchased from Mega Systems, consisting of: 2 computers at £1,950 each, 2 printers at £395 each and a photocopier at £2,470, all *less* $12\frac{1}{2}$% trade discount; 25 per cent was paid by cheque, the remainder on credit

10 Oct   I Hardrup, who owes the firm £603.50, has been declared bankrupt; a cheque for 20p in the pound of the amount owed has been received in full and final settlement of the debt, the remainder is to be written off as a bad debt

15 Oct   A delivery van has been sold for book value of £1,950 to R Groves on credit; a cheque for one-third has been received, the balance is to be paid on 15 December 20-1

You are required to show journal entries, with narrations, to record the above transactions.

(b) John Jennings' accounts were reviewed on 31 October and the following errors were discovered:
   (i) A cash payment of £143 to M Dyson had been entered in the cash book and posted to the ledger as £341
   (ii) Goods bought on credit from T Clark, costing £390, had been entered in J Clarkson's account
   You are required to show journal entries, with narrations, to record items (i) and (ii).

(c) John Jennings' financial year ends on 31 October. From the balances given below prepare the closing journal entries to transfer the figures to the final accounts:

General expenses £2,074
Carriage inwards £652
Discount allowed £890

☑ **28** Errors not affecting trial balance agreement

Taking out a trial balance is a way of *checking the book-keeping*. A trial balance which agrees indicates that for every debit entry there has been a corresponding credit entry, but it does *not* prove that *no errors have been made*. A trial balance has limitations, and for this reason it is considered to be only a *prima facie* proof of accuracy (*prima facie* means 'at first sight'). There are six types of error that will not affect the agreement of the trial balance:

1 Original errors
2 Errors of omission
3 Errors of commission
4 Errors of principle
5 Compensating errors
6 Complete reversal of entries.

Original errors

These happen when the *original document is incorrect*: the book-keeping entries made from that document will also be incorrect. For example: an error was made in the calculation of a sales invoice and double entry was carried out using the incorrect figure.

More often these errors occur when *copying figures from original documents*, such as invoices, credit and debit notes into the day books. For example: if an invoice for £459 received from James Cartright, a supplier, is entered in the supplier's account and the purchases account as £495, the trial balance *would still agree*, it would not show that this error has been made. When correcting errors there is no simple rule: you will need to consider the error and then decide what action is required to make the correction. When an error is discovered the correction is made first by preparing a journal entry, then by posting to the double entry accounts.

We can now look at this example: the amount posted to the double entry accounts was greater than the correct amount, the original invoice of £459 was entered in the accounts as £495. First we must calculate the amount involved (£495 *less* £459 = £36), this is the amount needed to correct the error. A *debit* entry of £36 in the supplier's account will make the necessary reduction with a corresponding *credit* entry in the purchases account. The journal entry would look like this:

The Journal

Date	Details	F	Dr	Cr
8 Mar	James Cartwright account Purchases account Correction of error, purchase invoice of £459 entered as £495		36.00	36.00

Errors of omission

As the name suggests, these are transactions which have been *completely omitted from the books*. Sometimes a document is mislaid before it is even entered into the books: neither the debit or credit entry has been made in the ledger so the trial balance *would still agree*. This is a typical example: an invoice of £499 from Office Supplies for a new printer had been mislaid and had not been entered in the accounts.

These types of errors are probably the easiest to correct because all you need to consider is the *double entry*. Clearly the account that has *received value* is the office equipment account (*debit* the receiver); Office Supplies who has not yet been paid, will be credited (*credit* the giver). When an error is discovered the correction is made, first by preparing a journal entry, then by posting to the double entry accounts. The journal entry for this example would look like this:

The Journal

Date	Details	F	Dr	Cr
4 Apr	Office Equipment account Office Supplies account Correction of omission of invoice for new printer		499.00	499.00

Errors of commission

The word *commission* means '*authority to take action*': an error of commission is one where the *action taken is incorrect*. Errors of commission happen when both the debit and credit entries are made but a wrong account is used. Frequently this type of error occurs when two debtors or creditors have the same or similar names: it is quite easy to post a debt to the wrong account. This is a typical example: on 7 May goods sold on credit to C Green costing £285.60 had been posted to C Gray's account.

The trial balance *would still agree* because the total debtors would be correct – it cannot distinguish between these two debtors. Probably the error would be discovered when C Gray was asked to pay for goods he had never ordered or received.

When an error is discovered the correction is made, first by preparing a journal entry, then by posting to the double entry accounts.

To correct this error a *debit* entry is needed in C Green's account (*debit* the receiver). C Gray's account will be *credited* to remove the amount posted in error. The journal entry would look like this:

The Journal

Date	Details	F	Dr	Cr
7 May	C Green account		285.60	
	C Gray account			285.60
	Correction of error posted to wrong personal account			

Errors of principle

This type of error occurs when a transaction is entered in the *wrong type of account*. It is a common mistake when purchasing assets to treat them as purchases of goods and include them in the purchases account. This type of error has a serious effect on the profits of a business. The trial balance would still agree but the assets figure would be less than it should be and the purchases figure would be too large. This is a typical example: on 17 June new office furniture costing £950 was purchased on credit from New Systems Ltd; this had been debited in error to the purchases account. One of the entries is wrong in principle, but the trial balance *would still agree* – it would not reveal this error.

When an error is discovered the correction is made, first by preparing a journal entry, then by posting to the double entry accounts. To correct this error, a *debit* entry is needed in the office furniture account; a *credit* entry in the purchases account will remove the amount posted in error. The journal entry would look like this:

The Journal

Date	Details	F	Dr	Cr
17 Jun	Office furniture account		950.00	
	Purchases account			950.00
	Correction of error, new office furniture posted to purchases account			

Compensating errors

These are errors which *cancel out each other*. They happen when two separate errors of the same amount have been made, one affecting the debit column and one affecting the credit column. The trial balance *would still agree* – the debit column and the credit column would be incorrect by the same amount, but the errors would cancel out each other.

These are often *addition errors* – for example: if the sales day book is overcast by £100 and the purchases day book is overcast by the same amount, the trial balance would still agree. The extra £100 in the sales account (*credit* column) will have been compensated by the extra £100 in the purchases account (*debit* column). Details of the correction would first be entered in the journal and then posted to the double entry accounts. To correct this error, we need a *debit* entry to reduce the sales account by £100 and a *credit* entry to reduce purchases by £100. The journal entry would look like this:

The Journal

Date	Details	F	Dr	Cr
30 Jun	Sales account Purchases account Correction of compensating errors, totals of sales and purchases day books incorrectly added		100.00	100.00

Complete reversal of entries

These errors occur when the *entries for a transaction are reversed* – the account which should have been debited is credited and vice versa. The correct amounts are entered in the correct accounts, but the entries are made at the *wrong side* of each account.

This is a typical example: a cheque of £450 paid to D Mason, a supplier, was entered at the debit side of the bank account and the credit side of the supplier's account; the trial balance *would still agree*, because a debit and credit entry for the same amount had been made.

These errors are more difficult to correct; it is not simply a matter of reversing the incorrect entries. To correct these errors, *double* the amount is needed. Entering only the original amount would merely cancel out the error leaving no entry of the transaction.

To correct this error, we need a *debit* entry of £900 in D Mason's account and a credit entry of £900 in the bank account. The journal entry would look like this:

The Journal

Date	Details	F	Dr	Cr
3 Aug	D Mason account Bank account Correction of error, payment by cheque of £450 was entered at debit side of Bank account and credit side of D Mason's account		900.00	900.00

Points to remember

- Errors can occur in many different ways; correcting errors depends upon a clear understanding of the *double entry system.* You will need to consider the error and then decide what action is required to make the correction.
- When an error is discovered the correction is made, first by preparing a *journal entry,* then by posting to the *double entry accounts.*
- 'Casting' is a term that is often used – *to cast* means 'to add up':
  - *Overcasting* means incorrectly adding up a column of figures to give an answer which is *greater* than it should be.
  - *Undercasting* means incorrectly adding up a column of figures to give an answer which is *less* than it should be.

Assignments

28.1
(a) Explain why a trial balance which agrees is not conclusive proof of the complete accuracy of the accounts.

(b) State **three** types of errors which will not affect the trial balance agreement.

28.2
(a) To what extent is the agreement of the trial balance proof of accuracy of the books? How would the omission of:

   (i) the opening stock, and
   (ii) the closing stock affect the trial balance?

(b) State the initial steps you would take to locate the error if the trial balance disagreed.

28.3

On 31 March 20-4 the following balances appeared in the ledger of Terry Dennis:

	£
Drawings	1,600
Rent and rates	350
Stock, 1 April 20-3	5,500
Bank overdraft	750
Wages	8,000
Petty cash	60
Creditor for office equipment	1,600
Selling expenses	3,100
Purchases	11,206
Trade creditors	2,746
Carriage outwards	410
Sales	26,532
Office expenses	4,730
Trade debtors	2,650
Commission received	520
Furniture and equipment	19,600
Discount allowed	428
Capital	?

You are required to:

(a) Prepare a trial balance as at 31 March 20-4 and calculate the capital account balance.
(b) State the procedures you would adopt if the trial balance does not agree.
(c) Certain types of error can occur even though the trial balance agrees. Name and describe **three** types of such errors.

28.4

Andrew Scott is a retailer selling newspapers and confectionery. On 29 February 20-8 the following trial balance was extracted from his books:

	£	£
Capital		40,100
Drawings	5,000	
Rent and rates	2,500	
Lighting and heating	2,400	
Advertising	220	
Motor expenses	1,200	
Wages and salaries	8,500	
Insurance	500	
Purchases	26,100	
Sales		55,320
Creditors		2,500
Motor vehicles	15,000	
Equipment	20,000	
Stock of goods: 1 March 20-7	12,000	
Cash in hand	100	
Cash at bank	4,400	
	97,920	97,920

After preparation of the trial balance the following errors were discovered:

(i) **15 Jun** A payment of £200 by cheque to D Smith, a creditor, had been debited to the account of D Smithson

(ii) **13 Aug** An invoice for the purchase of sweets and confectionery for £340 from R Wallis and Co had not been entered in the books

(iii) **24 Sep** A payment for repairs to the motor vehicles of £500 had been entered in the motor vehicles account

(iv) **30 Oct** Andrew Scott had bought petrol for his own use costing £200; this had been entered in the motor expenses account

You are required to:

(a) Prepare journal entries to correct these errors.
(b) Rewrite the trial balance *after* the errors have been corrected.

28.5

After a year's trading the following balances appeared in the ledger of Nicholas Davidson on 31 May 20-6:

	£
Stock	2,025
Drawings	1,396
Carriage outwards	194
Wages and salaries	16,830
Discount allowed	103
Creditors	2,405
General expenses	810
Purchases	10,092
Bad Debts	158
Sales	14,580
Returns inwards	175
Debtors	3,890
Discount received	369
Premises	38,500
Returns outwards	238
Petty cash	82
Cash at bank	1,837
Capital	?

A short time later the following information was discovered:

(i) Nicholas Davidson's private motor expenses had been entered in general expenses; these are estimated to be 20 per cent of general expenses

(ii) A Slowman, who owes the firm £240, has been declared bankrupt; a cheque for 15 per cent of the amount owed is received in full and final settlement of the debt, the remainder is to be written off as a bad debt

(iii) An invoice for £158 received from M Ramsden, a supplier, had not been entered in the books

(iv) Goods bought on credit from F Greenwood costing £350 had been incorrectly posted to the account of T Greenfield

You are required to:

(a) Prepare a trial balance as at 31 May 20-6 after considering the above information and calculate the capital account balance.

(b) Show journal entries to record items (i)–(iv). Full narrations are required.

(c) Clearly show the correct date against the stock item in your trial balance.

28.6

You work in the accounts department of Moortown Enterprises. On 30 April 20-9 the following balances appeared in the ledger:

	£
Stock	3,095
Carriage outwards	249
Drawings	2,586
Discount allowed	403
Creditors	5,409
Sundry expenses	1,608
Purchases	11,928
Bad debts	685
Sales	18,470
Returns inwards	430
Debtors	8,750
Discount received	682
Rates	1,206
Premises	68,500
Returns outwards	964
Bank overdraft	3,145
Petty cash	220
Wages and salaries	16,260
Capital	?

A short time later the following information was discovered:

(i) The bank statement showed that a payment for rates of £850 had been made by direct debit, but no entry had been made in the accounts

(ii) D Myers, who owes the firm £480, has been declared bankrupt; a cheque for 15 per cent of the amount owed is received in full and final settlement of the debt, the remainder is to be written off as a bad debt

(iii) Goods bought on credit from K Williams costing £578 had been incorrectly posted to K Williamson's account

(iv) An invoice for £202 received from A Oldridge had not been entered in the books

(v) A payment of £253 for repairs to the owner's private car had been entered in sundry expenses

You are required to:

(a) Prepare a trial balance as at 30 April 20-9 after considering the above information and calculate the capital account balance.

(b) Show journal entries to record items (i)–(v). Full narrations are required.

28.7

You work in the accounts department of Weetwood Enterprises. On 31 May 20-9 the following balances appeared in the ledger:

	£
Purchases	11,026
Creditors	3,862
Stock	3,252
Returns outwards	493
Discount received	495
Returns inwards	364
Bad debts	315
Petty cash	183
Debtors	6,396
Commission received	780
Carriage outwards	574
Discount allowed	402
Equipment	18,750
Carriage inwards	369
Drawings	2,040
Wages and salaries	16,865
General expenses	840
Sales	15,480
Bank balance	1,364
Capital	?

A short time later the following information was discovered:

(i)   A credit note for £76 received from R Foxwood had not been entered in the books
(ii) Goods bought on credit from M Kellerman costing £485 had been incorrectly posted to the account of M Keller
(iii) C Gulliver, who owes the firm £360, has been declared bankrupt; cheque for 15 per cent of the amount owed is received in full and final settlement of the debt, the remainder is to be written off as a bad debt
(iv) The owner's private motor expenses had been entered in general expenses; these are estimated to be $12\frac{1}{2}$ per cent
(v)   A customer, G Sanderson, had deducted £18 discount to which he was not entitled; this had been entered in the customer's account and the discount account

You are required to:

(a) Prepare a trial balance as at 31 May 20-9 after considering the above information and calculate the capital account balance.
(b) Show journal entries to record items (i)–(v). Full narrations are required.

☒ **29** Control accounts

In order to understand control accounts you must first appreciate why they are necessary. In a small business the accounts can easily and quickly be checked to find any errors. However, in a large business with hundreds of accounts any errors can be very difficult to find and extremely time consuming. Firms with large numbers of debtors and creditors often divide a ledger into alphabetical sections, for example: **A to F**, **G to L**, **M to S**, **T to Z**; they use *control accounts* to check on the accuracy of each ledger or section of the ledger. A control account contains the same information as the individual ledger accounts which it *controls*, but in total. Because totals are used they are often known as *total accounts*.

A control account can be maintained for any ledger or part of a ledger, but the two most frequently used control accounts are the sales ledger control account and the purchase ledger control account. They operate on the principle that whatever is entered in an individual account is also entered in the control account and the balance on the control account must equal the total of the individual balances on the ledger, or section of the ledger which it controls.

It must be emphasised that control accounts are not necessarily part of the double entry system. They are mathematical proofs performing the same function as a trial balance to a particular ledger or section of a ledger. When individual debtors' and creditors' accounts are kept on the double entry system, then the control account is *not*, otherwise the entries would be duplicated. It is usual to find control accounts in the same form as a normal account.

Control accounts are an excellent test of a student's ability and for this reason they regularly appear as examination questions.

Sales ledger control account

Accounts in the sales ledger will normally have *debit* balances because they are the *personal accounts of debtors*. Everyday entries are made in the sales ledger to record sales, returns inwards, cash and cheques received from customers, discounts allowed and any bad debts. A sales ledger control account is prepared using the *total* of all the individual items that have been entered in the debtors' accounts. We can now look at a typical example question.

Worked question

From the following information, prepare a sales ledger control account for the month of May, clearly showing the balance carried forward at 31 May 20-9:

		£
(i)	1 May Sales ledger balances	23,524
(ii)	Sales day book	19,870
(iii)	Returns inwards day book	670
(iv)	Cheques received from customers	17,450
(v)	Discount allowed	371
(vi)	Bad debts written off	300

When asked to prepare a sales ledger control account, you simply ask yourself, on each item: '*where would this appear on an ordinary debtor's account?*' This is because the items appear in exactly the same place in the sales ledger control account.

(i)   This is the total of all the individual debtor's balances; they would appear at the *debit* side of each debtor's account, so the total is placed at the *debit* side of the control account, like this:

Sales Ledger Control Account

20-9		£	20-9		£
1 May	Balance b/d	23,524			

(ii)   This is the total of the sales day book for the month of May (or the sales account if day books are not used). Sales are entered at the *debit* side of each customer's account, so the total sales for the month are placed at the *debit* side of the control account, like this:

Sales Ledger Control Account

20-9		£	20-9		£
1 May	Balance b/d	23,524			
31 May	Sales	19,870			

(iii)   This is the total of the returns inwards day book for the month of May (or the returns inwards account if day books are not used). Returns inwards are entered at the *credit* side of each customer's account, so the total for the month is placed at the *credit* side of the control account, like this:

Sales Ledger Control Account

20-9		£	20-9		£
1 May	Balance b/d	23,524	31 May	Returns inwards	670
31 May	Sales	19,870			

(iv) This is the total amount of cheques received from customers during the month of May. Money received is entered at the *credit* side of each customer's account, so the total for the month is placed at the *credit* side of the control account, like this:

Sales Ledger Control Account

20-9		£	20-9		£
1 May	Balance b/d	23,524	31 May	Returns inwards	670
31 May	Sales	19,870	31 May	Bank	17,450

(v) This is the total discount allowed to customers during the month of May. Discount allowed is entered at the *credit* side of each customer's account, so the total for the month is placed at the *credit* side of the control account, like this:

Sales Ledger Control Account

20-9		£	20-9		£
1 May	Balance b/d	23,524	31 May	Returns inwards	670
31 May	Sales	19,870	31 May	Bank	17,450
			31 May	Discount allowed	371

(vi) This is the total bad debts written off during the month of May. Bad debts are entered at the *credit* side of a customer's account, so the total for the month is placed at the *credit* side of the control account, like this:

Sales Ledger Control Account

20-9		£	20-9		£
1 May	Balance b/d	23,524	31 May	Returns inwards	670
31 May	Sales	19,870	31 May	Bank	17,450
			31 May	Discount allowed	371
			31 May	Bad debts	300

Now all we need to do is *balance the account*, like this:

Sales Ledger Control Account

20-9		£	20-9		£
1 May	Balance b/d	23,524	31 May	Returns inwards	670
31 May	Sales	19,870	31 May	Bank	17,450
			31 May	Discount allowed	371
			31 May	Bad debts	300
			31 May	Balance c/d	24,603
		43,394			43,394
1 Jun	Balance b/d	24,603			

Purchase ledger control account

Accounts in the purchase ledger will normally have *credit balances* because they are the *personal accounts of creditors*. Everyday entries are made in the purchase ledger to record purchases, returns outwards, cash and cheques paid to suppliers and discounts received. A purchase ledger control account is prepared using the *total* of all the individual items which have been entered in the creditors' accounts. We can now look at a typical example question.

Worked questions

From the following information, prepare a purchase ledger control account for the month of May, clearly showing the balance carried forward at 31 May 20-9:

		£
(i)	1 May Purchase ledger balances	20,690
(ii)	Purchase day book	8,760
(iii)	Returns outwards day book	490

(iv) Cheques paid to creditors   9,765
(v) Discount received   470

When asked to prepare a purchase ledger control account, you must ask yourself, on each item: '*where would this appear on an normal creditor's account?*' simply because the items appear in exactly the same place in the purchase ledger control account.

(i)   This is the total of all the individual creditor's balances; they would appear at the *credit* side of each creditor's account, so the total is placed at the *credit* side of the control account.
(ii)   This is the total of the purchases day book for the month of May (or the purchases account if day books are not used). Purchases are entered at the *credit* side of each supplier's account, so the total for the month is placed at the *credit* side of the control account.
(iii) This is the total of the returns outwards day book for the month of May (or the returns outwards account if day books are not used). Returns outwards are entered at the *debit* side of each creditor's account, so the total for the month is placed at the *debit* side of the control account.
(iv)   This is the total amount of cheques paid to creditors during the month of May. Money paid out is entered at the *debit* side of each creditor's account, so the total for the month is placed at the *debit* side of the control account.
(v)   This is the total discount received during the month of May. Discount received is entered at the *debit* side of each creditor's account, so the total for the month is placed at the *debit* side of the control account.

When these entries have been made, you would *balance the account,* and it would look like this:

Purchase Ledger Control Account

20-9		£	20-9		£
31 May	Returns outwards	490	1 May	Balance b/d	20,690
			31 May	Purchases	8,760
31 May	Bank	9,765			
31 May	Discount received	470			
31 May	Balance c/d	18,725			
		29,450			29,450
			1 Jun	Balance b/d	18,725

Some examination questions ask for the debtors or creditors accounts to be completed as well as the control account. This is a typical example:

Elaine Mellor has a small business which produces a wide range of educational toys and games. On 1 May 20-6 her sales ledger contained the following debtors:

	£
A Buckley	208.00
W Dixon	275.00
L Gibson	392.00

During the month of May the following transactions took place:

Sales

May	Goods £	VAT £	Total £
2 W Dixon	113.64	11.36	125.00
8 A Buckley	143.64	14.36	158.00
17 L Gibson	266.36	26.64	293.00

Returns Inwards

May	Goods £	VAT £	Total £
10 W Dixon	31.82	3.18	35.00
27 L Gibson	42.73	4.27	47.00

Payments received by cheque

May	Discount allowed £	Cheque value £
16 A Buckley	10.00	198.00
20 L Gibson	18.00	374.00
30 W Dixon	12.00	228.00

You are required to:

(a) Open ledger accounts for all debtors and enter the balances as at 1 May 20-6.
(b) Enter the transactions which have taken place during the month of May to the appropriate ledger accounts and balance the accounts at the end of the month.
(c) Show the entries which would appear in the sales, returns inwards and VAT accounts in the general ledger.
(d) Prepare a sales ledger control account for May 20-6 and reconcile the balance with the total debtors balances in the sales ledger.

This is a fully worked answer to this question:

A Buckley Account

20-6		£	20-6		£
1 May	Balance b/d	208	16 May	Bank	198
8 May	Sales	158	16 May	Discount allowed	10
			31 May	Balance c/d	158
		366			366
1 Jun	Balance b/d	158			

W Dixon Account

20-6		£	20-6		£
1 May	Balance b/d	275	10 May	Returns inwards	35
2 May	Sales	125	30 May	Bank	228
			30 May	Discount allowed	12
			31 May	Balance c/d	125
		400			400
1 Jun	Balance b/d	125			

L Gibson Account

20-6		£	20-6		£
1 May	Balance b/d	392	20 May	Bank	374
20 May	Sales	293	20 May	Discount allowed	18
			27 May	Returns inwards	47
			31 May	Balance c/d	246
		685			685
1 Jun	Balance b/d	246			

Sales Account

			20-6		£
			31 May	Total for month	523.64

Returns Inwards Account

20-6		£		
31 May	Total for month	74.55		

Value Added Tax Account

20-6		£	20-6		£
31 May	Total ret inwards	7.45	31 May	Total sales book	52.36

Sales Ledger Control Account

20-6		£	20-6		£
1 May	Balance b/d	875.00	31 May	Returns inwards	74.55
31 May	Sales	523.64	31 May	VAT	7.45
31 May	VAT	52.36	31 May	Bank	800.00
			31 May	Discount allowed	40.00
			31 May	Balance c/d	529.00
		1,451.00			1,451.00
1 Jun	Balance b/d	529.00			

Debtors' balances:	£
A Buckley	158.00
W Dixon	125.00
L Gibson	246.00
	529.00 = balance on Sales Ledger Control Account

Points to remember

- A control account contains the same information as the individual ledger accounts which it *controls*, but in total. Because totals are used they are often known as *total accounts*.
- Sales and purchase ledger control accounts are prepared using the *total* of all the individual items which have been entered in the debtors' and creditors' accounts.
- When preparing a control account you simply ask yourself, on each item: *where would this appear on a normal debtor's or creditor's account?* This is because the items appear in exactly the same place in the control account.
- The balance on the control account *must* equal the total of the individual balances on the ledger, or section of the ledger which it controls.
- Occasionally there could be a dishonoured cheque; this is a cheque returned by a debtor's bank unpaid. This would be entered at the *debit* side of the sales ledger control account.

Assignments

29.1
From the following information, prepare a sales ledger control account for the month of May, clearly showing the balance carried forward at 31 May 20-7:

		£
1 May	Sales ledger balances	4,760
	Sales day book	5,912
	Returns inwards day book	423
	Cheques received from customers	3,969
	Discount allowed	179
	Bad debts written off	57

29.2
From the following information, prepare a purchase ledger control account for the month of May, clearly showing the balance carried forward at 31 May 20-7:

		£
1 May	Purchase ledger balances	8,904
	Purchases day book	7,038
	Returns outwards day book	324
	Cheques paid to creditors	6,604
	Discount received	272

29.3
From the following information, prepare a sales ledger control account for the month of June, clearly showing the balance carried forward at 30 June 20-7:

		£
1 June	Sales ledger balances	6,869
	Sales day book	12,762
	Returns inwards day book	295
	Cash received from customers	187
	Cheques received from customers	11,230
	Discount allowed	536
	Bad debts written off	552
	Dishonoured cheque	119

29.4
From the following information, prepare a purchase ledger control account for the month of June, clearly showing the balance carried forward at 30 June 20-7:

		£
1 June	Purchase ledger balances	13,561
	Purchases day book	17,614

		£
	Returns outwards day book	232
	Cheques paid to creditors	12,760
	Discount received	101

29.5

Khalid Shah extracted the following balances from his books for the month of January 20-7:

		£
1 January	Purchase ledger balances	14,641
1 January	Sales ledger balances	17,542
	Totals for January	
	Purchases day book	135,652
	Sales day book	197,961
	Returns outwards day book	2,864
	Returns inwards day book	4,231
	Cheques paid to creditors	142,876
	Cash and cheques received from customers	197,580
	Discount allowed	5,180
	Discount received	2,708
	Bad debts written off	342
	Customers' cheques dishonoured	54

You are required to:

(a) Prepare a sales ledger control account for the month of January, clearly showing the balance carried forward at 31 January 20-7.

(b) Prepare a purchase ledger control account for the month of January, clearly showing the balance carried forward at 31 January 20-7.

29.6

The following information relates to the sales ledger control account for ledger number 2, K to R:

	£
Debit balances on 1 May 20-4	3,788
Cash received from customers	2,300
Cheques received from customers	14,568
Returns inwards	292
Bad debts written off	172
Discounts allowed	300
Sales	20,580
Debit balances on 31 May 20-4 as extracted from sales ledger	6,781

You are required to:

(a) Write up the sales ledger control account from the information given above.

(b) Comment on the significance of the closing figure as revealed by the control account with the figure for debtors as extracted from the sales ledger.

29.7

Emily McGregor has a small business which produces a wide range of educational toys and games. On 1 May 20-9 her sales ledger contained the following debtors:

	£
A Butler	804.62
W Dyson	472.95
L Grainger	628.38

During the month of May the following transactions took place:

Sales on credit

May	Goods £	VAT £	Total £
2 W Dyson	394.64	39.46	434.10
8 A Butler	418.83	41.88	460.71
17 L Grainger	626.90	62.69	689.59

Returns Inwards

May	Goods £	VAT £	Total £
10 W Dyson	62.72	6.27	68.99
27 L Grainger	48.34	4.83	53.17

Payments received by cheque

May	Discount allowed £	Cheque value £
16 A Butler	40.24	764.38
20 L Grainger	23.65	449.30
30 W Dyson	31.42	596.96

You are required to:

(a) Open ledger accounts for all debtors and enter the balances as at 1 May 20-9.
(b) Enter the transactions which have taken place during the month of May to the appropriate ledger accounts and balance the accounts at the end of the month.
(c) Show the entries which would appear in the sales, returns inwards and VAT accounts in the general ledger.
(d) Prepare a sales ledger control account for May 20-9 and reconcile the balance with the total debtors balances in the sales ledger.

29.8

Jean Oldridge has a small business which produces an exclusive range of sports wear. On 1 May 20-9 her sales ledger contained the following debtors:

	£
G Anderson	796.42
V Ellis	428.78
M Hariman	873.96

During the month of May the following transactions took place:

Sales on credit

May	Goods £	VAT £	Total £
2 V Ellis	593.20	59.32	652.52
8 G Anderson	847.92	84.79	932.71
17 M Hariman	735.70	73.57	809.27

Returns Inwards

May	Goods £	VAT £	Total £
10 V Ellis	63.82	6.38	70.20
27 M Hariman	77.64	7.76	85.40

Payments received by cheque

May	Discount allowed £	Cheque value £
16 G Anderson	39.82	756.60
20 M Hariman	43.70	830.26
30 V Ellis	21.44	407.34

You are required to:

(a) Open ledger accounts for all debtors and enter the balances as at 1 May 20-9.
(b) Enter the transactions which have taken place during the month of May to the appropriate ledger accounts and balance the accounts at the end of the month.
(c) Show the entries which would appear in the sales, returns inwards and VAT accounts in the general ledger.
(d) Prepare a sales ledger control account for May 20-9 and reconcile the balance with the total debtors balances in the sales ledger.

■ ⋮ **30** Capital and revenue expenditure and receipts

Whenever a firm spends money it *receives some form of value* in goods or services. However, the value received from the money spent varies in the length of time it is of benefit to the business. For example: if a firm buys a filing cabinet it may last 10 years, if a firm buys petrol it will last a much shorter time. The contrast between these two types of expense is the difference between *capital* and *revenue expenditure*.

Capital expenditure

Capital expenditure is when a firm spends money to *buy fixed assets* or when money is spent to *increase the value of an existing fixed asset*. Usually they will last a long time (*more than a year*) and provide the framework within which the business activities are carried out.

 Capital expenditure includes:

(i)   Buying fixed assets
(ii) Increasing the value of an existing fixed asset; this could be an extension to an existing building
(iii) Legal costs of buying or extending buildings
(iv) Cost of carriage and installation of new machinery
(v)   Any other cost needed to get a fixed asset ready for use.

Revenue expenditure

Money spent on the day to day running of a business is known as *revenue expenditure*. This includes goods purchased for resale, or materials which are purchased for manufacture before being sold. Also expenses such as: salaries, wages, lighting and heating, rent, rates and so on. Generally these costs are used up in *one year or less* and do not add to the value of fixed assets.

Differences between capital and revenue expenditure

Basically the difference between these two types of expenditure is the *length of time* the expenditure is of benefit to the business. A good general guideline is:

- *longer than one year* – capital expenditure
- *one year or less* – revenue expenditure.

Difficulty is sometimes experienced in what is generally referred to as *capitalisation* of revenue expenditure. This happens when a business incurs revenue expenditure on an item which is a fixed asset. This is best illustrated in the following example: wages are paid to the firm's workmen engaged in building a new office extension. Normally, wages are revenue expenditure, but in this example the wages are paid to workmen employed building a new office extension. The new building would be capital expenditure and because these wages costs are directly involved with *increasing the value of an existing fixed asset*, they would be capitalised and treated as capital expenditure.

Legal expenses are normally revenue expenditure. However, the legal charges incurred for conveyancing in the purchase of land or buildings, or an extension to an existing building, would be capital expenditure because these costs would be directly related to the purchase of a fixed asset.

Dealing with borderline cases

In some situations it is difficult to decide whether the expenditure is capital or revenue. For example, if a firm redecorates its premises every three years, is this capital or revenue expenditure? Generally it will last more than a year, but the expenditure has not provided a new asset, it has only ensured that the premises do not deteriorate. This type of expense is considered to be part of the *normal maintenance running costs* and is regarded as *revenue expenditure.*

The examples in Table 30.1 will illustrate the difference:

Table 30.1 **Types of expenditure**

Expenditure	Type of expenditure
Purchase of new motor van	Capital
Petrol costs for motor van	Revenue
Insurance for motor van	Revenue
Repairs to motor van	Revenue
Cost of building extension to factory	Capital
Cost of painting new extension	Capital
Repainting extension three years later	Revenue

Revenue expenditure is charged to the *trading or profit and loss account,* while capital expenditure will result in increased figures for fixed assets on the *balance sheet.*

Joint expenditure

Sometimes an item of expenditure will be *part capital and part revenue expenditure* – a typical example would be: the purchase of a motor van:

- *Buying* the motor van would be the purchase of a fixed asset, probably useful for a number of years, so this would be capital expenditure.
- However, *paying for insurance* to use the motor van would be revenue expenditure because it would be used up in a short time and does not add to the value of fixed assets.

Capital receipts

Capital receipts consist of the money received from the *sale of fixed assets.* For example, if a plot of land was sold, the money received would be a *capital receipt.* Similarly, if the owner of a business invested a further sum of money for use in the business, this would be treated as a capital receipt.

Revenue receipts

Revenue receipts consist of money received from sales, commission received for services supplied and all other *revenue received items* such as: rent received and discount received.

At the end of the financial year all items of revenue received are transferred to the profit and loss account to be set against the revenue expenses.

Points to remember

- *Capital expenditure* is the money spent to buy fixed assets or to increase the value of an existing fixed asset.
- *Revenue expenditure* is money spent on the daily running costs of a business.
- The difference between these two types of expenditure is the *length of time* the expenditure is of benefit to the business.
- When a fixed asset is sold the money received is called a *capital receipt.*
- *Revenue receipts* are money received from sales and all other revenue received items.

Assignments

30.1

Classify the following items under the heading of capital expenditure or revenue expenditure:

(a) Purchase of a new machine for use in the business
(b) Quarterly account for electricity
(c) Purchase of a new motor van
(d) Cost of road tax for new van
(e) Cost of repairs to photocopier
(f) Fire insurance premium

30.2

John Conway has a retail food business. Classify the following items under the heading of capital or revenue expenditure:

(a) Purchase of a refrigerated display counter
(b) Repainting shop door
(c) Repairs to meat slicer
(d) Purchase of new cash register
(e) Replacement of a broken window
(f) New tyres for the delivery van
(g) Installation of burglar alarm system
(h) Insurance premium for delivery van
(i) Wages of shop assistant

30.3

Angus Scott is in business as an estate agent, some of his transactions are given below:

(a) Rent
(b) Purchase of photocopying machine
(c) Commission received from builder
(d) Fees received from clients for professional services
(e) Wages of secretary
(f) Cost of new display equipment
(g) Cost of installing new display equipment
(h) Redecoration of shop front
(i) Proceeds from sale of old computer

You are required to:

(a) Explain the meaning of the following accounting terms:
   Capital expenditure   Revenue expenditure
   Capital receipts   Revenue receipts.
(b) Rule up four columns headed: Capital expenditure, Revenue expenditure, Capital receipt and Revenue receipt, and list items (a)–(i) in the appropriate columns.

30.4
The Pier View Garage paid for the items given below:

(a) Breakdown truck
(b) Paper for photocopier
(c) Sweets for sale in forecourt kiosk
(d) Insurance for breakdown truck
(e) New petrol pumps
(f) Repairs to forecourt lighting
(g) A secondhand car for resale
(h) Wages of forecourt cashier

You are required to:

(a) Briefly explain the term *revenue expenditure.*
(b) List items (a)–(h) as appropriate under the headings of capital or revenue expenditure.

30.5
A Rogers opened his own business as a newsagent and paid for the following:

(i)   Wages of shop assistant
(ii)   Purchase of a new cash register
(iii)   Repairs to leaking shop window
(iv)   Fire insurance premium
(v)   A new extension to the rear of the premises to provide more storage space
(vi)   Purchase of floor cleaning materials for use in the shop
(vii) Legal fees paid in connection with the building of the extension
(viii) Purchase of stock for resale

You are required to:

(a) For each item, state whether it is capital or revenue expenditure.
(b) Briefly explain the difference between these two types of expenditure.

30.6
Mr Brown has recently started a new business and is puzzled by the terms *capital expenditure* and *revenue expenditure.*

(a) Explain to him what 'capital expenditure' is.

(b) Mr Brown has purchased a new van; the details of the account were as follows:

	£
Van	13,000
Seat belts	124
Delivery charges	242
Number plates	15
Road tax	150
Insurance	320
	13,851

He has also received an account from his local builder, details of which are as follows:

	£
Redecorate shop front	400
Erect shelves in stock room	90
	490

You are required to list the items from both invoices under their respective headings of capital and revenue expenditure.

30.7

State whether the following transactions of Salford Engineering Company are *capital* or *revenue* expenditure:

(a) Purchase of motor van
(b) Yearly premium to insure motor van
(c) Cost of rebuilding factory wall damaged by frost
(d) Purchase of freehold land
(e) Cost of building extension to factory
(f) Cost of painting new extension
(g) Legal costs on acquiring land for the extension
(h) Repainting extension four years after completion
(i) Cost of repairs to motor van
(j) Repairing roof of extension

30.8

(a) Briefly explain the difference between capital and revenue expenditure.

(b) Identify each of the following items of expenditure as capital or revenue and state whether you would expect to find each item in the trading account, profit and loss account or balance sheet:

  (i)   £200 paid to hauliers for carriage inwards
  (ii) £125 paid to Better Garages for fitting seat belts to new van
  (iii) £300 for replacement of broken window
  (iv) £450 to Unicold for supply and installation of refrigerated shop counter.

30.9

During the month of February Thomas Wilding paid for the following items:

(i)   Fire insurance premium for factory
(ii) Cost of building new extension to factory
(iii) Legal fees paid in connection with new extension
(iv) Carriage costs on purchases
(v)   Cost of painting new extension
(vi) Cost of repairing photocopier

You are required to:

(a) List the items as appropriate, under the headings of Capital or Revenue Expenditure.
(b) State which items will be charged to the trading account, the profit and loss account or the balance sheet.

■ V **3 I** Reconciling ledger accounts

Most suppliers send a monthly statement to their customers listing the transactions that have taken place during the previous month. Statements must be carefully checked by the customer against the relevant ledger accounts to ensure that they contain the correct invoice values, any credit notes and payments made, including cash discounts.

Reconciliation statement

A *reconciliation statement* is prepared to confirm that, although there may be differences, on a particular date, between the two balances these are not usually because of errors, but more often result from a difference in timing. This is a typical example: Parkwood Garden Centre is one of your suppliers. Their account in your ledger is as follows:

Purchase Ledger
Parkwood Garden Centre Account

20-9		£	20-9		£
10 Nov	Returns outwards	28.00	1 Nov	Balance b/d	325.00
16 NOv	Bank	308.75	7 Nov	Purchases	170.00
16 Nov	Discount received	16.25	18 Nov	Purchases	165.00
26 Nov	Returns outwards	35.00	23 Nov	Purchases	180.00
30 Nov	Balance c/d	452.00			
		840.00			840.00
			1 Dec	Balance b/d	452.00

On 2 December the following statement of account is received from Parkwood Garden Centre:

Statement of Account

20-9		Debit £	Credit £	Balance £
1 Nov	Balance			325.00
4 Nov	Sales	170.00		495.00
14 Nov	Returns		28.00	467.00
15 Nov	Sales	165.00		632.00
19 Nov	Bank		308.75	323.25
19 Nov	Discount		16.25	307.00
21 Nov	Sales	180.00		487.00
28 Nov	Sales	195.00		682.00

You are required to prepare a reconciliation statement, **starting with the balance in your books of £452.00**, to explain the difference between the balance in your ledger and the closing balance on the statement of account.

The first step is to compare the two documents and eliminate those entries which appear correctly in both. Do this by placing a small tick against each item which can be identified on both, like this:

Parkwood Garden Centre Account

20-9			£	20-9			£
10 Nov	Returns outwards	✓	28.00	1 Nov	Balance b/d	✓	325.00
16 Nov	Bank	✓	308.75	7 Nov	Purchases	✓	170.00
16 Nov	Discount received	✓	16.25	18 Nov	Purchases	✓	165.00
26 Nov	Returns outwards		35.00	23 Nov	Purchases	✓	180.00
30 Nov	Balance c/d		452.00				
			840.00				840.00
				1 Dec	Balance b/d		452.00

On 2 December the following statement of account is received from Parkwood Garden Centre:

Statement of Account

20-9		Debit £	Credit £		Balance £
1 Nov	Balance			✓	325.00
4 Nov	Sales	✓ 170.00			495.00
14 Nov	Returns		✓ 28.00		467.00
15 Nov	Sales	✓ 165.00			632.00
19 Nov	Bank		✓ 308.75		323.25
19 Nov	Discount		✓ 16.25		307.00
21 Nov	Sales	✓ 180.00			487.00
28 Nov	Sales	195.00			682.00

The next step is to look at the entries in the ledger account that do not appear on the statement. Here there is only one item, on 26 November goods were returned to Parkwood Garden Centre which have not yet arrived; when they do it will reduce the balance on the statement by £35.00.

The next step is to look at the entries on the statement that do not appear in the ledger account. There is one invoice for £195.00 which is probably on its way, by post, but has not yet arrived. When it does, it will increase the balance in the ledger account.

These items are listed and adjusted on the reconciliation statement, which we can now prepare:

Reconciliation Statement as at 30 November 20-9

			£
Balance as per ledger account			452.00
Add: 26 November	returns outwards	35.00	
28 November	purchases	195.00	230.00
Balance as per statement:			682.00

A reconciliation statement explains that when all outstanding transactions have gone through the two businesses, the balances will agree.

We can now look at other possible reasons why differences may occur.

Payment by cheque to a creditor

Details of any payment made by cheque to a creditor would be entered in the cash book, then posted to the ledger account on the date the cheque was written and despatched. It may be several days later before the cheque is received by the creditor and the details entered in the relevant account. This is called *cash in transit*: clearly the difference is in timing.

Errors and omissions

Errors

Sometimes mistakes will occur, very often these errors are a *transposition of figures*. For example, an invoice for £124 is entered as £142, or an invoice appears on a statement for goods which have not been ordered or received. In these situations an *adjustment* for the difference would be required when reconciling the two balances.

Omissions

Usually these are items which have been *overlooked*. For example, an amount of cash discount for prompt payment has been omitted on the statement. An adjustment for the omission would be required when reconciling the two balances.

Contra entries

These happen when the same firm is both a supplier and a customer, because there would be an account in both the purchase and sales ledgers. To avoid needless transactions the two balances are offset against each other. This is done by transferring the account with the smaller balance into the account with the larger balance. This transfer is known as a *contra entry*.

Points to remember

- Statements should always be carefully checked by the customer against the *relevant ledger accounts.* This is to ensure that they contain the accurate invoice values, any credit notes and payments made, including cash discounts.
- First, compare the two documents and eliminate those entries which appear *correctly in both.* Do this by placing a small tick against each item which can be identified on both.
- Next, make a list of any entries in the *ledger account* which do not appear on the *statement.*
- Then, make a list of any entries on the *statement* which do not appear in the *ledger account.*
- Details of these outstanding items are listed and adjusted on a *reconciliation statement.*
- Make sure that the *opening balances* at the start of the month agree on both. If they do not agree, make a note of the difference. This usually occurs when a payment by cheque is in transit; details of the cheque and perhaps cash discount, will have been entered in the ledger account but the cheque will not have arrived before the statement was prepared. When this happens it will become evident before the matching procedure is completed.

Assignments

31.1

Hongtai Imports is one of your suppliers. Their account in your ledger is as follows:

Hongtai Imports Account

20-9		£	20-9		£
3 Apr	Returns outwards	28.50	1 Apr	Balance b/d	416.75
16 Apr	Bank	395.92	4 Apr	Purchases	184.25
16 Apr	Discount received	20.83	18 Apr	Purchases	219.54
25 Apr	Returns outwards	47.72			
30 Apr	Balance c/d	327.57			
		820.54			820.54
			1 May	Balance b/d	327.57

On 2 May the following statement of account is received from Hongtai Imports:

Statement of Account

20-9		Debit £	Credit £	Balance £
1 Apr	Balance			416.75
2 Apr	Sales	184.25		601.00
6 Apr	Returns		28.50	572.50
16 Apr	Sales	219.54		792.04
18 Apr	Bank		395.92	396.12
18 Apr	Discount		20.83	375.29
26 Apr	Sales	295.50		670.79

You are required to prepare a reconciliation statement, **starting with the balance in your books of £327.57**, to explain the difference between the balance in your ledger and the closing balance on the statement of account.

31.2

Aztec Sportswear is one of your suppliers. Their account in your ledger is as follows:

Aztec Sportswear Account

20-9		£	20-9		£
9 Feb	Returns outwards	36.75	1 Feb	Balance b/d	308.00
15 Feb	Bank	292.60	5 Feb	Purchases	214.95
15 Feb	Discount received	15.40	18 Feb	Purchases	196.70
26 Feb	Returns outwards	49.25			
28 Feb	Balance c/d	325.65			
		719.65			719.65
			1 Mar	Balance b/d	325.65

On 2 March the following statement of account is received from Aztec Sportswear:

Statement of Account

20-9		Debit £	Credit £	Balance £
1 Feb	Balance			308.00
3 Feb	Sales	214.95		522.95
14 Feb	Returns		36.75	486.20
16 Feb	Sales	196.70		682.90
17 Feb	Bank		292.60	390.30
22 Feb	Sales	296.90		687.20

You are required to prepare a reconciliation statement, **starting with the balance in your books of £325.65**, to explain the difference between the balance in your ledger and the closing balance on the statement of account.

31.3
Grangeway Products is one of your suppliers. Their account in your ledger is as follows:

Grangeway Products Account

20-9		£	20-9		£
2 May	Bank	428.00	1 May	Balance b/d	450.00
2 May	Discount received	22.00	6 May	Purchases	275.00
14 May	Purchase returns	35.00	18 May	Purchases	199.00
28 May	Bank	263.00			
28 May	Discount received	12.00			
29 May	Purchase returns	44.00			
31 May	Balance c/d	120.00			
		924.00			924.00
			1 Jun	Balance b/d	120.00

On 2 June the following statement of account is received from Grangeway Products:

Statement of Account

20-9		Debit £	Credit £	Balance £
1 May	Balance			450.00
4 May	Bank		428.00	22.00
4 May	Sales	275.00		297.00
16 May	Returns		35.00	262.00
17 May	Sales	199.00		461.00
28 May	Sales	257.00		718.00

You are required to prepare a reconciliation statement, **starting with the balance in your books of £120.00**, to explain the difference between the balance in your ledger and the closing balance on the statement of account.

31.4
J S Kingsley is one of your suppliers. Their account in your ledger is set out below:

J S Kingsley Account

20-6		£	20-6		£
29 Jan	Bank	350.00	1 Jan	Balance b/d	150.00
31 Jan	Balance c/d	350.00	7 Jan	Purchases	200.00
			17 Feb	Purchases	350.00
		700.00			700.00
			1 Feb	Balance b/d	350.00

On 2 February the following statement of account is received from J S Kingsley:

Statement of Account

20-6		Debit £	Credit £	Balance £
1 Jan	Balance			350.00
3 Jan	Sales	200.00		550.00
4 Jan	Bank		200.00	350.00
11 Jan	Sales	350.00		700.00
27 Jan	Sales	250.00		950.00
29 Jan	Sales	190.00		1,140.00

You are required to prepare a reconciliation statement, **starting with the balance in your books of £350.00**, to explain the difference between the balance in your ledger and the closing balance on the statement of account.

31.5
Alan Brown is one of your suppliers. His account in your ledger is set out below:

Alan Brown Account

20-1		£	20-1		£
4 May	Bank	4,056.00	1 May	Balance b/d	4,160.00
4 May	Discount		10 May	Purchases	3,120.00
	received	104.00	16 May	Purchases	1,313.00
9 May	Purchase		31 May	Purchases	1,310.00
	returns	193.00			
28 May	Bank	4,134.00			
28 May	Discount				
	received	106.00			
31 May	Balance c/d	1,310.00			
		9,903.00			9,903.00
			1 Jun Balance b/d		1,310.00

On 2 June the following statement of account is received from Alan Brown

Statement of Account

		Debit	Credit	Balance
20-1		£	£	£
1 May	Balance			4,160.00
6 May	Bank		4,056.00	104.00
9 May	Sales	3,120.00		3,224.00
14 May	Returns		193.00	3,031.00
15 May	Sales	1,313.00		4,344.00
28 May	Sales	1,310.00		5,654.00

You are required to prepare a reconciliation statement, **starting with the balance in your books of £1,310.00**, to explain the difference between the balance in your ledger and the closing balance on the statement of account.

31.6
Vantage Products are one of your suppliers. Their account in your ledger is as follows:

Vantage Products Account

20-8		£	20-8		£
12 Oct	Purchase returns	75	1 Oct	Balance b/d	1,625
28 Oct	Bank	1,570	10 Oct	Purchases	1,050
28 Oct	Discount	55	21 Oct	Purchases	1,675
30 Oct	Purchase returns	105			
31 Oct	Balance c/d	2,545			
		4,350			4,350
			1 Nov	Balance b/d	2,545

On 2 November the following statement of account is received from Vantage Products:

Statement of Account

		Debit	Credit	Balance
20-8		£	£	£
1 Oct	Balance			3,175
3 Oct	Bank		1,500	1,675
3 Oct	Discount		50	1,625
8 Oct	Sales	1,050		2,675
15 Oct	Returns inwards		75	2,600
19 Oct	Sales	1,675		4,275
28 Oct	Sales	1,550		5,825

You are required to:

(a) Prepare a reconciliation statement, **starting with the balance in your books of £2,545**, to explain the difference between the balance in your ledger and the closing balance on the statement of account.
(b) If the outstanding balance in your ledger on 1 November was settled *less* $2\frac{1}{2}$ per cent cash discount:
   (i) State the amount of discount.
   (ii) State the amount of the cheque.

31.7
E Patterson is one of your suppliers. His account in your books is set out below:

E Pattesson Account

20-9		£	20-9		£
6 May	Bank	6,780	1 May	Balance b/d	6,800
6 May	Discount	20	13 May	Purchases	1,350
12 May	Purchase returns	150	18 May	Purchases	1,120
23 May	Bank	1,325			
23 May	Discount	25			
31 May	Balance c/d	970			
		9,270			9,270
			1 Jun	Balance b/d	970

On 2 June the following statement of account is received from E Patterson:

Statement of Account

		Debit	Credit	Balance
20-9		£	£	£
1 May	Balance			6,800
9 May	Bank		6,780	20
9 May	Sales	1,350		1,370
14 May	Returns inwards		150	1,220
17 May	Sales	1,120		2,340
30 May	Sales	1,470		3,810

You are required to:

(a) Prepare a reconciliation statement, **starting with the balance in your books of £970** to explain the difference between the balance in your ledger and the closing balance on the statement of account.

(b) If the outstanding balance in your ledger on 1 June was settled *less* 5 per cent cash discount:
(i)   State the amount of discount.
(ii) State the amount of the cheque.

31.8
Excel Products are one of your suppliers. Their account in your ledger is as follows:

Excel Products Account

20-9		£	20-9		£
14 Oct	Purchase returns	95	1 Oct	Balance b/d	1,350
29 Oct	Bank	1,330	8 Oct	Purchases	1,850
29 Oct	Discount	20	22 Oct	Purchases	1,050
30 Oct	Purchase returns	75			
31 Oct	Balance c/d	2,730			
		4,250			4,250
			1 Nov	Balance b/d	2,730

On 2 November the following statement of account is received from Excel Products:

Statement of Account

		Debit	Credit	Balance
20-9		£	£	£
1 Oct	Balance			2,775
3 Oct	Bank		1,400	1,375
3 Oct	Discount		25	1,350
6 Oct	Sales	1,850		3,200
16 Oct	Returns inwards		95	3,105
20 Oct	Sales	1,050		4,155
28 Oct	Sales	1,550		5,705

You are required to:

(a) Prepare a reconciliation statement, **starting with the balance in your books of £2,730**, to explain the difference between the balance in your ledger and the closing balance on the statement of account.

(b) Briefly explain why a supplier may disallow a cash discount.

(c) If the outstanding balance in your ledger on 1 November was settled *less* $2\frac{1}{2}$ per cent cash discount:

    (i) State the amount of discount.

    (ii) State the amount of the cheque.

▐ Ⅴ **32** Wages and salaries

The distinction between salaries and wages is not clearly defined, but generally *salaries* are paid on a *monthly basis*. They are usually expressed as a fixed amount for a year: for example, an employee is paid an annual salary of £13,500. The amount of each month's pay is calculated by dividing the annual amount by twelve, making the gross pay for each month £1,125. Generally salaries are paid directly into the employee's bank account.

Wages are usually considered to be earnings which are calculated on a *weekly basis* and paid in cash. Wages can be earned and calculated on a *time rate* or a *piece rate* basis.

Time rate wages

With this system, the employee is paid an agreed amount for each hour worked up to a given number of hours. This is known as the basic or standard rate of pay; work done in addition to normal hours might be paid at a higher rate, known as *overtime rate*. There may be several different overtime rates according to the number of hours worked. Overtime rates are generally quoted as *time and a quarter, time and a half* and *double time*. If the standard rate of pay is £6.00 per hour, then:

Time and a quarter would be £6.00 *plus* a quarter £1.50 = £7.50
Time and a half would be £6.00 *plus* a half £3.00 = £9.00
Double time would be £6.00 plus £6.00 = £12.00.

This is a typical example: An employee is paid a basic wage of £6.00 per hour for a 40 hour week; any hours worked in excess of this are paid at time and a half. During the week ended 17 June 20-9 the employee worked a total of 46 hours. The gross wage would be calculated like this:

	£
40 hours at £6.00 per hour	240.00
6 hours at £9.00 per hour	54.00
Gross pay	294.00

Gross pay is the total amount earned *before* any deductions have been made.

Piece rate wages

With this method of payment wages are based on *results*. Earnings are calculated on the quantity of good work produced. A figure is agreed between the management and the workers and payment is made according to the number of items produced.

This is a typical example: J Bond works in the assembly unit of a local factory. The firm operates a piece work system; piece rates are paid at a rate of £30.00 for every 100 items produced. During the week ended 24 June J Bond assembled 900 items. The gross wage would be calculated like this:

900 divided by 100 = 9 multiplied by £30
Gross wage   £270.00

Deductions from pay

Statutory deductions are *compulsory* deductions from pay. It is the responsibility of the employer to deduct Income Tax and National Insurance contributions from the wages and salaries of the employees.

Income Tax – Pay As You Earn

This is a statutory deduction. In the United Kingdom the wages and salaries of all employees are liable to have Income Tax deducted from them; the system is known as *Pay As You Earn*, which is usually abbreviated to PAYE. Pay As You Earn means just that: it has to be deducted on every pay date, whether it be weekly or monthly.

For every employee the Inland Revenue sends the employer a Notice of Coding and on this is shown a *code number*. The code number is based upon the personal circumstances of the employee.

The Inland Revenue sends a set of tax tables to each employer, showing rates of tax on both a weekly and monthly basis. The actual calculation is done by comparing both the amount of gross pay and the code number with the tax tables.

Most employees will have a *tax-free allowance*, which means that part of their gross pay will be free of tax and only the amount above the allowance will be taxed. All PAYE deducted from employees is eventually paid over to the Inland Revenue.

Each year in his budget, the Chancellor of the Exchequer announces the rates of income tax for the following year. Because the annual rate varies frequently, the rates of income tax shown in this book are for illustration purposes only, they are *not* the actual rates of income tax at the time you are reading this book.

Employee's National Insurance contributions

This is also a statutory deduction. In the UK employees are also liable to pay National Insurance contributions. This deduction is carried out by the employer at the same time as the PAYE deductions are made.

The payment of National Insurance contributions is to ensure that the employee will have the benefit of the extensive services provided by the state: such as health services, sickness, unemployment and retirement benefits. The percentages used in this book are for illustration purposes only.

Employer's National Insurance contributions

Employers also have to pay National Insurance contributions to the Inland Revenue. However, this is *not* deducted from the employee's wages but is an expense of the employer.

Superannuation contributions

Many firms have superannuation schemes. These are schemes whereby the employee will receive a pension on retiring from the firm and, very often, a lump sum payment in cash. Usually both the employer and the employee will make contributions towards financing a superannuation scheme.

Other deductions

Many employees also make voluntary contributions to various organisations. These include: local or national charities, union membership fees, private medical schemes, social and welfare clubs and savings schemes. Most employers will agree to deduct these types of voluntary contributions from the wages and salaries of their employees.

Net pay

This is the *actual amount received by the employee* after the statutory and voluntary deductions have been made. It is the responsibility of the wages clerk to deal with the work of paying the employees their wages or salaries and of keeping detailed records of all such payments. In most organisations, each employee will be given a reference number for identification purposes.

Each employee receives a *pay advice slip* giving details of their gross pay, income tax, National Insurance contributions, any other deductions and clearly showing the amount of net pay. We can now look at two typical examples:

Worked example 1

James Miller is paid a standard rate of £6.00 per hour for a 40 hour week; any hours worked in excess of this are paid at time and a half. During the week ended 17 June 20-9 he worked a total of 52 hours. His deductions for the week were:

Income tax   25 per cent of all earnings in excess of £60 per week

National Insurance   10 per cent of his gross pay
Union membership fee £2.50 per week

You are required to:

(a) Calculate his gross pay.
(b) Show the amount of each deduction and set out his pay slip for the week ended 17 June 20-9.

Solution
James Miller
Week ended 17 June 20-9

		£
40 hours at £6.00 per hour		240.00
12 hours at £9.00 per hour		108.00
	Gross pay	348.00
Deductions	£	
Income tax	72.00	
National Insurance	34.80	
Union membership fee	2.50	
		109.30
	Net pay	238.70

Worked example 2

Jean Bond works in the assembly unit of a local factory. The firm operates a piece work system; piece rates are paid at a rate of £30.00 for every 100 items produced. During the week ended 24 June 20-9, Jean Bond assembled 900 items. Her deductions for the week were:

Income tax   25 per cent of all earnings in excess of £40 per week
National Insurance   10 per cent of her gross pay
Social club   £1.50 per week

You are required to:

(a) Calculate her gross pay.
(b) Show the amount of each deduction and set out her pay slip for the week ended 24 June 20-9.

Solution
Jean Bond
Week ended 24 June 20-9

			£
900 items at £30.00 per 100		Gross pay	270.00
Deductions	£		
Income tax	57.50		
National Insurance	27.00		
Social club	1.50		
			86.00
		Net pay	184.00

Making up pay packets

If there are more than one or two employees you will need to calculate the number of notes and coins that will be required to make up the wage packets with the correct amounts. This procedure is known as preparing a *note and coin analysis.*

Usually there will be local agreements with employees regarding the value of the notes to be used. An employee earning £200.05 in a week would probably complain if the wages were given to him in four £50 notes and a five pence coin! Notes for larger amounts can be difficult to change.

This is a typical example using the net pay for six employees:

	£
G Collins	124.39
A Sandford	103.94
H Williams	97.45
K Douglas	118.72
M Stephenson	125.68
R Ford	109.87

Assume the following agreement has been reached:

> *£10 is the highest value note to be used and each employee must receive at least one £1 coin.*

To carry out the calculation you will need to make a list of the note and coin values across the top, then list each employee down the side, like this:

Employees	Net pay £	£10	£5	£2	£1	50p	20p	10p	5p	2p	1p
G Collins	124.39	12		1	2		1	1	1	2	
A Sandford	103.94	10		1	1	1	2			2	
H Williams	97.45	9	1		2		2		1		
K Douglas	118.72	11	1	1	1	1	1			1	
M Stephenson	125.68	12		2	1	1		1	1	1	1
R Ford	109.87	10	1	1	2	1	1	1	1	1	
	680.05	64	3	6	9	4	7	3	4	7	1

Your calculations can be verified liked this:

£

$64 \times £10 = 640.00$
$3 \times £5 = 15.00$
$6 \times £2 = 12.00$
$9 \times £1 = 9.00$
$4 \times 50p = 2.00$
$7 \times 20p = 1.40$
$3 \times 10p = 30$
$4 \times 5p = 20$
$7 \times 2p = 14$
$1 \times 1p = 01$

680.05 ✓

Points to remember

- *Salaries* are usually paid monthly and stated as an amount for a year. One month's pay is calculated by dividing the annual amount by twelve.
- *Wages* are usually considered to be earnings which are calculated on a weekly basis and paid in cash. Wages can be earned and calculated on a *time rate* or a *piece rate* basis. When preparing salaries or wages accurate calculations are essential.
- Certain deductions are required to be made by law; these are know as *statutory deductions*. Other deductions which are agreed by the employee are known as *voluntary deductions*.
- Examination questions which require candidates to prepare a *note/coin analysis* often state details of an agreement regarding the value of notes to be used, for example: *£10 is the highest value note to be used and each employee must receive a minimum of five £1 coins in the wage packet.* Always read the question carefully to make sure you comply with the instructions. Often candidates fail to read the question properly and completely ignore the special instructions.

Assignments

32.1

Paul Davies is paid at a basic rate of £7.50 per hour for a 38 hour week; all overtime is paid at time and half. During the week ended 30 July 20-9 Paul Davies worked a total of 50 hours.

His deductions for the week were:

Income Tax	30 per cent of all earnings in excess of £55 per week
National Insurance	5 per cent of gross wage
Social and Athletic Club	£2.50 per week

You are required to:

(a) Calculate his gross pay.
(b) Show the amount of each deduction and set out his pay slip for the week ended 30 July 20-9.

32.2

The following information relates to two employees for the week ending 8 August 20-9:

Name	Number of items produced
G Forbes	4,800
B Carr	5,200

The firm operates a piece work system at a rate of £3.00 per 50 items produced and a productivity bonus of £20 is paid to each employee who completes in excess of 5,000 units in a working week.

G Forbes pays Income Tax at 30 per cent on all earnings in excess of £60 per week. National Insurance contributions are 10 per cent of gross pay.

B Carr pays Income Tax at 30 per cent on all earnings in excess of £50 per week. National Insurance contributions are 10 per cent of gross pay.

You are required to:

(a) Calculate the gross pay for each employee.
(b) Show the amount of each deduction and set out their pay slips for the week ended 8 August 20-9.

32.3

Jasvinder Patel is paid a basic wage of £8.40 per hour for a 35 hour week. The first five hours in excess of this are paid at time and a quarter; any further hours are paid at time and a half.

During the week ended 15 August 20-9 Jasvinder Patel worked a total of $42\frac{1}{2}$ hours. In addition to her basic pay and overtime she received a productivity bonus of £25.

Deductions for the week were:

Income Tax	25 per cent of all earnings in excess of £40 per week
National Insurance	10 per cent of gross pay
Company Pension Fund	5 per cent of basic pay
Social Club	£2.00 per week

You are required to:

(a) Calculate her gross pay.
(b) Show the amount of each deduction and set out her pay slip for the week ended 15 August 20-9.

32.4

David King works in the assembly unit of a local factory, his clock number is 17. The firm operates a piece work system; piece rates are paid at a rate of £17.25 for every 25 items produced.

During the week ending 31 October 20-9, D King assembled 450 items. Deductions are to be calculated as follows:

Company pension scheme	6 per cent of gross pay
National Insurance	8 per cent of gross pay
PAYE	25 per cent of all earnings in excess of £50 per week
Social club	£2.50

You are required to:

(a) Calculate his gross pay.
(b) Show the amount of each deduction and set out his pay slip for the week ended 31 October 20-9.

32.5

Donah Romero is paid a basic wage of £7.40 per hour for a 37 hour week. Any hours worked in excess of this are paid at time and a half, except for hours worked on a Sunday, which are paid at double time. During the week ending 17 June 20-9 she worked a total of 46 hours, 4 of which were on Sunday.

Deductions for the week were:

Company Pension Fund	4 per cent of basic wage
National Insurance	7 per cent of gross wage
PAYE	30 per cent of all earnings in excess of £40 per week
Sports and Social Club	£1.50 per week

You are required to:

(a) Calculate her gross pay.
(b) Show the amount of each deduction and set out her pay slip for the week ended 17 June 20-9.

32.6

Valiant Sportswear runs a small factory. The following information relates to four employees for a typical week.

Name	Hours worked Basic	Overtime	Number of items produced
J Oldridge	36		3,400
K Bullard	40	10	5,400
H Downing	40	7	5,600
L Beech	40	8	4,900

Valiant Sportswear pays a basic rate of £6.45 per hour with an overtime rate of time and a third. They are offering to pay piece rates of £6.00 per 100 items produced.

You are required to:

(a) Calculate the gross pay for each employee at time rates and at piece rates.
(b) Indicate which would be most favourable to each one.
(c) When calculating net pay, statutory and voluntary deductions may be made from gross pay. State which of the following are statutory deductions and which are voluntary deductions:
Income Tax
Contributions to a firm's social club
Trade Union contributions
National Insurance contributions.

32.7

You are employed as a wages clerk by Harewood Builders. The following are the net wages of six employees working on a local building site for the week ending 3 August 20-9:

	£
H Greenwood	74.85
P Summers	98.67
D Connors	83.96
F Marshall	79.33
A Harrison	91.90
K Caldwell	89.74

You are required to:

(a) Prepare a summarised notes and coin analysis. Calculate the number of notes and coins required to make up the wage packets for the six employees. Your firm does not use notes greater than £20 and each employee must receive the *lowest* number of notes and coins possible.
(b) Total and verify your analysis to prove your figures and state the amount of the cheque required for the payroll.

32.8

You are employed as a wages clerk by Adel Secretarial Services. The following are the net wages of the employees for the week ending 8 October 20-9:

	£
F Gibson	94.11
T Simpson	133.99
M Jackson	87.81
G Smith	91.19
W Mellor	124.62
A Fell	111.75
E Jones	103.33
S Moore	98.96
C Wood	82.57
V Bean	123.49
P West	131.36
T Camp	74.67
B Dixon	80.80

You are required to:

(a) Prepare a summarised notes and coin analysis. Calculate the number of notes and coins required to make up the wage packets for the employees. An agreement has been reached with the employees, so your firm does not use notes greater than £10 and each employee must have a minimum of five £1 coins in the wage packet. Each employee must receive *lowest* number of notes and coins possible.

(b) Total and verify your analysis to prove your figures and state the amount of the cheque required for the payroll.

32.9

You are employed as a wages clerk by Superfoam Products. The following are the net wages of the employees for the week ending 15 October 20-9:

	£
B Gill	274.63
P Farraday	191.17
H Oliver	182.58
R Watt	248.76
T Yeoman	187.80
R Cook	236.95

You are required to:

(a) Prepare a summarised notes and coin analysis. Calculate the number of notes and coins required to make up the wage packets for the six employees. Your firm does not use notes greater than £20 and each employee must receive the *lowest* number of notes and coins possible.

(b) Total and verify your analysis to prove your figures and state the amount of the cheque required for the payroll.

32.10
You are employed as a wages clerk by M & D Caterers. The following are the net wages of the employees for the week ending 6 November 20-9:

	£
S Farrar	194.11
L Crisp	203.72
A Hurst	180.95
B Walker	177.63
M Dyson	215.48
S Craven	196.26

You are required to:

(a) Prepare a summarised notes and coin analysis. Calculate the number of notes and coins required to make up the wage packets for the six employees. Your firm does not use notes greater than £10 and each employee must receive the *lowest* number of notes and coins possible.

(b) Total and verify your analysis to prove your figures and state the amount of the cheque required for the payroll.

32.11
You are employed as a wages clerk by Newlooks Decorators. The following are the net wages of six employees working on a local building site for the week ending 20 November 20-9:

	£
W Kelly	184.63
S Munro	158.97
M Franks	182.78
B Malik	176.55
D Rogers	153.14
H Khan	189.43

You are required to:

(a) Prepare a summarised notes and coin analysis. Calculate the number of notes and coins required to make up the wage packets for the six employees. Your firm does not use notes greater than £20 and each employee must receive the *lowest* number of notes and coins possible.

(b) Total and verify your analysis to prove your figures and state the amount of the cheque required for the payroll.

▮ ⌄ **33** Stock records

Importance of recording stock levels

It is essential to keep some *record of stock* to ensure that we never run out of items that are essential to keep production lines going. The profitability of a business could be seriously affected if adequate stock levels are not maintained in order to meet the usual anticipated demand.

Accurate information should always be available regarding the number of items in stock of small parts, components or materials for manufacture. Records of stock can be kept on a computerised system or some firms use *stock record cards* or *bin cards* for every item of stock. With a computerised system all the information can be brought up on screen, receipts and issues are entered using the keyboard, the balance in stock is automatically updated. Computerised systems can quickly provide reports showing which items need reordering and the total value of the stock held. With a stock card system one record card is made out for each item of stock. Although stock record cards can vary slightly, they generally include:

- A *description* of the item and/or the reference number
- They begin with the *number in stock*.

The following points are also very important:

- They *must be* completed in *date order* with a *running balance*
- When *new stock* is received, the date and invoice number are entered in the relevant column, the number received is entered in the quantity received column and then added to the balance in stock
- When *supplies are issued*, the date and requisition number are entered in the relevant column, the number issued is entered in the quantity issued column and then deducted from the balance in stock.

If accurate records are kept and care is taken issuing stock, the figures shown on the record card should agree with the *actual number of items in stock*. From time to time, in order to verify that the record cards are correct, a *stock check* is carried out. A stock check, or 'stocktaking,' means physically counting the actual number of items in the stores.

Very often small parts or components are known by a *reference code* – for example, a garage may classify a cylinder head gasket as item CHG.

Worked example

This is a typical example:

Smart Garage is a firm that services and repairs motor vehicles. They use stock cards to record receipts and issues of the various items held in the stores.

On 1 May there were 250 units in stock of item CHG/34. During the month of May the following stock movements took place:

Date	Receipts	Items	Date	Issues	Items
2 May	Invoice 7719	20	4 May	Requisition Number 370	14
18 May	Invoice 8081	50	8 May	Requisition Number 385	37
24 May	Invoice 8214	60	12 May	Requisition Number 401	12
28 May	Invoice 9122	65	21 May	Requisition Number 414	34
			23 May	Requisition Number 422	46
			26 May	Requisition Number 436	28
			31 May	Requisition Number 453	25

You are required to complete a stock record card, in date order, for the month of May.

Solution
Look at Figure 33.1.

Stock Record Card				
Item No.: CHG/34				
Date	Reference	Receipts	Issues	Balance
1 May	Balance b/d			250
2 May	Invoice 7719	20		270
4 May	Requisition 370		14	256
8 May	Requisition 385		37	219
12 May	Requisition 401		12	207
18 May	Invoice 8081	50		257
21 May	Requisition 414		34	223
23 May	Requisition 422		46	177
24 May	Invoice 8214	60		237
26 May	Requisition 436		28	209
28 May	Invoice 9122	65		274
31 May	Requisition 453		25	249

Figure 33.1

Quantity and value

Some firms like their stock record cards to include details of both quantity and value.

Worked example

This is a typical example:

Adelgrove is a small engineering firm. They use stock cards to record receipts and issues of the various components held in the stores. It is the firm's policy to keep up to date records of both the quantity and value of stock items.

On 1 February there were 100 units in stock of item MN/84. The cost price per unit is £5.00. During the month of February the following stock movements took place:

Date	Receipts	Items	Date	Issues	Items
4 Feb	Invoice 915	50	6 Feb	Requisition Number 55	60
8 Feb	Invoice 930	20	10 Feb	Requisition Number 63	70
17 Feb	Invoice 946	45	15 Feb	Requisition Number 69	25
27 Feb	Invoice 976	60	24 Feb	Requisition Number 78	55

You are required to complete a stock record card, in date order, for the month of May:

- First calculate and enter the value of the opening stock: 100 units at £5.00 per unit = £500
- In date order, enter the details of each receipt and issue.

Solution
Look at Figure 33.2.

Stock Record Card							
Item No.: MN/84							
Date	Details	Receipts		Issues		Balance	
		Units	£	Units	£	Units	£
1 Feb	Balance b/d					100	500
4 Feb	Invoice 915	50	250			150	750
6 Feb	Requisition 55			60	300	90	450
8 Feb	Invoice 930	20	100			110	550
10 Feb	Requisition 63			70	350	40	200
15 Feb	Requisition 69			25	125	15	75
17 Feb	Invoice 946	45	225			60	300
24 Feb	Requisition 78			55	275	5	25
27 May	Invoice 976	60	300			65	325

Figure 33.2

Points to remember

- *Stock cards* are kept for each stock item and are always completed *in date order*.
- Stock cards always begin with the *number of items in stock*; a *running balance* gives a total after each addition or subtraction.
- When supplies are received these are *added* to the balance.
- When stock is issued these are *deducted* from the balance. The balance column shows the number of items in stock.
- To verify that the record cards are correct a *stock check* is carried out. A stock check, or 'stocktaking', means physically counting the actual number of items in the stores.

Assignments

33.1

Botica Plastics use stock cards to record receipts and issues of the various items held in the stores.

On 1 March there were 225 units in stock of item DWT/8. During the month of March the following stock movements took place:

Date	Receipts	Items	Date	Issues	Items
2 Mar	Invoice 767	60	4 Mar	Requisition Number 454	20
15 Mar	Invoice 786	50	6 Mar	Requisition Number 467	28
21 Mar	Invoice 812	70	10 Mar	Requisition Number 476	35
28 May	Invoice 865	85	18 Mar	Requisition Number 482	43
			22 Mar	Requisition Number 491	26
			24 Mar	Requisition Number 498	34
			30 Mar	Requisition Number 502	36

You are required to:

(a) Rule up a stock record card with suitable column headings.
(b) Complete the stock record card, in date order, for the month of March.

33.2

The Bestly Bottle Company supplies various sizes of bottles to the retail trade. Deliveries of bottles are made to the warehouse and orders are sent to customers from the despatch department.

On 1 October there was an opening balance of 530 bottles. During October the following quantities of half-litre clear glass bottles were received and issued:

Date	Receipts	Bottles	Date	Issues	Bottles
6 Oct	Invoice 684	120	7 Oct	Requisition Number 54	35
9 Oct	Invoice 732	50	8 Oct	Requisition Number 55	70
22 Oct	Invoice 786	135	15 Oct	Requisition Number 56	40
24 Oct	Invoice 789	50	28 Oct	Requisition Number 57	80

There was a stock check on 10 October and 3 bottles were found to be broken.

You are required to:

(a) Rule up a stock record card with suitable column headings.
(b) Complete the stock record card, in date order, for the month of October.

33.3

Seven Arches is a small engineering firm. They use stock cards to record receipts and issues of the various components held in the stores.

On 1 May there were 39 items in stock of component number MN/348. During the month of May the following stock movements took place:

Date	Receipts	Items	Date	Issues	Items
5 May	Invoice 2916	60	6 May	Requisition Number 142	26
13 May	Invoice 3060	55	9 May	Requisition Number 166	19
22 May	Invoice 3214	75	15 May	Requisition Number 209	25
29 May	Invoice 3327	65	23 May	Requisition Number 232	35
			25 May	Requisition Number 246	46
			30 May	Requisition Number 264	29

You are required to:

(a) Rule up a stock record card with suitable column headings.
(b) Complete the stock record card, in date order, for the month of May.

33.4

Leda Components supplies various sizes of plastic containers to their customers.

On 1 April there was an opening balance of 728 containers. During April the following quantities of 8 mm white plastic containers were received and issued:

Date	Receipts	Items	Date	Issues	Items
3 Apr	Invoice 574	450	2 Apr	Requisition Number 217	149
14 Apr	Invoice 612	250	5 Apr	Requisition Number 232	75
21 Apr	Invoice 720	350	10 Apr	Requisition Number 251	125
28 Apr	Invoice 815	200	16 Apr	Requisition Number 272	80
			24 Apr	Requisition Number 315	95
			30 Apr	Requisition Number 334	68

On 15 April there was a stock check and 6 containers were scrapped because they were damaged.

You are required to:

(a) Rule up a stock record card with suitable column headings.
(b) Complete the stock record card, in date order, for the month of April.

33.5

Selcom is a small engineering firm. They use stock cards to record receipts and issues of the various components held in the stores. It is the firm's policy to keep records of both the quantity and value of stock items.

On 1 April there were 200 units in stock of item DN/X. The cost price per unit is £6.00. During the month of April the following stock movements took place:

Date	Receipts	Items	Date	Issues	Items
4 Apr	Invoice 6120	60	3 Apr	Requisition Number 122	50
9 Apr	Invoice 6220	40	7 Apr	Requisition Number 131	25
18 Apr	Invoice 6317	50	11 Apr	Requisition Number 139	35
30 Apr	Invoice 6424	70	22 Apr	Requisition Number 150	44

You are required to:

(a) Rule up a stock record card with suitable column headings.
(b) Complete the stock record card, in date order, for the month of April.

33.6

Zannit Products use stock cards to record receipts and issues of the various components held in the stores. It is the firm's policy to keep records of both the quantity and value of stock items.

On 1 May there were 158 units in stock of item MN/8. The cost price per unit is £8.00. During the month of May the following stock movements took place:

Date	Receipts	Items	Date	Issues	Items
4 May	Invoice 212	150	3 May	Requisition Number 642	30
18 May	Invoice 249	80	8 May	Requisition Number 651	42
24 May	Invoice 274	70	12 May	Requisition Number 674	78
31 May	Invoice 305	50	20 May	Requisition Number 715	69
			26 May	Requisition Number 736	56

You are required to:

(a) Rule up a stock record card with suitable column headings.
(b) Complete the stock record card, in date order, for the month of May.

33.7

Marsdens use stock cards to record receipts and issues of the various stock items held in the stores. It is the firm's policy to keep records of both the quantity and value of stock items.

On 1 June there were 75 units in stock of item DN/76. The cost price per item is £3.00. During the month of June the following stock movements took place:

Date	Receipts	Items	Date	Issues	Items
5 Jun	Invoice 1029	55	2 Jun	Requisition Number 25	18
14 Jun	Invoice 1072	40	9 Jun	Requisition Number 38	24
20 Jun	Invoice 1180	65	15 Jun	Requisition Number 46	32
30 Jun	Invoice 1262	75	26 Jun	Requisition Number 54	26

You are required to:

(a) Rule up a stock record card with suitable column headings.
(b) Complete the stock record card, in date order for the month of June.

■ ▼ 34 Receipts and payments accounts and income and expenditure accounts

Most people run a business primarily to *make profit*, while clubs, societies and other non-profit making organisations are run for the *benefit of their members*. These types of organisations are not concerned in trading as such or in profit making, they are established by people who have joined together to pursue a common interest. Their main purpose is to promote activities which interest them. The final accounts for these types of organisations are different from those prepared by businesses.

In most cases, the financial affairs of a club or similar organisation are managed by a *committee* which is elected by the members. The committee consists of elected officers, such as a chairperson, treasurer and secretary.

The *treasurer* is the committee member responsible for collecting subscriptions from the members and paying the bills. The treasurer must also prepare suitable final accounts to submit to the committee at the Annual General Meeting (often abbreviated to AGM). In the case of a small club these final accounts are called *receipts and payments accounts*. Larger organisations, particularly those with substantial assets, present their final accounts in the form of *income and expenditure accounts*, together with a balance sheet.

Cash book of a club

Many clubs use an analysed cash book. With this type of cash book the money received and the payments which occur most frequently will be given a separate analysis column. Obviously, the number of analysis columns will depend on what each club finds useful. At the end of the year, all the analysis columns are totalled to show the entire amount received and spent under each heading.

Receipts and payments account

A receipts and payments account is the simplest way a treasurer can present the final accounts. It is prepared using the totals of the analysis columns from the club's cash book. A receipts and payments account commences with the balance of cash/bank in hand, then lists all money received and all payments made during the year, ending with the closing balance; this represents the amount of cash remaining at the end of the year.

Worked example

This is a typical example:

For the year ended 31 December 20-9 the following information is available for the Queensway Cricket Club:

	£
Bank balance at 1 January 20-9	872
Light and heat	820
Ground maintenance	358
Members' subscriptions	2,920
Travelling expenses	752
Purchase of new equipment	395
Insurance	295
Rent	1,450
Proceeds of Jumble Sale	382
Sundry expenses	168
Bar sales	4,972
Bar purchases	1,856
Bar staff wages	650

You are required to prepare a receipts and payments account for the year ended 31 December 20-9.

Solution

Queensway Cricket Club
Receipts and Payments Account for the year ended 31 December 20-9

20-9		£	20-9		£
1 Jan	Balance b/d	872		Light and heat	820
	Subscriptions	2,920		Ground maintenance	358
	Jumble sale	382		Travelling expenses	752
	Bar sales	4,972		New equipment	395
				Insurance	295
				Rent	1,450
				Sundry expenses	168
				Bar purchases	1,856
				Bar staff wages	650
			31 Dec	Balance c/d	2,402
		9,146			9,146

Only very small organisations would produce their final accounts in the form of a receipts and payments account, for the following reasons:

- A receipts and payments account simply lists all money received and all payments made during the year. It gives no details of any *existing assets* already owned by the club, other than the cash balance and any assets purchased during the current year.
- There is no mention of any *outstanding liabilities*: there may be some unpaid bills at the end of the year.
- Members cannot see if a *profit* or *loss* was made on any particular activity.

For these important reasons it is more usual for a club or organisation to present their final accounts in much greater detail, in the form of an income and expenditure account and a balance sheet.

Bar trading accounts

Although the main purpose of a club is to pursue a common interest they often carry out some activities to provide additional income; for example running a bar, a dance, a raffle or a jumble sale. These types of activities are intended to make a profit and in order to find out if a profit has been made a separate trading account may be prepared for each activity.

Particularly when a club provides a bar for its members it is usual to prepare a *bar trading account*: this information will tell them whether the prices they charge for drinks are too high, or too low.

Bar trading accounts for clubs are no different from the normal trading accounts of a business and are prepared in exactly the same way. When additional expenses are incurred, such as bar staff wages, these would be charged to the bar trading account because these costs are directly related to running the bar.

To illustrate this we can now prepare a bar trading account for the Queensway Cricket Club. There was an opening bar stock of £674 and on 31 December 20-9 there was a stock of drinks valued at £720. We also need to use some items from the receipts and payments account:

Queensway Cricket Club
Receipts and Payments Account for the year ended 31 December 20-9

20-9		£	20-9		£
1 Jan	Balance b/d	872		Light and heat	820
	Subscriptions	2,920		Ground	
	Jumble sale	382		maintenance	358
	Bar sales ✓	4,972		Travelling expenses	752
				New equipment	395
				Insurance	295
				Rent	1,450
				Sundry expenses	168
				Bar purchases ✓	1,856
				Bar staff wages ✓	650
			31 Dec	Balance c/d	2,402
		9,146			9,146

Bar Trading Account for the year ended 31 December 20-9

	£		£
Opening stock	674	Bar sales	4,972
Add bar purchases	1,856		
	2,530		
Less closing stock	720		
Cost of goods sold	1,810		
Add bar staff wages	650		
	2,460		
Profit on bar to income	2,512		
and expenditure account			
	4,972		4,972

Income and expenditure account

Because clubs do not exist primarily to make profits, but rather for the benefit of their members, these types of organisations do not calculate a *profit* or *loss*. Instead, they produce an income and expenditure account which results in the calculation of a *surplus* or a *deficit*. An income and expenditure account follows exactly the same principles as a profit and loss account. We may have to make year end *adjustments* in club accounts just as we do in an ordinary business.

Adjustments

Once again the rule is that final accounts must be prepared in such a way that all the *income* that belongs to the accounting period under consideration is included, whether it has actually been received or not. Set against this should be all *expenses* incurred during that period, even if they have not actually been paid. This principle is known as the *matching rule* because the incomes and expenditures are matched with one another. Examination questions will often include notes giving details of any adjustments which need to be made for prepayments and accruals.

Subscriptions

Subscriptions may have to be adjusted for subscriptions paid in advance or in arrears:

Subscriptions in advance: subscriptions which have been paid in advance for next year are *deducted* from the subscriptions figure for the current year. Subscriptions paid in advance are a *liability*, because the club has received payment before providing the benefit of the facilities. On the balance sheet the amount of subscriptions paid in advance is shown under *Current liabilities*.

Subscriptions in arrears: these are members who have not paid their subscriptions for the current year. Most clubs observe the 'prudence concept' and do not adjust for subscriptions in arrears at the year end. This is because some members leave without notice and no attempt is made to collect their outstanding subscriptions. However, in examination questions, unless an instruction is given to the contrary, you will be expected to include subscriptions in arrears in your calculations. Subscriptions in arrears at the year end are *added* to the subscriptions total for the current year. On the balance sheet the amount of subscriptions in arrears are shown under *Current assets*.

Prepare a set of *workings* to assist you *before* you commence the income and expenditure account. You may need to revise the procedure, adjustments are fully detailed in Unit 26.

Like a profit and loss account, income is entered on the *credit* side, expenditure is entered on the *debit* side. A surplus is transferred to the accumulated fund, to increase the fund, in the same way that the net profit increases the sole trader's capital. A deficit would decrease the accumulated fund.

An income and expenditure account, like the profit and loss account, is a *revenue account*, and follows the same rules. Any capital expenditure, such as the purchase of new equipment is **never** entered in the income and expenditure account. Any new equipment purchased during the current year would be added to the existing equipment and shown under fixed assets on the balance sheet. When no previous equipment exists, the new equipment would be entered, under fixed assets on the balance sheet.

Accumulated fund

A sole trader would have a capital account. A non-profit making organisation has an *accumulated fund*: a *surplus* is *added* to the accumulated fund, a *deficit* is *deducted*.

In effect, the accumulated fund is the same as capital and is calculated in the same way: it is the difference between *assets* and *liabilities*. To illustrate this, if we list the assets and liabilities of the Queensway Cricket Club at the start of the year we can calculate the accumulated fund:

Assets	£
Bar stock	674
Equipment	950
Cash at bank	872
	2,496

Less liabilities:	
Unpaid bill for travelling expenses	56
Accumulated fund at *1 January 20-9* =	2,440

When final accounts are prepared for the first year a club has been in existence there would be no accumulated fund at the beginning of the year. At the end of the first year any surplus is entered as the accumulated fund on the balance sheet.

Balance sheet

Balance sheets for non-profit making organisations follow the same principles and layout as those prepared for sole traders. The accumulated fund occupies the same position as the capital of a sole trader.

Now we can look at the preparation of an income and expenditure account and a balance sheet for the Queensway Cricket Club.

On 1 January 20-9 the Queensway Cricket Club had the following assets and liabilities: bar stock £674, equipment £950, cash at bank £872, unpaid bill for travelling expenses £56.

During the year ended 31 December 20-9 the following receipts and payments were made:

	£
Bank balance at 1 January 20-9	872
Light and heat	820
Ground maintenance	358
Members' subscriptions	2,920
Travelling expenses	752
Purchase of new equipment	395
Insurance	295
Rent	1,450

Proceeds of Jumble Sale	382
Sundry expenses	168
Bar sales	4,972 ✓
Bar purchases	1,856 ✓
Bar staff wages	650 ✓

On 31 December 20-9 the following adjustments had not been made:

(i)   There was an unpaid bill for travelling expenses of £72
(ii) Insurance prepaid was £75
(iii) Closing bar stock was valued at £720

You are required to:

(a) Prepare an income and expenditure account for the year ended 31 December 20-9.
(b) Calculate the accumulated fund at 1 January 20-9.
(c) Prepare a balance sheet as at 31 December 20-9.

To prepare the income and expenditure account we must use the remaining items in the above list, include the profit on the bar and make the necessary adjustments. (Items ticked have already been used to prepare the bar trading account.)

Adjustments at 31 December 20-9

(i)   There was an unpaid bill for travelling expenses of £72.
      Your *workings* would look like this:

Income and expenditure entry		**Balance sheet entry**
Travelling expenses	752	under *Current liabilities*
Less owing on 1 Jan 20-9	56	Travelling
	696	expenses owing £72
Add owing on 31 Dec 20-9	72	
	768	

(ii) Insurance prepaid was £75.
      Your *workings* would look like this:

Income and expenditure entry		**Balance sheet entry**
Insurance	295	under *Current assets*
Less prepaid	75	Insurance prepaid £75
	220	

Queensway Cricket Club
Income and Expenditure Account for the year ended 31 December 20-9

	£		£
Light and heat	820	Profit on bar	2,512
Ground maintenance	358	Subscriptions	2,920
Travelling expenses		Proceeds of Jumble Sale	382
(752 – 56 + 72)	768		
Insurance (295 – 75)	220		
Rent	1,450		
Sundry expenses	168		
Surplus	2,030		
	5,814		5,814

Note: Calculation of surplus: total income *less* total expenditure:

	£
Total income	5,814
Less total expenditure	3,784
Surplus	2,030

Balance Sheet as at 31 December 20-7

	£	£		£	£
Fixed Assets			Accumulated fund		
			at 1 Jan 20-9	2,440	
Equipment	950		Add surplus	2,030	4,470
Add new					
equipment	395	1,345			
Current Assets			**Current Liabilities**		
Bar stock	720		Travelling expenses		
Insurance prepaid	75		accrued		72
Bank balance	2,402	3,197			
		4,542			4,542

Points to remember

- A receipts and payments account is prepared using the *totals of the analysis columns* from a club's cash book. It commences with the balance of cash/bank in hand, then lists all money received and all payments made during the year, ending with the closing balance: this represents the amount of cash remaining at the end of the year.
- An income and expenditure account, like the profit and loss account, is a *revenue account* and follows the same rules. Any capital expenditure, such as the purchase of new equipment is *never* entered in the income and expenditure account. Any new equipment purchased during the current year is added to the existing equipment and shown under fixed assets on the balance sheet.
- *Adjustments* for final accounts follow the principle known as the *matching rule*. They must be prepared in such a way that all *income* that belongs to the accounting period under consideration is included, whether it has *actually been received or not*. Set against this should be all *expenses* incurred during that period, even if they have not *actually been paid*. Examination questions generally include notes giving details of any adjustments which need to be made. It is the *adjusted figure* that is used in the income and expenditure account and the amount of the prepayment or accrual which will appear on the balance sheet.
- The accumulated fund occupies the same position as the capital on a balance sheet: a surplus will *increase* it, a *deficit* will decrease it.

This unit provides the underpinning knowledge you will need to prepare club accounts. Now you should attempt the assignments, which are all recent examination questions, to gain practice in the method and procedures.

Assignments

34.1
On 1 January 20-9 the Oakdale Youth Club had the following assets: furniture and fittings £1,500, games equipment £640, motor van £5,000, cash at bank £460. There were no liabilities.

During the year ended 31 December 20-9 the following receipts and payments were made:

	£
Subscriptions 284 members at £6 each	
Electricity	905
Repairs to equipment	138
Proceeds of annual fete	852
Motor expenses	496
New games equipment	420
Postage and stationery	184
Insurance	375
General expenses	118

On 31 December 20-9 the following information was also available:

(i) There was an electricity bill outstanding of £107
(ii) Insurance prepaid was £115

You are required to:

(a) Prepare a receipts and payments account for the year ended 31 December 20-9.
(b) Prepare an income and expenditure account for the year ended 31 December 20-9.
(c) Calculate the accumulated fund at 1 January 20-9.
(d) Prepare a balance sheet as at 31 December 20-9.

34.2
On 1 June 20-8 the Northside Sports Club had the following assets and liabilities: sports equipment £1,580, furniture £1,090, cash at bank £692, sundry expenses owing £76, stock of drinks £708.

The following is a summary of the receipts and payments of the club for the year ended 31 May 20-9:

Receipts	£	Payments	£
Subscriptions	3,750	Expenses of annual dance	432
Annual dance	974	Rent	1,595
Locker rents	548	New tables	360
Competition fees	396	Prizes for competitions	158
Bar sales	2,836	Sundry expenses	612
		Bar purchases	1,574
		Insurance	495

On 31 May 20-9 the following adjustments had not been made:

(i) Bar stock valued at £692
(ii) Insurance prepaid was £78
(iii) There was £145 owing for rent

You are required to:

(a) Calculate the club's bank balance at 31 May 20-9.
(b) Prepare a bar trading account for the year ended 31 May 20-9.

(c) Prepare an income and expenditure account for the year ended 31 May 20-9.

(d) Calculate the accumulated fund at 1 June 20-8.

(e) Prepare a balance sheet as at 31 May 20-9.

34.3

On 1 June 20-4 the assets and liabilities of the Ambrose Cricket Club were as follows:

	£
Club premises	65,000
Equipment	12,500
Cash at bank	7,370
Unpaid bill for travelling expenses	55

During the year ended 31 May 20-5 the following receipts and payments were made:

	£
Members' subscriptions	7,500
Purchase of new grass cutting machine	1,695
Insurance premium	830
Travelling expenses to away matches	1,315
Rates	920
Stationery and postage	163
Purchases of refreshments	738
Payment of league entry fees	250
Wages of groundsman	1,400
Printing expenses	97
Refreshment bar takings	1,576
Lighting and heating	410
Interest received from bank	74

The following adjustments have not yet been made:

(i) On 31 May 20-5 there was an invoice for printing of £49 which had not been paid

(ii) There was an unused stock of stationery valued at £35 and unused postage stamps valued at £18

You are required to:

(a) Prepare a receipts and payments account for the year ending 31 May 20-5.

(b) Prepare an income and expenditure account for the year ending 31 May 20-5.

(c) Calculate the accumulated fund at 1 June 20-4.

(d) Prepare a balance sheet as at 31 May 20-5.
   The profit or loss on the refreshment bar should be shown.
   You should show clearly how you have dealt with the adjustments.

34.4

On 1 January 20-2 the Adelmead Tennis Club had the following assets and liabilities: equipment £9,000, cash at bank £850, cash in hand £270, unpaid electricity bill £45.

During the year, receipts and payments were:

	£
Subscriptions	4,250
Postage and stationery	45
Fees received for tournament	660
Prizes for tournament	215
Electricity	150
Wages of groundsman	1,450
Rent	935
Purchase of new equipment	411
Insurance	387

On 31 December 20-2 the following information is available:

	£
Tournament fees not paid	40
Rent owing	85
Insurance prepaid	67
Cash in hand	237

You are required to:

(a) Prepare a receipts and payments account for the year ended 31 December 20-2.
(b) Prepare an income and expenditure account for the year ended 31 December 20-2.
(c) Prepare a balance sheet as at 31 December 20-2.

34.5

On 1 June 20-6 the Woodside Sports Club had the following assets and liabilities: equipment £450, cash in hand £173, cash at bank £1,690, rent due but unpaid £75.

During the year receipts and payments were as follows:

	£
Subscriptions: 96 full members, each paying	65
34 part-time members, each paying	35
Fees received for competitions	492
Insurance	385
Lighting and heating	1,463
General expenses	472
Rent paid	1,296
Prizes for competitions	284
Deposit paid on new equipment costing £690	150

	£
On 31 May 20-7	
Insurance was prepaid	35
Rent owing was	108
Cash in hand	96
There was an unpaid bill for general expenses	152

You are required to:

(i) Prepare a receipts and payments account for the year ending 31 May 20-7.
(ii) Prepare an income and expenditure account for the year ending 31 May 20-7.
(iii) Prepare a balance sheet as at 31 May 20-7.
Show clearly how you have dealt with the adjustments.
Full and part-time members are listed and accounted for quite separately.

34.6
On 1 November 20-6 the Lawnswood Tennis Club had the following assets and liabilities: club premises £45,500, equipment £12,750, bar stock £980, bank balance £5,220, cash £326, creditor for bar supplies £450.

The following receipts and payments were made during the year ended 31 October 20-7:

	£
Subscriptions: 98 full-time members, each paying	250
45 part-time members, each paying	125
Travelling expenses to away matches	1,454
Payments to suppliers for bar purchases	8,428
Lighting and heating	2,962
Payment of league entry fees	545
Rent received from private functions	1,485
General expenses	3,835
Rates	3,180
Insurance premium	2,472
Bar staff wages	5,950
Purchase of new equipment	5,790
Stationery and postage	508
Bar sales	16,592

On 31 October 20-7 the following information was available:

(i) Rent of £395 was owing to the club for private functions
(ii) Insurance prepaid was £1,854
(iii) There was a stock of stationery valued at £96 and a stock of drinks valued at £1,080; there were no bar creditors

You are required to:

(a) Prepare a bar trading account for the year ended 31 October 20-7.
(b) Prepare a receipts and payments account for the year ended 31 October 20-7.
(c) Prepare an income and expenditure account for the year ended 31 October 20-7.

Note: A balance sheet is *NOT* required.

Clearly show how you have dealt with the adjustments.

Full and part-time members are listed and accounted for separately.

◼ ✓ **35** Continuous balance ledger accounts

All the accounts previously shown in this book are known as *traditional accounts* – that is, they have *debit* and *credit* sides to the account and are balanced off at the end of the month. Although traditional accounts are the most useful, especially in gaining a real understanding of the principles of double entry book-keeping, most computer systems use a different style of ledger account.

Accounts prepared using computerised systems

When accounts are prepared using computerised systems the principles involved are identical to those of a manual system. However, the style of the ledger account is different. Often it appears as three columns of figures, one column for debit entries, another column for credit entries and the last column for the balance. They are called *continuous balance* or *running balance* accounts, which simply means that every time we make an entry the computer automatically calculates the running balance on the account. It is a real advantage to immediately have the current balance on every account, and everyday business transactions can be efficiently carried out in a fraction of the time taken by manual methods. When traditional methods are used it would be tedious and time consuming to calculate a new balance after each transaction. It also means that there would be a greater possibility of errors. For these reasons it is usual for students to use two-sided accounts. However, it is important to realise that there is no difference in principle, the final balances are the same using either method.

This is a typical example of a customers account, in a sales ledger prepared in traditional style:

B Senior Account

20-9		£	20-9		£
1 Apr	Balance b/d	235.50	10 Apr	Returns inwards	49.25
5 Apr	Sales	250.20	28 Apr	Bank	235.50
20 Apr	Sales	139.50	30 Apr	Balance c/d	340.45
		625.20			625.20
1 May	Balance b/d	340.45			

Now we can look at the same account, but this time prepared in three-column style with a continuous balance. As you can see, the debit and credit columns indicate the type of entry. *Sales* are entered in the *debit* column and then *added* to the balance: this is because the amount owed by the customer has now increased. Similarly, *returns inward* and *bank* are entered in the *credit* column and then *deducted* from the balance: this is because the amount owed has been reduced. (Balance column usually indicates whether debit or credit balance.)

Name:	B Senior			
Address:	34 Courtway			
	LEEDS LS16 8ER			
Account Number: SL/18				

Date	Details	Debit	Credit	Balance
1 Apr	Balance b/d			235.50 Dr
5 Apr	Sales	250.20		485.70 Dr
10 Apr	Returns inwards		49.25	436.45 Dr
20 Apr	Sales	139.50		575.95 Dr
28 Apr	Bank		235.50	340.45 Dr

As you can see, the final balances are the same using either method. Here is another illustration, this is a typical example of a supplier's account in a purchase ledger, prepared in traditional style.

N Davidson Account

20-9		£	20-9		£
12 Apr	Returns outwards	58.20	1 Apr	Balance b/d	365.30
20 Apr	Bank	365.30	7 Apr	Purchases	215.50
30 Apr	Balance c/d	485.75	18 Apr	Purchases	328.45
		909.25			909.25
			1 May	Balance b/d	485.75

Now we can look at the same account, but this time prepared in three-column style with a continuous balance. As you can see, the debit and credit columns indicate the type of entry. *Purchases* are entered in the *credit* column and then *added* to the balance: this is because the amount owed by the firm has now increased. Similarly, *returns* outwards and *bank* are entered in the *debit* column and then *deducted* from the balance: this is because the amount owed has been reduced. (Balance column usually indicates whether debit or credit balance.)

Name:	N Davidson			
Address:	8 Broomfield			
	BRADFORD BD90 7MN			
Account Number:	PL/10			

Date	Details	Debit	Credit	Balance
1 Apr	Balance b/d			365.30 Cr
7 Apr	Purchases		215.50	580.80 Cr
12 Apr	Returns outwards	58.20		522.60 Cr
18 Apr	Purchases		328.45	851.05 Cr
20 Apr	Bank	365.30		485.75 Cr

Points to remember

- When accounts are prepared using computerised systems the principles involved are identical to those of a manual system. However, the style of the ledger account is different. Often it appears as *three* columns of figures – one column for *debit* entries, another column for *credit* entries and the last column for the *balance*.
- Some examinations require candidates to manually prepare three-column ledger accounts with a running balance. Usually candidates are given a list of balances. These balances must be entered in the appropriate accounts first *before* you begin to record any other transactions. Follow these guidelines:
  1 *Open an account* for each of the balances given, enter the date, balance b/d and the amount stated in the balance column. (Indicate whether debit or credit balance.)
  2 *Enter each transaction*, making the entries in the correct column and calculate the new balance.
- Remember the principles are exactly the same whether you prepare three-column ledger accounts with a continuous balance or two-sided traditional accounts.

The following Assignments will help you gain confidence in both method and procedure.

Assignments

35.1

You are an employee of Parkwood Garden Centre and you have been given the following information. All opening balances are as 1 May 20-9:

		£	
A Bannister	– opening balance	202.56	Cr
D Lenton	– opening balance	274.80	Cr
Adam & Sons	– opening balance	345.93	Dr
C Groves	– opening balance	307.28	Dr
Bank	– opening balance	5,931.60	Dr
Capital	– opening balance	4,860.50	Cr
General expenses	– opening balance	492.75	Dr
Purchases	– opening balance	938.80	Dr
Purchase returns	– opening balance	236.20	Cr
Sales	– opening balance	2,581.94	Cr
Sales returns	– opening balance	139.64	Dr

During the month of May the following transactions took place:

Purchases on credit		£	Sales on credit		£
2 May	D Lenton	150.92	4 May	C Groves	230.44
4 May	A Bannister	208.80	9 May	Adam & Sons	384.12
14 May	D Lenton	195.94	18 May	C Groves	196.38
15 May	A Bannister	124.46	24 May	Adam & Sons	379.64

Purchase returns		£	Sales returns		£
12 May	A Bannister	32.50	15 May	Adam & Sons	38.20
24 May	D Lenton	30.68	23 May	C Groves	26.92

Payments received by cheque		£	Payments made by cheque		£
16 May	C Groves	153.64	8 May	General expenses	49.20
28 May	Adam & Sons	345.93	17 May	A Bannister	202.56
			20 May	General expenses	64.50
			22 May	D Lenton	274.80

You are required to:

(a) Open the appropriate ledger accounts and enter the balances as at 1 May 20-9.

(b) Enter the transactions which have taken place during the month of May to the appropriate ledger accounts and correct the running balance after each entry.

35.2

You are an employee of Nikas Sportswear and you have been given the following information. All opening balances are as 1 April 20-9.

		£	
Airedale Fabrics	– opening balance	376.94	Cr
Hollywell Mills	– opening balance	290.46	Cr
Activity Centre	– opening balance	485.30	Dr
Spot Sport	– opening balance	398.92	Dr
Bank	– opening balance	4,372.86	Dr
Capital	– opening balance	8,264.68	Cr
Equipment	– opening balance	3,650.50	Dr
Purchases	– opening balance	1,295.48	Dr
Purchase returns	– opening balance	258.30	Cr
Rent	– opening balance	740.00	Dr
Sales	– opening balance	2,704.62	Cr
Sales returns	– opening balance	312.38	Dr
Sundry expenses	– opening balance	639.56	Dr

During the month of April the following transactions took place:

Purchases on credit		£	Sales on credit		£
4 Apr	Hollywell Mills	390.26	3 Apr	Spot Sport	429.36
6 Apr	Airedale Fabrics	286.30	5 Apr	Activity Centre	384.62
15 Apr	Hollywell Mills	319.52	12 Apr	Spot Sport	275.28
20 Apr	Airedale Fabrics	352.84	20 Apr	Activity Centre	307.54

Purchase returns		£	Sales returns		£
10 Apr	Hollywell Mills	38.28	9 Apr	Activity Centre	32.60
25 Apr	Airedale Fabrics	40.96	18 Apr	Spot Sport	40.58

Payments received by cheque		£	Payments made by cheque		£
6 Apr	Spot Sport	398.92	2 Apr	Rent	165.00
22 Apr	Activity Centre	485.30	3 Apr	Equipment	495.95
			8 Apr	Airedale Fabrics	188.47
			15 Apr	Sundry expenses	59.25
			20 Apr	Hollywell Mills	290.46
			24 Apr	Sundry expenses	79.70
			28 Apr	Airedale Fabrics	474.77

You are required to:

(a) Open the appropriate ledger accounts and enter the balances as at 1 April 20-9.
(b) Enter the transactions which have taken place during the month of April to the appropriate ledger accounts and correct the running balance after each entry.

35.3

You are an employee of Focus Lighting and you have been given the following information. All opening balances are as 1 May 20-9:

Purchase Ledger

		£	
Court Fabrics	– opening balance	314.68	Cr
Walkers Ltd	– opening balance	428.90	Cr
Yorkshire Supplies	– opening balance	294.24	Cr

Sales Ledger

Aladdin Lamps	– opening balance	826.92	Dr
Megson Trading Co	– opening balance	493.30	Dr
Supreme Designs	– opening balance	684.80	Dr

Nominal Ledger

Capital	– opening balance	10,725.76	Cr
Machinery	– opening balance	16,580.50	Dr
Purchases	– opening balance	9,492.96	Dr
Purchase returns	– opening balance	683.52	Cr
Sales	– opening balance	19,105.10	Cr
Sales returns	– opening balance	574.68	Dr
Sundry expenses	– opening balance	1,790.99	Dr
VAT	– opening balance	812.80	Cr
Bank	– opening balance	1,920.85	Dr

During the month of May the following transactions took place:

Focus Lighting Purchases Day Book

Date 20-9	Detail	Goods £ p	VAT £ p	Invoice total £ p
2 May	Yorkshire Supplies	392.12	68.62	460.74
4	Walkers Ltd	376.46	65.88	442.34
15	Court Fabrics	270.93	47.41	318.34
20	Walkers Ltd	404.80	70.84	475.64
25	Yorkshire Supplies	283.26	49.57	332.83
31 May		1,727.57	302.32	2,029.89

Purchases Returns Day Book

Date 20-9	Detail	Goods £ p	VAT £ p	Total £ p
12 May 13	Yorkshire Supplies Walkers Ltd	49.50 36.80	8.66 6.44	58.16 43.24
31 May		86.30	15.10	101.40

Sales Day Book

Date 20-9	Detail	Goods £ p	VAT £ p	Invoice total £ p
3 May 5 10 15 20 22 26	Megson Trading Co Aladdin Lamps Megson Trading Co Supreme Designs Aladdin Lamps Supreme Designs Megson Trading Co	472.69 505.32 372.12 250.69 649.83 340.69 649.83	82.72 88.43 65.12 43.87 113.72 59.62 113.72	555.41 593.75 437.24 294.56 763.55 400.31 763.55
31		3,241.17	567.20	3,808.37

Sales Returns Day Book

Date 20-9	Detail	Goods £ p	VAT £ p	Total £ p
20 May 29	Aladdin Lamps Megson Trading Co	69.60 48.24	12.18 8.44	81.78 56.68
31		117.84	20.62	138.46

Payments received by cheque	£	Payments made by cheque	£
4 May Megson Trading Co	246.65	3 May Sundry expenses	79.95
15 May Supreme Designs	342.40	5 May Walkers Ltd	228.00
24 May Aladdin Lamps	413.46	12 May Court Fabrics	157.34
		23 May Machinery	750.75
		29 May Yorkshire Supplies	147.12
		30 May Walkers Ltd	200.90

You are required to:

(a) Open the appropriate ledger accounts and enter the balances as at 1 May 20-9.

(b) Enter the transactions which have taken place during the month of May to the appropriate ledger accounts and correct the running balance after each entry.

35.4

You are an employee of Homestyle and you have been given the following information. All opening balances are as 1 May 20-9:

Purchase Ledger

		£	
Fairburn & Lawson	– opening balance	372.48	Cr
Pudsey & Co	– opening balance	436.50	Cr
J C Vickers	– opening balance	295.76	Cr

Sales Ledger

Country Kitchens	– opening balance	1,562.84	Dr
Handforth Interiors	– opening balance	1,849.62	Dr
Woodcraft	– opening balance	2,638.96	Dr

Nominal Ledger

Capital	– opening balance	15,750.00	Cr
Fixtures and fittings	– opening balance	17,520.00	Dr
General expenses	– opening balance	2,893.74	Dr
Purchases	– opening balance	12,620.95	Dr
Purchase returns	– opening balance	993.51	Cr
Sales	– opening balance	21,790.28	Cr
Sales returns	– opening balance	254.60	Dr
VAT	– opening balance	861.47	Cr
Bank	– opening balance	1,159.29	Dr

During the month of May the following transactions took place:

Homestyle Purchases Day Book

Date	Detail	Goods £ p	VAT £ p	Invoice total £ p
5 May	J C Vickers	412.35	72.16	484.51
7	Fairburn & Lawson	178.63	31.26	209.89
12	J C Vickers	220.00	38.50	258.50
19	Pudsey & Co	636.58	111.40	747.98
28	Fairburn & Lawson	135.89	23.78	159.67
31 May		1,583.45	277.10	1,860.55

Purchases Returns Day Book

Date	Detail	Goods £ p	VAT £ p	Total £ p
16 May	J C Vickers	68.23	11.94	80.17
28	Fairburn & Lawson	39.32	6.88	46.20
29	J C Vickers	54.58	9.55	64.13
31 May		162.13	28.37	190.50

Sales Day Book

Date	Detail	Goods £ p	VAT £ p	Invoice total £ p
6 May	Handforth Interiors	626.58	109.65	736.23
14	Country Kitchens	450.12	78.77	528.89
18	Woodcraft	372.63	65.21	437.84
22	Country Kitchens	405.43	70.95	476.38
24	Handforth Interiors	428.29	74.95	503.24
29	Woodcraft	564.75	98.83	663.58
31 May		2,847.80	498.36	3,346.16

Sales Returns Day Book

Date	Detail	Goods £ p	VAT £ p	Total £ p
20 May	Handforth Interiors	90.23	15.79	106.02
25	Country Kitchens	64.75	11.33	76.08
31 May		154.98	27.12	182.10

Payments received by cheque	£	Payments made by cheque	£
4 May Handforth Interiors	945.40	2 May General expenses	74.62
		4 May J C Vickers	195.00
16 May Country Kitchens	781.42	15 May Pudsey & Co	436.50
		26 May Fairburn & Lawson	372.48
29 May Woodcraft	1,319.48	28 May General expenses	193.25
		28 May J C Vickers	100.76
		30 May Shop fittings	395.95

You are required to:

(a) Open the appropriate ledger accounts and enter the balances as at 1 May 20-9.

(b) Enter the transactions which have taken place during the month of May to the appropriate ledger accounts and correct the running balance after each entry.

■ ⌄ Answers to assignments

Unit 1

1.1 *Assets*   *Liabilities*
    Motor van   Creditors
    Cash at bank
    Office equipment
    Stock of goods
1.2 *Assets*   *Liabilities*
    Premises   Creditors
    Debtors   Capital
    Motor vehicle
    Office furniture
    Cash in hand
1.3 Total assets £25,000
1.4 Total liabilities £20,500
1.5 Total assets £21,000
1.6 (a) £24,700 (b) £26,500 (c) £59,750 (d) £48,700 (e) £25,000
1.7 (a) £31,800 (b) £92,200 (c) £18,950 (d) £48,830 (e) £81,000
1.8 (a) £32,750 (b) £44,650 (c) £59,450 (d) £31,100 (e) £24,800
1.9 (a) £28,950 (b) £35,050 (c) £56,700 (d) £13,900 (e) £22,100
1.10 Balance sheet totals: £25,600
1.11 Balance sheet totals: £32,400
1.12 Balance sheet totals: £30,250
1.13 Balance sheet totals: £21,500
1.14 Balance sheet totals: £10,800
1.15 Balance sheet totals: £14,500
1.16 Balance sheet totals: £15,600

Unit 2

2.1 *Account to be debited*   *Account to be credited*
    (a) Machinery   Mitchells Ltd
    (b) Cash   Motor van
    (c) M Fieldhouse   Bank
    (d) Cash   D Nelson (Loan)

	(e) Office equipment	Bank
	(f) Cash	B Dixon

2.2 *Account to be debited*   *Account to be credited*

(a) Motor van	Cash
(b) B Groves	Bank
(c) Office furniture	Modern Offices Ltd
(d) Bank	K Williams (Loan)
(e) Machinery	Cash
(f) Cash	W Preston

2.3 K Chippendale

Capital Account

			1 May	Cash	2,000

Cash Account

1 May	Capital	2,000	12 May	Office furniture	500
24 May	L Gibson (Loan)	500	30 May	Crossways Garage	950

Motor Van Account

3 May	Crossways Garage	950

Crossways Garage Account

30 May	Cash	950	3 May	Motor van	950

Office Furniture Account

12 May	Cash	500

L Gibson (Loan) Account

			24 May	Cash	500

2.4 S Curtis

Capital Account

			1 Apr	Bank	5,000

Bank Account

1 Apr	Capital	5,000	10 Apr	Motor van	1,500
20 Apr	D Lester (Loan)	2,000	23 Apr	Machinery	500
			29 Apr	Design Centre	450

Office Furniture Account

4 Apr	Design Centre	450

Design Centre Account

29 Apr	Bank	450	4 Apr	Office furniture	450

Motor Van Account

10 Apr	Bank	1,500

D Lester (Loan) Account

			20 Apr	Bank	2,000

Machinery Account

23 Apr	Bank	500

2.5 J Patel

Capital Account

			1 Jun	Cash	7,000

Cash Account

1 Jun	Capital	7,000	3 Jun	Bank	6,500
14 Jun	P Wilson (Loan)	1,000			

Bank Account

3 Jun	Cash	6,500	6 Jun	Motor van	1,950
			23 Jun	Machinery	750
			30 Jun	Elite Supplies	350

Motor Van Account

6 Jun	Bank	1,950

Office Furniture Account

9 Jun	Elite Supplies	500	20 Jun	Elite Supplies	150

Elite Supplies Account

20 Jun	Office furniture	150	9 Jun	Office furniture	500
30 Jun	Bank	350			

P Wilson (Loan) Account

			14 Jun	Cash	1,000

Machinery Account

23 Jun	Bank	750

2.6 M Sanchez

Capital Account

			1 Oct	Bank	5,000

Bank Account

1 Oct	Capital	5,000	5 Oct	Cash	250
12 Oct	S Ramsden (Loan)	2,000	10 Oct	Motor van	1,750
			20 Oct	Machinery	250
			26 Oct	Systems Ltd	694

Office Equipment Account

3 Oct	Systems Ltd	750	15 Oct	Systems Ltd	56

Systems Ltd Account

15 Oct	Office equipment	56	3 Oct	Office equipment	750
26 Oct	Bank	694			

Cash Account

5 Oct	Bank	250	23 Oct	Shop fittings	175
31 Oct	Shop fittings	60			

Motor Van Account

10 Oct	Bank	1,750

S Ramsden (Loan) Account

			12 Oct	Bank	2,000

Machinery Account

20 Oct	Bank	250

Shop Fittings Account

23 Oct	Cash	175	31 Oct	Cash	60

2.7 P Fleming

Capital Account

			1 Dec	Cash	4,000

Cash Account

1 Dec	Capital	4,000	6 Dec	Bank	3,500
30 Dec	J Oldridge	150	22 Dec	Office furniture	75

Motor Van Account

3 Dec	Ringways Garage	2,500			

Ringways Garage Account

28 Dec	Bank	2,500	3 Dec	Motor van	2,500

Bank Account

6 Dec	Cash	3,500	9 Dec	Office furniture	275
15 Dec	J Gillow (Loan)	3,000	12 Dec	Machinery	800
			28 Dec	Ringways Garage	2,500

Office Furniture Account

9 Dec	Bank	275			
22 Dec	Cash	75			

Machinery Account

12 Dec	Bank	800	18 Dec	J Oldridge	150

J Gillow (Loan) Account

			15 Dec	Bank	3,000

J Oldridge Account

18 Dec	Machinery	150	30 Dec	Cash	150

Unit 3

3.1

Account to be debited	Account to be credited
(a) Purchases	R Sykes
(b) Cash	Sales
(c) Bank	Machinery
(d) Purchases	Cash
(e) J. Cook	Sales
(f) Bank	Sales

3.2

Account to be debited	Account to be credited
(a) Purchases	Bank
(b) Cash	Sales
(c) Office furniture	Cash
(d) G Clarke	Sales
(e) Purchases	Cash
(f) Bank	H Gibson

3.3

Account to be debited	Account to be credited
(a) L Morgan	Sales
(b) D Sadler	Cash
(c) Purchases	W James
(d) P Ellis	Bank

(e) Cash   Sales

(f) Purchases   Bank

3.4   M Donaldson

Capital Account

			1 Mar	Cash	5,000

Cash Account

1 Mar	Capital	5,000	3 Mar	Office equipment	750
			8 Mar	Bank	4,000
			18 Mar	Purchases	120

Office Equipment Account

3 Mar	Cash	750

Bank Account

8 Mar	Cash	4,000	12 Mar	Motor van	1,900
21 Mar	Sales	85			
30 Mar	M Jackson	150			

Purchases Account

10 Mar	J Lyons	500
18 Mar	Cash	120
25 Mar	J Lyons	275

J Lyons Account

			10 Mar	Purchases	500
			25 Mar	Purchases	275

Motor Van Account

12 Mar	Bank	1,900

M Jackson Account

15 Mar	Sales	150	30 Mar	Bank	150

Sales Account

			15 Mar	M Jackson	150
			21 Mar	Bank	85

3.5 J Singh

Capital Account

			1 May	Cash	8,000

Cash Account

1 May	Capital	8,000	3 May	Bank	7,000
20 May	Sales	50	30 May	Purchases	75

Bank Account

3 May	Cash	7,000	9 May	Office furniture	700
			25 May	G Moore	350

Purchases Account

5 May	G Moore	350
30 May	Cash	75

G Moore Account

25 May	Bank	350	5 May	Purchases	350

Office Furniture Account

9 May	Bank	700

Sales Account

			14 May	F Green	450
			20 May	Cash	50

F Green Account

14 May	Sales	450

Motor Van Account

17 May	Newtown Motors	5,000

Newtown Motors Account

			17 May	Motor van	5,000

3.6 S Munro

Capital Account

			1 Jun	Bank	5,000

Bank Account

1 Jun	Capital	5,000	15 Jun	Motor vehicle	2,000
5 Jun	Sales	250	22 Jun	C Clifton	150
20 Jun	T Wilson (Loan)	1,000	26 Jun	Purchases	70

Purchases Account

3 Jun	C Clifton	150
9 Jun	Cash	50
11 Jun	K Ingram	660
26 Jun	Bank	70

C Clifton Account

22 Jun	Bank	150	3 Jun	Purchases	150

Sales Account

			5 Jun	Bank	250
			7 Jun	Cash	150
			14 Jun	E Mason	500
			30 Jun	G Spink	90

Cash Account

7 Jun	Sales	150	9 Jun	Purchases	50

K Ingram Account

			11 Jun	Purchases	660

E Mason Account

14 Jun	Sales	500

Motor Vehicle Account

15 Jun	Bank	2,000

T Wilson (Loan) Account

			20 Jun	Bank	1,000

G Spink Account

30 Jun	Sales	90

3.7   C Gulliver

Capital Account

			1 Aug	Cash	10,000

Cash Account

1 Aug	Capital	10,000	2 Aug	Bank	8,500
15 Aug	Sales	200	3 Aug	Purchases	150
			26 Aug	Purchases	450
			27 Aug	Nelsons Ltd	250

Bank Account

2 Aug	Cash	8,500	29 Aug	Display equipment	350
28 Aug	F Fieldhouse	100	30 Aug	J Black	650
31 Aug	Sales	220			

Purchases Account

3 Aug	Cash	150
12 Aug	J Black	650
26 Aug	Cash	450

Sales Account

			5 Aug	F Fieldhouse	100
			15 Aug	Cash	200
			24 Aug	J Smith	150
			31 Aug	Bank	220

F Fieldhouse Account

5 Aug	Sales	100	28 Aug	Bank	100

Office Equipment Account

7 Aug	Nelsons Ltd	250

Nelsons Ltd Account

27 Aug	Cash	250	7 Aug	Office equipment	250

J Black Account

30 Aug	Bank	650	12 Aug	Purchases	650

Motor Van Account

20 Aug	Bright Motors	4,000

Bright Motors Account

			20 Aug	Motor van	4,000

J Smith Account

24 Aug	Sales	150

Display Equipment Account

29 Aug	Bank	350

3.8 M Gonzalas

Capital Account

			1 Nov	Bank	5,000
			14 Nov	Cash	500

Bank Account

1 Nov	Capital	5,000	3 Nov	Cash	250
20 Nov	E Somes	150	16 Nov	Motor van	1,500
30 Nov	F Armitage	220	26 Nov	W Rycroft	490

Cash Account

3 Nov	Bank	250	4 Nov	Purchases	175
7 Nov	Sales	225	18 Nov	Purchases	420
14 Nov	Capital	500	21 Nov	Shop fittings	150
24 Nov	Sales	190			
27 Nov	J Buckley	325			

Purchases Account

2 Nov	W Rycroft	490
4 Nov	Cash	175
9 Nov	G Stewart	595
9 Nov	W Rycroft	355
18 Nov	Cash	420
22 Nov	G Stewart	225
28 Nov	G Stewart	395

Sales Account

			5 Nov	J Buckley	325
			7 Nov	Cash	225
			12 Nov	F Armitage	220
			12 Nov	J Buckley	295
			24 Nov	Cash	190

W Rycroft Account

26 Nov	Bank	490	2 Nov	Purchases	490
			9 Nov	Purchases	355

J Buckley Account

5 Nov	Sales	325	27 Nov	Cash	325
12 Nov	Sales	295			

Display Equipment Account

6 Nov	Thompson Ltd	550	10 Nov	E Somes	150

Thompson Ltd Account

			6 Nov	Display equipment	550

G Stewart Account

			9 Nov	Purchases	595
			22 Nov	Purchases	225
			28 Nov	Purchases	395

E Somes Account

10 Nov	Display equipment	150	20 Nov	Bank	150

F Armitage Account

12 Nov	Sales	220	30 Nov	Bank	220

Motor Van Account

16 Nov	Bank	1,500

Shop Fittings Account

21 Nov	Cash	150

Unit 4

4.1 *Account to be debited*   *Account to be credited*

	Debited	Credited
(a)	D Marshall	Sales
(b)	Purchases	Cash
(c)	T Newman	Returns outwards
(d)	Bank	Sales
(e)	Returns inwards	D Marshall
(f)	Bank	R Goodman

4.2 *Account to be debited*   *Account to be credited*

	Debited	Credited
(a)	Purchases	E Russell
(b)	Office furniture	Newstyle Ltd
(c)	F King	Sales
(d)	E Russell	Returns outwards
(e)	L Curtis	Cash
(f)	Newstyle Ltd	Office furniture

4.3 *Account to be debited*   *Account to be credited*

	Debited	Credited
(a)	Cash	Sales
(b)	Returns inwards	G Jennings
(c)	Purchases	B Dixon
(d)	Project Design	Display equipment
(e)	Motor van	Smart Motors
(f)	B Dixon	Returns outwards

4.4 Dean Sayer

Capital Account

			1 May	Cash	7,000

Cash Account

1 May	Capital	7,000	2 May	Bank	6,500
10 May	Sales	50	20 May	Purchases	145

Bank Account

2 May	Cash	6,500	9 May	Office furniture	300
18 May	Sales	75	26 May	M Trenholme	440
31 May	D Davey	210	29 May	Linton Garages	250

Purchases Account

3 May	M Trenholme	500
15 May	R Marples	750
20 May	Cash	145
28 May	R Marples	350

Sales Account

			8 May	D Davey	250
			10 May	Cash	50
			18 May	Bank	75
			24 May	K Bradshaw	221

Returns Inwards Account

12 May	D Davey	40
27 May	K Bradshaw	21

M Trenholme Account

6 May	Returns outwards	60	3 May	Purchases	500
26 May	Bank	440			

Returns Outwards Account

		6 May	M Trenholme	60
		22 May	R Marples	80
		30 May	R Marples	25

Motor Van Account

5 May	Linton Garages	3,000

Linton Garages Account

29 May	Bank	250	5 May	Motor van	3,000

D Davey Account

8 May	Sales	250	12 May	Returns inwards	40
			31 May	Bank	210

Office Furniture Account

9 May	Bank	300

R Marples Account

22 May	Returns outwards	80	15 May	Purchases	750
30 May	Returns outwards	25	28 May	Purchases	350

K Bradshaw Account

24 May	Sales	221	27 May	Returns inwards	21

4.5 M Daswani

Capital Account

		1 Jun	Bank	10,000

Bank Account

1 Jun	Capital	10,000	20 Jun	Cash	500
28 Jun	V Reed	350	25 Jun	M Webb	775

Cash Account

12 Jun	Sales	300	30 Jun	Euro Designs	250
20 Jun	Bank	500			

Purchases Account

2 Jun	M Webb	900
6 Jun	T Ross	500

Sales Account

		8 Jun	V Reed	425
		12 Jun	Cash	300
		17 Jun	F Redman	350
		27 Jun	F Redman	230

Returns Inwards Account

15 Jun	V Reed	75
22 Jun	F Redman	25

Returns Outwards Account

		7 Jun	M Webb	125
		11 Jun	T Ross	50

M Webb Account

7 Jun	Returns outwards	125	2 Jun	Purchases		900
25 Jun	Bank	775				

Display Equipment Account

4 Jun	Euro Designs Ltd	250	

Euro Designs Ltd Account

30 Jun	Cash	250	4 Jun	Display equipment	250

T Ross Account

11 Jun	Returns outwards	50	6 Jun	Purchases	500

V Reed Account

8 Jun	Sales	425	15 Jun	Returns inwards	75
			28 Jun	Bank	350

F Redman Account

17 Jun	Sales	350	22 Jun	Returns inwards	25
27 Jun	Sales	230			

4.6 Jill O'Connor

Capital Account

			1 Aug	Cash	5,000

Cash Account

1 Aug	Capital	5,000	5 Aug	Bank	4,500
18 Aug	Sales	124	30 Aug	Purchases	320
31 Aug	T Williams	129			

Purchases Account

3 Aug	T Mann	875
10 Aug	Bank	420
15 Aug	T Mann	300
30 Aug	Cash	320

T Mann Account

7 Aug	Returns outwards	75	3 Aug	Purchases	875
22 Aug	Returns outwards	30	15 Aug	Purchases	300
29 Aug	Bank	1,070			

Bank Account

5 Aug	Cash	4,500	8 Aug	Office furniture	295
20 Aug	J Kelly (Loan)	3,000	10 Aug	Purchases	420
			25 Aug	Greens Garages	200
			29 Aug	T Mann	1,070

Returns Outwards Account

		7 Aug	T Mann	75
		22 Aug	T Mann	30

Office Furniture Account

8 Aug	Bank	295

Sales Account

9 Aug	James Seymore	580
14 Aug	T Williams	165
18 Aug	Cash	124
28 Aug	James Seymore	175

James Seymore Account

9 Aug	Sales	580	13 Aug	Returns inwards	40
28 Aug	Sales	175			

Motor Van Account

12 Aug	Greens Garages	4,500

Greens Garages Account

25 Aug	Bank	200	12 Aug	Motor van	4,500

Returns Inwards Account

13 Aug	James Seymore	40
19 Aug	T Williams	36

T Williams Account

14 Aug	Sales	165	19 Aug	Returns inwards	36
			31 Aug	Cash	129

J Kelly (Loan) Account

20 Aug	Bank	3,000

Unit 5

5.1 *Account to be debited*   *Account to be credited*

	Account to be debited	*Account to be credited*
(a)	Motor expenses	Cash
(b)	Rent	Bank
(c)	Drawings	Cash
(d)	Rates	Bank
(e)	Cash	Commission received
(f)	Insurance	Bank

5.2 *Account to be debited*   *Account to be credited*

	Account to be debited	*Account to be credited*
(a)	Purchases	Cash
(b)	Bank	Rent received
(c)	Motor expenses	Bank
(d)	J Kendall	Sales
(e)	Motor van	Leaders Garages
(f)	Wages	Cash

5.3 *Account to be debited*   *Account to be credited*

	Account to be debited	*Account to be credited*
(a)	Electricity	Bank
(b)	Cash	Sales
(c)	Bank	Commission received
(d)	Returns inwards	J Kilburn
(e)	Office furniture	Bank
(f)	Drawings	Cash

5.4 *Account to be debited*   *Account to be credited*

	Account to be debited	*Account to be credited*
(a)	R Bright	Returns outwards

(b) Rates   Bank
(c) K Williams   Sales
(d) Drawings   Purchases
(e) Returns inwards   K Williams
(f) Cash   Rates

5.5 A Oldridge

Bank Account

1 May	Capital	5,000	4 May	Cash	500
9 May	Sales	250	12 May	Rent	75
16 May	Rent received	30	29 May	Drawings	50
24 May	K Stead	126	30 May	J Richardson	710

Capital Account

| | | | 1 May | Bank | 5,000 |

Purchases Account

| 2 May | J Richardson | 750 |
| 19 May | S Ramsden | 950 |

J Richardson Account

| 6 May | Returns outwards | 40 | 2 May | Purchases | 750 |
| 30 May | Bank | 710 | | | |

Cash Account

4 May	Bank	500	7 May	Drawings	100
25 May	Sales	88	15 May	Motor expenses	58
			22 May	Wages	150
			28 May	Office furniture	200
			31 May	Rent	75

Returns Outwards Account

| | | | 6 May | J Richardson | 40 |
| | | | 27 May | S Ramsden | 68 |

Drawings Account

| 7 May | Cash | 100 |
| 29 May | Bank | 50 |

K Stead Account

| 11 May | Sales | 150 | 14 May | Returns inwards | 24 |
| | | | 24 May | Bank | 126 |

Sales Account

			9 May	Bank	250
			11 May	K Stead	150
			11 May	M Day	229
			25 May	Cash	88
			26 May	T Barnett	122
			26 May	M Day	159

M Day Account

| 11 May | Sales | 229 |
| 26 May | Sales | 159 |

Rent Account

12 May	Bank	75
31 May	Cash	75

Returns Inwards Account

14 May	K Stead	24

Motor Expenses Account

15 May	Cash	58

Rent Received Account

			16 May	Bank	30

S Ramsden Account

27 May	Returns outwards	68	19 May	Purchases	950

Wages Account

22 May	Cash	150

T Barnett Account

26 May	Sales	122

Office Furniture Account

28 May	Cash	200

5.6 K Wilson

Capital Account

			1 Jun	Cash	10,000

Cash Account

1 Jun	Capital	10,000	2 Jun	Purchases	500
9 Jun	Commission received	50	3 Jun	Rent	100
26 Jun	Sales	265	6 Jun	Bank	9,000
			12 Jun	Drawings	75
			22 Jun	Stationery	18
			30 Jun	Motor expenses	55

Rent Account

3 Jun	Cash	100

Purchases Account

2 Jun	Cash	500
10 Jun	A Dawson	329
10 Jun	C Page	172
20 Jun	Bank	750

Bank Account

6 Jun	Cash	9,000	18 Jun	Rates	150
27 Jun	Commission received	28	20 Jun	Purchases	750
28 Jun	J Stevens	225	24 Jun	Drawings	120

Sales Account

			8 Jun	J Stevens	250
			23 Jun	G Blackman	495
			26 Jun	Cash	265

J Stevens Account

8 Jun	Sales	250	14 Jun	Returns inwards	25
			28 Jun	Bank	225

Commission Received Account

			9 Jun	Cash	50
			27 Jun	Bank	28

A Dawson Account

		10 Jun	Purchases	329

C Page Account

16 Jun	Returns outwards	22	10 Jun	Purchases	172

Drawings Account

12 Jun	Cash	75
24 Jun	Bank	120

Returns Inwards Account

14 Jun	J Stevens	25
29 Jun	G Blackman	58

Motor Van account

15 Jun	Northtown Garages	4,000

Northtown Garages Account

	15 Jun	Motor van	4,000

Returns Outwards Account

	16 Jun	C Page	22

Rates Account

18 Jun	Bank	150

Stationery Account

22 Jun	Cash	18

G Blackman Account

23 Jun	Sales	495	29 Jun	Returns inwards	58

Motor Expenses Account

30 Jun	Cash	55

5.7 D Shelley

Bank Account

1 Aug	Capital	5,000	5 Aug	Purchases	675
15 Aug	Sales	150	10 Aug	Cash	300
18 Aug	R Cawood (Loan)	2,000	16 Aug	Insurance	30
30 Aug	Insurance refund	5	20 Aug	Smith & Weston	330
31 Aug	H Dale	181	23 Aug	Electicity	68
			26 Aug	Newstylax	460

Capital Account

	1 Aug	Bank	5,000

Purchases Account

2 Aug	Smith & Weston	359
5 Aug	Bank	675
29 Aug	Cash	45

Smith & Weston Account

7 Aug	Returns outwards	29	2 Aug	Purchases	359
20 Aug	Bank	330			

Office Furniture Account

4 Aug	Newstylax	460

Newstylax Account

26 Aug	Bank	460	4 Aug	Office furniture	460

Returns Outwards Account

		7 Aug	Smith & Weston	29

Sales Account

		9 Aug	H Gibson	450
		15 Aug	Bank	150
		24 Aug	J Youngman	278
		24 Aug	H Dale	181

H Gibson Account

9 Aug	Sales	450	19 Aug	Returns inwards	40
			21 Aug	Cash	200

Cash Account

10 Aug	Bank	300	12 Aug	Drawings	50
21 Aug	H Gibson	200	14 Aug	Rent	200
28 Aug	Rent received	50	22 Aug	Wages	175
			29 Aug	Purchases	45

Drawings Account

12 Aug	Cash	50

Rent Account

14 Aug	Cash	200

Insurance Account

16 Aug	Bank	30	30 Aug	Bank	5

R Cawood (Loan) Account

		18 Aug	Bank	2,000

Returns Inwards Account

19 Aug	H Gibson	40
27 Aug	J Youngman	58

Wages Account

22 Aug	Cash	175

Electricity Account

23 Aug	Bank	68

J Youngman Account

24 Aug	Sales	278	27 Aug	Returns inwards	58

H Dale Account

24 Aug	Sales	181	31 Aug	Bank	181

Rent Received Account

		28 Aug	Cash	50

5.8 T Garside

Bank Account

1 Oct	Capital	7,000	3 Oct	Rates	75
9 Oct	Commission received	75	21 Oct	T Richie	750
14 Oct	Rates refund	20	25 Oct	R Kemp	902
16 Oct	A Goldman (Loan)	4,000	28 Oct	Drawings	150
18 Oct	A Andrews	152	30 Oct	Abbot Garages	150
26 Oct	D Jenkins	425			

Capital Account

			1 Oct	Bank	7,000
			1 Oct	Cash	500

Cash Account

1 Oct	Capital	500	7 Oct	Insurance	150
8 Oct	Sales	65	12 Oct	Motor expenses	35
13 Oct	Sales	150	15 Oct	Wages	250
24 Oct	Commission received	95	20 Oct	Purchases	150
31 Oct	Sales	96	24 Oct	Wages	200
			27 Oct	Motor expenses	22

Purchases Account

2 Oct	T Richie	750			
2 Oct	R Kemp	375			
2 Oct	P Douglas	480			
10 Oct	R Kemp	267			
10 Oct	W Wallace	290			
19 Oct	R Kemp	360			
20 Oct	Cash	150			

T Richie Account

21 Oct	Bank	750	2 Oct	Purchases	750

R Kemp Account

6 Oct	Returns outwards	45	2 Oct	Purchases	375
22 Oct	Returns outwards	55	10 Oct	Purchases	267
25 Oct	Bank	902	19 Oct	Purchases	360

P Douglas Account

			2 Oct	Purchases	480

Rates Account

3 Oct	Bank	75	14 Oct	Bank	20

Motor Van Account

4 Oct	Abbot Garages	2,000			

Abbot Garages Account

30 Oct	Bank	150	4 Oct	Motor van	2,000

Sales Account

			5 Oct	D Jenkins	295
			5 Oct	A Andrews	190
			8 Oct	Cash	65
			13 Oct	Cash	150
			23 Oct	D Jenkins	130
			23 Oct	R Smythe	276
			31 Oct	Cash	96

D Jenkins Account

5 Oct	Sales	295	26 Oct	Bank	425
23 Oct	Sales	130			

A Andrews Account

5 Oct	Sales	190	11 Oct	Returns inwards	38
			18 Oct	Bank	152

Returns Outwards Account

			6 Oct	R Kemp	45
			22 Oct	R Kemp	55

Insurance Account

7 Oct	Cash	150			

Commission Received Account

			9 Oct	Bank	75
			24 Oct	Cash	95

W Wallace Account

			10 Oct	Purchases	290

Returns Inwards Account

11 Oct	A Andrews	38			
29 Oct	R Smythe	26			

Motor Expenses Account

12 Oct	Cash	35			
27 Oct	Cash	22			

Wages Account

15 Oct	Cash	250			
24 Oct	Cash	200			

A Goldman (Loan) Account

			16 Oct	Bank	4,000

Office Fixtures Account

17 Oct	Burton Supplies	195			

Burton Supplies Account

			17 Oct	Office fixtures	195

R Smythe Account

23 Oct	Sales	276	29 Oct	Returns inwards	26

Drawings Account

28 Oct	Bank	150			

5.9 F Patel

Capital Account

			1 Nov	Bank	4,000
			1 Nov	Cash	350

Bank Account

1 Nov	Capital	4,000	5 Nov	Rates	212
4 Nov	J Franks (Loan)	2,500	10 Nov	Insurance	55
13 Nov	Rates refund	25	17 Nov	Electricity	124
24 Nov	S Grey	378	20 Nov	Stationery	47
26 Nov	J Armitage	357	22 Nov	Drawings	150
			23 Nov	J Dean	775
			28 Nov	Websters Garages	1,500

Cash Account

1 Nov	Capital	350	8 Nov	Motor expenses	35
3 Nov	Sales	150	9 Nov	Drawings	80
12 Nov	Sales	245	14 Nov	Wages	130
18 Nov	Rent received	55	25 Nov	Office fixtures	150
25 Nov	Sales	200	27 Nov	Wages	75

Purchases Account

2 Nov	J Dean	650
2 Nov	R Reagan	467
2 Nov	M Nichols	265
11 Nov	R Reagan	330
11 Nov	J Dean	125
19 Nov	M Nichols	356
19 Nov	B Harris	95
29 Nov	B Harris	450

J Dean Account

23 Nov	Bank	775	2 Nov	Purchases	650
			11 Nov	Purchases	125

R Reagan Account

15 Nov	Returns outwards	45	2 Nov	Purchases	467
			11 Nov	Purchases	330

M Nichols Account

21 Nov	Returns outwards	38	2 Nov	Purchases	265
			19 Nov	Purchases	356

Sales Account

			3 Nov	Cash	150
			7 Nov	E Barker	221
			7 Nov	J Armitage	357
			7 Nov	S Grey	128
			12 Nov	Cash	245
			16 Nov	E Barker	325
			16 Nov	S Grey	250
			25 Nov	Cash	200

L Franks (Loan) Account

			4 Nov	Bank	2,500

Rates Account

5 Nov	Bank	212	13 Nov	Bank	25

Motor Van Account

6 Nov	Websters Garages	1,500

Websters Garages Account

28 Nov	Bank	1,500	6 Nov	Motor van	1,500

E Barker Account

7 Nov	Sales	221
16 Nov	Sales	325

J Armitage Account

7 Nov	Sales	357	26 Nov	Bank	357

S Grey Account

7 Nov	Sales	128	24 Nov	Bank	378
16 Nov	Sales	250			

Motor Expenses Account

8 Nov	Cash	35

Drawings Account

9 Nov	Cash	80
22 Nov	Bank	150

Insurance Account

10 Nov	Bank	55

Wages Account

14 Nov	Cash	130
27 Nov	Cash	75

Returns Outwards Account

15 Nov	R Reagan	45
21 Nov	M Nichols	38
30 Nov	B Harris	65

Electricity Account

17 Nov	Bank	124

Rent Received Account

18 Nov	Cash	55

B Harris Account

30 Nov	Returns outwards	65	19 Nov	Purchases	95
			29 Nov	Purchases	450

Stationery Account

20 Nov	Bank	47

Office Fixtures Account

25 Nov	Cash	150

Unit 6

6.1
(b) Real
(c) Nominal
(d) Real
(e) Personal
(f) Real

6.2
(b) Nominal
(c) Personal
(d) Real
(e) Nominal
(f) Personal

6.3 Personal accounts only

D Hall Account

| 26 Jan | Bank | 348 | 1 Jan | Purchases | 348 |

L Walker Account

9 Jan	Returns outwards	55	1 Jan	Purchases	576
31 Jan	Balance c/d	646	4 Jan	Purchases	125
		701			701
			1 Feb	Balance b/d	646

B Hagston Account

9 Jan	Returns outwards	50	1 Jan	Purchases	850
31 Jan	Balance c/d	800			
		850			850
			1 Feb	Balance b/d	800

B Dickson Account

18 Jan	Returns outwards	67	4 Jan	Purchases	367
30 Jan	Cash	300	16 Jan	Purchases	146
31 Jan	Balance c/d	146			
		513			513
			1 Feb	Balance b/d	146

J Dunn Account

| 31 Jan | Balance c/d | 85 | 16 Jan | Purchases | 85 |
| | | | 1 Feb | Balance b/d | 85 |

6.4 Personal accounts only

M Harding Account

1 Feb	Sales	360	12 Feb	Returns inwards	60
			15 Feb	Cash	300
		360			360

J Johnson Account

1 Feb	Sales	98	6 Feb	Returns inwards	24
			28 Feb	Cash	74
		98			98

E Briggs Account

1 Feb	Sales	450	6 Feb	Returns inwards	50
18 Feb	Sales	220	25 Feb	Bank	400
27 Feb	Sales	90	28 Feb	Balance c/d	310
		760			760
1 Mar	Balance b/d	310			

T Myers Account

1 Feb	Sales	212	20 Feb	Returns inwards	52
9 Feb	Sales	152	28 Feb	Balance c/d	552
18 Feb	Sales	240			
		604			604
1 Mar	Balance b/d	552			

R Godfrey Account

3 Feb	Sales	330	28 Feb	Balance c/d	465
9 Feb	Sales	135			
		465			465
1 Mar	Balance b/d	465			

P Ellis Account

3 Feb	Sales	421	19 Feb	Bank	421

R Kemp Account

27 Feb	Sales	350	28 Feb	Balance c/d	350
1 Mar	Balance b/d	350			

6.5 Personal accounts only

J Radcliffe	no balance		P Coates	credit balance	295
W James	credit balance	847	P Williams	credit balance	240
J Burns	no balance		S Daniel	debit balance	700
D Hall	debit balance	422	P Harper	debit balance	245
J Allen	credit balance	497	J Nixon	debit balance	225

6.6 Personal accounts only

R Pearson	credit balance	231	S Dean	credit balance	760
L Gregg	no balance		N Banks	credit balance	475
P Lodge	debit balance	390	D Simons	debit balance	407
J Watson	debit balance	564	R Sutcliffe	debit balance	480
T Barnsdale	debit balance	155	F McKay	no balance	
K Stocks	credit balance	455	J Carlton	credit balance	150

6.7 All accounts

Bank	debit balance	2,505	Capital	credit balance	2,500
Purchases	debit balance	1,750	M Seal	credit balance	335
J Green	credit balance	610	S Sutcliffe	no balance	
Sales	credit balance	841	E Phillips	debit balance	160
W Lodge	debit balance	436	Cash	debit balance	100

Returns					
outwards	credit balance	55	Rent	debit balance	150
Drawings	debit balance	100	G Normanton	credit balance	1,000
Stationery	debit balance	45	Insurance	debit balance	95

6.8 All accounts

Bank	debit balance	3,961	Cash	debit balance	502
Capital	credit balance	6,250	B Lewis	credit balance	1,262
Purchases	debit balance	3,159	E Daley	credit balance	982
Stationery	debit balance	24	Returns outwards	credit balance	94
Rent	debit balance	125	Sales	credit balance	939
Machinery	debit balance	191	Groves & Bean	credit balance	316
Wages	debit balance	140	D Mills	debit balance	248
J Kendall	no balance		W Barry	no balance	
Rent received	credit balance	25	Returns inwards	debit balance	45
Motor vehicle	debit balance	1,750	Lockwood Motors	no balance	
B Freeman	no balance		Drawings	debit balance	100
D Trent	no balance		B Todd	credit balance	425
Motor expenses	debit balance	48			

Unit 7

7.1

Trial Balance as at 31 March 20-8

	Dr	Cr
Bank	4,111	
Capital		6,000
Office Fixtures	400	
Purchases	1,640	
Rent	420	
Sales		1,050
Cash	260	
Insurance	74	
Wages	90	
Returns outwards		45
Returns inwards	40	
Drawings	60	
	7,095	7,095

7.2

Trial Balance as at 31 January 20-8

	Dr	Cr
Capital		6,800
A Frazer		1,732
Motor vehicle	3,800	
A Hodges	1,603	
J Jennings	590	
Bank	1,460	
Office equipment	560	
Sales		2,230
Purchases	1,830	
Returns inwards	37	
Drawings	500	
Returns outwards		98
Salaries	480	
	10,860	10,860

7.3

Trial Balance as at 30 November 20-8

	Dr	Cr
Premises	6,250	
P Cave	810	
R Webster	1,640	
V Bruce	130	
Bank	900	
Capital		9,000
G Franks (Loan)		2,000
T Cummings		1,654
G Fenland		1,060
Sales		1,420
H Crossley	480	
Purchases	2,394	
I Shaw		295
Purchase returns		115
Motor van	2,000	
Rates	600	
Motor expenses	90	
Drawings	250	
	15,544	15,544

7.4

Trial Balance as at 31 May 20-4

	Dr	Cr
Sales		21,255
Purchases	13,255	
General expenses	5,344	
Fixtures	2,500	
K Gibson	555	
T Lowe		485
Bank	1,828	
Drawings	3,100	
Capital		7,228
Stock	2,386	
	28,968	28,968

7.5

Trial Balance as at 31 October 20-6

	Dr	Cr
G Rogers	70	
A Lewis		120
Bank	1,120	
Capital		1,080
General expenses	40	
Purchases	120	
Sales		150
	1,350	1,350

7.6

Trial Balance as at 31 October 20-8

	Dr	Cr
Capital		8,525
Bank	8,940	
R Johnson	1,006	
S Desmonds	3,560	
Returns outwards		110
L Morgan		740
G Edwards		3,830
Sales		2,325
Purchases	1,965	
Returns inwards	59	
	15,530	15,530

Unit 8

8.1 (a) General
(b) Purchase

8.2 (a) General
(b) Sales

(c) General	(c) General	
(d) Sales	(d) General	
(e) General	(e) Private	
(f) General	(f) Purchase	
8.3 (a) General	8.4 (a) General	
(b) Private	(b) Cash Book	
(c) General	(c) Sales	
(d) Sales	(d) Purchase	
(e) Purchase	(e) General	
(f) Purchase	(f) Cash Book	

Unit 9

9.1 Total cash 928.50   Cheques 469.26   Total credit 1,397.76
9.2 Old balance 3,113.18   This cheque 1,842.75   New balance 1,270.43
9.3 Total cash 536.30   Cheques 492.33   Total credit 1,028.63
9.4 Old balance 925.75   This cheque 349.05   New balance 576.70
9.5 (a) Liability (b) Cheque serial number (c) Withdrawn
    (d) Payment made to specified person, on stated date for stated amount
    (e) (i) Refer to drawer (ii) Insufficient funds (f) 45 overdrawn

Unit 10

10.1

Cash Book

Date	Particulars	F	Cash	Bank	Date	Particulars	F	Cash	Bank
May 1	Balances b/d		262.00	2756.00	May 3	Stationery		37.00	
2	R Douglas			368.00	4	Office furniture			560.00
5	Sales		125.00		8	Insurance			48.00
10	M Curtis			149.00	9	Purchases		62.00	
12	J Singh		375.00		11	Drawings		100.00	
17	Sales		250.00		15	Motor repairs			97.00
19	S Myers			595.00	22	Wages		450.00	
24	Sales		172.00		25	D Nicholas			368.00
					26	Drawings		100.00	
					30	Display Equipment			695.00
					31	Balances c/d		435.00	2100.00
			1184.00	3868.00				1184.00	3868.00
June 1	Balances b/d		435.00	2100.00					

10.2

Cash Book									
Date	Particulars	F	Cash	Bank	Date	Particulars	F	Cash	Bank
June 1	Balances b/d		435.00	2100.00	June 3	Rates			1500.00
2	L Goodman			650.00	5	Insurance			450.00
4	Rent received		230.00		8	Marcus Ltd			106.00
5	Sales		170.00		9	Office stationery		34.00	
12	Sales		96.00		10	Purchases		52.00	
15	B Matthews			275.00	11	C M Lupton			139.00
19	Sales		185.00		16	Drawings		200.00	
22	M Dixon			1650.00	17	Office furniture			158.00
23	Rates			28.00	18	Motor expenses		75.00	
30	J Oldridge		45.00		24	Drawings		100.00	
					25	Purchases		65.00	
					26	Wages			750.00
					30	Balances c/d		635.00	1600.00
			1161.00	4703.00				1161.00	4703.00
July 1	Balances b/d		635.00	1600.00					

10.3	Totals:	Cash 1880	Bank 5200
	balances	cash debit 515	bank debit 2558
10.4	Totals:	Cash 1800	Bank 3509
	balances	cash debit 500	bank debit 2017
10.5	Totals:	Cash 1014	Bank 5474
	balances	cash debit 255	bank debit 3952
10.6	Totals:	Cash 6758	Bank 5726
	balances	cash debit 229	bank debit 4729
10.7	Totals:	Cash 1164	Bank 4250
	balances	cash debit 50	bank debit 2122
10.8	Totals:	Cash 1565	Bank 4578
	balances	cash debit 169	bank credit 304

Unit 11

11.1

					Cash Book						
Date	Particulars	F	Discount allowed	Cash	Bank	Date	Particulars	F	Discount received	Cash	Bank
Aug 1	Balances b/d			168.00	2998.00	Aug 4	Display equipment				248.00
3	Sales			160.00		5	Bank	C		250.00	
5	Cash	C			250.00	9	Stationery			34.00	
6	S Driver		18.00		357.00	10	Cash	C			250.00
10	Bank	C		250.00		11	Purchases			128.00	
12	J Scott		8.00		146.00	13	Wages			90.00	
17	B Jones			180.00		18	Bank	C		200.00	
18	Cash	C			200.00	19	B Dixon		3.00		57.00
20	Sales			140.00		26	M Dean			45.00	
23	S Ryder		12.00		196.00	27	Cash	C			150.00
27	Bank	C		150.00		28	B Wilson		2.00	78.00	
						29	Motor van				950.00
						30	Drawings			120.00	
						31	Balances c/d			103.00	2492.00
			38.00	1048.00	4147.00				5.00	1048.00	4147.00
Sep 1	Balances b/d			103.00	2492.00						

11.2

					Cash Book						
Date	Particulars	F	Discount allowed	Cash	Bank	Date	Particulars	F	Discount received	Cash	Bank
Nov 1	Balances b/d			76.00	2641.00	Nov 4	Cash	C			250.00
2	D Chadley		16.00		378.00	5	R Fox		4.00		156.00
3	Sales			150.00		6	Drawings			125.00	
4	Bank	C		250.00		8	Purchases			72.00	
7	M Richardson		12.00		192.00	11	Bank	C		250.00	
9	D Sellers		14.00		278.00	13	Motor expenses				197.00
10	D Crofton			198.00		15	R Keaton		16.00		304.00
11	Cash	C			250.00	17	Cash	C			200.00
14	R Best		8.00		595.00	18	Purchases			162.00	
16	Sales			45.00		20	Rates				170.00
17	Bank	C		200.00		24	W Temple		5.00		195.00
21	T Bramley			98.00		28	Bank	C		200.00	
26	Rent received				45.00	30	Balances c/d			208.00	3272.00
28	Cash	C			200.00						
29	B Matthews		13.00		165.00						
			63.00	1017.00	4744.00				25.00	1017.00	4744.00
Dec 1	Balances b/d			208.00	3272.00						

11.3 Totals: Cash 1396.50   Bank 3654.65
                  Discount allowed 46.85   Discount received 76.77
        balances cash debit 561.50   bank debit 1271.12
11.4 Totals: Cash 1245.00   Bank 3242.38
                  Discount allowed 61.95   Discount received 23.05
        balances cash debit 205.35   bank debit 1127.08

11.5 Totals: Cash 1428.00 Bank 2937.60
Discount allowed 66.10 Discount received 32.85
balances cash debit 397.00 bank credit 553.70
11.6 Totals: Cash 2574.40 Bank 3227.00
Discount allowed 3.00 Discount received 15.00
balances cash debit 74.40 bank debit 2166.50
T Duke no balance B Prince credit balance 125.00
R Knight credit balance 241.30 J Lord no balance
11.7 2200 (F) 20 (C) 380 (L) 160 (D) 95 (J)
750 (E) 55 (K) 440 (B)

Unit 12

12.1 John Dawson

Bank Cash Book									
Date	Particulars	Discount allowed	Details	Bank	Date	Particulars	Discount received	Details	Bank
		£	£	£			£	£	£
01-Jan	Balance b/d			2252.58	02-Jan	D Guy	5.60		114.40
02-Jan	S Peters	17.80	338.20		03-Jan	Wages		350.00	
02-Jan	Sales		142.00		03-Jan	Petty cash		76.80	
02-Jan	J Myers		67.00	547.20	03-Jan	Drawings		100.00	526.80
04-Jan	Sales		167.80		04-Jan	S Barnes			127.00
04-Jan	D Adams	13.00	137.00		05-Jan	Office equipment			365.20
04-Jan	M Cliff		48.00	352.80	06-Jan	Rates			125.00
05-Jan	B Groves		92.00		06-Jan	B Mills	24.00		456.00
05-Jan	Commission received		30.00		06-Jan	Balance c/d			2830.83
05-Jan	Sales		126.20	248.20					
06-Jan	Sales		238.95						
06-Jan	G Spink		750.00						
06-Jan	T Denton	4.50	155.50	1144.45					
		35.30		4545.23			29.60		4545.23
07-Jan	Balance b/d			2830.83					

12.2 Graham Dean

Bank Cash Book									
Date	Particulars	Discount allowed	Details	Bank	Date	Particulars	Discount received	Details	Bank
		£	£	£			£	£	£
01-Mar	Balance b/d			1376.30	02-Mar	Insurance			150.00
02-Mar	Sales			236.65	02-Mar	W Kay	11.00		209.00
03-Mar	Sales		276.55		03-Mar	E Franks			76.60
03-Mar	Rent received		35.00		04-Mar	Rent			120.00
03-Mar	C Prince	5.00	145.00	456.55	05-Mar	F Peters	22.50		427.50
04-Mar	Machinery		150.00		06-Mar	Petty cash		68.65	
04-Mar	Sales		122.20	272.20	06-Mar	Drawings		150.00	218.65
06-Mar	P Timms	18.20	347.50		06-Mar	Balance c/d			1826.75
06-Mar	Sales		178.80						
06-Mar	J Jacques	6.26	160.50	686.80					
		29.46		3028.50			33.50		3028.50
07-Mar	Balance b/d			1826.75					

12.3 Totals: Bank 2961.40 Discount allowed 25.00 Discount received
20.00 balance b/d debit 2001.00

12.4 Totals: Bank 3560.84 Discount allowed 17.51 Discount received
28.80 balance b/d debit 1740.74

12.5 Totals: Bank 7520.00 Discount allowed 102.00 Discount received
69.00 balance b/d debit 4910.00

12.6 Totals: Bank 3070.00 Discount allowed 23.00 Discount received
15.00 balance b/d credit 520.00

Unit 13

13.1	(a) 14.80	(b) 64.30	(c) 75.35	(d) 20.75	(e) 50.00
13.2	(a) 100.00	(b) 20.00	(c) 14.92	(d) 85.08	(e) 84.50
	(f) 85.08	(g) 85.08			

13.3 Total payments 90.24 Balance c/d 9.76 Wages 46.80
Postage 5.14 Stationery 5.70 Motor expenses
20.20

Ledger 12.40

13.4 Total payments 168.55 Balance c/d 31.45 Travelling 20.30
Motor expenses 79.10 Postage and Ledger 42.40
stationery 26.75

13.5 Total payments 146.15 Balance c/d 3.85 Cleaning 43.75
Motor expenses 32.95 Travelling 18.70 Post/stationery
20.05

Ledger 30.70

13.6

Total payments 79.95	Balance c/d 20.05	Sundry expenses 6.82
Cleaning 33.00	Motor expenses 19.54	Post/stationery 15.48
VAT 5.11		

13.7

Total payments 119.36	Balance c/d 30.64	Sundry expenses 28.98
Travel 20.80	Cleaning 27.82	Post/stationery 33.45
VAT 8.31		

13.8

Total payments 192.74	Balance c/d 7.26	Sundry expenses 37.00
Cleaning 25.00	Motor expenses 53.57	Post/stationery 57.24
VAT 19.93		

13.9

Total payments 81.40	Balance c/d 18.60	Travelling 26.90
Cleaning 16.90	Post/stationery 19.50	Ledger 18.10
Totals: Bank 2646.87	Discount allowed 2.50	
Discount received 20.00	balance b/d debit 1220.17	

13.10

Total payments 29.00	Balance c/d 21.00	Post and stationery 12.30
Travel expenses 4.70	Ledger 12.00	
Totals: Bank 2174.39	Discount allowed 2.50	
Discount received 6.00	balance b/d credit 610.39	

13.11

Total payments 75.98	Balance c/d 74.02	Sundry expenses 27.79
Travel 8.50	Post/stationery 20.91	Ledger 18.78
Totals: Bank 1789.95	Discount allowed 75.30	
Discount received 48.21	balance b/d credit 286.77	

13.12

Total payments 114.97	Balance c/d 85.03	Sundry expenses 28.90
Cleaning 33.00	Post/stationery 11.95	Ledger 41.12
Totals: Bank 2309.74	Discount allowed 26.10	
Discount received 33.57	balance b/d credit 809.35	

Unit 14

14.1

Cash Book

31 May	Balance b/d		2500.00	31 May	Insurance	S/O	135.00
31 May	Investment			31 May	Annual sub	S/O	50.00
	dvd	C/T	250.00				
				31 May	Balance c/d		2565.00
			2750.00				2750.00
1 Jun	Balance b/d		2565.00				

Bank Reconciliation Statement as at 31 May 20-4

Balance as per Cash Book		2565.00
Add: unpresented cheque		125.00
		2690.00
Less: bank lodgement not yet entered on bank statement:		590.00
Balance as per bank statement:		2100.00

14.2

Cash Book

30 Jun	Balance b/d		583.00	30 Jun	Rates	S/O	175.00
30 Jun	B. Groves	C/T	985.00	30 Jun	Bank charges	D/D	68.00
				30 Jun	Balance c/d		1325.00
			1568.00				1568.00
1 Jun	Balance b/d		1325.00				

Bank Reconciliation Statement as at 30 June 20-4

Balance as per Cash Book		1325.00
Add: unpresented cheque		150.00
		1475.00
Less: bank lodgement not yet entered on bank statement:		230.00
Balance as per bank statement:		1245.00

14.3 Cash Book total: 3212   Balance c/d 2510

Bank Reconciliation Statement as at 31 October 20-4

Balance as per Cash Book		2510
Add: unpresented cheques (238 + 376)		614
		3124
Less: bank lodgement		834
Balance as per bank statement		2290

14.4 Cash Book total: 2950   Balance c/d 2651
      Bank Reconciliation Statement as at 31 March 20-4
      Balance as per Cash Book   2651
      Add: unpresented cheques (128 + 364)   492
                                                              3143
      Less bank lodgement   259
      Balance as per bank statement   2884

14.5 Cash Book total: 2586   Balance c/d 1958
      Bank Reconciliation Statement as at 30 April 20-9
      Balance as per Cash Book   1958
      Add: unpresented cheques (492 + 580)   1072
                                                              3030
      Less bank lodgement   278
      Balance as per bank statement   2752

14.6 Cash Book total 1100   Balance c/d 900
      Bank Reconciliation Statement as at 30 April 20-5
      Balance as per Cash Book   900
      Add: unpresented cheques (380 + 242)   622
                                                              1522
      Less bank lodgement   74
      Balance as per bank statement   1448

14.7 (a) Bank Cash Book   Balance c/d 3191
           Totals: Bank 5794   Discount allowed 45   Discount received 40
      (b) Bank total: 3691   Balance c/d 2941
      (c) **Bank Reconciliation Statement as at 31 May 20-9**
           Balance as per Cash Book   2941
           Add: unpresented cheques (358 + 500)   858
                                                              3799
           Less bank lodgement   1170
           Balance as per bank statement   2629

14.8 (a) Bank Cash Book   Balance c/d 1580
           Totals: Bank 4596   Discount allowed 32   Discount received 23
      (b) Bank total: 1830   Balance c/d 1688
      (c) **Bank Reconciliation Statement as at 31 October 20-9**
           Balance as per Cash Book   1688
           Add: unpresented cheques (599 + 434)   1033
                                                              2721
           Less bank lodgement   718
           Balance as per bank statement   2003

14.9 (a) Bank Cash Book   Balance c/d 520
           Totals: Bank 3070   Discount allowed 29   Discount received 15
      (b) Bank total: 758   Balance c/d 47

(c) **Bank Reconciliation Statement as at 31 May 20-5**

Balance as per Cash Book	47
Add: unpresented cheques (384 + 699)	1083
	1130
Less bank lodgement	368
Balance as per bank statement	762

Unit 15

15.1 (a) Micro Electronics   680
         Hitech (UK) Ltd   668
         Systems Unlimited   675
     (b) Hitech (UK) Ltd

15.2   **Sales Day Book**

Date	Name	Invoice Number	F	£ p
2 May	G A Coleman	3481	SL	187.42
9 May	Kota Supplies	3482	SL	338.00
15 May	B Newton	3483	SL	96.90
22 May	Moss Linton	3484	SL	207.00
30 May	L Gibson & Son	3485	SL	304.17
	Transferred to Sales Account		GL	1,133.49

Sales Ledger

G A Coleman Account
2 May   Sales   187.42
Kota Supplies Account
9 May   Sales   338.00
B Newton Account
15 May   Sales   96.90
Moss Linton Account
22 May   Sales   207.00
L Gibson & Son Account
30 May   Sales   304.17
General Ledger

Sales Account
31 May   Total for month   1133.49

15.3

Sales Day Book

Date	Name	Invoice Number	F	£ p
1 Jun	James Mcmillan	5724	SL	219.37
5 Jun	J Sanderson	5725	SL	146.16
12 Jun	B Sinclair	5726	SL	216.58
19 Jun	T Matthews	5727	SL	164.00
30 Jun	L Booth	5728	SL	179.40
	Transferred to Sales Account		GL	925.51

15.4

Sales Day Book

Date	Name	Invoice Number	F	£ p
1 Aug	Adel Garden Shop	395	SL	204.42
4 Aug	George Riley	396	SL	751.50
8 Aug	T Newbury	397	SL	173.60
14 Aug	B J Lacey	398	SL	467.50
20 Aug	S Stocks	399	SL	167.62
25 Aug	H Crossley	400	SL	625.00
31 Aug	Thornton Supplies	401	SL	208.80
	Transferred to Sales Account		GL	2,598.44

15.5

Sales Day Book

Date	Name	F	£ p
1 Sep	G Miller	SL	113.62
5 Sep	T Bennett	SL	96.00
8 Sep	B Watkinson	SL	30.60
14 Sep	L Roberts	SL	214.69
22 Sep	A Dixon	SL	192.10
30 Sep	D Hewitt	SL	72.60
	Transferred to Sales Account	GL	719.61

Unit 16

16.1

Purchases Day Book

Date	Name	Invoice Number	F	£ p
2 Feb	General Supplies Ltd	G9054	PL	246.51
7 Feb	Jones Manufacturing Ltd	37516	PL	89.60
15 Feb	General Supplies Ltd	G9168	PL	201.15
22 Feb	Thomas Dean Ltd	5073	PL	64.69
28 Feb	Peter Simmonds	06814	PL	274.13
	Transferred to Purchases Account		GL	876.08

Purchase Ledger

General Supplies Ltd Account

	2 Feb	Purchases	246.51
	15 Feb	Purchases	201.15

Jones Manufacturing Ltd Account

	7 Feb	Purchases	89.60

Thomas Dean Ltd Account

	22 Feb	Purchases	64.69

Peter Simmonds Account

	28 May	Purchases	274.13

General Ledger

Purchases Account

28 Feb   Total for month   876.08

16.2

Purchases Day Book

Date	Name	Invoice Number	F	£ p
2 Mar	Kenneth Ingram	67413	PL	81.60
4 Mar	Graham Clifton	49216	PL	538.12
8 Mar	Stewart Brothers	2963	PL	107.06
16 Mar	Frederick Rycroft	F/5087	PL	75.15
24 Mar	Robert Linton	38525	PL	364.33
30 Mar	Vincent Hood	2416	PL	622.80
	Transferred to Purchases Account		GL	1,789.06

Purchase Ledger

Kenneth Ingram Account

	2 Mar	Purchases	81.60

Graham Clifton Account

	4 Mar	Purchases	538.12

Stewart Brothers Account

	8 Mar	Purchases	107.06

Frederick Rycroft Account

	16 May	Purchases	75.15

Robert Linton Account

	24 Mar	Purchases	364.33

Vincent Hood Account

	30 Mar	Purchases	622.80

General Ledger

Purchases Account

31 Mar   Total for month   1,789.06

16.3 Purchases Day Book total   2156. 50
Sales Day Book total   2456. 00

Unit 17

17.1

Sales Day Book

Date	Name	F	£ p
1 Jun	G Spink	SL	218.00
1 Jun	J Goodall	SL	127.00
1 Jun	Scott Bros	SL	92.00
5 Jun	B Moss	SL	117.00
5 Jun	L Gibson	SL	138.00
5 Jun	P Andrews	SL	242.00
5 Jun	F Benn	SL	189.00
11 Jun	F Myers	SL	233.00
11 Jun	B Moss	SL	186.00
20 Jun	J Goodall	SL	149.00
20 Jun	F Benn	SL	256.00
23 Jun	K Williams	SL	212.00
23 Jun	G Spink	SL	306.00
30 Jun	B Moss	SL	290.00
30 Jun	E Nelson	SL	135.00
30 Jun	Transferred to Sales Account	GL	2,890.00

Returns Inwards Day Book

Date	Name	F	£ p
8 Jun	J Goodall	SL	21.00
8 Jun	Scott Bros	SL	17.00
14 Jun	L Gibson	SL	28.00
14 Jun	P Andrews	SL	32.00
27 Jun	F Benn	SL	37.00
	Transferred to Returns Inwards Account	GL	135.00

17.1 *Sales Ledger*

G Spink Account

1 Jun	Sales	218.00			
23 Jun	Sales	306.00			

J Goodall Account

1 Jun	Sales	127.00	8 Jun	Returns inwards	21.00
20 Jun	Sales	149.00			

Scott Bros Account

1 Jun	Sales	92.00	8 Jun	Returns inwards	17.00

B Moss Account

5 Jun	Sales	117.00			
11 Jun	Sales	186.00			
30 Jun	Sales	290.00			

L Gibson Account

5 Jun	Sales	138.00	14 Jun	Returns inwards	28.00

P Andrews Account

| 5 Jun | Sales | 242.00 | 14 Jun | Returns inwards | 32.00 |

F Benn Account

| 5 Jun | Sales | 189.00 | 27 Jun | Returns inwards | 37.00 |
| 20 Jun | Sales | 256.00 | | | |

F Myers Account

| 11 Jun | Sales | 233.00 |

K Williams Account

| 23 Jun | Sales | 212.00 |

E Nelson Account

| 30 Jun | Sales | 135.00 |

General Ledger

Sales Account

| | | 30 Jun | Total for month | 2890.00 |

Returns Inwards Account

| 30 Jun | Total for month | 135.00 |

17.2

Purchases Day Book

Date	Name	F	£ p
1 Aug	W Lawrence	PL	258.00
4 Aug	J Barrymore	PL	316.00
4 Aug	T Groves	PL	192.00
4 Aug	H Roper	PL	257.00
4 Aug	D Passmore	PL	168.00
10 Aug	T Groves	PL	388.00
10 Aug	P Armstrong	PL	219.00
10 Aug	H Roper	PL	242.00
10 Aug	W Jones	PL	312.00
18 Aug	W Lawrence	PL	280.00
18 Aug	M Hardy	PL	116.00
24 Aug	J Barrymore	PL	185.00
30 Aug	F King	PL	395.00
31 Aug	Transferred to Purchases Account	GL	3,328.00

Returns Outwards Day Book

Date	Name	F	£ p
8 Aug	W Lawrence	PL	17.00
12 Aug	J Barrymore	PL	56.00
12 Aug	D Passmore	PL	35.00
20 Aug	T Groves	PL	28.00
28 Aug	M Hardy	PL	15.00
31 Aug	Transferred to Returns Outwards Account	GL	151.00

Purchase Ledger

W Lawrence Account

8 Aug	Returns outwards	17.00	1 Aug	Purchases	258.00
			18 Aug	Purchases	280.00

J Barrymore Account

12 Aug	Returns outwards	56.00	4 Aug	Purchases	316.00
			24 Aug	Purchases	185.00

T Groves Account

20 Aug	Returns outwards	28.00	4 Aug	Purchases	192.00
			10 Aug	Purchases	388.00

H Roper Account

4 Aug	Purchases	257.00
10 Aug	Purchases	242.00

D Passmore Account

12 Aug	Returns outwards	35.00	4 Aug	Purchases	168.00

P Armstrong Account

10 Aug	Purchases	219.00

W Jones Account

10 Aug	Purchases	312.00

M Hardy Account

28 Aug	Returns outwards	15.00	18 Aug	Purchases	116.00

F King Account

30 Aug	Purchases	395.00

General Ledger

Purchases Account

31 Aug	Total for month	3,328.00

Returns Outwards Account

	31 Aug	Total for month	151.00

17.3 Day Book totals:

Purchases	1408.75	Purchase returns	78.50
Sales	1221.00	Sales returns	78.00

17.4 (a) Debtor   (b) Purchase   (c) Dawn Gwinnett
   (d) 5 per cent   (e) Cash discount   (f) Returns outwards
   (g)   (i) 44.00   (ii) 1716.00

17.5 Check goods were ordered
Check all goods have been received and details correspond with order
Check prices charged on invoice are correct
Check all calculations are accurate.

17.6 (a) J Hunt
   (b) 1 Feb   Amount owing by R J Cook
        6 Feb   Invoice for goods purchased by R J Cook
        8 Feb   Cheque paid by R J Cook
        8 Feb   Cash discount allowed to R J Cook

			12 Feb	Goods returned by R J Cook to J Hunt
			26 Feb	Invoice for goods purchased by R J Cook
	(c)	Invoice		Sender: J Hunt
				Receiver: R J Cook
	(d)	Debtor		R J Cook
		Creditor		J Hunt
		312.36		Owing on 28 February 20-4.

17.7 (a) Customer's account should be inspected to ascertain if payments are being received promptly on due dates.
Ensure new order will not exceed credit limit.

(b) A new customer may be required to supply trade references, or bankers reference to establish credit worthiness.

Unit 18

18.1

Sales Day Book

Date	Name	F	Total	Goods	VAT
2 Apr	J Wilson	SL	275.00	250.00	25.00
5 Apr	K Allen	SL	195.80	178.00	17.80
10 Apr	F Stones	SL	539.00	490.00	49.00
15 Apr	R Lockwood	SL	170.50	155.00	15.50
22 Apr	B McKenzie	SL	233.20	212.00	21.20
30 Apr	M Newman	SL	400.40	364.00	36.40
			1,813.90	1,649.00	164.90

Sales Ledger

J Wilson Account

2 Apr   Sales   275.00

K Allen Account

5 Apr   Sales   195.80

F Stones Account

10 Apr   Sales   539.00

R Lockwood Account

15 Apr   Sales   170.50

B McKenzie Account

22 Apr   Sales   233.20

M Newman Account

30 Apr   Sales   400.40

General Ledger

Sales Account

30 Apr   Total for month   1,649.00

Value Added Tax Account

30 Apr   Total SDB   164.90

18.2

Purchases Day Book

Date	Name	F	Total	Goods	VAT
1 May	M Booth	PL	260.48	236.80	23.68
4 May	J Price	PL	405.90	369.00	36.90
8 May	B Ramsden	PL	172.04	156.40	15.64
14 May	L Nelson	PL	240.24	218.40	21.84
20 May	M Senior	PL	147.73	134.30	13.43
25 May	D Rawdon	PL	273.90	249.00	24.90
			1,500.29	1,363.90	136.39

Purchase Ledger

M Booth Account

1 May   Purchases   260.48

J Price Account

4 May   Purchases   405.90

B Ramsden Account

8 May   Purchases   172.04

L Nelson Account

14 May   Purchases   240.24

M Senior Account

20 May   Purchases   147.73

D Rawdon Account

25 May   Purchases   273.90

General Ledger

Purchases Account

31 May   Total for month   1,363.90

Value Added Tax Account

31 May   Total PDB   136.39

18.3   Invoice total 809.60

18.4

Purchases day book	Total 979.99	Goods 890.90	VAT 89.09
Sales day book	Total 1,238.60	Goods 1,126.00	VAT 112.60
Purchase returns book	Total 61.60	Goods 56.00	VAT 5.60
Sales returns book	Total 82.50	Goods 75.00	VAT 7.50

18.5

Purchases day book	Total 2,034.34	Goods 1,849.40	VAT 184.94
Sales day book	Total 1,432.20	Goods 1,302.00	VAT 130.20
Purchase returns book	Total 128.59	Goods 116.90	VAT 11.69
Sales returns book	Total 100.10	Goods 91.00	VAT 9.10

18.6

Purchases day book	Total 721.60	Goods 656.00	VAT 65.60
Sales day book	Total 902.00	Goods 820.00	VAT 82.00
Returns outwards book	Total 83.60	Goods 76.00	VAT 7.60
Returns inwards book	Total 22.00	Goods 20.00	VAT 2.00

18.7

Sales day book	Total 1,714.90	Goods 1,559.00	VAT 155.90
Purchases day book	Total 876.70	Goods 797.00	VAT 79.70

| Sales returns book | Total 51.70 | Goods 47.00 | VAT 4.70 |
| Purchase returns book | Total 44.00 | Goods 40.00 | VAT 4.00 |

18.8

Ace Furnishings Account

| 5 May | Sales | 330.00 |

Comfy Chair Co Account

| 10 May | Sales | 594.00 |

Top Woodworkers Account

| | | | 18 May | Purchases | 343.20 |

Jones Account

| | | | 20 May | Shop fittings | 110.00 |

Shop Fittings Account

| 20 May | Jones | 100.00 |

Sales Account

| | | | 5 May | Ace Furnishings | 300.00 |
| | | | 10 May | Comfy Chair | 540.00 |

Purchases Account

| 18 May | Top Woodworkers | 312.00 |

Value Added Tax Account

18 May	Top Woodworkers	31.20	5 May	Ace Furnishings	30.00
20 May	Jones	10.00	10 May	Comfy Chair	54.00
31 May	Balance c/d	42.80			
		84.00			84.00
			1 Jun	Balance b/d	42.80

Balance on Value Added Tax Account is owed to Customs and Excise

Unit 19

19.1

Analysed Purchases Day Book

Date	Details	Total invoice	General household	Garden accessories	VAT
2 Apr	Self Paste Ltd	2,411.20	2,192.00		219.20
15 Apr	Green Fingers Ltd	1,102.20		1,002.00	100.20
20 Apr	G A Coleman & Son	217.80	198.00		19.80
		3,731.20	2,390.00	1,002.00	339.20

Purchase Ledger

Self Paste Ltd Account

| | | | 2 Apr | Purchases | 2,411.20 |

Green Fingers Ltd Account

| | | | 15 Apr | Purchases | 1,102.20 |

G A Coleman & Son Account

| | | | 20 Apr | Purchases | 217.80 |

General Ledger

Purchases Account – General Household

30 Apr	Total for month	2,390.00	

Purchases Account – Garden Accessories

30 Apr	Total for month	1,002.00	

Value Added Tax Account

30 Apr	Total PDB	339.20	

19.2

Analysed Purchases Day Book

Date	Details	Total invoice	Furniture dept	Electrial dept	VAT
5 May	Overland	1,100.00	1,000.00		100.00
13 May	Pelican Co Ltd	572.00		520.00	52.00
25 May	Overland	396.00	360.00		36.00
		2,068.00	1,360.00	520.00	188.00

Purchase Ledger

Overland Furniture Account

	5 May	Purchases	1,100.00
	25 May	Purchases	396.00

Pelican Co Ltd Account

	13 May	Purchases	572.00

General Ledger

Purchases Account – Furniture

31 May	Total for month	1,360.00	

Purchases Account – Electrical

31 May	Total for month	520.00	

Value Added Tax Account

31 May	Total PDB	188.00	

19.3

Sales Day Book

Date	Details	Total invoice	Garden furniture	Camping equipment	VAT
5 May	Dalesman Products	299.64		272.40	27.24
8 May	Parkway Garden Centre	327.25	297.50		29.75
16 May	Sun Valley Campers	239.25		217.50	21.75
20 May	Woodland Supplies	134.64	38.25	84.15	12.24
		1,000.78	335.75	574.05	90.98

Sales Returns Day Book

Date	Details	Total invoice	Garden furniture	Camping equipment	VAT
27 May	Dalesman Products	19.98		18.16	1.82

19.4

Purchases Day Book

Date	Details	Total	China	Cutlery	VAT
6 Oct	Coglin Supplies	105.60	96.00		9.60
14 Oct	Simmonds Services	148.50		135.00	13.50
16 Oct	Jenson Ltd	140.25	127.50		12.75
		394.35	223.50	135.00	35.85

Purchase Returns Day Book

Date	Details	Total	China	Cutlery	VAT
18 Oct	Coglin Supplies	10.56	9.60		.96

19.5

Sales Day Book

Date	Details	Total invoice	Sports goods	Camping equipment	VAT
3 Oct	Aire Valley Campers	540.80		491.64	49.16
12 Oct	Arena Centre	471.80	191.76	237.15	42.89
18 Oct	Lakeside Golf Club	95.04	86.40		8.64
		1,107.64	278.16	728.79	100.69

Sales Returns Day Book

Date	Details	Total invoice	Sports goods	Camping equipment	VAT
24 Oct	Arena Centre	11.68		10.62	1.06

19.6

Sales Day Book

Date	Details	Total invoice	Kitchen utensils	Crockery and glass	Electrical appliances	VAT
4 May	Bridge House Motel	448.80		120.00	288.00	40.80
10 May	Cosy Cafe	354.86	25.60	162.00	135.00	32.26
15 May	Sidlow Grange	198.00		180.00		18.00
17 May	Bridge House Motel	102.85	93.50			9.35
26 May	Riverside Hotel	176.00			160.00	16.00
		1,280.51	119.10	462.00	583.00	116.41

Sales Returns Day Book

Date	Details	Total invoice	Kitchen utensils	Crockery and glass	Electrical appliances	VAT
8 May	Bridge House Motel	13.20		12.00		1.20

Unit 20

20.1   **Trading and Profit and Loss Account for the year ended 31 December 20-6**

Purchases	15,269	Sales	20,662
Less closing stock	2,868		
Cost of goods sold	12,401		
Gross profit c/d	8,261		
	20,662		20,662
Rent	650	Gross profit b/d	8,261
Insurance	155		
Motor expenses	545		
Wages	2,568		
Net profit	4,343		
	8,261		8,261

Balance Sheet as at 31 December 20-6

Fixed Assets			Capital at start	6,000	
Equipment	2,850		Add net profit	4,343	
Motor vehicle	1,100	3,950		10,343	
			Less drawings	925	9,418
Current Assets			Current Liabilities		
Stock	2,868		Creditors		1,682
Debtors	2,350				
Bank	1,864				
Cash	68	7,150			
		11,100			11,100

20.2

Trading and Profit and Loss Account for the year ended 31 December 20-7

Purchases	14,650	Sales	18,874
Less closing stock	3,235		
Cost of goods sold	11,415		
Gross profit c/d	7,459		
	18,874		18,874
Rates	720	Gross profit b/d	7,459
General expenses	490		
Wages and salaries	3,105		
Motor expenses	382		
Insurance	220		
Net profit	2,542		
	7,459		7,459

Balance Sheet as at 31 December 20-7

Fixed Assets			Capital at start	18,000	
Premises	7,700		Add net profit	2,542	
Fixtures and fittings	1,750			20,542	
Motor vehicles	3,900	13,350	Less drawings	1,250	19,292
Current Assets			Current Liabilities		
Stock	3,235		Creditors		1,926
Debtors	2,865				
Bank	1,646				
Cash	122	7,868			
		21,218			21,218

20.3 Gross profit 8,319   Net profit 3,197   Fixed assets 9,250
Current assets 14,273   Current liabilities 2,018

20.4 Gross profit 6,738   Net loss 1,071
Fixed assets 29,400   Current assets 10,229
Long-term liabilities 6,000   Current liabilities 6,450

20.5 Gross profit 15,781   Net profit 8,224
Fixed assets 19,000   Current assets 44,788
Long-term liabilities 5,000   Current liabilities 13,864

20.6 (a) Fixed assets 25,950   Current assets 14,325
Current liabilities 1,025

(b)

Drawings Account

31 Mar	Bank	1,250	31 Dec	Capital	5,000
30 Jun	Bank	1,250			
30 Sep	Bank	1,250			
31 Dec	Bank	1,250			
		5,000			5,000

Capital Account

31 Dec	Drawings	5,000	1 Jan	Balance b/d	25,750
31 Dec	Balance c/d	39,250	31 Dec	Net profit	18,500
		44,250			44,250
			1 Jan	Balance b/d	39,250

20.7 (a) Fixed assets 68,250   Current assets 10,250
Long-term liabilities 5,000   Current liabilities 5,530

(b)

Drawings Account

31 Aug	Bank	1,750	31 May	Capital	7,000
30 Nov	Bank	1,750			
28 Feb	Bank	1,750			
31 May	Bank	1,750			
		7,000			7,000

Capital Account

31 May	Drawings	7,000	1 Jun	Balance b/d	45,250
31 May	Balance c/d	67,970	31 May	Net profit	29,720
		74,970			74,970
			1 Jun	Balance b/d	67,970

Unit 21

21.1   **Trading and Profit and Loss Account for the year ended 31 December 20-7**

Opening stock	21,190	Sales	98,650
Add purchases	76,990	*Less* returns inwards	562
	98,180		98,088
Less returns outwards	415		
	97,765		
Add carriage inwards	204		
	97,969		
Less closing stock	22,560		
Cost of goods sold	75,409		
Gross profit c/d	22,679		
	98,088		98,088
Rent	1,855	Gross profit b/d	22,679
Wages and salaries	9,890		
Carriage outwards	251		
Insurance	365		
Motor expenses	932		
General expenses	428		
Net profit	8,958		
	22,679		22,679

Balance Sheet as at 31 December 20-7

Fixed Assets			Capital	30,200	
Furniture and					
fittings	4,420		*Add* net profit	8,958	
Motor vehicle	5,500	9,920		39,158	
			Less drawings	2,330	36,828
			Long-term liabilities		
			Loan – D. Conway		5,000
Current Assets			*Current Liabilities*		
Closing Stock	22,560		Creditors		10,735
Debtors	14,950				
Bank	4,620				
Cash	513	42,643			
		52,563			52,563

21.2   **Trading and Profit and Loss Account for the year ended 30 September 20-7**

Opening stock	9,842	Sales	69,480
Add purchases	45,612	*Less* returns inwards	872
	55,454		68,608
Less returns outwards	684		
	54,770		
Add carriage inwards	485		
	55,255		
Less closing stock	8,975		
Cost of goods sold	46,280		
Gross profit c/d	22,328		
	68,608		68,608
Salaries and wages	7,838	Gross profit b/d	22,328
Insurance	556	Discount received	452
Rent and rates	740		
Carriage outwards	414		
Motor expenses	526		
Discount allowed	322		
Net profit	12,384		
	22,780		22,780

Balance Sheet as at 30 September 20-7

Fixed Assets			Capital	16,900	
Fixtures and fittings	2,900		*Add* net profit	12,384	
Motor vehicles	7,500	10,400		29,284	
			Less drawings	2,500	26,784
Current Assets			*Current Liabilities*		
Closing Stock	8,975		Creditors		8,984
Debtors	10,765				
Bank	5,628	25,368			
		35,768			35,768

21.3 Gross profit 17,880   Net profit 7,080
      Fixed assets 25,900   Current assets 9,880
      Long-term   Current liabilities 6,060
        liabilities 3,000

21.4 Gross profit 10,970   Net profit 3,592   Fixed assets 9,700
      Current assets 20,162   Current liabilities 5,980

21.5 Gross profit 10,455   Net loss 728
     Fixed assets 17,900   Current assets 15,800
     Long-term   Current liabilities 8,540
       liabilities 5,000

21.6 Gross profit 24,117   Net profit 12,320   Fixed assets 28,500
     Current assets 18,660   Current liabilities 4,950

Unit 22

22.1 Cost $20,000 - 5,000 = 15,000$ divided by $5 = 3,000$
     $20,000 - 3,000 = 17,000 - 3,000 = 14,000 - 3,000$
     $= 11,000 - 3,000 = 8,000 - 3,000 = 5,000$

22.2 Cost $8,000 - 2,400 = 5,600 - 1,680 = 3,920 - 1,176 = 2,744$

22.3 (a) Straight line: Cost $10,500 - 2,520 = 7,980$ divided by $4 = 1,995$
         $10,500 - 1,995 = 8,505 - 1,995 = 6,510 - 1,995 = 4,515 - 1,995 = 2,520$
     (b) Reducing balance: Cost $10,500 - 3,150 = 7,350 - 2,205$
         $= 5,145 - 1,544 = 3,601 - 1,080 = 2,521$

22.4 (a) Straight line: Cost $3,000 - 712 = 2,288$ divided by $5 = 458$
         $3,000 - 458 = 2,542 - 458 = 2,084 - 468 = 1,626 - 458$
         $= 1,168 - 458 = 710$
     (b) Reducing balance: $3,000 - 750 = 2,250 - 563 = 1,687 - 422$
         $= 1,265 - 316 = 949 - 237 = 712$

22.5 Cost $6,500 - 1,300 = 5,200 - 1,040 = 4,160 - 832 = 3,328$
     Cost $7,500 - 1,125 = 6,375 - 1,275 = 5,100$

22.6 Machine 'M'   Cost $3,000 - 825 = 2,175 - 653 = 1,522 - 457 = 1,065$
     Machine 'D'   Cost $4,000 - 600 = 3,400 - 1,020 = 2,380 - 714 = 1,666$
     Machine 'W'   Cost $5,000 - 125 = 4,875 - 1,463 = 3,412 - 1,024 = 2,388$
     Machine 'B'   Cost $6,000 - 600 = 5,400 - 1,620 = 3,780$

Unit 23

23.1   **Machinery Account**
       Apr   Bank   3,000

Provision for Depreciation Account

31 Dec	Balance c/d	750	31 Dec	Profit and loss	750
31 Dec	Balance c/d	1,312	1 Jan	Balance b/d	750
			31 Dec	Profit and loss	562
		1,312			1,312
31 Dec	Balance c/d	1,734	1 Jan	Balance b/d	1,312
			31 Dec	Profit and loss	422
		1,734			1,734
Dec 31	Balance c/d	2,050	1 Jan	Balance b/d	1,734
			31 Dec	Profit and loss	316
		2,050			2,050
31 Dec	Balance c/d	2,287	1 Jan	Balance b/d	2,050
			31 Dec	Profit and loss	237
		2,287			2,287
			1 Jan	Balance b/d	2,287

23.2 (a)
Vehicle Account

1 Jan	Bank	23,000

Provision for Depreciation Account

31 Dec	Balance c/d	4,000	31 Dec	Profit and loss	4,000
31 Dec	Balance c/d	8,000	1 Jan	Balance b/d	4,000
			31 Dec	Profit and loss	4,000
		8,000			8,000
31 Dec	Balance c/d	12,000	1 Jan	Balance b/d	8,000
			31 Dec	Profit and loss	4,000
		12,000			12,000
Dec 31	Balance c/d	16,000	1 Jan	Balance b/d	12,000
			31 Dec	Profit and loss	4,000
		16,000			16,000
31 Dec	Balance c/d	20,000	1 Jan	Balance b/d	16,000
			31 Dec	Profit and loss	4,000
		20,000			20,000
			1 Jan	Balance b/d	20,000

(b) *Balance sheet entries* at 31 December:

20-3 Vehicle 23,000 *less* depreciation 4,000 = 19,000
20-4 Vehicle 23,000 *less* depreciation 8,000 = 15,000
20-5 Vehicle 23,000 *less* depreciation 12,000 = 11,000
20-6 Vehicle 23,000 *less* depreciation 16,000 = 7,000
20-7 Vehicle 23,000 *less* depreciation 20,000 = 3,000

23.3 *Machinery Account*   1 Oct 20-7 balance b/d 12,800

Depreciation Account

20-5 30 Sep	Machinery	5,000	20-5 30 Sep	Profit and loss	5,000
20-6 30 Sep	Machinery	4,000	20-6 30 Sep	Profit and loss	4,000
20-7 30 Sep	Machinery	3,200	20-7 30 Sep	Profit and loss	3,200

Profit and loss account entries: 20-5 Depreciation 5,000
20-6 Depreciation 4,000
20-7 Depreciation 3,200

Balance sheet entries: 20-5 Machinery 25,000 *less* 5,000 = 20,000
20-6 Machinery 20,000 *less* 4,000 = 16,000
20-7 Machinery 16,000 *less* 3,200 = 12,800

23.4 (a)   **Motor Van Account**

1 Jun	Bank	10,800	1 Jun	Disposal	10,800

Disposal Account

1 Jun	Motor van	10,800	1 Jun	Depreciation	7,600
			1 Jun	Cash	3,000
			31 May	Profit and loss	200
		10,800			10,800

(b) *Profit and loss account entries:* (c) Balance sheet entries:

20-6 Depreciation – Motor   Motor van 10,800
van 3,600   – 3,600 = 7,200

20-7 Depreciation – Motor   Motor van 10,800
van 2,400   – 6,000 = 4,800

20-8 Depreciation – Motor   Motor van 10,800
van 1,600   – 7,600 = 3,200

20-9 Loss on sale – Motor van 200

23.5 (a)   **Machinery Account**

4 Jan	Bank	15,500	3 Jan	Disposal	15,500

(b) *Provision for Depreciation Account*
1 January 20-9 Balance b/d 12,500

(c)   **Disposal Account**

3 Jan	Machinery	15,500	3 Jan	Depreciation	12,500
31 Dec	Profit and loss	250	3 Jan	Bank	3,250
		15,750			15,750

(d)

Profit and loss account entries: Balance sheet entries:

20-5 Depreciation – Machinery 3,125   Machinery 15,500
– 3,125 = 12,375

20-6 Depreciation – Machinery 3,125   Machinery 15,500
– 6,250 = 9,250

20-7 Depreciation – Machinery 3,125   Machinery 15,500
– 9,375 = 6,125

20-8 Depreciation – Machinery 3,125   Machinery 15,500
– 12,500 = 3,000

20-9 Profit on sale – Machinery 250

23.6 (a)   **Motor Lorries Account**
         1 Jan Bank   4,800   1 Jan   Disposal   4,800
         1 Jan Bank   4,800   31 Dec Balance c/d   9,600
         1 Jan Bank   4,800
                               14,400   14,400
         1 Jan Balance b/d   9,600

    (b)   **Disposal Account**
         1 Jan Motor lorries   4,800   1 Jan   Depreciation   1,800
                                          1 Jan   Bank   2,500
                                          31 Dec Profit and loss   500
                                  4,800   4,800

    (c) *Provision for Depreciation Account*
        1 January 20-9 Balance b/d 5,400

23.7

    AB 101 T   500 per annum   CD 202 V   600 per annum
    EF 303 W   400 per annum   GH 404 X   700 per annum

    (a) (i) *Motor Van Account*
             31 December 20-2   Balance b/d   5,500
         (ii) Provision for Depreciation Account
             31 December 20-2   Balance c/d   1,500
         (iii) Disposal Account – 20-2 totals: 3,200

    (b) *Profit and loss entries:*
        19-9   Depreciation – Motor van 500
        20-0   Depreciation – Motor vans 1,100
        20-1   Depreciation – Motor vans 1,000   Loss on sale of van 500
        20-2   Depreciation – Motor vans 1,100   Profit on sale of van 200

    (c) *Balance sheet entries:*
        19-9   Motor van 2,500 – 500 = 2,000
        20-0   Motor vans 5,500 – 1,600 = 3,900
        20-1   Motor vans 5,000 – 1,600 = 3,400
        20-2   Motor vans 5,500 – 1,500 = 4,000

Unit 24

24.1   **D Nelson Account**
         1 Mar Balance b/d   76.50   30 Mar Bad debts   76.50
                          Bad Debts Account
        30 Mar D Nelson   76.50
24.2   **Alan Senior Account**
         1 Nov Balance b/d   350.00   30 Nov Bank   175.00
                                       30 Nov Bad debts   175.00
                               350.00   350.00

Bad Debts Account

30 Nov	Alan Senior	175.00

24.3

A Baxter Account

1 Apr	Balance b/d	175.00	15 Apr	Cash	78.75
			15 Apr	Bad debts	96.25
		175.00			175.00

Bad Debts Account

15 Apr	A Baxter	96.25

24.4

Bank Account

3 Aug	Bad debt (J London)	220.00

Bad Debts Account

3 Aug	Bank (J London)	220.00

24.5 (i) A new customer may be required to supply trade references or a bankers reference.

(ii) Cash only basis or proforma invoice.

24.6 (a) Bad debts are debts that are likely never to be paid. It is necessary to write off bad debts because the amount owed can no longer be regarded as an asset to a business.

Bad Debts Account

30 Jun	A Noble	160.00	1 Dec	Bank (P Jones)	6.00
31 Aug	P Jones	120.00	31 Dec	Profit and loss	654.00
31 Oct	R Scott	250.00			
30 Nov	L Skirrow	130.00			
		660.00			660.00

24.7

Bad Debts Account

31 Jul	J Brown	220.40	31 Mar	Profit and loss	615.20
30 Sep	K Lawson	157.50			
31 Dec	B Nicholas	114.30			
28 Feb	M Swan	123.00			
		615.20			615.20

24.8 (a)

Provision for Bad Debts Account

31 Dec	Balance c/d	450.00	31 Dec	Profit and loss	450.00
31 Dec	Balance c/d	500.00	1 Jan	Balance b/d	450.00
			31 Dec	Profit and loss	50.00
		500.00			500.00
			1 Jan	Balance b/d	500.00

(b) **Profit and loss entries:**

20-5 Provision for bad debts 450
20-6 Provision for bad debts 50

(c) **Balance sheet entries:**

Debtors 9,000 *less* 450 = 8,550
Debtors 10,000 *less* 500 = 9,500

24.9 (a) **Bad Debts Account**

20-1			20-1		
Dec 31	Sundry debtors	750.00	Dec 31	Profit and loss	750.00
20-2			20-2		
Dec 31	Sundry debtors	4,085.00	Dec 31	Profit and loss	4,085.00
20-3			20-3		
Dce 31	Sundry debtors	2,900,00	Dec 31	Profit and loss	2,900.00

(b) **Provision for Bad Debts Account**

31 Dec	Balance c/d	700.00	1 Jan	Balance b/d	500.00
20-1			31 Dec	Profit and loss	200.00
		700.00			700.00
31 Dec	Balance c/d	1,000.00	1 Jan	Balance b/d	700.00
20-2			31 Dec	Profit and loss	300.00
		1,000.00			1,000.00
31 Dec	Profit and loss	250.00	1 Jan	Balance b/d	1,000.00
31 Dec	Balance c/d	750.00			
		1,000.00			1,000.00
			1 Jan	Balance b/d	750.00

(c) **Balance sheet entries**:
  20-1 Debtors 14,000 *less* provision 700 = 13,300
  20-2 Debtors 10,000 *less* provision 1,000 = 9,000
  20-3 Debtors 15,000 *less* provision 750 = 14,250

24.10 (a) **Provision for Bad Debts Account**

30 Sep	Balance c/d	1,186.00	30 Sep	Profit and loss	1,186.00
30 Sep	Profit and loss	186.00	1 Oct	Balance b/d	1,186.00
30 Sep	Balance c/d	1,000.00			
		1,186.00			1,186.00
			1 Oct	Balance b/d	1,000.00

(b) **Profit and loss entries**   (c) **Balance sheet entries:**

20-7 Bad debts 140
    Provision for bad debts 1,186 Debtors 11,860 *less*
                                   1,186 = 10,674
20-8 Decrease provision 186   Debtors 10,000 *less*
                                   1,000 = 9,000

24.11 (a) A debt which is considered irrecoverable is written off as a bad debt. A provision for doubtful debts is created to provide a reserve fund to guard against the possibility of some debtors failing to pay their debts.

      (b) A Balance Sheet should always present a true and fair view of the total debtors.

      To prepare in advance by having a reserve fund available.

(c) A previously written off bad debt which is recovered at a later date

The amount recovered would be transferred to the credit side of the profit and loss account.

(d) (i)   **Provision for Bad Debts Account**

31 Dec	Profit and loss	100.00	1 Jan	Balance b/d	500.00
31 Dec	Balance c/d	400.00			
		500.00			500.00
31 Dec	Balance c/d	550.00	1 Jan	Balance b/d	400.00
			31 Dec	Profit and loss	150.00
		550.00			550.00
			1 Jan	Balance b/d	550.00

(ii)   **Profit and loss account entries:**

20-4   Decrease provision 100   20-5   Increase provision 150

Unit 25

25.1   **Rent Account**

4 Jan	Bank	500.00	1 Jan	Accrued b/d	500.00
3 Apr	Bank	500.00	31 Dec	Profit and loss	2,000.00
5 Jul	Bank	500.00			
8 Oct	Bank	500.00			
31 Dec	Accrued c/d	500.00			
		2,500.00			2,500.00
			1 Jan	Accrued b/d	500.00

25.2   **Rates Account**

4 Jan	Prepaid b/d	525.00	31 Dec	Profit and loss	2,250.00
30 Apr	Bank	1,150.00	31 Dec	Prepaid c/d	575.00
5 Oct	Bank	1,150.00			
		2,825.00			2,825.00
1 Jan	Prepaid b/d	575.00			

25.3 Totals: 2,090   Profit and loss 1,803

25.4 Totals: 1,625   Profit and loss 1,045

25.5 Totals: 2,466   Profit and loss 1,678

25.6 Totals   Rent 2,700   Profit and loss 2,700

      Totals: Rent received 675   Profit and loss 600

25.7 Totals: Rent 1,200   Profit and loss 1,200

      Totals: Rent received 520   Profit and loss 480

      Totals: Electricity 437   Profit and loss 363

25.8 Totals: Rent 5,712   Profit and loss 5,712

      Totals: Sundry expenses 2,854   Profit and loss 2,356

      Totals: Rates 3,678   Profit and loss 2,528

      Totals: Rent received 2,976   Profit and loss 2,480

Unit 26

26.1

Trading, Profit and Loss Account for the year ended 31 December 20-5

Stock	3,800	Sales	82,000
Purchases	60,000		
	63,800		
Less closing stock	4,000		
Cost of goods sold	59,800		
Gross profit c/d	22,200		
	82,000		82,000
Salaries	9,100	Gross profit b/d	22,200
Discount allowed	820	Discount received	640
Rates	650		
Insurances (150 – 25)	125		
Telephone (100 + 30)	130		
Net profit	12,015		
	22,840		22,840

Balance Sheet as at 31 December 20-5

Fixed Assets			Capital	31,660	
Land and					
Buildings	28,000		*Add* net profit	12,015	
Fixtures & fit	1,800			43,675	
Motor van	2,200	32,000	*Less* drawings	4,500	39,175
Current Assets			*Current Liabilities*		
Stock	4,000		Creditors	1,800	
Debtors	2,400		Tel accrued	30	1,830
Ins prepaid	25				
Bank	1,980				
Cash	600	9,005			
		41,005			41,005

26.2

Trading, Profit and Loss Account for the year ended 31 December 20-6

Stock	3,112	Sales	32,484
Purchases	23,821		
	26,933		
Add Carriage inwards	138		
	27,071		
Less closing stock	2,477		
Cost of goods sold	24,594		
Gross profit c/d	7,890		
	32,484		32,484
Rent and rates	1,340	Gross profit b/d	7,890
Wages and salaries			
(2,711 + 42)	2,753		
Bad debts	88		
Office exps (488 – 56)	432		
Sundry expenses	797		
Net profit	2,480		
	7,890		7,890

Balance Sheet as at 31 December 20-6

Fixed Assets			Capital	11,700	
Motor vehicles		7,037	*Add* net		
			profit	2,480	
				14,180	
			Less drawings	2,100	12,080
Current Assets			*Current Liabilities*		
Stock	2,477		Creditors	1,535	
Debtors	3,840		Wages		
Stat stock	56		Accrued	42	1,577
Bank	247	6,620			
		13,657			13,657

26.3 Net profit 14,618

Fixed assets 31,600   Current assets 5,719

Long-term liabilities 4,000   Current liabilities 570

26.4 Gross profit 32,125   Net profit 4,250

Fixed assets 21,500   Current assets 25,500

Current liabilities 18,100

26.5 Gross profit 18,920   Net loss 1,610
     Fixed assets 25,500   Current assets 10,100
     Long-term liabilities 5,000   Current liabilities 7,570
26.6 Net profit 9,414   Fixed assets 6,375
     Current assets 1,406   Current liabilities 876
26.7 Net profit 20,878
     Fixed assets 93,100   Current assets 9,836
     Long-term liabilities 25,000   Current liabilities 3,638
26.8 Gross profit 17,400   Net profit 10,100
     Fixed assets 4,500   Current assets 43,600
     Long-term liabilities 6,000   Current liabilities 14,400
26.9 Gross profit 19,620   Net profit 6,060
     Fixed assets 11,500   Current assets 19,070
     Current liabilities 11,180

Unit 27

27.1

			Dr	Cr
4 Feb	Shop fittings		8,600	
	Arthur Blake			8,600
	Purchase on credit of new shop fittings			
15 Feb	Peter Payne		400	
	Shop fittings			400
	Sale on credit of old fittings			
18 Feb	Bad debts		51	
	Simon Bates			51
	Irrecoverable debt written off			
29 Feb	Harry Albert Jones		210	
	Henry Jones			210
	Correction of error in posting			

27.2

			Dr	Cr
3 June	Office furniture		4,500	
	Crescent Furniture Ltd			4,500
	Purchase on credit of new office furniture			
7 June	Bad debts		470	
	Philip Richards			470
	Irrecoverable debt written off			
9 June	John Belling		150	
	John Bell			150
	Correction of error in posting			
10 June	Car Trader		70	
	Motor van			70
	Sale on credit of old van			

27.3

Opening Journal entry: Assets 46,089   Liabilities 11,565   Capital 34,524

6 May	Dr	Fixtures	950	Cr	Micawber & Sons	950
8 May	Dr	Micawber & Sons	60	Cr	Fixtures	60
12 May	Dr	Bad debts	64	Cr	A Baker	64
22 May	Dr	Gatt & Co	90	Cr	Fixtures	90
29 May	Dr	T Davies	130	Cr	T Davis	130

27.4

7 May	Dr	Rent	40	Cr	Rates	40
16 May	Dr	Motor van	2,400	Cr	Purchases	2,400
18 May	Dr	Tom Boon	250	Cr	John Boon	250
22 May	Dr	Sales	45	Cr	Cash	45

27.5

Opening Journal entry: Assets 39,820   Liabilities 6,190   Capital 33,630

(i)	Dr	T Marsden	350	Cr	T Marsland	350
(ii)	Dr	Bank	95	Cr	F Ryder	95
	Dr	Bad debts	380	Cr	F Ryder	380
(iii)	Dr	Drawings	326	Cr	Purchases	176
				Cr	Cash	150
(iv)	Dr	B Clifton	65	Cr	Discount allowed	65
(v)	Dr	D Anderson	790	Cr	Bank	790

27.6

Opening Journal entry: Assets 33,930   Liabilities 2,530   Capital 31,400

7 May	Dr	Motor van	4,750	Cr	Cash	1,000
				Cr	Better Motors	3,750
14 May	Dr	A Baker	250	Cr	Fixtures and fittings	250
18 May	Dr	Bad debts	100	Cr	J Smith	100
21 May	Dr	Sales	25			
	Dr	Purchases	25	Cr	T Murphy	50

27.7

3 Oct	Dr	Office equipment	6,265.00	Cr	Bank	1,566.25
				Cr	Mega Systems	4,698.75
10 Oct	Dr	Bank	120.70			
	Dr	Bad debts	482.80	Cr	I Hardrup	603.50
15 Oct	Dr	Bank	650.00			
	Dr	R Groves	1,300.00	Cr	Delivery van	1,950.00
31 Oct	Dr	Cash	198.00	Cr	M Dyson	198.00
31 Oct	Dr	J Clarkson	390.00	Cr	T Clark	390.00
31 Oct	Dr	Profit and loss	2,074.00	Cr	General exps	2,074.00
31 Oct	Dr	Trading account	652.00	Cr	Carriage in	652.00
31 Oct	Dr	Profit and loss	890.00	Cr	Dis allowed	890.00

Unit 28

28.1

    (a) A trial balance has limitations. There are six types of errors which can occur that will not be revealed by taking out a trial balance.

    (b) Original error; Error of omission; Compensating error.

28.2

    (a) A trial balance is a '*prima facie*', at first sight, indication of accuracy. It is a test only of the arithmetical accuracy of the postings.

       (i) Debit column would be understated by the amount of the opening stock.

      (ii) No effect – not included in trial balance.

    (b) Recheck totals. Check location of balances i.e. debit balances incorrectly entered in credit column and vice versa.

28.3 (a) Trial balance totals: 57,634   Capital 25,486

    (b) Recheck totals. Check location of balances, i.e. debit balances incorrectly entered in credit column and vice vaersa.

    (c) **Original error:** where an error in made on an original document, such as an invoice, and double entry is carried out using the incorrect figure.

    Error of omission: where a transaction is completely omitted from the books

    Compensating errors: these are errors that cancel out each other.

28.4 Trial balance totals: 98,260

15 Jun	Dr	D Smith	200	Cr	D Smithson	200
13 Aug	Dr	Purchases	340	Cr	R Wallis & Co	340
24 Sep	Dr	Motor expenses	500	Cr	Motor vehicles	500
30 Oct	Dr	Drawings	200	Cr	Motor expenses	200

28.5 Trial balance totals: 76,250   Capital 58,500

(i)	Dr	Drawings	162	Cr	General expenses	162
(ii)	Dr	Bank	36			
	Dr	Bad debts	204	Cr	A Slowman	240
(iii)	Dr	Purchases	158	Cr	M Ramsden	158
(iv)	Dr	T Greenfield	350	Cr	F Greenwood	350

28.6 Trial balance totals: 116,900   Capital 87,250

(i)	Dr	Rates	850	Cr	Bank	850
(ii)	Dr	Bank	72			
	Dr	Bad debts	408	Cr	D Myers	480
(iii)	Dr	K Williamson	578	Cr	K Williams	578
(iv)	Dr	Purchases	202	Cr	A Oldridge	202
(v)	Dr	Drawings	253	Cr	Sundry expenses	253

28.7 Trial balance totals: 62,740   Capital 41,630

(i) Dr	R Foxwood	76	Cr	Returns outwards	76
(ii) Dr	M Keller	485	Cr	M Kellerman	485
(iii) Dr	Bank	54			
Dr	Bad debts	306	Cr	C Gulliver	360
(iv) Dr	Drawings	105	Cr	General expenses	105
(v) Dr	G Sanderson	18	Cr	Discount allowed	18

Unit 29

29.1

Sales Ledger Control Account

1 May	Balance b/d	4,760	31 May	Returns inwards	423
31 May	Sales	5,912	31 May	Bank	3,969
			31 May	Discount allowed	179
			31 May	Bad debts	57
			31 May	Balance c/d	6,044
		10,672			10,672
1 Jun	Balance b/d	6,044			

29.2

Purchase Ledger Control Account

31 May	Returns outwards	324	1 May	Balance b/d	8,904
31 May	Bank	6,604	31 May	Purchases	7,038
31 May	Discount received	272			
31 May	Balance c/d	8,742			
		15,942			15,942
			1 Jun	Balance b/d	8,742

29.3 Totals: 19,750   Balance c/d 6,950

29.4 Totals: 31,175   Balance c/d 18,082

29.5 *Sales ledger control account:* Totals: 215,557   Balance c/d 8,224
     Purchase ledger control account: Totals: 150,293   Balance c/d 1,845

29.6 (a) Totals: 24,368   Balance c/d 6,736
     (b) The closing balance on the sales ledger control account does not agree with the debit balances as extracted from ledger 2, K-R. this section will require detailed checking to discover the error(s).

29.7 Debtors' balances:

A Butler	460.71
W Dyson	209.68
L Grainger	791.85
	1,462.24 = balance on sales ledger control account

29.8 Debtors' balances:

G Anderson	932.71
V Ellis	582.32
M Harriman	723.87
	2,238.90 = balance on sales ledger control account

Unit 30

30.1 (a) Capital   (b) Revenue   (c) Capital   (d) Revenue
    (e) Revenue   (f) Revenue

30.2 (a) Capital   (b) Revenue   (c) Revenue   (d) Capital
    (e) Revenue   (f) Revenue   (g) Capital   (h) Revenue
    (i) Revenue

30.3 (a) Revenue expenditure   (b) Capital expenditure
    (c) Revenue receipt   (d) Revenue receipt
    (e) Revenue expenditure   (f) Capital expenditure
    (g) Capital expenditure   (h) Revenue expenditure
    (i) Capital receipt

30.4 (a) Capital   (b) Revenue   (c) Revenue   (d) Revenue
    (e) Capital   (f) Revenue   (g) Revenue   (h) Revenue

30.5 (a) Revenue   (b) Capital   (c) Revenue   (d) Revenue
    (e) Capital   (f) Revenue   (g) Capital   (h) Revenue

30.6

Capital expenditure	*Revenue expenditure*
Van	Road tax
Seat belts	Insurance
Delivery charges	Redecorate shop front
Number plates	
Erect shelves in stockroom	

30.7 (a) Capital   (b) Revenue   (c) Revenue   (d) Capital   (e) Capital
    (f) Capital   (g) Capital   (h) Revenue   (i) Revenue
    (j) Revenue

30.8

(i) Revenue	expenditure	Trading account
(ii) Capital	expenditure	Balance sheet
(iii) Revenue	expenditure	Profit and loss account
(iv) Capital	expenditure	Balance sheet

30.9

(i) Revenue	expenditure	Profit and loss account
(ii) Capital	expenditure	Balance sheet
(iii) Capital	expenditure	Balance sheet
(iv) Revenue	expenditure	Trading account
(v) Capital	expenditure	Balance sheet
(vi) Revenue	expenditure	Profit and loss account

Unit 31

31.1 Reconciliation Statement as at 30 April 20-9

Balance as per ledger account			327.57
Add: Returns outwards	47.72		
Purchases	295.50		343.22
Balance as per statement			670.79

31.2 Reconciliation Statement as at 28 February 20-9

Balance as per ledger account			325.65
Add: Discount received	15.40		
Returns outwards	49.25		
Purchases	296.90		361.55
Balance as per statement			687.20

31.3 Reconciliation Statement as at 31 May 20-9

Balance as per ledger account			120.00
Add: Discount received	22.00		
Bank	263.00		
Discount received	12.00		
Purchase returns	44.00		
Purchases	257.00		598.00
Balance as per statement			718.00

31.4 Reconciliation Statement as at 31 January 20-6

Balance as per ledger account			350.00
Add: Bank	350.00		
Purchases	250.00		
Purchases	190.00		790.00
Balance as per statement			1,140.00

31.5 Reconciliation Statement as at 31 May 20-1

Balance as per ledger account			1,310.00
Add: Discount received	104.00		
Bank	4,134.00		
Discount received	106.00		
			4,344.00
Balance as per statement			5,654.00

31.6 (a)   Reconciliation Statement as at 31 October 20-8

Balance as per ledger account			2,545.00
Add: Bank	1,570.00		
Discount	55.00		
Purchase returns	105.00		
Purchases	1,550.00		3,280.00
Balance as per statement			5,825.00

(b)   (i) 63.63   (ii) 2,481.37

31.7 (a)   **Reconciliation Statement as at 31 May 20-9**

Balance as per ledger account		970.00
Add: Discount	20.00	
Bank	1,325.00	
Discount	25.00	
Purchases	1,470.00	2,840.00
Balance as per statement		3,810.00

(b)   (i) 48.50   (ii) 921.50

31.8 (a)   **Reconciliation Statement as at 31 October 20-9**

Balance as per ledger account		2,730.00
Add: Bank	1,330.00	
Discount	20.00	
Purchase returns	75.00	
Purchases	1,550.00	2,975.00
Balance as per statement		5,705.00

(b)   A supplier may disallow a cash discount if payment is not received by the due date

(c)   (i) 68.25   (ii) 2,661.75

Unit 32

32.1   **Paul Davies**

Week ended 30 July 20-9

38 hours at £7.50 per hour		285.00
12 hours at £11.25 per hour		135.00
	Gross pay	420.00
Deductions		
Income tax	109.50	
National Insurance	21.00	
Social club	2.50	133.00
	Net pay	287.00

32.2   **G Forbes**

Week ended 8 August 20-9

4,800 items at £3 per 50	Gross pay	288.00
Deductions		
Income tax	68.40	
National Insurance	28.80	97.20
	Net pay	190.80

B Carr

Week ended 8 August 20-9

5,200 items at £3 per 50		312.00
Productivity Bonus		20.00
	Gross pay	332.00

Deductions

Income tax	84.60	
National Insurance	33.20	117.80
	Net pay	214.20

32.3   Gross pay 403.00 Deductions 147.75 Net pay 255.25

32.4   Gross pay 310.50 Deductions 111.10 Net pay 199.40

32.5   Gross pay 388.50 Deductions 144.20 Net pay 244.30

32.6   J Oldridge   Gross pay: Time rate 232.20   Piece rate 204.00
Time rate most favourable
K Bullard   Gross pay: Time rate 344.00   Piece rate 324.00
Time rate most favourable
H Downing   Gross pay: Time rate 318.20   Piece rate 336.00
Piece rate most favourable
L Beech   Gross pay: Time rate 326.80   Piece rate 294.00
Time rate most favourable

32.7   Cheque required for payroll 518.45

	£20	£10	£5	£2	£1	50p	20p	10p	5p	2p	1p
Analysis totals:	22	4	3	8	3	5	7	3	3	4	2

32.8   Cheque required for payroll 1,338.65

	£10	£5	£2	£1	50p	20p	10p	5p	2p	1p
Analysis totals:	118	11	12	72	8	11	8	8	10	5

32.9   Cheque required for payroll 1,321.89

	£20	£10	£5	£2	£1	50p	20p	10p	5p	2p	1p
Analysis totals:	63	3	3	5	3	5	4	3	4	3	3

32.10   Cheque required for payroll 1,168.15

	£10	£5	£2	£1	50p	20p	10p	5p	2p	1p
Analysis totals:	114	3	4	2	3	6	2	3	3	4

32.11 Cheque required for payroll 1,045.50

	£20	£10	£5	£2	£1	50p	20p	10p	5p	2p	1p
Analysis totals:	49	3	3	7	3	4	5	2	3	6	3

Unit 33

Stock Record Card

Item No: DWT/8

Date	Reference	Receipts	Issues	Balance
1 Mar	Balance b/d			225
2 Mar	Invoice 767	60		285
4 Mar	Requisition 454		20	265
6 Mar	Requisition 467		28	237
10 Mar	Requisition 476		35	202
15 Mar	Invoice 786	50		252
18 Mar	Requisition 482		43	209
21 Mar	Invoice 812	70		279
22 Mar	Requisition 491		26	253
24 Mar	Requisition 498		34	219
28 Mar	Invoice 865	85		304
30 Mar	Requisition 502		36	268

33.1

Stock Record Card

Half litre clear glass bottles

Date	Reference	Receipts	Issues	Balance
1 Oct	Balance b/d			530
6 Oct	Invoice 684	120		650
7 Oct	Requisition 54		35	615
8 Oct	Requisition 55		70	545
9 Oct	Invoice 732	50		595
10 Oct	Stock check		3	592
15 Oct	Requisition 56		40	552
22 Oct	Invoice 786	135		687
24 Oct	Invoice 789	50		737
28 Oct	Requisition 57		80	657

33.2

33.3 Balance at 30 May – 114

33.4 Balance at 30 April – 1,380

33.5 Balance at 30 April – 266 units value £1,596

33.6 Balance at 31 May – 233 units value £1,864

33.7 Balance at 30 June – 210 units value £630

Unit 34

34.1

Oakdale Youth Club:

(a) **Receipts and Payments Account for the year ended 31 December 20-4**

1 Jan	Balance b/d	460		Electricity	905
	Subscriptions	1,704		Repairs to equipment	138
	Annual fete	852		Motor expenses	496
				New equipment	420
				Postage and stationery	184
				Insurance	375
				General expenses	118
			31 Dec	Balance c/d	380
		3,016			3,016

(b) **Income and Expenditure Account for the year ended 31 December 20-4**

Electricity (905 + 107)	1,012	Subscriptions	1,704
Repairs to equipment	138	Annual fete	852
Motor expenses	496		
Postage and stationery	184		
Insurance (375 – 115)	260		
General expenses	118		
Surplus	348		
	2,556		2,556

(c) Accumulated Fund at 1 January 20-4 – £7,600

(d)   **Balance Sheet as at 31 December 20-4**

Fixed Assets			Accumulated Fund		
Furn and fittings	1,500		at 1 Jan 20-4	7,600	
Games			*Add* surplus	348	7,948
equipment	1,060				
Motor van	5,000	7,560			
Current Assets			Current Liabilities		
Insurance			Electricity accrued		107
prepaid	115				
Bank	380	495			
		8,055			8,055

34.2 (a) *Northside Sports Club*: bank balance at 31 May 20-9 – £3,970

(b)   **Bar Trading Account for the year ended 31 May 20-9**

Opening stock	708	Bar sales	2,836
Add bar purchases	1,574		
	2,282		
Less closing stock	692		
Cost of goods sold	1,590		
Profit on bar	1,246		
	2,836		2,836

(c)   **Income and Expenditure Account for the year ended
31 May 20-9**

Annual dance expenses	432	Profit on bar	1,246
Rent (1,595 + 145)	1,740	Subscriptions	3,750
Competition prizes	158	Annual dance	974
Sundry expenses	536	Locker rents	548
Insurance (495 – 78)	417	Competition fees	396
Surplus	3,631		
	6,914		6,914

(d) Accumulated Fund at 1 June 20-8 – £3,994

(e)   **Balance Sheet as at 31 May 20-9**

Fixed Assets			*Accumulated Fund*		
Sports			at 1 June 20-8	3,994	
equipment	1,580				
Furniture	1,450	3,030	*Add* surplus	3,631	7,625
Current Assets			*Current Liabilities*		
Bar stock	692		Rent accrued		145
Insurance					
prepaid	78				
Bank	3,970	4,740			
		7,770			7,770

34.3
- (a) Receipts and payments account: balance at 31 May 20-5 – 8,702
- (b) Income and expenditure account: surplus 3,086
- (c) Accumulated Fund at 1 June 20-4 – 84,815
- (d) Fixed assets 79,195   Current assets 8,755   Current liabilities 49

34.4
- (a) Receipts and payments account: balance at 31 December 20-2 – 2,437
- (b) Income and expenditure account: surplus 1,795
- (c) Fixed assets 9,411   Current assets 2,544   Current liabilities 85

34.5
- (i) Receipts and payments account: balance at 31 May 20-7 – 5,735
- (ii) Income and expenditure account: surplus 3,872
- (iii) Fixed assets 1,140   Current assets 5,770   Current liabilities 800

34.6
- (a) Bar trading account: profit on bar 2,764
- (b) Receipts and payments account: balance at 31 October 20-7 – 18,624
- (c) Income and expenditure account: surplus 21,763

Unit 35

35.1   *A Bannister Account*

Date	Details	Debit	Credit	Balance	
1 May	Balance b/d			202.56	Cr
4 May	Purchases		208.80	411.36	Cr
12 May	Purchase returns	32.50		378.86	Cr
15 May	Purchases		124.46	503.32	Cr
17 May	Bank	202.56		300.76	Cr

D Lenton Account

Date	Details	Debit	Credit	Balance	
1 May	Balance b/d			274.80	Cr
2 May	Purchases		150.92	425.72	Cr
14 May	Purchases		195.94	621.66	Cr
22 May	Bank	274.80		346.86	Cr
24 May	Purchase returns	30.68		316.18	Cr

Adams & Sons Account

Date	Details	Debit	Credit	Balance	
1 May	Balance b/d			345.93	Dr
9 May	Sales	384.12		730.05	Dr
15 May	Sales returns		38.20	691.85	Dr
24 May	Sales	379.64		1,071.49	Dr
28 May	Bank		345.93	725.56	Dr

C Groves Account

Date	Details	Debit	Credit	Balance	
1 May	Balance b/d			307.28	Dr
4 May	Sales	230.44		537.72	Dr
16 May	Bank		153.64	384.08	Dr
18 May	Sales	196.38		580.46	Dr
23 May	Sales returns		26.92	553.54	Dr

Bank Account

Date	Details	Debit	Credit	Balance	
1 May	Balance b/d			5,931.60	Dr
8 May	General expenses		49.20	5,882.40	Dr
16 May	C. Groves	153.64		6,036.04	Dr
17 May	A. Bannister		202.56	5,833.48	Dr
20 May	General expenses		64.50	5,768.98	Dr
22 May	D. Lenton		274.80	5,494.18	Dr
28 May	Adam & Sons	345.93		5,840.11	Dr

Capital Account

Date	Details	Debit	Credit	Balance	
1 May	Balance b/d			4,860.50	Cr

General Expenses Account

Date	Details	Debit	Credit	Balance	
1 May	Balance b/d			492.75	Dr
8 May	Bank	49.20		541.95	Dr
20 May	Bank	64.50		606.45	Dr

Purchases Account

Date	Details	Debit	Credit	Balance	
1 May	Balance b/d			938.80	Dr
31 May	Total PDB	680.12		1,618.92	Dr

Purchase Returns Account

Date	Details	Debit	Credit	Balance	
1 May	Balance b/d			236.20	Cr
31 May	Total PRDB		63.18	299.38	Cr

Sales Account

Date	Details	Debit	Credit	Balance	
1 May	Balance b/d			2,581.94	Cr
31 May	Total SDB		1,190.58	3,772.52	Cr

Sales Returns Account

Date	Details	Debit	Credit	Balance	
1 May	Balance b/d			139.64	Dr
31 May	Total SRDB	65.12		204.76	Dr

35.2
Airedale Fabrics Account

Date	Details	Debit	Credit	Balance	
1 Apr	Balance b/d			376.94	Cr
6 Apr	Purchases		286.30	663.24	Cr
8 Apr	Bank	188.47		474.77	Cr
20 Apr	Purchases		352.84	827.61	Cr
25 Apr	Purchase returns	40.96		786.65	Cr
28 Apr	Bank	474.77		311.88	Cr

Hollywell Mills Account

Date	Details	Debit	Credit	Balance	
1 Apr	Balance b/d			290.46	Cr
4 Apr	Purchases		390.26	680.72	Cr
10 Apr	Purchase returns	38.28		642.44	Cr
15 Apr	Purchases		319.52	961.96	Cr
20 Apr	Bank	290.46		671.50	Cr

Activity Centre Account

Date	Details	Debit	Credit	Balance	
1 Apr	Balance b/d			485.30	Dr
5 Apr	Sales	384.62		869.92	Dr
9 Apr	Sales returns		32.60	837.32	Dr
20 Apr	Sales	307.54		1,144.86	Dr
22 Apr	Bank		485.30	659.56	Dr

Spot Sport Account

Date	Details	Debit	Credit	Balance	
1 Apr	Balance b/d			398.92	Dr
3 Apr	Sales	429.36		828.28	Dr
6 Apr	Bank		398.92	429.36	Dr
12 Apr	Sales	275.28		704.64	Dr
18 Apr	Sales returns		40.58	664.06	Dr

Bank Account

Date	Details	Debit	Credit	Balance	
1 Apr	Balance b/d			4,372.86	Dr
2 Apr	Rent		165.00	4,207.86	Dr
3 Apr	Equipment		495.95	3,711.91	Dr
6 Apr	Spot Sport	398.92		4,110.83	Dr
8 Apr	Airedale Fabrics		188.47	3,922.36	Dr
15 Apr	Sundry expenses		59.25	3,863.11	Dr
20 Apr	Hollywell Mills		290.46	3,572.65	Dr
22 Apr	Activity Centre	485.30		4,057.95	Dr
24 Apr	Sundry expenses		79.70	3,978.25	Dr
28 Apr	Airedale Fabrics		474.77	3,503.48	Dr

Capital Account

Date	Details	Debit	Credit	Balance	
1 Apr	Balance b/d			8,264.68	Cr

Equipment Account

Date	Details	Debit	Credit	Balance	
1 Apr	Balance b/d			3,650.50	Dr
3 Apr	Bank	495.95		4,146.45	Dr

Purchases Account

Date	Details	Debit	Credit	Balance	
1 Apr	Balance b/d			1,295.48	Dr
30 Apr	Total PDB	1,348.92		2,644.40	Dr

Purchase Returns Account

Date	Details	Debit	Credit	Balance	
1 Apr	Balance b/d			258.30	Cr
30 Apr	Total PRDB		79.24	337.54	Cr

Rent Account

Date	Details	Debit	Credit	Balance	
1 Apr	Balance b/d			740.00	Dr
2 Apr	Bank	165.00		905.00	Dr

Sales Account

Date	Details	Debit	Credit	Balance	
1 Apr	Balance b/d			2,704.62	Cr
30 Apr	Total SDB		1,396.80	4,101.42	Cr

Sales Returns Account

Date	Details	Debit	Credit	Balance	
1 Apr	Balance b/d			312.38	Dr
30 Apr	Total SRDB	73.18		385.56	Dr

Sundry Expenses Account

Date	Details	Debit	Credit	Balance	
1 Apr	Balance b/d			639.56	Dr
15 Apr	Bank	59.25		698.81	Dr
24 Apr	Bank	79.70		778.51	Dr

35.3 Closing balances:
Purchase Ledger

Court Fabrics	475.68	Cr
Walkers Ltd	874.74	Cr
Yorkshire Supplies	882.53	Cr

Sales Ledger

Aladdin Lamps	1,688.98	Dr
Megson Trading Co	1,946.17	Dr
Supreme Designs	1,037.27	Dr

Nominal Ledger

Capital	10,725.76	Cr
Machinery	17,331.25	Dr
Purchases	11,220.53	Dr
Purchase returns	769.82	Cr
Sales	22,346.27	Cr
Sales returns	692.52	Dr
Sundry expenses	1,870.94	Dr
VAT	1,072.16	Cr
Bank	1,359.30	Dr

35.4 Closing balances:
Purchase Ledger

Fairburn & Lawson	323.36	Cr
Pudsey & Co	747.98	Cr
J C Vickers	598.71	Cr

Sales Ledger

Country Kitchens	1,710.61	Dr
Handforth Interiors	2,037.67	Dr
Woodcraft	2,420.90	Dr

Nominal Ledger

Capital	15,750.00	Cr
Fixtures and fittings	17,915.95	Dr
General expenses	3,161.61	Dr
Purchases	14,204.40	Dr
Purchase returns	1,155.64	Cr
Sales	24,638.08	Cr
Sales returns	409.58	Dr
VAT	1,083.98	Cr
Bank	2,437.03	Dr

■ ﹀ Index